Evolving Entrepreneurial Education

Innovation in the Babson Classroom

Evolving Entrepreneurial Education

Innovation in the Babson Classroom

Edited By

Victoria L. Crittenden
Kathryn Esper
Nathaniel Karst
Rosa Slegers
Babson College, USA

United Kingdom − North America − Japan
India − Malaysia − China

Emerald Group Publishing Limited
Howard House, Wagon Lane, Bingley BD16 1WA, UK

First edition 2015

Copyright © 2015 Emerald Group Publishing Limited

Reprints and permissions service
Contact: permissions@emeraldinsight.com

British Library Cataloguing in Publication Data
A catalogue record for this book is available from the British Library

ISBN: 978-1-78560-201-6

ISOQAR certified
Management System,
awarded to Emerald
for adherence to
Environmental
standard
ISO 14001:2004.

ISOQAR
REGISTERED

Certificate Number 1985
ISO 14001

INVESTOR IN PEOPLE

Contents

Part 2   Cross-Disciplinary Learning and Teaching

List of Contributors

Jennifer Bailey	Technology, Operations, and Information Management Division
Anjali Bal	Marketing Division
David M. Blodgett	Mathematics & Science Division
Candida Brush	Entrepreneurship Division
Allan R. Cohen	Management Division
Andrew Corbett	Entrepreneurship Division
Victoria L. Crittenden	Marketing Division
Susan Duffy	Center for Women's Entrepreneurial Leadership
Kathryn Esper	Center for Engaged Learning & Teaching
Marjorie Feld	History & Society Division
Sebastian K. Fixson	Technology, Operations, and Information Management Division
Mary Gale	Entrepreneurship Division
Bradley George	Entrepreneurship Division
Steven Gordon	Technology, Operations, and Information Management Division
Danna N. Greenberg	Management Division
Patricia Greene	Entrepreneurship Division
Dhruv Grewal	Marketing Division
Richard C. Hanna	Marketing Division
Carolyn Hotchkiss	Dean of Faculty
James Hunt	Management Division
Paul R. Joseph	Adjunct Lecturer

Nathaniel Karst	Mathematics & Science Division
Cheryl Kiser	The Lewis Institute
Nan Langowitz	Management Division
Julie Levinson	Arts & Humanities Division
Benjamin Luippold	Accounting & Law Division
Meghan G. MacLean	Mathematics & Science Division
Mahdi Majbouri	Economics Division
Heidi Neck	Entrepreneurship Division
Salvatore Parise	Technology, Operations, and Information Management Division
Virginia Rademacher	Arts & Humanities Division
Amir Reza	Vice Provost, International & Multicultural Education
Anders Richtnér	Visiting Scholar, The Lewis Institute
Vikki L. Rodgers	Mathematics & Science Division
Anne L. Roggeveen	Marketing Division
Jodi H. Schaefer	Mathematics & Science Division
Victor P. Seidel	Technology, Operations, and Information Management Division
Ganesan Shankaranarayanan	Technology, Operations, and Information Management Division
J. Janelle (Jan) Shubert	The Lewis Institute
Rosa Slegers	Arts & Humanities Division
Janet Strimaitis	Arthur M. Blank Center for Entrepreneurship
Peter R. Wilson	Accounting & Law Division
Charles Winrich	Mathematics & Science Division
Beth Wynstra	Arts & Humanities Division
Andrew Zacharakis	Entrepreneurship Division

List of External Reviewers

Gerald Albaum
University of New Mexico

Anne Balazs
Eastern Michigan University

Lauren Beitelspacher
Portland State University

Terrence Cahill
Seton Hall University

Colin Campbell
Kent State University

Jeffrey Cohen
Boston College

William Crittenden
Northeastern University

Kimberly Eddleston
Northeastern University

Keith Ferguson
Grand Rapids Community College

Linda Ferrell
University of New Mexico

O. C. Ferrell
University of New Mexico

Derek Hassay
University of Calgary

Amy Henley
Kennesaw State University

Kenneth Kahn
Virginia Commonwealth University

Lucy Matthews
Trine University

Vince Wayne Mitchell
City University London

Jamie Murphy
The Australian School of Management

Michael Parent
Simon Fraser University

Torsten Pieper
Kennesaw State University

Leyland Pitt
Simon Fraser University

Andrew Rohm
Loyola Marymount University

J. Michael Simmons
Butler University

Scott Swenseth
University of Nebraska

Donald Weatherman
Lyon College

Jim Weber
Duquesne University

Kelly Weidner
Dominican University

David Williams
Dalton State College

Elizabeth Wilson
Suffolk University

Evolving Entrepreneurial Education

Innovation in the Babson Classroom

> Behind the classroom door the key factor in the success of a lesson, in determining whether the students actually learn something that matters, is the creative ability of the teachers.
>
> Stafford (2006)

The ability to enrich student learning is fundamental to the educational process and requires a broad range of talents. A truly great educator will inspire students through a well-grounded approach to stimulating intellectual curiosity and growth, while maintaining high standards of performance. This inspiration and stimulation require a great deal of effort in course and program development, delivery, and performance. Glassick, Huber, and Maeroff (1997) suggest that excellence in teaching necessitates more than just the act of teaching. Excellence in teaching also requires educators to explore new approaches to student learning and to share the details of such explorations publicly so as to facilitate peer review and reflection.

While there are several business education journals in the marketplace that seek to publish innovative teaching ideas and other educational scholarship (e.g., *Academy of Management Learning & Education, Journal of Marketing Education, Marketing Education Review, Decision Sciences Journal of Innovative Education, Journal of Education for Business, Journal of Teaching in International Business, Journal of Entrepreneurship Education*), it has been left to the time and prowess of the individual educator to locate articles on the subject of teaching and learning. This monograph brings together educational scholarship that focuses upon the varied roles of both teachers and students in the entrepreneurial leader learning process, making this book a one-stop shop for educators seeking to deliver quality classroom content.

In their book, Greenberg, McKone-Sweet, and Wilson (2011) focused on the intellectual journey that creates entrepreneurial leaders. When the book was released, the themes within Entrepreneurial Thought and Action® (ET&A®) were in the early stages of integration into the Babson College curriculum. The individual entrepreneurial leader is at the core of ET&A®, and this current monograph offers insight and detail into the "how" of ET&A®; that is, how *self and contextual awareness*, one of the pillars of ET&A®, is created and delivered at Babson College. According to researchers at the George Lucas Educational Foundation, great teachers help create great students (Edutopia Team, 2008). We at Babson College believe that great teachers enable students to become aware of both themselves and different contexts.

In this monograph, educational scholars from a variety of academic disciplines share their experiences. These scholars view teaching as both a serious responsibility and a wonderful opportunity and have created a learning environment that enhances intellectual growth and practical achievement. In short, this book is written by educators for educators who want to engage the next generation of leaders in the classroom.

Teaching Knowledge

Without a doubt, there is an art and a science to great teaching. According to Marzano (2007), knowing what instructional strategies to use in the classroom is a science yet knowing when to use them and with whom is an art. Knowledge about teaching is a fundamental cornerstone of great teaching, whether an art or a science. Kreber and Cranton (2000) suggest that the ongoing learning about teaching and the demonstration of teaching knowledge are of critical importance to faculty development. Engagement in teaching and demonstration of teaching knowledge make it imperative that we have a wealth of teaching knowledge to draw from, and Kreber and Cranton (1997) offered three different, yet interrelated, domains of knowing about teaching: instructional knowledge, curricular knowledge, and pedagogical knowledge. Instructional knowledge focuses on strategies used in the actual classroom teaching; curricular knowledge addresses issues of why we teach the way we do; pedagogical knowledge seeks to understand how student learn. This monograph encapsulates all three of these knowledge domains in the various parts of the book.

Part 1 of this monograph, *The Role of Educational Scholarship: Navigating the Creative Process*, explores the important role and responsibility of educators in sharing pedagogical knowledge with colleagues worldwide. Bailey, Saparito, Kressel,

Christensen, and Hooijberg (1997) argue that teaching and research are complementary and so intermeshed that they become functionally identical and, as such, can both be treated as reflective knowledge practices. The contributions in this first part explore the creative process in which educational scholarship is crafted, transformed, and shared. Within the context of Babson College, various aspects of knowledge generation are examined — from the audiences with whom we interact to what makes the college number one in entrepreneurship to how we create both learning and teaching opportunities together with our students. This part of the book takes a very broad view of learning and teaching and how it transforms into educational scholarship.

The second part of this monograph, *Cross-Disciplinary Learning and Teaching*, portrays the breadth and depth of Entrepreneurial Thinking and Action®. The entrepreneurial leader engages critical thinking skills that do not lie in one particular discipline; rather, this skill set has to be crafted through an awareness brought to light via a variety of cross-disciplinary endeavors. Essentially, Babson College students receive a truly cross-functional education without falling prey to the implementation problems that ensue from creating cross-disciplinary learning environments (Crittenden, 2005). Part 2 of the book provides concrete examples of teaching and learning across functional boundaries.

The teaching environment in our schools of business fosters a set of responsibilities among our faculty to ensure a value-added educational experience for our students. To be successful educators, we must create and deliver a rigorous, practice-oriented learning experience that is well-organized and utilizes the most valuable learning materials, and the latest thinking regarding the field of study. This process of creating new and innovative pedagogy spans a variety of venues. Part 3, *Pedagogical Innovation for Entrepreneurial Thought & Action® and Self & Contextual Awareness*, describes a variety of pedagogical innovations — from course innovations to process innovations to project innovations. Details are provided so that educators can use the innovative teaching techniques in their own classrooms. At the same time, the examples are framed within broader educational approaches so as to provide solid backdrops and support for educational scholarship in action.

Babson College is the home to many Centers that provide opportunities for both students and faculty to have an impact on pedagogy across campus and at colleges and universities around the globe, and the final part of this monograph, *The Role of Centers in Enhancing the Educational Environment*, highlights several of the Centers on campus. By drawing upon Babson's core competencies, methodologies, and commitment to high quality teaching and learning, the Centers create and provide resources for the teaching of improved business techniques and innovative education programs, events, and research.

This monograph captures the best-of-the-best in terms of classroom innovation and educational scholarship. Each contribution in the book focuses on specifics with regards to creating and delivering teaching knowledge, and each chapter has been through a double-blind review process, thus capturing the essence of the traditional demands of educational scholarship. The contents of this book are relevant to all educators. Not only will educators be intrigued by the examples offered as far as classroom pedagogical tools and techniques, the cross-disciplinary nature of the curricular programming will provide valuable insights for educators in both the business and liberal arts domains.

Center for Engaged Learning and Teaching

Indicative of Babson College's belief in the need for strong teachers for our next generation of leaders, this monograph is the result of efforts supported by the College's Center for Engaged Learning and Teaching (CELT). CELT's mission is *to deepen the faculty's impact on pedagogy on campus and at Colleges and Universities around the globe — through distribution of the Babson Collection teaching materials*; this monograph clearly enables the fulfillment of that mission. As depicted in Figure 1, CELT engages in activities related to faculty development, teaching innovation, and case/teaching materials.

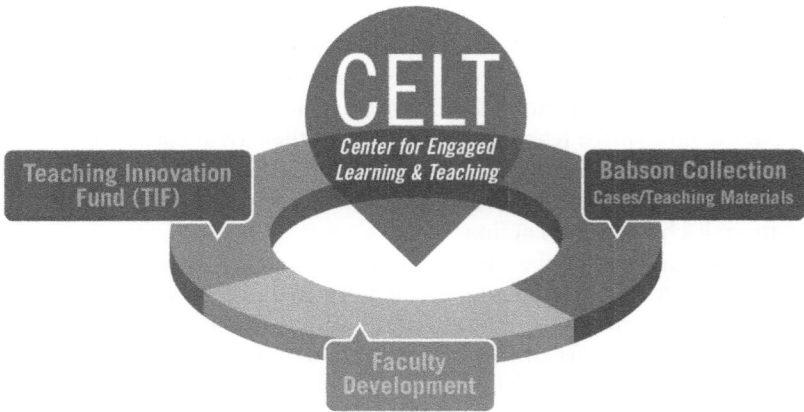

Figure 1:   Center for Engaged Learning and Teaching.

While the structure, publications, players, and programs of the CELT evolve and grow, the purpose of the Center is to sustain and deepen the already strong community and culture that exists among Babson College's faculty. CELT serves educators who actively seek opportunities to convene, encourage, and facilitate innovative learning and teaching. Its programs focus on: (1) infusing creativity into an already solid pedagogical foundation, (2) crossing disciplines, and (3) experiential learning.

Internal programs and external opportunities support excellence in teaching methods and materials. For example, faculty development programs facilitate and sponsor a small number of programs each academic year that go "deep with less." Investing time, money, and energy in high-potential faculty and cutting-edge teaching initiatives, these programs are intentionally kept small, focused, and concentrated. This provides the time, space, and structure needed to appreciate the reflective and cross-disciplinary aspects of teaching innovation.

The CELT also provides programs that are larger in scope. This monograph was born out of a day-long *Faculty Learn & Share*, which is a faculty development event held annually. This 2014 Faculty Learn & Share focused on "Translating Pedagogy into Educational Scholarship." Its purpose was to provide Babson College faculty the opportunity to share innovative classroom experiences with the broader campus community. The topics for this day of educational scholarship evolved from practical (the what, why, and how of educational scholarship) to inspirational (specific, innovative examples from Babson's own classrooms) to interactive (where one's classroom innovations intersected with that of their colleagues — especially across disciplines). It was at this event that this monograph began to take shape, and the 29 chapters about innovation in the Babson classroom are the result of this CELT-created opportunity.

References

Bailey, J. R., Saparito, P., Kressel, K., Christensen, E. W., & Hooijberg, R. (1997). A model for reflective pedagogy. *Journal of Management Education, 21*, 155–167.

Crittenden, V. (2005). Cross-functional education: The need for case development. *Journal of Business Research, 58*, 955–959.

Edutopia Team. (2008). *Why is teacher development important?: Because students deserve the best*. Retrieved from http://www.edutopia.org/teacher-development-introduction

Glassick, C. E., Huber, M. T., & Maeroff, G. I. (1997). *Scholarship assessed: Evaluation of the professoriate*. San Francisco, CA: Jossey-Bass.

Greenberg, D., McKone-Sweet, K., & Wilson, H. J. (2011). *The new entrepreneurial leader: Developing leaders who create social and economic opportunity.* San Francisco, CA: Berrett-Koehler.

Kreber, C., & Cranton, P. A. (1997). Teaching as scholarship: A model for instructional development. *Issues and Inquiry in College Learning and Teaching, 19*(2), 4–13.

Kreber, C., & Cranton, P. A. (2000). Exploring the scholarship of teaching. *The Journal of Higher Education, 71*(4), 476–795.

Marzano, R. J. (2007). *The art and science of teaching: A comprehensive framework for effective instruction.* Alexandria, VA: Association for Supervision and Curriculum Development.

Stafford, J. T. (2006). The importance of educational research in the teaching of history. *Canadian Social Studies, 40*(1), 1–8.

PART 1
The Role of Educational Scholarship: Navigating the Creative Process

1

Academic Scholarship: A Stakeholder Analysis

Victoria L. Crittenden and
Carolyn Hotchkiss

As educators, teaching is fundamental to who we are and what we do. Unfortunately, there has long been friction between teaching and research, with the two seen as very different, almost mutually exclusive, priorities in the life of an educator (Balkin & Mello, 2012). The great perceived divide between the two is that time spent on one activity is time not spent on the other activity (Loyd, Kern, & Thompson, 2005). However, Bailey, Saparito, Kressel, Christensen, and Hooijberg (1997) argue that not only are teaching and research complementary, they are also so intermeshed that they become functionally identical and could be treated as reflective practices. The intent here, however, is not to engage in the debate with regards to the tension between teaching and research since as noted by Bailey (2006), it would be disingenuous to deny the tension. Rather, this chapter explores scholarship from the perspective of the various stakeholders so as to highlight how a variety of academic scholarship types can reach and impact the various publics for whom we, at Babson College, serve in our educational role.

For our purposes at Babson College, we refer to academic scholarship as the various types of teaching, research, and learning that reach and engage a variety of stakeholders. As the world continues to change with regards to knowledge and information sharing, we do not put boundaries on our teaching, research, and learning. Boundaries would inhibit the creativity in our sharing of knowledge and information. Thus, we engage in boundary spanning, not boundary delimitation, so as to innovate in terms of teaching, research, and learning in ways that engage with our various stakeholders.

In this contribution, we explore the connection between teaching, research, and learning within the context of Babson College, a college with the mission of educating "entrepreneurial leaders who create great economic and social value — everywhere." Each of the two authors of this chapter serves the college in an administrative capacity, engages with students in the classroom, and continues to be active in professional arenas via both research and service. Thus, while informed by the literature, firsthand experience is also brought to bear in the discussion that follows.

The Scholarship of Teaching, Research, and Learning

Historically, and as described by Balkin and Mello (2012), the tension between teaching and traditional forms of scholarship is rooted in the norm that research has to have scientific, theoretical, and empirical implications and that pedagogical or applied research does not allow for such implications. As such, business schools have tended to give higher priority to discipline-based research over teaching almost as though the two require different types of professors to engage successfully in one or the other. Table 1 shows the factors Balkin and Mello (2012) suggest contribute to the tension between the teaching and discipline-based research.

This tension between the art and science of teaching and traditional research is not necessarily imposed on the professoriate by some higher being, however. Juxtaposing the art of teaching versus the science of research is often portrayed in even the published documents as related to teaching and learning. For example, Walck

Table 1: Three Major Factors That Contribute to the Tension between Teaching and Research.

1. Tradition

The academy's measurement of teaching, research, and service as three separate and distinct activities and responsibilities

2. Doctoral training

The emphasis in doctoral programs on the preparation for research without commensurate emphasis on preparation for teaching

3. Resource allocation

The greater allocation of resources toward research-related activities rather than toward teaching-related activities (even the notion of release from teaching for scholarly research)

Source: Balkin and Mello (2012).

(1997) writes about "teaching as an art" and the "art of teaching"; Bickford and Van Vleck (1997) use art as a metaphor to reframe teaching as an engaging, creative, holistic, collaborative learning process between the student and teacher; and Dehler and Welsh (1997) discuss "artful teaching." Loyd, Kern, and Thompson (2005), however, proffer the scientific approach by introducing a new research paradigm of classroom research, which is suggested to be a way to push knowledge frontiers in the classroom. Thus, even professors themselves tend to allow the great divide of art versus science to filter into their own thinking and writing.

Regardless of the art and science of teaching, research, and learning, its efficacy and meaningfulness to a broad audience was the object of attention by Boyer (1990) in his report, *Scholarship Reconsidered*, and then later in the 1997 follow-up publication, *Scholarship Assessed* (Glassick, Huber, & Maeroff, 1997). The importance of teaching as scholarly work began to take hold in business research, and an educator could see his/her excellence in teaching/pedagogy as a valued component of a school's mission without compromising his/her integrity as a scholar (Bailey et al., 1997).

Glassick et al. (1997) suggest that excellence in teaching necessitates more than just the act of teaching. Excellence in teaching also requires educators to explore new approaches to student learning and to share the details of such explorations publicly so as to facilitate peer review and reflection. Not only is the peer review process critical in informing teaching excellence, but the opinions of a wide variety of stakeholders such as recruiters, students, and practicing managers can also help create an environment of excellence in our classrooms (Behrman & Levin, 1984; Linder & Smith, 1992).

Various stakeholders have begun seeking evidence of the relationship between teaching practices and student learning/business impact (Dean & Forray, 2014). Thus, the scholarship of teaching, research, and learning, in which life-long learning and educational research are recognized and rewarded, has enabled a niche marketplace in which the compatibility between teaching and research is now recognized as critical to the success of business schools (Fukami, 1997).

According to Hutchings and Shulman (1999), engaging in the scholarship of teaching and learning is not just about excellent teaching. Whether designing a new course, facilitating classroom activities via project or process innovations, or other programmatic contributions, entering into the territory of scholarship implies the sharing of insights with others and engages these other stakeholders into a broader set of practices (Hutchings, Huber, & Ciccone, 2011). As noted by McKinney (2006), the scholarship of teaching and learning involves the public sharing of such work. At this juncture is where the traditional thinking about research begins to bear fruit in the verbal and written delivery of teaching and learning, as the demand is for that delivery to engage the methods of scholarly research with regards to theoretical framing of educational scholarship.

It is this public sharing of educational scholarship that drives the need for a stakeholder approach to understanding academic scholarship. Applying the stakeholder analysis paradigm to the scholarship of teaching and learning depicts the impact that educational scholarship can have for a college that educates entrepreneurial leaders who create economic and social value in all walks of life.

Stakeholder Analysis

An apparently widely held misconception about the nature of colleges and universities is that they only exist to further the discovery of new knowledge. While that is certainly one of the functions of some institutions of higher education, it is less relevant to many excellent colleges and universities whose reason for existence lies elsewhere. At Babson College, the broader view is that the College exists for many reasons, from discovery of new knowledge to having an impact on our students' lives to changing business practice. The hallmarks of the Babson College education are our thoughtful, practical, and creative students who graduate and change the world. We not only follow the standards of our accrediting bodies in our overall academic program (i.e., the New England Association of Schools and Colleges (NEASC)) and our business education program (i.e., AACSB International and EQUIS), we also include the Principles of Responsible Management Education (PRME) as our guide for educational practices. As such, we must assess teaching and scholarship with a wide lens.

With our mission, it would not make sense for Babson College to follow a purely traditional model of academic scholarship. To limit our faculty to the discipline-based research of academic discovery would stifle in our faculty the kind of creativity we hope to inspire in our students. Instead, we have collectively chosen to have a different conversation about intellectual vitality. To this end, Gross and Godwin (2005) suggest that a stakeholder analysis is a business strategy that begs to be utilized in the academic arena.

STAKEHOLDER THEORY

Stakeholder theory suggests that organizations must actively deal with a multitude of constituent groups and that management should broaden its vision of responsibilities to incorporate the concerns of these various constituent groups (Freeman, 1984; Mitchell, Agle, & Wood, 1997). According to Donaldson and Preston (1995), stakeholder theory identifies a number of different actors (i.e., stake-holders) for whom there are often multiple and incongruent objec-tives. The intention is to address the key question of "Which groups are stakeholders deserving or requiring management attention, and which are not?" (Mitchell et al., 1997, p. 855). Additionally, there are four assumptions in depicting the relationships: (1) firms have relationships with a multitude of stakeholders who have different rights, objectives, expectations, and responsibilities and each of these stakeholders has the power to influence performance, (2) decisions are made by top managers, (3) the divergent interests among various stakeholders may not be in harmony and can result in conflict, and (4) competitive pressures can have an effect on behavior, yet ineffi-cient behavior may not necessarily be penalized in the short run (Hult, Mena, Ferrell, & Ferrell, 2011).

The multitude of stakeholders can be categorized as primary or secondary stakeholders (Hult et al., 2011). Primary stakeholders are motivated by the resource dependency theory (Pfeffer & Salancik, 1978) and are generally highly visible since there is a desire to respond to the demands of these primary stakeholders. Secondary stakeholders are those that "influence or affect, or are influenced or affected by, the corporation, but they are not essential for its survi-val" (Clarkson, 1995, p. 107). Essentially, secondary stakeholders can mobilize public opinion for or against the organization's actions and practices (Hult et al., 2011).

With regards to the primary and secondary stakeholders, Hult et al. (2011) found that there is failure to examine multiple stake-holders simultaneously and Sisodia, Sheth, and Wolfe (2007, p. xxx) maintained that stakeholders "are part of a complex net-work of interests that function in a matrix of interdependences." Stakeholder theory within the business context has identified the six primary stakeholders of customers, employees, shareholders, regula-tors, suppliers, and community and the five secondary stakeholders of special interest groups, competitors, trade associations, mass media, and social media (Hult et al., 2011). In considering a holistic stakeholder analysis of academic scholarship at Babson College, we must take into account both primary and secondary stakeholders as well as the assumptions about relationships.

A Holistic Stakeholder Analysis of Babson College Academic Scholarship

The descriptive/empirical approach to stakeholder theory seeks to describe and explain the interactions with various stakeholders (Hult et al., 2011), and it is this descriptive/empirical approach followed by Babson College with regards to teaching, research, and learning. Following this approach requires two actions: (1) each faculty member identifies the primary and secondary stakeholders for his/her work and (2) each faculty member creates the metrics to show the impact of his/her work on the intended audience. Thus, the faculty member is assessed on the value that is created for each stakeholder group. Initially, however, the assumptions underlying the college's stakeholder approach to academic scholarship had to be clarified.

The four assumptions underlying stakeholder relations in business had to be adapted to accommodate the academic context. With regards to stakeholder influence, the targeting of one's academic scholarship is highly dependent upon the expectations of the various stakeholders. For example, if a piece of academic scholarship is related to pedagogy, the successful acceptance of the contribution will depend upon the objectives, expectations, and responsibilities of the stakeholder recipient. The college does not attempt to manage the targeting process; rather, each individual faculty member must possess the ability to understand the needs of differing stakeholder outlets. With that said, however, the college administrators have all made a commitment to acknowledge, and show appreciation for, quality output within a variety of stakeholder outlets. Thus, there is not a list of approved journals within each discipline, the use and gaming of citation indices are avoided, and impact factor calculations that are limited in scope to a group of journals that speak only to one group of stakeholders (namely other academics) are used sparingly.

College administrators have made it quite clear that the value of each and every piece of academic scholarship must be assessed via faculty-identified metrics. This metric ties closely to inefficient behavior in the marketplace, in that a faculty member should not take short-term risks with low quality journals as this could be potentially harmful to both the faculty member's and the college's reputation. Finally, faculty members have to recognize that the varying stakeholders will likely not appreciate the same types of academic scholarship and that a Babson College faculty member must be able to speak to a variety of audiences in order to deliver on the college's mission.

Rather than attempt to force the corporate acumen for stakeholder groupings into the academic domain, faculty and administrators at Babson College have identified four primary and three secondary stakeholder groups. Primary stakeholders include discipline and cross-disciplinary basic research faculty, practitioners, students/teachers, and public policy makers. Secondary stakeholders are the general public, media, and competitor educational institutions. It is understood that the stakeholders are likely to evolve over the span of an academic career. The institutional task is to ensure that the overall balance of faculty work supports the mission of the college, while the faculty member's task is to create the story of his/her work and to hone the measurements of quality.

Unlike assessment in business, there is not one overarching stakeholder group. For example, Webster (1992) identified customer relationships as the most important business asset, yet Babson College has resisted any tendencies to identify a "customer" stakeholder group. Each faculty member is encouraged to identify the stakeholder(s) for his/her academic research and to develop a plan to achieve the metrics for success in satisfying the needs of the stakeholder(s). Additionally, the idea of a range of metrics is now recognized as part of the AACSB (2013) Business Standards.

PRIMARY STAKEHOLDERS

Discipline and Cross-Disciplinary Basic Research Faculty

The scholarly work of the faculty at Babson College addresses concerns identified by peer groups in the academic audience. With regards to this stakeholder group, the impetus is basic research that can be accessed via the double-blind review process. According to Bailey, Hair, Hermanson, and Crittenden (2012), publication in peer-reviewed journals is critical to an individual faculty member's success in his/her career and, institutionally, faculty publication in peer-reviewed scholarly journals correlates to an academic institution's reputation.

Here, faculty members often rely on traditional measures of impact: the quality of the journal as measured by the various lists of top journals, the peer review process, impact factor analysis, citation indices (e.g., Google Scholar), and awards/honors for academic work. These measures of value are fairly standard among academic institutions and readily available publicly.

Practitioners

This audience is an important stakeholder institutionally for Babson College. Business is inherently a practical discipline, with applications in every field. Babson College has a large, active, and global school of executive and enterprise education with the purpose to influence and change the practice of business. Some of the College's faculty members in non-business disciplines also have the opportunity to structure their work to impact the practitioner audience. For example, an ethnomusicologist may discover and bring to light musical scores that become part of the professional singer's repertoire. Applied mathematicians and statisticians may explore research questions with applications in technology, sport, medicine, and other fields of practice. Babson College explicitly recognizes work for practitioner audiences in its definition of academic vitality.

The question here is how to evaluate quality. In some instances, professional associations have created measures and equivalencies. For example, the Association for Theatre in Higher Education (ATHE, 2014) has a set of conditions which, when met, indicate the task of directing a theater production open to the public as equivalent to a peer review journal. In the business disciplines, the tendency is to use SSCI impact factors and the size of the outlet's readership.

Students and Teachers

The third stakeholder group for the scholarly work of Babson College faculty is that of students and teachers. Babson College is an institution where teaching matters. One of the stimulants of any conversation among faculty is the subject of pedagogy. The College is home to the Center for Engaged Learning and Teaching (CELT). The CELT exists to deepen the faculty's impact on pedagogy, both on campus, through programs that support curriculum redesign, and off campus, through distribution of the Babson Collection's cases and teaching materials to colleges and universities around the world.

Collectively, we have chosen to be clear that work in the scholarship of pedagogy and work aimed at student audiences are publications that we value. With respect to this stakeholder group, we rely on various measures of impact. Scholarly work published in pedagogical journals relies upon traditional measures of impact such as journal rankings and citation indices. Material such as textbooks or cases is gauged against sales figures and industry data for popularity among the intended audience. This book is a living example of one kind of work that sees other teaching faculty as stakeholders.

Policy Makers

Babson College recognizes that academic research can (and should) provide grounding and data useful to those who make public policy decisions. For example, financial research can provide useful data to exchanges, congressional committees, and the overall regulatory process. In business law, faculty research might be cited in briefs before courts and in judicial opinions. Additionally, expert witnessing is likely rooted in a faculty member's ability to draw reasoned opinions from his/her research. At Babson College, studies such as the Global Entrepreneurship Monitor (GEM) provide valuable insights into job creation and conditions for entrepreneurs. For example, the U.S. Department of State's Bureau of Business and Economic Affairs (2014) cited GEM in the speech to launch

Celebrating Partnerships for Launch of Africa's WECREATE Centers in August 2014.

With regard to metrics, reports such as the GEM generate hundreds of thousands of downloads, thousands of media mentions, and serve as the basis for governmental recommendations on job creation. Babson College recognizes the efforts involved in collecting, organizing, and reporting the data that informs public policy.

SECONDARY STAKEHOLDERS

Secondary stakeholders have different types of relationships with organizations, and these relationships can be either collaborative or confrontational (Arenas, Lozano, & Albareda, 2009). As such, it is often difficult to assess the value of various types of stakeholder engagements. Of Babson College's secondary stakeholders, the general public tends to be most easily assessable while media and competitor colleges and universities are often difficult, if not impossible, to enable an assessment metric.

As noted by Handelman and Arnold (1999) and Drumwright (1996), consumer support of an organization can enhance its image, and community members are often considered to be primary stakeholders (Hult et al., 2011). However, the College has deemed that the lack of direct influence on academic scholarship places community members in the role of secondary stakeholder with regards to power and influence. However, some faculty members may have an audience for their work that consists of the general public. For example, a historian may write a biography that is sold and read widely. A management professor could write a regular column for investors. Other professors might maintain a group blog in a leading business publication (e.g., *Inc., Forbes,* or *The Economist*) or an individual blog that relates to topical interest. Also, a poet could have her poetry set to music and performed for the public (e.g., List & Pinard, 2014). While the general public is a secondary stakeholder, it is still an audience that recognizes quality and one that enhances the ability of the college to impact a wider world.

The benefits accrued to the College are substantial when a faculty member is noted in the media, either through positive actions that he/she has taken or via invited comments. Thus, Babson College invests considerable time and energy with the college marketing group to ensure that newsworthy events are highlighted as much as possible and that our faculty members are sought after commentators. Media cites enhance both the college and the faculty member in terms of external reputation.

Finally, another secondary stakeholder that Babson College acknowledges with regards to a faculty member's academic pursuits is that of the conveyed perception among competing institutions of individual faculty members and their recognition and expertise. Thus, invitations to give plenary talks and make various types of presentations at competitors' campuses are important in creating a general sense of the activities that transpire among faculty members at Babson College. Naturally, the fear is that the competitor will entice the faculty member to change employers and that an invitation to speak is a foray into recruiting. However, it is a risk that the College is willing to take as it is an honor to be asked to speak at a competing institution.

Among secondary stakeholders, academic scholarship for the general public, media, and competitors presents a somewhat difficult assessment process. However, the college does acknowledge the benefits that can be gained personally and professionally in engagements with the public constituencies. In cases such as this, the individual faculty might rely on the prominence of the popular press publication outlet, sales figures, followers on digital media, invitations to speak, and overall "marketability" in terms of impact among secondary stakeholders.

Conclusions

We find that a stakeholder analysis allows Babson College professors to understand the greater impact of their efforts with regards to teaching, research, and learning. Thinking creatively is a hallmark of Babson College, and thinking creatively about the value of teaching, research, and learning allows us to align the intellectual activities of the faculty with the mission of the college. We then honor and reward the scholarly activities, as measured against stakeholder value/impact, that support the mission of the College. It would not make sense at Babson College to confine our faculty members to the purely discipline-based research of academic discovery as this would stifle our faculty and our students.

At the same time, we recognize that our form of stakeholder analysis is a differentiator for Babson College in the recruiting of new faculty members. A candidate trained in the ways of purely basic research with teaching as almost a sideline, for example, will likely not be successful (or even happy) at Babson College. Therefore, we have to look closely when engaged in recruiting and seek to identify the relevant stakeholders for a candidate's academic work. Then, we have to make the difficult decision as to the person's fit with the college and relevant stakeholders.

While we know that each college and university will be different in terms of primary and secondary stakeholders, resulting in a different balance among the different forms of teaching, research, and learning, we advocate strongly for a stakeholder approach to faculty engagement and assessment. Inviting faculty members to consider multiple and alternative audiences for their work encourages an open discussion about quality, relevance, and impact.

References

AACSB. (2013). *Examples of impact metrics in support of documentation.* Retrieved from http://www.aacsb.edu/en/accreditation/standards/2013-business/appendix/

Arenas, D., Lozano, J. M., & Albareda, L. (2009). The role of NGOs in CSR: Mutual perceptions among stakeholders. *Journal of Business Ethics, 88*(1), 175–197.

ATHE. (2014). *Tenure and promotion guidelines.* Retrieved from http://www.athe.org/?page=TP_Guide

Bailey, C. D., Hair, J. F., Hermanson, D. R., & Crittenden, V. L. (2012). Marketing academics' perceptions of the peer review process. *Marketing Education Review, 22*(3), 263–278.

Bailey, J. R. (2006). From the editor: Integrating the professorial mission. *Academy of Management Learning & Education, 5*(2), 149–151.

Bailey, J. R., Saparito, P., Kressel, K., Christensen, E., & Hooijberg, R. (1997). A model for reflective pedagogy. *Journal of Management Education, 21*(2), 155–167.

Balkin, D. B., & Mello, J. A. (2012). Facilitating and creating synergies between teaching and research: The role of the academic administrator. *Journal of Management Education, 36*(4), 471–494.

Behrman, J. N., & Levin, R. I. (1984). Are business schools doing their job? *Harvard Business Review, 62*, 140–147.

Bickford, D. J., & Welsh, J. (1997). Reflections on artful teaching. *Journal of Management Education, 21*(4), 448–472.

Boyer, E. L. (1990). *Scholarship reconsidered: Priorities of the professoriate.* Princeton, NJ: Carnegie Foundation for the Advancement of Teaching.

Clarkson, M. (1995). A stakeholder framework for analyzing and evaluating corporate social performance. *Academy of Management Review, 20*(1), 92–117.

Dean, K. L., & Forray, J. M. (2014). How do we know what we know ... and how do we show it? *Journal of Management Education, 38*(6), 779–783.

Dehler, G. E., & Welsch, M. A. (1997). Discovering the keys: Spirit in teaching and the journey of learning. *Journal of Management Education, 21*(4), 496–508.

Donaldson, T., & Preston, L. E. (1995). The stakeholder theory of the corporation: Concepts, evidence, and implications. *Academy of Management Review, 20*(1), 65–91.

Drumwright, M. E. (1996). Company advertising with a social dimension: The role of noneconomic criteria. *Journal of Marketing, 60*(4), 71–87.

Freeman, R. E. (1984). *Strategic management: A stakeholder approach.* Marshfield, MA: Pitman Publishing Inc.

Fukami, C. (1997). Struggling with balance. In R. Andre & P. J. Frost (Eds.), *Researchers hooked on teaching.* Thousand Oaks, CA: Sage.

Glassick, C. E., Huber, M. T., & Maeroff, G. I. (1997). *Scholarship assessed: Evaluation of the professoriate.* San Francisco, CA: Jossey-Bass.

Gross, K., & Godwin, P. (2005). Education's many stakeholders. University Business. Retrieved from http://www.universitybusiness.com/article/educations-many-stakeholders

Handelman, J. M., & Arnold, S. J. (1999). The role of marketing actions with a social dimension: Appeals to the institutional environment. *Journal of Marketing, 63*(3), 33–48.

Hult, G. T. M., Mena, J. A., Ferrell, O. C., & Ferrell, L. (2011). Stakeholder marketing: A definition and conceptual framework. *AMS Review, 1*(1), 44–65.

Hutchings, P., Huber, M., & Ciccone, A. (2011). *The scholarship of teaching and learning reconsidered*. San Francisco, CA: Jossey-Bass.

Hutchings, P., & Shulman, L. E. (1999). The scholarship of teaching: New elaborations, new developments. *Change, 31*(5), 10–15.

Linder, J. C., & Smith, H. J. (1992). The complex case of management education. *Harvard Business Review, 70*, 16–33.

List, A., & Pinard, M. (2014). *On the wing: A celebration of birds in music and spoken word*. Retrieved from http://www.babson.edu

Loyd, D. L., Kern, M. C., & Thompson, L. (2005). Classroom research: Bridging the ivory divide. *Academy of Management Learning & Education, 4*(1), 8–21.

McKinney, K. (2006). Attitudinal and structural factors contributing to challenges in the work of the scholarship of teaching and learning. *New Directions for Institutional Research, 129*, 37–50.

Mitchell, R. K., Agle, B. R., & Wood, D. J. (1997). Toward a theory of stakeholder identification and salience: Defining the principle of who and what really counts. *Academy of Management Review, 22*(4), 853–886.

Pfeffer, J., & Salancik, G. R. (1978). *The external control of organizations: A resource dependence perspective*. New York, NY: Harper & Row.

Sisodia, R., Sheth, J. N., & Wolfe, D. B. (2007). *Firms of endearment*. Upper Saddle River, NJ: Wharton School Publishing.

U.S. Department of State Bureau of Business and Economic Affairs. (2014). Retrieved from http://www.state.gov/e/eb/rls/rm/2014/230362.htm

Walck, C. L. (1997). A teaching life. *Journal of Management Education, 21*(4), 473–482.

Webster, F. E., Jr. (1992). The changing role of marketing in the corporation. *Journal of Marketing, 56*(4), 1–17.

2

Staying on Top: How Babson Achieves Excellence in Teaching

Anders Richtnér

Introduction

Given that "teaching is one of the most complex, important, and demanding of all occupations; to be effective as an educator takes years of intense effort and constant reflection and dialogue" (Bennett, 2010, p. 67), it is reasonable to ask two questions. First, how do teachers develop excellence in their teaching? And second, what sort of environment will help them do so? This chapter unpacks organizational routines in microfoundational terms (Salvato & Rerup, 2010) to find answers to these two questions.

Organizational routines, defined as repeatable patterns of inter-dependent behaviors, are a central construct in organization theory (Nelson & Winter, 1982). A strong motivation for unpacking routines in microfoundational terms is that it helps us understand what drives differences in the behavior and performance of firms (Felin, Foss, Heimeriks, & Madsen, 2012). Research suggests that progress has been made on understanding routines and how they change at the organizational level, but the underlying microfoundations have not received enough attention (Felin et al., 2012). A well-known example of an organizational routine is Intel's "Copy Exactly," an improvement program for replicating the firm's best manufacturing routines (Szulanski & Winter, 2002). However, many organizations do not have the option to find and copy practices (Bresman, 2013), because their working conditions are characterized by constant change, scarce resources, and short-time horizons (Brown & Eisenhardt, 1997). Additionally, many organizations rely on individual experts to perform critical tasks (Zellmer-Bruhn, 2003). In these environments, the challenge is less about replicating useful routines in new areas, more about continuously developing those already in use (cf. Bresman, 2013).

In this chapter, I extend our knowledge of organizational routines and how they change at the micro-level of origin (Felin et al., 2012) by examining how routines are tried out and changed. I address the following two-part research question: *How do organizational actors change their routines in order to develop excellence in teaching, and how does the environment in which they act influence changes in routines?* To answer this question, I build upon recent advances by Felin et al. (2012), who argue that microfoundations consist of three building blocks: individuals, processes, and structure.

I used qualitative research methodology (Yin, 1994) to study what teachers at Babson College, a private business school in Massachusetts, USA, do in order to achieve excellence in their teaching, and how the environment affects them. Babson was chosen first because, despite operating in a highly dynamic and competitive environment, it has consistently outperformed the market. The school has ranked number one for entrepreneurship for 18 consecutive years (undergraduate teaching) and 21 consecutive years (graduate). Second, Babson prides itself on its entrepreneurial ethos and approach (Greenberg, McKone-Sweet, & Wilson, 2011); it expects, if not demands, that teachers change routines continually. Teachers are expected and incentivized to make their approaches more efficient and effective, and share these changes with Babson's teaching community. This offers a natural setting for studying change in routines. Using an inductive approach, I examined patterns in routine changes as teachers developed, conducted, and followed up their courses. Based on my observations, I propose a process model explaining the dynamics of how excellence is created in teaching.

Several insights emerge from the model that contributes to current theory on organizational routines and its building blocks on the microfoundational level. First, concerning individuals, my findings mirror recent findings on the group level — i.e., that approaches to new routines range from straightforward copying (Szulanski & Winter, 2002) to extensive adaptation (Bresman, 2013). The study also shows that the environment that the teacher is part of is highly influential, as individual beliefs and expectations are shaped by other actors in the organization, which affects which routines are changed and aggregated to a collective level, and how this happens (Felin & Zenger, 2009). Second, concerning processes and interactions, I find that formal processes are stable over time, creating many fairly rigid routines. However, these stable formal routines are complemented by an expectation of flexibility in the organization, such that teachers can change courses "on the fly," in real time. This facilitates a balance between the stability of formal routines and the option for adaptability and variation within the routine.

Theoretical Background

EXCELLENCE IN TEACHING

What excellence in teaching is, and what it consists of, is a hotly contested question (Harden & Wilkinson, 2011). This is perhaps surprising, since the instructional skills of teachers are seen as a keystone of school effectiveness (Marzano, 2010b). There are some studies that focus at the level of the individual teacher, but far fewer on how schools achieve teaching excellence on a collective level.

At the individual level, Bain (2004) explains what makes the best college teachers effective in terms of having the most sustained, substantial, and positive influence on the way students think and act. His observations fall into six categories. First, the teachers know their subject really well, and believe that learning means little unless it significantly and sustainably influences the way students *act, think,* and *feel.* Second, every session is treated as an intellectual intervention, which calls for *serious preparation.* Third, the teachers *expect "more" of their students;* in contrast with less meaningful "high" expectations across the board, this indicates that the teachers aim to help each student learn and develop on a personal level. Fourth, the teachers aim to create a *natural learning environment –* one in which students can try, fail, and receive feedback, but one that also instills curiosity and motivation. Fifth, effective teachers believe that students want to learn and can do so, and they *treat students with simple decency.* Finally, the teachers *systematically assess their own performance* and make appropriate changes, primarily concentrating on learning objectives.

The key theme underlying Bain's findings is the emphasis on *students learning,* as opposed to teachers teaching. Similar arguments can be found elsewhere. Whetten (2007) points to the importance of course design, and argues that predictors of student learning reflect choices made during the course-design process. Marzano (2010a, p. 237) goes one step further, arguing that the "ultimate criterion for successful teaching must be student learning." Kreber (2002) points to the nature of teaching scholarship, which involves not only being an expert on teaching, but also sharing public accounts of teaching in a manner that can be peer-reviewed and used by other members of the teaching community.

In line with these arguments, I define excellence in teaching as a purposeful way of facilitating student learning in which teachers "draw on formal and personal sources of knowledge construction about teaching, effectively combine this with their knowledge of the discipline to construct pedagogical content knowledge, continuously further this knowledge through self-regulated learning processes, and validate their knowledge through peer-review" (Kreber, 2002, p. 18). While advances have been made at the level of the individual teacher trying to identify how they achieve excellence, it has been pointed out that the focus is still more on their own knowledge, rather than how they facilitate learning (Weimer, 2013).

Nye, Konstantopoulos, and Hedges (2004) examined teaching effectiveness and revealed substantial differences among teachers in their ability to elicit achievement gains from their students. But little is known on how to systematically develop and reproduce teaching excellence (Marzano, 2010a). To answer this question, we must first understand the organizational routines that underlie excellence in teaching, and how they change over time.

ORGANIZATIONAL ROUTINES

Prior work defines organizational routines as "regularities in organizational behaviors, cognitions, and performance" (Salvato & Rerup, 2010, p. 472) or "recurrent patterns of collective activity" (Becker, 2004, p. 645). Routines are viewed as "effortful accomplishments" (Pentland & Rueter, 1994, p. 488) that involve, and are performed by, multiple actors (Becker, Lazaric, Nelson, & Winter, 2005; Feldman, 2003; Feldman & Pentland, 2003), making actors and their interactions central to the idea of routines. It follows that actors in an organization have a choice between passively following organizational routines, or adjusting them (Feldman & Rafaeli, 2002; Pentland & Rueter, 1994). Since actors can adapt and create routines (Witt, 2011), routines exhibit qualities of both stability and change (Feldman, 2003).

Earlier research has analyzed the way organizational routines change over time at the organizational level (Becker, Knudsen, & March, 2006), but less so at the micro-level of origin (Felin et al., 2012). Thus, we understand how to copy manufacturing routines (Szulanski & Winter, 2002), but know far less about what happens to routines in working conditions characterized by constant change, scarce resources, or short-time horizons (Brown & Eisenhardt, 1997), or those where organizations rely on individual experts to perform critical tasks (Zellmer-Bruhn, 2003). Such environments make it difficult to identify and copy practices (Bresman, 2013).

This study focuses on how organizational actors change their routines in order to develop excellence in teaching, and how the environment influences such changes. By exploring this research question, we can examine how routines are developed, tried out, and changed in response to feedback from other actors in the organization. Our concern is not with the daily tasks of individual teachers — how they deal with their emails, which meetings they go to, etc. — but with how individuals and the organization create an environment that demands and expects excellence, and the sharing of knowledge about excellence.

Building upon recent advances by Felin et al. (2012), I examine the three microfoundational building blocks of routines: individuals, processes and interactions, and structure. As the authors note, these building blocks don't operate in a vacuum, but interact with each other. To explore how they contribute to developing excellence in teaching in terms of individuals and their environment, I chose a qualitative research methodology, outlined below.

Methodology

I chose a qualitative case-study design as the basis for inductive theory development, as existing literature did not allow for deductive hypothesis development related to the research question (Edmondson & McManus, 2007). Specifically, I sought to develop a theoretical explanation for how excellence in teaching is achieved. Therefore, I needed detailed data on the motives and actions of actors, which is best collected from qualitative data sources such as interviews (Yin, 1994). With a qualitative research approach, I could tap multiple, complementary data sources and generate a comprehensive analysis of excellence in teaching.

The research setting is Babson College ("Babson"), a business school in Massachusetts, USA, that specializes in entrepreneurship. Babson has been ranked number one in its field by authorities including *Money* magazine, *U.S. News & World Report*, *The Princeton Review*, and *Entrepreneur* magazine. Moreover, this is not a one-off achievement. Babson has been consistently recognized as a leader for two decades by the *U.S. News & World Report* (2014), which has ranked the college as the top undergraduate school for entrepreneurship for 18 consecutive years, and the top graduate school for entrepreneurship for 21 consecutive years.

Since it was founded in 1919, Babson has pursued a differentiation strategy based upon its capacity to expand the notion of entrepreneurship, and has continuously changed and disrupted its *modus operandi* over the years. Currently, it extols the concept of "Entrepreneurial thought and action®" (Greenberg et al., 2011). Babson's unique culture emphasizes preparing students for the realities of the business world, with the focus on practical experience as opposed to lectures. This approach can be traced to the early influence of its founder, Roger Babson. He wanted to create a college with a radically different approach to business education where the ambition was to aim at the hearts and minds of the students by blending the real with the ideal form, which Babson called "practical idealism" (Mulkern, 1994). In this context of continuous disruption and outward-looking adaptation, it is reasonable to believe routines will change. Therefore, the setting is well suited for investigating how teachers at Babson change their routines in order to achieve excellence in teaching.

In the empirical setting, routines can be found throughout the lifecycle of a course: before the course begins, during the course, and after the course. Examples of pre-course routines include setting up a course website, creating a course syllabus, and crafting learning objectives. During a course, teachers deliver lectures and give feedback on assignments. After a course, teachers assess students' performance, and their own. Some routines, such as handing out standardized course evaluations, are executed the same way year after year. Others are always part of the course process, but their execution differs depending on the teacher and the context; conducting a lecture is one example.

DATA COLLECTION

The primary source of data was semi-structured individual interviews. I conducted 14 interviews, plus numerous follow-up and informal discussions. All interviews were audio-recorded. Interviews ranged in duration from 45 to 90 minutes, but typically lasted around 60 minutes. I sampled my interviewees using Babson teaching awards as the selection criterion. Each year, Babson gives a Dean's award for excellence in teaching. The choice of recipient is based on student opinion surveys, innovative teaching, skill at teaching in integrated and cross-disciplinary settings, and engagement with course and curriculum design. Thus, the award goes beyond teaching performance to encompass a *scholarship of teaching* (Kreber, 2002). An award for excellence in teaching is made in each of five categories: (1) as adjunct faculty member, (2) at undergraduate level, (3) at graduate level, (4) in executive education teaching, and (5) teaching in any program. I listed the winners of the award over the preceding three years (2011–2013) and added seven teachers who had received multiple awards over the last 10 years. In total, 16 teachers agreed to take part in the study.

During the interviews, I asked each interviewee to elaborate on their experience as a teacher. I particularly encouraged them to focus on concrete activities that illustrated what did and didn't work in the classroom, and what happened before, during, and after a course. I used an interview guide based on the six overarching themes previously identified as distinguishing top-performing teachers (Bain, 2004).

I triangulated the interviews with other sources (Jick, 1979). First, I conducted participant observations, that is, sitting in the classroom during lectures. These observations lasted for 1.5–3 hours. I followed up with an informal interview (not audio-recorded) to get the teacher's thoughts about the session. Second, I referred to Blackboard (the course website), which included all the content related to the course, such as the syllabus, newsletters/mail, lecture slides, exercises, and take-home exams. In cases where I could not access Blackboard, I had access to the course syllabus. Third, I collected archive documents such as books, exercises developed, and cases written by teachers, along with public information from press announcements, newspaper articles, and public interviews. Table 1 summarizes the data sources and their use in the analysis.

Table 1:   Data Sources.

Source of Data	Type of Data	Use in Analysis
Interviews	Fourteen interviews conducted with teachers who had received the Dean's teaching award 2011–2013, and/or multiple teaching awards over the years. All interviews audio-recorded.	Gather data regarding how excellence in teaching is created, the relational context, the learning journey, and knowledge base. Identify patterns cutting across teachers.
Observation	Twelve classroom observations. Not all teachers had classes in the period of the study.	Triangulate data on framing the "why," dynamics in the classroom, relational context, and the learning journey.
Course website/ course syllabus	Access to course website (Blackboard): seven courses, including course syllabus, handouts, course announcements, etc. Course syllabus: five courses	Triangulate data on framing the "why," dynamics in the classroom, relational context, and the learning journey.
History narratives	Books (three), Babson.edu website, narrating the development of teaching at Babson.	Triangulate data on relational context; provide clues on excellence in teaching, the learning journey and knowledge base.
Internal documents	Internal company documents (30) such as product leaflets, presentations, reports, collected from websites (external and Babson internal), libraries.	Triangulate data on relational context; provide clues on excellence in teaching, the learning journey and knowledge base.

DATA ANALYSIS

To make sense of the qualitative data I used selective coding to identify recurring and dominant themes (Neuman, 2000; Strauss, 1987). The first step in the analysis was to re-read each of the interviews, manually identifying routines and issues that had an impact on how excellence in teaching is achieved and assessed. These *empirical observations* were then compared and contrasted across the interviews to identify common patterns. In the second step, I identified interactions by identifying which empirical observations shaped, leveraged, or were incorporated into other observations, forming *theoretical observations*. Finally, I developed explanations for the observed dynamics by creating *theoretical categories*. I developed my theory by going back and forth iteratively between the raw interview data and existing theoretical concepts on organizational routines, refining and rewording my observations, and developing theoretical observations (second-order themes; Gioia, Corley, & Hamilton, 2013) and theoretical categories. This process entailed repeated reading of the transcribed interview files and reviewing secondary data and the literature, enabling me to go beyond initial impressions to explore − rather than prejudge or ex-ante determine − how teaching excellence is achieved and assessed (Glaser & Strauss, 1967). The data structure is illustrated in the appendix.

Findings

KEY ELEMENTS OF THE DYNAMICS OF TEACHING EXCELLENCE

To explain the dynamics of excellence in teaching, I structure the key findings into three categories directly related to a course: preparation, execution, and conclusion, followed by three categories concerned with the environment: Babson, course development, and professional development.

Course Preparation

Teachers at Babson prepare for courses in two ways. First, they identify the "big question" that the course will answer. Whetten (2007) and Bain (2004) both discuss the importance of beginning with explicit, high-level learning objectives that are personally relevant to the students. During the interviews, in the classroom, and also in course syllabi, I observed teachers' ambition almost to transcend the nature of the course itself. For example: "*You will be able to apply this knowledge and assess the probable ecological impacts of your own lives ... and the major global developmental trends of human society and technology*" (course syllabus). It was also evident that teachers strove to make course content personally relevant. One professor noted that a course must be practical and usable. A course syllabus put it thus: "*Regardless of your ultimate objectives, you are invited to participate on this journey to discover how you will think and act entrepreneurially in your professional lives*" (course syllabus).

Second, teachers think carefully about the "story" or "flow" of the course. Many spoke about the importance of painting a coherent picture, framing the course as a dynamic journey in which every class is also a journey in itself. Several noted that the "story" needs a beginning, middle, and end, and that the teacher's job is to play the role of storyteller. And although some key points and theories remain constant, the way the story is told, and the characters within it, change over time. As one professor put it, "*[The] final goal of what they have to learn is the same, but the process is different*" (Professor 12).

The key finding is that in order to achieve excellence, teachers strive to *frame the "why" of the course.* The "why" might change slightly over the years, but it is always there. Second, this "big question" must be addressed by a compelling story that is reflected in the flow of the course. All these elements are decided before a course, and the decision to change them can have profound effects on how things are executed during the course — that is, routines may or may not change depending upon these decisions.

Course Execution

The literature offers several suggestions for how to choose activities that foster active, engaged learning, ranging from problem-based learning approaches to assigning time for reflection (e.g., Whetten, 2007). The teachers in the study understood this and applied it in the classroom. Specifically, many spoke of the importance of focusing on the energy within the classroom. One professor expressed it as a balance between light and heavy, while another spoke about the importance of not wasting people's time. Teachers used different tactics for maintaining classroom energy. Some divided every class into shorter 10-minute chunks. Others said they came to class with 10–11 key points, of which four were "must have" and six or seven were "optional to have" — but seven key points had to be covered in every class, in order to maintain the flow.

The suggestions above follow advice in the literature on how to create a dynamic environment in the classroom. However, what stood out in the interviews, and was also highly visible during my classroom visits, was the rapport between teachers and students. Rapport does not just happen, but is deliberately cultivated in a process that begins even before the course. As one professor said, "*When you walk into your class, you should know where your people are coming from — I mean experience, work experience … it is not only about reciting their names, it is about knowing who to call and when based upon their particular experiences they had, so I use their information on their personal background in my teaching"* (Professor 10). As another professor expressed it, *"It [is] a relationship that can be … I mean the classroom can be a terrifying place if you are coming into it not authentic, not caring … I think my students know from the beginning we are partners in learning"* (Professor 11). Others pointed to a relationship that develops during a course, but continues after the course is finished: *"We meet only twice a week, but we become so close … They feel so close each other, so whenever they have to apply for like other graduate schools, or job-related interviews, they always come to me … I say, 'Why?' and they say, they feel so close to me"* (Professor 12).

This rapport is closely linked to learning. Teachers explained that once they had established rapport with students, they could then go on to "blow their minds." However, as was pointed out, this is not a "walk in the park," because in order to learn, one must often unlearn first. Others noted that it was necessary to have tough challenges, and even discomforting questions, in order to push the students to stretch their horizons. An underlying ambition amongst the teachers was to encourage pattern recognition, so students would know how to tackle challenging situations in the future.

The key finding is that teachers work hard to **create dynamics during a course**. How dynamics are created and maintained depends on the teacher – and as several teachers pointed out, it is important to be authentic, to be oneself. The implication is that in order to create a dynamic classroom environment, teachers continuously changed and experimented with structures and approaches – that is, routines changed on a continuous and ongoing basis.

Course Conclusion

The literature on excellence in teaching suggests that the best teaching is "both an intellectual creation and a performing art" (Bain, 2004, p. 174). I coded the way teachers developed and assessed excellence in teaching in three distinct but not exclusive categories: concluding the course, after graduation, and lifelong learning. All three categories consisted of evidence of intellectual creativity, both at the end of the course and afterwards. One professor said: *"On course evaluations, the most interesting line for me is 'professor made me think.' The rest is beauty contest – it's bullshit. What I tell them my job is, is to provoke them. Provoke their thinking. And the highest complement they can pay me is to return the complement. To provoke me back. I feel strongly about that"* (Professor 10).

In terms of cultivating lifelong learning, one professor commented, *"I always try to leave them with a little something to keep them engaged and think about what is going to happen when the course is over"* (Professor 7). Several professors also pointed to the importance of adaptation during the course to allow for spontaneous learning, yet without compromising on learning objectives. As one professor said, *"By the time we get wherever we're supposed to get, or when the time runs out, which is probably more accurate, that everybody feels that like they've had a transformative experience, but maybe in different places"* (Professor 3). Finally, many teachers discussed their relationships and interactions with students long after the course had officially ended. As one explained, *"I try to make it so the course does not end ... guess what, your students can find you if they need advice or assistance, so let them know there is a support network out there, but you have to make them self-sufficient, so they understand what's out there"* (Professor 7).

Some teachers also commented on the performative aspects of a course, which often involved "closing the loop" by linking the end of the course back to the beginning. Some said the ending of the course depended on what had happened during it, making the ending different each time, calling for an ability to change continuously and in real time. There was agreement among the professors that the ending should always be inspiring, and linked to the ambition that learning should be a never-ending journey, with the course as a point of departure.

The key finding is that excellent teachers believe in, and emphasize, ***never-ending learning***. Their paramount objective is to have students rethink and question what they know, to foster a curiosity and thirst for more learning. The way to get there differs between teachers and changes over the years, but it is always about reaching both mind and heart. This is not an easy task, which is why teachers make changes up until the very end of the course to ensure learning continues beyond the end of it.

The Environment at Babson

Before coming to Babson, many of the professors in the study had been faculty or earned their PhDs at other well-known schools such as Harvard, MIT, and Stanford, to name a few. Without exception, they all said that Babson stands out in several ways. First, and perhaps foremost, teaching is taken seriously at Babson. It is the number-one priority. It is because teaching is so central to the Babson ethos that so many improve their teaching skills at the college. Others acknowledge the role of self-selection — that is, if you come to Babson you need to like teaching, and be good at it too. Natural selection also plays a role: if you are not good at teaching, you will (have to) leave. For instance, on the tenure track, teaching is the number-one criterion, and failure to reach a certain level will lead to tenure being denied. Several teachers spoke of competition between staff, and the need to achieve a certain standard if your class is after a "rock-star professor."

Two other key factors are the teachers' background and the students themselves. Babson teachers often have entrepreneurship experience, have started their own business and/or been involved in a start-up(s), or have significant operational experience, which reflects the quest for practical and relevant knowledge in courses. Students also influence the teaching, in several ways. They bring (often positive) experience from other classes, heightening their expectations for courses that follow. Teachers describe them as being action-oriented and eager to test out new things beyond the school, which underscores the need for actionable knowledge. Finally, students are at a crucial, formative stage of their lives, and teachers speak of their responsibility to prepare them for future challenges, but also help them become good citizens and empathic leaders.

The key finding is that there is an *(evolving)* **relational context** at Babson. The constant expectation that all teachers should be on their toes creates a need to revisit teaching materials over and over again. Hence, improving teaching is more of a continuous process than a static goal. Additionally, there is a true hunger among teachers to learn and be inspired; reflective teaching is taken very seriously indeed. Finally, teachers actively look for cross-disciplinary working opportunities, avoiding the "silo" mentality often found in both academia and business.

Environment for Course Development

Students' learning journeys are under constant scrutiny. First, professors continuously innovate in two dimensions: content and process. Concerning content, everyone in the study referred to the need to keep material up to date. Some are very systematic, and said they deliberately change 20–30% of the content every year. At the extreme, one professor literally threw everything (cases, teaching notes, etc.) into the trash every second or third year in order to have an up-to-the-minute course. Others spoke of the need to drop content whenever they felt bored with it; sometimes this meant small changes, sometimes a radical overhaul. The key point the professors made was that nothing is set in stone; content is constantly refreshed. Concerning the process, that is, what takes place during a course, some professors made changes during a course by asking for feedback from participants. Some did this by sending out mid-term surveys, some asked for feedback on each class, and others talked about the importance of informal discussions with students.

The professors in the study also explained how excellence is achieved by engaging with other teachers at Babson. For instance, many revealed that they would attend other people's classes for inspiration. Others said that they learned a lot by co-teaching. Some said a key for learning was to study other people's slide decks, and then discuss them with their author. A few professors were very systematic in evaluating their own performance after each class, and also when the course ended, focusing on one simple question: If I teach this course again, how can it be improved further? Finally, some teachers spoke about discussions with colleagues after classes and at the end of courses, which helped them see what to keep and what to change.

The key finding is that teachers at Babson continuously *(re)frame the learning journey* in order to achieve excellence. This impacts not only course content and the way it is taught (process), but also the way in which input from others (students and peer teachers) is sought.

Environment for Professional Development

The professors made sure they were always up to speed with the latest thinking — not only from research, but also from practice. Many spoke about the importance of reading extensively and widely, going way beyond the boundaries of their own discipline. For instance, one professor was given Steve Martin's book *Born Standing Up: A Comic's Life* by the president of Babson with the suggestion, "Read it and think about teaching." Many of the professors mentioned the importance of being "on the edge", which is achieved by sitting on company boards, doing consulting work, and engaging with society at large. Several systematically go through the news, both reading and watching, in order to find things that can be brought into the classroom. As already mentioned, colleagues and cross-disciplinary work are also fruitful sources of ideas.

The key finding is that being a teacher at Babson requires a *continuously developing (personal) knowledge base*. How this is done is a personal choice, but not doing it is not an option, according to the teachers in the study.

A MODEL OF EXCELLENCE IN TEACHING

Figure 1 shows how the six key findings from the empirical material explain how excellence in teaching is achieved over time. At the heart of the process model are organizational routines that show how never-ending learning is cultivated. Decisions on whether to change organizational routines to create dynamics during the course are triggered by the "why" of the course. Teachers incorporate the evolving relational context and the reframing of the learning journey as they create dynamics in the course. The dynamics created in the course is also leveraged in decisions about how never-ending learning is developed. Eventually, developing never-ending learning in

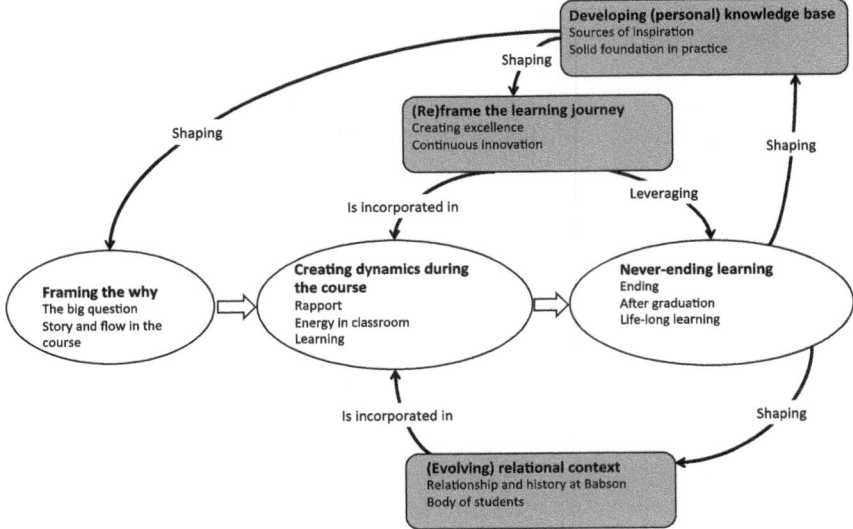

Figure 1:   A Model Explaining Dynamics of Excellence in Teaching.

teaching shapes the knowledge base, as new knowledge is created over time, and also the relational context, as new relationships are formed. As the knowledge base is developed, it shapes both the learning journey and the framing of the "why." All these elements must be taken into account to understand how and why organizational routines at the individual level are changed.

Discussion

Although research has provided a deeper understanding of routines at the organizational level, calls have been made for research that extends knowledge on the microfoundations, or micro-origins, of organizational routines, and how actors in organizations develop their routines (Felin et al., 2012). Prior work on organizational routines centers on the idea that routines are "recurrent patterns of collective activity" (Becker, 2004, p. 645) performed by multiple actors (Becker et al., 2006; Feldman, 2003; Feldman & Pentland, 2003), making actors and their intersection central to the idea of routines (Brauer & Laamanen, 2014). In this study, I begin to extend this knowledge by examining how organizational actors change their routines in order to achieve excellence in teaching, and how the environment in which the teachers act influences such changes. This study therefore contributes to our understanding of how routines arise (Felin et al., 2012; Salvato & Rerup, 2010) and are recreated at the micro level (Brauer & Laamanen, 2014).

Using an inductive approach, the study unpacks how organizational routines are formed and continuously developed over time in order to achieve excellence in teaching. The emergent model reveals a process that illustrates how actors change their routines over time, and the impact of the environment. More specifically, the model not only shows the process as such, it also helps to explain the interactions between members of the organization, how individuals themselves work, and finally, how the overall structure creates a context and enables individuals in the organization to act. To develop the theoretical implications of this study, I build upon the work by Felin et al. (2012), who argue that microfoundations consist of three building blocks: individuals, processes, and structure. The findings in the study suggest implications for individuals and processes, but not structure.

BUILDING BLOCK 1: INDIVIDUALS

Every organization depends on individuals within it. Therefore, to understand routines, we must acknowledge the role of individuals (Felin & Hesterly, 2007). Previous research has shown that individuals affect the behavior, evolution, and performance of organizations (Brauer & Laamanen, 2014), but without explaining how. This study takes a first step by showing how the evolving relational context is incorporated in the way dynamics are created during courses at Babson. By drawing on a wide variety of stakeholders with relevant knowledge, from students to researchers and people in the business community, teachers identified how they should change the way content was delivered in order to create specific classroom dynamics. Examples of changes in organizational routines as a result of interactions with stakeholders included using electronic "clickers" to vote on key questions; a more problem-based learning approach; inviting guest speakers to present challenges that the students then work toward solving; and changing how interactions outside the classroom took place, both formally and informally — for example, using Twitter to respond to students' queries.

Furthermore, by showing that the ambition to encourage never-ending learning shapes the relational context and the need to develop (teachers' own) knowledge bases, we can see how a virtuous circle that reproduces teaching excellence can be created. This is in line with recent contributions (Felin & Zenger, 2009) on how individuals theorize about the future and imagine novel options. The model in this study also suggests that the development of the knowledge base shapes not only the learning journey but also the framing of the "why."

BUILDING BLOCK 2: PROCESSES AND INTERACTIONS

A process is a sequence of independent events. Putting a process into action requires interaction between individuals, and the way individuals and processes interact shapes routines (Felin et al., 2012). Studies have examined coordination that is both formal (e.g., standard operating procedures), within and across firms, and informal (experience, norms, values) (Becker, 2004). While this work is important, it only partly addresses the microfoundations of routines (Felin et al., 2012), leaving unanswered questions such as the relationship between the rigidity and flexibility of routines, and the benefits of each. This study highlights that formal processes appear to remain stable over time: teachers stay with the same approach in areas such as scheduling year after year, and course evaluations remain the same, etc., which creates many fairly rigid routines. However, these formal routines are complemented by the flexibility to make real-time changes in the content of a course "on the fly." In this study, teachers conducted several short surveys so they could adapt and change what was happening in the classroom (process), and also make changes to assignments and readings (content) — provided such changes did not compromise the overall learning goals. This allowed them to balance the tension between formal routines and the need for adaptability and variation within them.

PRACTICAL IMPLICATIONS

The findings in this study offer implications for actors (both individuals and organizations) who want to foster excellence in teaching. First, as the process model shows, it is necessary to acknowledge that developing excellence is not simple; it has many elements that may, or may not, come together to form a virtuous circle in which routines are (re)created over and over again. The fundamental reason for the recreation of routines is the view that learning extends outside the boundaries of the course *per se*, and the key is to learn and challenge the way students think, remember, and draw conclusions (cf. Bain, 2004). This means it is necessary to encourage teachers to continuously develop the knowledge base, which in turn shapes the learning journey and frames the "big picture" in the course — that is, the desired learning outcomes (Whetten, 2007). This study also highlights the fact that in order to make predictions about excellence, one must know which relational context the actors are drawing on, as this influences dynamics during the course.

The advice for teachers is to work through each of the three steps in the middle of the process model with a critical mindset, imagining and considering what should be done at each step. To initiate this process, one can ask two critical questions: "What is the biggest question the course will help students answer?" and "What major abilities will the course help students to develop?" (Bain, 2004). The answers will probably affect several of the routines within the course. Having done that, the teacher should "zoom out" and ask whether and how the (personal) knowledge base should be developed, what the learning journey looks like and how it has (or hasn't) changed over the years, and how the relational context influences what is done within courses. Whereas this may seem trivial at first, this study shows that simple questions have complex outcomes, due to interdependencies within the model.

Conclusion

The dynamic model developed here describes a phenomenon of key concern for higher education establishments: how to develop excellence in teaching. The analysis shows that developing excellence depends on the ability to recreate routines, which is done by individuals interacting in a relational context, but also by individuals developing their knowledge base. The model also helps explain how flexibility and rigidity of routines can be balanced, in that the organization can develop formal routines that are stable over time, and at the same time give individuals the flexibility and autonomy to develop and change informal routines. In so doing, they can create a virtuous circle in which excellence in teaching can be (re)produced.

Acknowledgments

This research has benefited from the comments of Niklas Modig, Pär Mårtensson, Janelle (Jan) Schubert, Ebba Sjögren, and two anonymous reviewers. Financial support from Carl Silfvéns stipendiefond and Institute of Management and Technology (IMIT) is gratefully acknowledged.

References

Bain, K. (2004). *What the best college teachers do.* Cambridge, MA: Harvard University Press.

Becker, M. C. (2004). Organizational routines: A review of the literature. *Industrial and Corporate Change, 13*(4), 643–678.

Becker, M. C., Knudsen, T., & March, J. G. (2006). Schumpeter, winter, and the sources of novelty. *Industrial and Corporate Change, 15*(2), 353–371.

Becker, M. C., Lazaric, N., Nelson, R. R., & Winter, S. G. (2005). Applying organizational routines in understanding organizational change. *Industrial and Corporate Change, 14*(5), 775–791.

Bennett, B. (2010). The artful science of instructional integration. In R. J. Marzano (Ed.), *On excellence in teaching* (pp. 65−91). Bloomington, IN: Solution Tree Press.

Brauer, M., & Laamanen, T. (2014). Workforce downsizing and firm performance: An organizational routine perspective. *Journal of Management Studies, 51*(8), 1311−1333.

Bresman, H. (2013). Changing routines: A process model of vicarious group learning in pharmaceutical R&D. *Academy of Management Journal, 56*(1), 35−61.

Brown, S. L., & Eisenhardt, K. M. (1997). The art of continuous change: Linking complexity theory and time-paced evolution in relentlessly shifting organizations. *Administrative Science Quarterly, 42*(1), 1−34.

Edmondson, A. C., & McManus, S. E. (2007). Methodological fit in management field research. *Academy of Management Review, 32*(4), 1246−1264.

Feldman, M. S. (2003). A performative perspective on stability and change in organizational routines. *Industrial and Corporate Change, 12*(4), 727−752.

Feldman, M. S., & Pentland, B. T. (2003). Reconceptualizing organizational routines as a source of flexibility and change. *Administrative Science Quarterly, 48*(1), 94−118.

Feldman, M. S., & Rafaeli, A. (2002). Organizational routines as sources of connections and understandings. *Journal of Management Studies, 39*(3), 309−331.

Felin, T., Foss, N. J., Heimeriks, K. H., & Madsen, T. L. (2012). Microfoundations of routines and capabilities: Individuals, processes, and structure. *Journal of Management Studies, 49*(8), 1351−1374.

Felin, T., & Hesterly, W. S. (2007). The knowledge-based view, nested heterogeneity, and new value creation: Philosophical considerations on the locus of knowledge. *Academy of Management Review, 32*(1), 195−218.

Felin, T., & Zenger, T. R. (2009). Entrepreneurs as theorists: On the origins of collective beliefs and novel strategies. *Strategic Entrepreneurship Journal, 3*(2), 127−146.

Gioia, D. A., Corley, K. G., & Hamilton, A. L. (2013). Seeking qualitative rigor in inductive research: Notes on the Gioia methodology. *Organizational Research Methods, 16*(1), 15−31.

Glaser, B. G., & Strauss, A. L. (1967). *The discovery of grounded theory: Strategies for qualitative research.* Hawthorn, NY: Aldine de Gruyter.

Greenberg, D., McKone-Sweet, K., & Wilson, H. J. (2011). *The new entrepreneurial leader: Developing leaders who shape social and economic opportunity.* San Francisco, CA: Berrett-Koehler Publishers.

Harden, R. M., & Wilkinson, D. (2011). Excellence in teaching and learning in medical schools. *Medical Teacher, 33*(2), 95−96.

Jick, T. D. (1979). Mixing qualitative and quantitative methods: Triangulation in action. *Administrative Science Quarterly, 24*(4), 602−611.

Kreber, C. (2002). Teaching excellence, teaching expertise, and the scholarship of teaching. *Innovative Higher Education, 27*(1), 5−23.

Marzano, R. J. (2010a). Developing expert teachers. In R. J. Marzano (Ed.), *On excellence in teaching* (pp. 213−245). Bloomington, IN: Solution Tree Press.

Marzano, R. J. (2010b). A focus on teaching. In R. J. Marzano (Ed.), *On excellence in teaching* (pp. 1−6). Bloomington, IN: Solution Tree Press.

Mulkern, J. R. (1994). *Continuity and change.* Babson Park, MA: Babson College.

Nelson, R. R., & Winter, S. G. (1982). *An evolutionary theory of economic change.* Cambridge, MA: Belknap Press.

Neuman, W. L. (2000). *Social research methods: Qualitative and quantitative approaches* (4th ed.). Boston, MA: Allyn and Bacon.

Nye, B., Konstantopoulos, S., & Hedges, L. V. (2004). How large are teacher effects? *Educational Evaluation and Policy Analysis, 26*(3), 237–257.

Pentland, B. T., & Rueter, H. H. (1994). Organizational routines as grammars of action. *Administrative Science Quarterly, 39,* 484–510.

Salvato, C., & Rerup, C. (2010). Beyond collective entities: Multilevel research on organizational routines and capabilities. *Journal of Management.*

Strauss, A. L. (1987). *Qualitative analysis for social scientists.* New York, NY: Cambridge University Press.

Szulanski, G., & Winter, S. (2002). Getting it right the second time. *Harvard Business Review, 80*(1), 62–69, 125.

USNWR (U.S. News & World Report). (2014). Retrieved from http://www.usnews.com/education

Weimer, M. (2013). *Learner-centered teaching: Five key changes to practice* (2nd ed.). San Francisco, CA: Jossey-Bass.

Whetten, D. A. (2007). Principles of effective course design: What I wish I had known about learning-centered teaching 30 years ago. *Journal of Management Education, 31*(3), 339–357.

Witt, U. (2011). Emergence and functionality of organizational routines: An individualistic approach. *Journal of Institutional Economics, 7*(2), 157–174.

Yin, R. (1994). *Case study research: Design and methods* (5th ed.). London: Sage.

Zellmer-Bruhn, M. E. (2003). Interruptive events and team knowledge acquisition. *Management Science, 49*(4), 514–528.

APPENDIX: DATA STRUCTURE

3

A Practice-Based Approach to Entrepreneurship Education

Candida Brush, Heidi Neck and
Patricia Greene

Introduction

It is incredibly interesting when you think about it. Entrepreneurship
is characterized by uncertainty, experimentation, and action but the
most common approach to teaching entrepreneurship is the antithesis
of this (Kuratko, 2005; Neck, Greene, & Brush, 2014a). The vast
majority of teaching pedagogies, textbooks, and syllabi are associated
with an overly defined and linear process approach that can mislead
students into thinking that if a series of steps is followed, success is
inevitable. A typical process model of entrepreneurship generally
involves identifying an opportunity, evaluating the pros and cons, then
creating a plan for executing and acting on the opportunity (Hitt,
Ireland, Camp, & Sexton, 2001; Shane & Venkataraman, 2000;
Zahra & Dess, 2001). In the classroom, what generally happens is
that the focus is on the crafting of the plan, or "planning" all elements
for implementation of a new venture (e.g., pro-forma financials, market projections, team planning) with very little "real" action
(Sarasvathy, 2001). In other words, the focus is on the content and the
"what" of the discipline, following a predictive logic approach. Less
focus is on the actual implementation and action or the "how." But,
our responsibility as educators is changing given this more competitive, more uncertain, ever-changing environment that characterizes
today. Every business educator, regardless of discipline, must create a
classroom where "being entrepreneurial" is a baseline behavior. In

order to be entrepreneurial, students must do things (i.e., take action) rather than just plan. The reality is that the process approach is neither the most realistic nor the most effective approach for the current environment.

In order to address the deeper need for action and doing, we maintain that entrepreneurship can be taught as a method, one that focuses on the *how* at least as much as the *what*, but the method requires practice and the room for practice must be built into the learning and teaching approach. This is not to say that the *what*, or the content of an entrepreneurship course, is less important – course content is indeed central to entrepreneurship education. However, there is often less focus on the *how*, so for this chapter we highlight how entrepreneurship might be taught using practice theory as our theoretical foundation.

The remainder of this chapter provides a brief background on the history of entrepreneurship education and pedagogies, explaining the process approach and elaborating on entrepreneurship as a method. We draw from the theory that defines practice "as the enactment of activities and interactions that constitutes the occupation" (Billet, 2010, p. 22). We present five practices that comprise a method of teaching entrepreneurship – empathy, play, creation, experimentation, and reflection. Each practice is grounded in actionable theories from across a variety of disciplines and together constitutes a method of thinking and acting entrepreneurially, regardless of context (Neck et al., 2014a). Following a framework from educational scholarship, we provide examples of how a practice-based approach to teaching entrepreneurship can be applied in different contexts: independent classes, executive education, across a curriculum, in co-curricular settings, and across a nondegree program.

A Brief History of Entrepreneurship Education and Pedagogy

Entrepreneurship education has grown dramatically over the past 60 years, largely because entrepreneurship is deemed a catalyst for economic development and job creation around the world (Amoros & Bosma, 2014; Xavier, Kelley, Kew, Herrington, & Vorderwülbecke, 2012). Since the early 1960s, teaching courses in colleges, universities, and the private sector was recognized as an effective means for entrepreneurial learning (Timmons, 1989; Vesper, 1987). By 1979, it was estimated that 179 schools offered entrepreneurship courses and, today, it is estimated that more than 2,200 courses are offered in the United States alone at more than 1,600 colleges and universities

(Katz, 2003).[1] This same study showed that virtually all schools with an AACSB accredited MBA or four-year degree and nearly all nationally ranked schools are teaching entrepreneurship. Internationally, the growth in entrepreneurship courses is also skyrocketing. For one notable example, the Malaysian government launched the Higher Education Entrepreneurship Development Policy in 2010[2] with a goal of graduating college students with a greater ability to think and act entrepreneurially as a "catalyst for the achievement of economic transformation of the country from a middle to high income economy."

The past 60 years of entrepreneurship education has evolved through three phases: the Genesis Phase, the Apprentice Phase, and the Academic Phase.[3] The Genesis Phase really began with the first courses in entrepreneurship in 1947 at the Harvard School of Economic History, followed by a course taught by Peter Drucker in 1953 at NYU. In most of these early courses, students heard real-world experiences from speakers, a valuable exercise because this gave them role models. But, this approach left limited ability for students to actually practice entrepreneurship, while at the same time, association with any theory was very limited, mostly because academic entrepreneurship research was nascent at best. The vast majority of courses were focused either on small business management or starting a new venture. In 1984, Jeff Timmons brought together practitioners and academics to learn from each other and explore effective means of teaching through the Price-Babson Symposium for Entrepreneurship Educators (SEE) at Babson College.[4] The early years of Price-Babson SEE attempted to explicitly and intentionally link practice and theory in more experiential ways, even though the development of entrepreneurship theory had not yet caught up with practice. Today, an updated version of the program continues at Babson College and is regarded as one of the most action-oriented teacher training experiences available today.

The next wave of entrepreneurial pedagogy, the Apprentice Phase, was informed by strategic management whereby the case method became central to teaching entrepreneurship. Starting with the seminal text out of Harvard Business School, *New Business Ventures and the Entrepreneur* by Stevenson, Roberts, and Grousebeck (1989), entrepreneurship courses began to mimic strategy and policy courses by putting students in the role of the

---

[1] http://www.slu.edu/eweb/connect/for-faculty/infrastructure/entrepreneurship-education-chronology
[2] http://www.mohe.gov.my/portal/en/pelajar/program-keusahawanan.html
[3] Adapted from Figure 1.1 (p. 9), Neck et al. (2014a).
[4] http://www.babson.edu/executive-education/education-educators/Pages/price-babson-symposium.aspx

decision-maker or entrepreneur, akin to an apprentice model (Neck et al., 2014a). By the early 1990s, scores of teaching cases were written and schools began to include courses on entrepreneurial leadership, growing a venture, family business, and entrepreneurial financing.

Following the venture capital boom of the late 1990s, entrepreneurship education and pedagogy shifted to the Academic Phase — to an emphasis on the business plan where analytical skills became paramount (Honig, 2004). The focus of teaching was to analyze markets in order to determine gaps, create lengthy business plans that included detailed financial analysis, and predicted returns and market share. One quick survey of business plan competitions shows that every year, nationwide, there are more than 230 business plan competitions and, in any year given month, there are between 30 and 70 events for business plan competitions encompassing numerous administrative phases (submissions, presentations, final presentations, awards). More than $9.5 million is awarded annually to the winners of these competitions.[5] Today, many entrepreneurship programs continue to be heavily ensconced in the Academic Phase.

While all three phases of entrepreneurship pedagogy served as the foundation for a plethora of textbooks, case materials, and articles, they were all rooted in an overly linear process approach. In the process approach, entrepreneurship is taught in a stepwise fashion, starting with identifying an opportunity, then developing the concept, followed by assessing and acquiring the necessary array of resources, eventually implementing the business and finally selling or harvesting (Morris, 1998). The process is seemingly predictive because it assumes that opportunities can be identified, that it is possible to evaluate the pros and cons, and then that ultimately the projected outcome can be reached by following an executable plan (Neck & Greene, 2011). This approach tended to give false hope and an unrealistic sense of security to potentially overly optimistic entrepreneurship students.

More recently, scholars and teachers have increased interest in a more open view of entrepreneurship as a method of creation (Neck & Greene, 2011). This approach starts with the sense that each person has initial building blocks of resources and starting endowments that serve as an entrepreneurial foundation (Brush, Greene, & Hart, 2001). Going further down this path, Sarasvathy (2001, p. 245) posits an effectuation perspective and articulates this process as selecting between possible effects that can be created with a set of means; in other words, starting and taking action with what you have rather than waiting for what you need. She argues that

---

[5]http://www.bizplancompetitions.com/competitions/

effectual logic is rooted in what entrepreneurs have, who they know, and what they can afford to lose. Instead of a bias toward a particular end or outcome, entrepreneurs create their environment through action, using the resources or means they have available and bringing along other stakeholders who can help (Dew, Read, Sarasvathy, & Wiltbank, 2009). Other recent work on bricolage (Baker & Nelson, 2005) and improvisation (Hmieleski & Corbett, 2006) suggests that entrepreneurial actions can be characterized by trial and error, serendipity, or other creative approaches.

Creative actions, experimentation to clarify opportunities, and the discovery of new stakeholders are each embedded in a social context (Burt, 1992; Granovetter, 1985; Jack & Anderson, 2002). A creative approach to entrepreneurial action leverages resources and relationships at hand and "within reach" – both in the founding process and as a course for venture development – versus fitting and acquiring resources from a pre-created plan (e.g., human resources, financial resources, physical resources). A creative approach recognizes implicitly that all entrepreneurial actors are embedded in, working in, and shaping idiosyncratic social structures. In sum, entrepreneurship is inherently social and, therefore, largely cannot be predicted.

It is important to differentiate between the creative and predictive logics as they represent two forms of thinking and ways of teaching entrepreneurship. While the predictive logic dominated the Academic Phase of entrepreneurship education, the creative logic represents a more modern and relevant view of entrepreneurship education. Table 1 highlights the competing assumptions of the two logics.

Table 1: Predictive and creative logics.

Predictive Approach	Assumptions	Creative Approach	Assumptions
Identify the opportunity	Known inputs	Self-understanding	Skills/capabilities of individuals
Identify and quantify the resources needed	Known outcomes	Observation and reflection	Opportunities can be made or created
Systematically evaluate options	Identified steps, precision approach	Bring stakeholders along	Interactive
Create the plan	Predictive linear	Action and experiment	Creative and iterative
Execute and measure results	Tested	Build on results	Means driven Unknown inputs

Source: Adapted from Noyes and Brush (2012).

Despite the growing interest and evidence that entrepreneurs are utilizing creative and effectual approaches (Baker & Nelson, 2005; Dew et al., 2009; Hmieleski & Corbett, 2006), popular pedagogical approaches in the entrepreneurship classroom still heavily favor predictive ways of thinking. Of course, there are times when a predictive approach is appropriate and mandated, where resources, time, and information are available to conduct appropriate analyses. (Ansoff, 1988; Mintzberg, 1978). But, this information is less available in uncertain, entrepreneurial contexts. While it is agreed that some aspects of the venture creation and growth process, no matter what the context (social, corporate, family, de novo start up), require a predictive approach, analysis, or heuristics, especially when seeking funding, contracting with suppliers, or customers (Honig, 2004). But, an overemphasis on predictive logic as the underpinning of pedagogy means we may not be providing our students with the most relevant and robust tools to encourage entrepreneurial action. In other words, the predictive, more process-driven approaches dominate our pedagogies and how we teach, which is shortchanging our students' development for a more entrepreneurial world.

Moving from the Process Approach to Entrepreneurship as a Method

The process approach implies that one will get to a desired outcome if prescribed steps are followed. Importantly, the word "process" assumes known inputs and known outputs. Another way to consider this is to use a car manufacturing analogy (Neck & Greene, 2011). Think about building a car on an assembly line. Great thought and engineering are involved in designing the process where the required parts that enter the manufacturing process are known, there are precise specifications of how the parts are to be assembled, and it is known with great certainty what the car will look like as it comes off the line. The process is quite predictable. Can we really expect entrepreneurship to be such a process? Is entrepreneurship really that predictable? The answer is most certainly no, but the strong influence of strategic management and economics on the field of entrepreneurship has resulted in educators traditionally accepting a process view of teaching. This is also problematic because a process approach may not work in the dynamically changing social, technological, and global environments where entrepreneurship takes place.

We argue that the process model as a pedagogy for teaching entrepreneurship is outdated because entrepreneurial environments are unpredictable, uncertain, ambiguous, and therefore require a specific type of mindset. To better manage this type of environment, we propose that that entrepreneurship needs to include a creative logic that recognizes different phases of learning. It needs an action focus and it needs to be collaborative and iterative — entrepreneurship as a method. Learning entrepreneurship requires a student investment in their learning, not from a financial perspective, but in their commitment level to acquiring entrepreneurship knowledge. It also must be collaborative, going beyond any long held stereotypes to recognize the value of working with other people. Approaching entrepreneurship as a method means teaching a way of thinking and acting built on a set of assumptions using a portfolio of practices to encourage creating. Teaching entrepreneurship means reframing the process approach to a method that forces students to go beyond understanding, knowing, and talking. It requires using, applying, and acting. The method requires continuous practice (Neck et al., 2014a). Figure 1 summarizes the differences between the two approaches, method and process.

Teaching entrepreneurship as a method encourages our students to go beyond rote memorization of the content of a discipline and, instead, to *navigate* the discipline. A method represents a body of skills or techniques that help students develop a set of practices that implore students to think and act more entrepreneurially. We believe that introducing entrepreneurship as a method of practices is just as impactful, if not more so, than the current content so often seen in the textbooks. Basic information is a commodity today; therefore, "we need to teach methods that stand the test of dramatic changes in content and context" (Neck & Greene, 2011, p. 62).

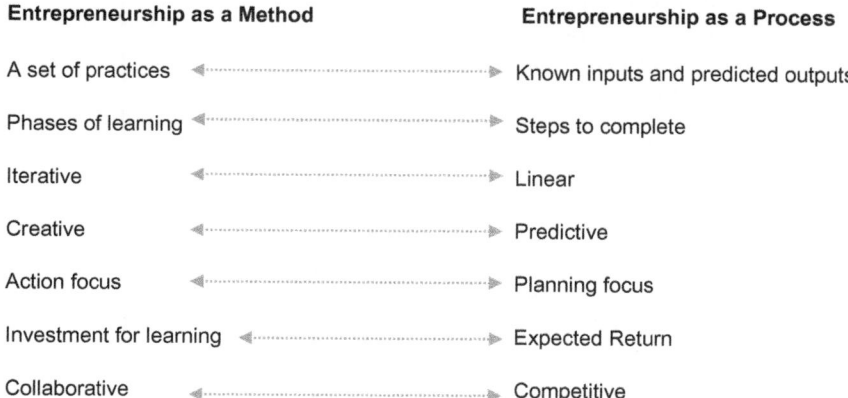

Entrepreneurship as a Method   **Entrepreneurship as a Process**

A set of practices   ⬸⋯⋯⋯⋯⋯⋯⋯⋯⋯⋯⬾   Known inputs and predicted outputs

Phases of learning   ⬸⋯⋯⋯⋯⋯⋯⋯⋯⋯⋯⬾   Steps to complete

Iterative   ⬸⋯⋯⋯⋯⋯⋯⋯⋯⋯⋯⬾   Linear

Creative   ⬸⋯⋯⋯⋯⋯⋯⋯⋯⋯⋯⬾   Predictive

Action focus   ⬸⋯⋯⋯⋯⋯⋯⋯⋯⋯⋯⬾   Planning focus

Investment for learning   ⬸⋯⋯⋯⋯⋯⋯⋯⋯⬾   Expected Return

Collaborative   ⬸⋯⋯⋯⋯⋯⋯⋯⋯⋯⋯⬾   Competitive

Figure 1: Method versus Process. *Source*: From Neck et al. (2014a, Figure 1.2, p. 12).

Teaching Entrepreneurship as a Practice

We argue that entrepreneurship needs to be practiced in order to be learned. We promote a practice-based approach as a model of learning to more effectively support entrepreneurial action. Teaching entrepreneurship as a method means teaching entrepreneurship as a series of practices that allow students to learn from doing and experiencing (Kolb, 1984). A practice defined within the realm of practice theory is "the enactment of the kinds of activities and interactions that constitutes the occupation" (Billet, 2010, p. 22). There is a long tradition of research that supports learning through practice.

> [Learning] can be enhanced by particular kinds of pedagogic activities which, as instanced, required the practitioner to represent their tacit learning in some way. This requirement creates an imbedded practice that has significant pedagogic qualities in so far as it generates the kinds of knowledge structures that make explicit what was tacit, and generates richer understanding about practice, but from and through practice, not on behalf of it. (Billet, 2010, p. 29)

The predominant themes found in practice theory (Rouse, 2006) capture why we elect to take a practice-based approach to entrepreneurship education:

1. Practices are meaningful performances governed by social rules and norms;
2. Practices create culture and act as a platform for social construction;
3. Practices require continuous interaction with others and the environment leading to expanded knowledge structures and mindfulness in the practice;
4. Practices create shared meaning among participants through the use of language, frameworks, tools, and common experiences.

We identify five specific practices that comprise a method of teaching entrepreneurship that through continued practice can develop the entrepreneurial thinking and acting abilities of students. These five practices are play, empathy, creation, experimentation, and reflection.

THE PRACTICE OF PLAY

The first practice is *play*. This is about developing a free and imaginative mind, allowing one to see a wealth of possibilities, a world of opportunities, and a pathway to more innovative ways of being entrepreneurial. There are three forms of play that represent different cognitive levels (Stone, 1995). Neck, Greene, and Brush (2014b) discuss the different forms with associated examples from entrepreneurship education, and we reiterate them here.

The first play form is *Sociodramatic* play that is based on imagination and fantasy. An example of this type of play is facilitating an idea generation exercise where students are forced to brainstorm the most fanciful, whacky, magical, ludicrous, or nonsensical ideas possible. The second play form is *Functional* play that requires interacting with the environment. Take for example the popular business model canvas (Osterwalder & Pigneur, 2010). An example of functional play is creating a card game using the nine components of the business model canvas and asking student teams to put the components in order from the most important component to address to the least important. Students are physically moving cards around and discussing each part of the business model canvas while competing with other teams for the "correct" order. The final play form is *Constructive* play. This type encourages students to build, create, or problem solve. Consider the popular marshmallow challenge (http://marshmallowchallenge.com/Welcome.html). Teams are given 20 sticks of dried spaghettis, one yard of tape, one yard of string, and one marshmallow and asked to build the tallest structure they can with the marshmallow on top.

Building the three forms of play in the classroom helps students develop a practice of play that aid in the developments of skills that include idea generation, lateral thinking, business model understanding, teamwork, learning from trial and error, and so on. As suggested by Education Professor Wasserman (1992, p. 137), "virtually every important concept to be taught — whether it be at the primary, intermediate, or graduate level or whether it be in science, math, economics, or business management — can be taught through the medium of serious play."

THE PRACTICE OF EMPATHY

A teacher in Orlando, Florida, spent his summer vacation living as a homeless person (Kavanagh, 2014). After years of helping the homeless, Thomas Rebman wanted to gain insights into what it is like to truly live homeless. What he discovered could only happen through empathy. Though threatened, scared, and hungry on most days, what he did not expect was how he *felt*. Rebman noted, "The big issue is how you are treated. It amazes me the things people do and say every day" (Kavanagh, 2014). Rebman's story is one that represents the second practice — empathy. Empathy borrows heavily from psychology, neuroscience, and design thinking and is defined as "a social and emotional skill that helps us feel and understand the emotions, circumstances, intentions, thoughts, and needs of others, such that we can offer sensitive, perceptive, and appropriate communications and support" (McLaren, 2013, p. 11).

The origins of empathy as an area of academic inquiry began in art history (Titchener, 1909). Empathy was used to describe the artist unable to separate himself from the objects portrayed in the art. As other disciplines began studying empathy (theology, philosophy, psychology, neuroscience), the complexity of the construct grew (Preston & Waal, 2002). Empathy does require practice because it has been proven that empathy can be developed over time by creating experiences or scenarios (Kouprie &Visser, 2009).

Given that empathy can be developed, this practice is important to entrepreneurship education for two reasons (Neck et al., 2014a). First, students need to develop empathy in order to better understand and relate to the lives of the entrepreneurs. By doing so, a student has a more realistic view of what it takes and how it can feel to be an entrepreneur. A starting point is a simple "interview-an-entrepreneur" assignment, which can help students develop empathy for a practicing entrepreneur while also assessing their own ability to become an entrepreneur. The second reason for building a practice of empathy is that students to connect with customers, users, and other stakeholders in more meaningful and authentic ways in order to identify unmet needs — the antecedent of innovation. Introducing students to design thinking (Brown & Katz, 2009; Norman, 1988) can further develop their practice of empathy since observing and subsequently understanding the needs of humans is a central tenet of design thinking. Simply assigning students a space to observe for two hours (without talking) can produce profound reactions from students.

THE PRACTICE OF CREATION

The practice of creation combines effectuation theory (Sarasvathy, 2001) and creativity theory (Amabile, 1983; Csikszentmihalyi, 1996; De Bono, 1985) and relates to "unleashing the creative ability of students to produce something of value with what they have rather than not producing because of constraints based on what they think is needed" (Neck et al., 2014b, p. 13). The practice is complex and includes opportunity creation, identification, and exploitation as well as a general openness to the world – an entrepreneurial mindset.

Creativity can be taught and everyone can be creative in some manner (Amabile & Kramer, 2011). Thus, the practice of creation is about harnessing that creative potential to start something from basically nothing. Imagine an exercise where student teams are given US$5 and two hours to generate as much profit as they can (http://ecorner.stanford.edu/authorMaterialInfo.html?mid=2268). Lessons learned from this exercise range from the necessary ability of entrepreneurs to bootstrap to the realization that cash can often be a constraint in starting new ventures. Resources abound if one is able to creatively leverage what they have around them. Helping students develop a practice of creation requires two things. First students need to believe that they are creative (or can be), but it must be harnessed and unleashed through immersion. In other words, creative practice builds creative muscles. Second, such immersion requires tools that can aid the creative development. The perspective that new ideas come from a light bulb moment is a myth. "Even when an idea seems sudden, our minds have actually been working on it all along" (Sawyer, 2006, p. 474). In other words, creation of new ideas requires development and practice.

THE PRACTICE OF EXPERIMENTATION

The practice of experimentation involves trying something, seeing what the results are, learning from the results, and then trying it again. The practice involves interacting with people, places, and objects in the environment in order to acquire new knowledge (Fletcher, 2009; Zahorik, 1995). The practice of experimentation borrows from theories related to problem-based learning (Barrows, 1985), evidence-based learning (Howard, McMillen, & Pollio, 2003), and sensemaking (Weick, 1995).

Experimentation is a practice where the predictive and the creative approaches really do come together. Problem-based learning builds on a sense of cognitive conflict as a stimulus for learning. There is a need, a concern, or an issue that must be resolved and the starting point for evidence-based learning is the existing information. Examining what is known, including identifying what is yet not known, serves as the starting point. Figuring out what this "evidence" means involves sensemaking, a way of making this personal to the students. This step gives meaning to the students in the context of their lives and their environments. According to Weick (1993), sensemaking is "an ongoing accomplishment that emerges from efforts to create order and make retrospective sense of what occurs." It is through experimentation, done in a wide variety of ways, that students learn to take action, analyze, and learn from that action, and try again based on what they learned (Schlesinger, Keifer, & Brown, 2012).

The practice of experimentation is best described as "students acting in order to learn rather than learning before acting or applying" (Neck et al., 2014b, p. 15). Popular entrepreneurship education tools such as the Business Model Canvas (Osterwalder & Pigneur, 2010) or the Innographer Toolkit (Bruton, 2014) all require actions through experimentation, getting out of the building, and collecting new and real information to validate assumptions and answer questions associated with new ideas.

THE PRACTICE OF REFLECTION

The practice of reflection actually connects the other four practices together. The previous four practices (play, empathy, creation, and experimentation) all require a lot of *action* and *doing*; therefore, reflection is necessary to allow students to pause and think, allowing them to codify and examine their learning experiences. This is perhaps the most integrating of all the practices, because there is evidence that practicing reflection can enhance each of the other practices (Schön, 1983).

The theoretical foundations of this practice are from Schön's reflective practitioner work (1983, 1987) and Brockbank and McGill's (2007) dense and rigorous treatment of reflection in higher education. The purpose of reflection is to go beyond surface learning into deep learning, which requires critical thinking enabling students to connect concepts, principles, and ideas in ways that lead to longer term retention and future application (Case, 2008).

Reflection requires practice because a simple journaling assignment without guidance is not sufficient in entrepreneurship. We offer six types of reflection (Brockbank & McGill, 2007; Neck et al., 2014a) that can be used to get to the desired deeper learning from the other practices:

1. Narrative reflection: Student describes what happened in a class, exercise, or event.
2. Emotional reflection: Student focuses on what they were feeling, why, and how the emotions were managed during a class, exercise, or event.
3. Percipient reflection: Student must identify and consider the perceptions (theirs and others) and how it affected the class, exercise, or experience.
4. Analytical reflection: Student explains the processes or important elements of the class, exercise, or experience, and how they are connected or related.

5. Evaluative reflection: Student assesses the class, exercise, or experience and identifies the criteria used for the evaluation.
6. Critical reflection: Student identifies alternatives or contradictions in the class, exercise, or experience while also reflecting on what was learned about student, his or herself, in the process.

In general, each type of reflection represents a different level of depth and learning. Asking students specific questions related to each type of reflection can produce a more intense and relevant reflection experience. Reflection is also considered the overarching practice, in that it is the tool for reinforcing what has been learned through any of the other practices. Given that any entrepreneurship course or program is going to include a portfolio of practices, reflection allows students to cross over assignments, exercises, and even courses, to assimilate and embed what they have learned. Figure 2 shows how the five practices flow from play, to empathy, to creation, to experimentation, and to reflection in a cycle.

The next section provides illustrations of how these five practices for entrepreneurial education can be applied in three different contexts: a co-curricular setting, a nondegree practitioner program, and an educator program.

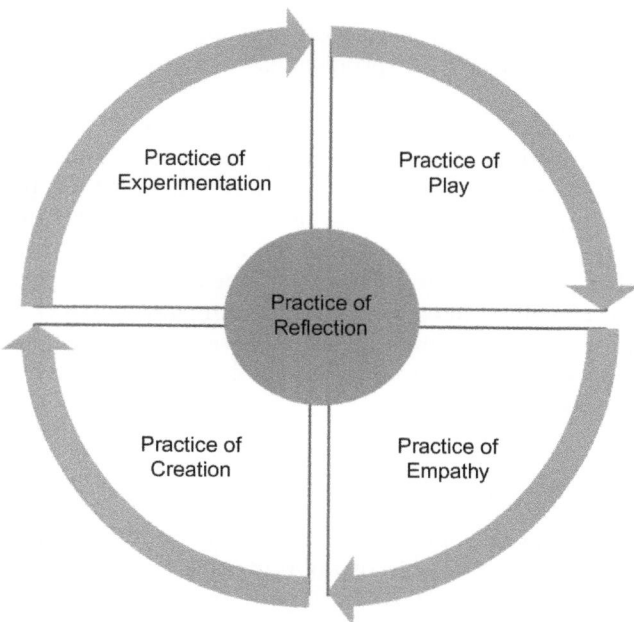

Figure 2: The Practices of Entrepreneurship Education. Source: Neck et al. (2014a).

Practicing Entrepreneurship Beyond the "Official Curriculum"

In addition to the classroom examples provided in the previous section, we next consider a variety of contexts for practicing entrepreneurship to illustrate how the five practices can be applied beyond the traditional classroom. Each practice is explained along with an activity, the faculty role, and the learner assessment.

BABSON COLLEGE SUMMER VENTURE PROGRAM – A CO-CURRICULAR ACTIVITY

The Babson College Summer Venture Program (SVP) is a 10-week intensive experience designed to accelerate the development of student entrepreneurial ventures. The Summer Venture Program supports the most promising graduate and undergraduate entrepreneurs from Babson, Olin College of Engineering, and Wellesley College. Approximately 15 teams are chosen to participate in the program each summer. Teams receive housing, work space, advisors, a speaker series, and other resources to help them and their businesses develop throughout the 10 weeks. The program ends each year with the Summer Venture Showcase. This event serves as a culmination of the students' hard work and allows them to showcase their accomplishments to professional investors and the local community.

A key activity is participation in the "Hot Seat" sessions. Students learn to critique each other's presentations, and to develop engaging sales and investor pitches. Students deliver their presentations and then reflect on their learning and customer experiences to answer questions from their peers and outside advisors. At the same time, other participants feel "empathy" for the hot seat participant because they will be next. They use their empathetic experiences to prepare for their own time to share. Vicarious learning takes place as students learn to listen to questions and empathize with the entrepreneur in the "hot seat."

GOLDMAN SACHS *10,000 SMALL BUSINESSES*

Our practice-based approach to teaching entrepreneurship is also valid when teaching outside of the traditional classroom to individuals who already own their businesses and are working to grow them. The curriculum for *10,000 Small Businesses* includes the full portfolio of practices. Two key examples can be seen in the practices of play and of reflection. The business owners are guided through an exercise called the Idea Lab[6] which starts with their idea for a pathway to business growth and has them play with that idea, stretching it out and shrinking it to various sizes, twisting it around and poking it to test various market assumptions, and finally allowing it to settle into a space that feels like a business fit with them as the business owner. The faculty members not only guide the exercise process, but also encourage the business owners to examine all of their currently held assumptions about how a business "should" be grown and consider innovative approaches to not just their product or service but also to their business itself.

Reflection also plays a critical role in *10,000 Small Businesses*. The business owners are each directed to select a reflection tool that best fits them, be it a small notebook, a mobile app, or something in between. The faculty guide them through a reflection process, emphasizing the importance of going beyond just the narrative of the phenomena being examined to consider other approaches such as trying to reflect from a change of perspective (someone else's eye) or reflecting on the emotions raised and the reason for those emotions. The final step is generally a movement toward "what do I do now?" Business owners often find the reflection process difficult, describing themselves as feeling like they need to "do something." The teaching challenge is to help them learn that reflection, thinking, is actually doing something.

BABSON SYMPOSIUM FOR ENTREPRENEURSHIP EDUCATORS (SEE)

SEE programs are delivered at Babson and in international locations around the globe. Each program is typically four days long and designed to train and develop all types of educators in the "Babson Way" of teaching entrepreneurship. Program participants are immersed in all five of the practices because each session is designed to engage participants in the same ways we engage our students. In other words, participants assume two roles. They are not only an educator reflecting on their experience as they move through the program but also a student experiencing similar thoughts, feelings, emotions, and motivations of their own student. Participants *play* games and participate in simulations. They *create* and pitch new ideas that will enhance entrepreneurship education. They develop *empathy* for their own students as they participate in classroom discussions, assignments, and activities that are often uncomfortable, challenging, and even ambiguous. Participants are also encouraged to *experiment* with new approaches learned in the program and reminded that the only path to change and growth is

---

[6]See Neck et al. (2014a, pp. 194–200).

experimentation in the classroom. Finally, participants are asked to reflect at the end of each day using an assignment reflection questions. Sometimes, participants are asked to post their reflection on an electronic discussion board; other times they are asked to report out the following morning. Because each SEE program models the expected teaching and learning behaviors of our own Babson classrooms, it is expected that all the practices are in play throughout the program.

Conclusion

Entrepreneurship education is now seen as of increased importance as individuals express desires to create their own organizations and as governmental bodies at all levels (towns, states, countries, etc.) look to entrepreneurial endeavors as a means of economic and social development. While the question of whether one can teach or learn entrepreneurship is less frequently asked, the question of *how* one teaches entrepreneurship remains paramount. The overemphasis on a linear predictive process actually does a disservice to those enrolled in entrepreneurship classes with a true mind to start and build something of their own. A teaching portfolio based on the five practices of play, empathy, creation, experimentation, and the ubër practice of reflection help each student, no matter of their educational category or level, develop his/her own toolkit to help him/her think and act entrepreneurially. Teaching entrepreneurship is no longer a luxury in higher education, it is a necessity. More than ever the world needs students and leaders who think and act entrepreneurially in order to act on opportunities that generate economic and social value everywhere.

References

Amabile, T. (1983). *The social psychology of creativity*. New York, NY: Springer-Verlag.

Amabile, T., & Kramer, S. (2011). *The progress principle: Using small wins to ignite joy, engagement and creativity at work*. Boston, MA: Harvard Business School Press.

Amoros, J. E., & Bosma, N. (2014). *The 2013 global entrepreneurship monitor report*. Wellesley, MA: Babson College.

Ansoff, I. (1988). *The new corporate strategy*. New York, NY: Wiley.

Baker, T., & Nelson, R. (2005). Creating something from nothing: Resource construction through entrepreneurial bricolage. *Administrative Sciences Quarterly*, 50(3), 329–366.

Barrows, H. (1985). A taxonomy of problem based learning methods. *Medical Education, 20*, 481–486.

Billet, S. (2010). *Learning through practice: Models, traditions, orientations and approaches.* London: Springer.

Brockbank, A., & McGill, I. (2007). *Facilitating reflective learning in higher education* (2nd ed.). New York, NY: McGraw-Hill.

Brown, T., & Katz, B. (2009). *Change by design: How design thinking transforms organization and inspires innovation.* New York, NY: HarperCollins E-books.

Brush, C. G., Greene, P. G., & Hart, M. M. (2001). From initial idea to unique advantage: The entrepreneurial challenge of constructing a resource base. *Academy of Management Executive, 15*(1), 64–78.

Bruton, A. (2014). *The really big idea — The Innographer.* Retrieved from www.innographer.com. Accessed on February 16, 2015.

Burt, R. S. (1992). *Structural holes.* Cambridge, MA: Harvard University Press.

Case, J. (2008). *Education theories on learning.* Higher Education Academy Engineering Subject Center. Retrieved from http://exchange.ac.uk/downloads/scholar-art/education-theories.pdf

Csikszentmihalyi, M. (1996). *Creativity flow and the psychology of discovery and invention.* New York, NY: HarperCollins.

De Bono, E. (1985). *Six thinking hats.* New York, NY: Little, Brown & Company.

Dew, N., Read, S., Sarasvathy, S. D., & Wiltbank, R. (2009). Effectual versus predictive logics in entrepreneurial decision-making: Differences between experts and novices. *Journal of Business Venturing, 24*(4), 287–309.

Drucker, P. (1998). The discipline of innovation. *Harvard Business Review, 76*(6), 149–157.

Fletcher, J. D. (2009). From behaviorism to constructivism. In S. Tobias & T. M. Duffy (Eds.), *Constructivist theory applied to instructions: Success or failure?* (pp. 242–263). New York, NY: Taylor & Francis.

Granovetter, M. (1985). Economic action, social structure, and embeddedness. *American Journal of Sociology, 91*, 481–510.

Hitt, M. A., Ireland, R. D., Camp, M., & Sexton, D. L. (2001). Integrating entrepreneurship and strategic management actions to create firm wealth. *Academy of Management Perspectives, 15*(1), 49–63.

Hmieleski, K. M., & Corbett, A. C. (2006). Proclivity for improvisation as a predictor of entrepreneurial intentions. *Journal of Small Business Management, 44*(1), 45–63.

Honig, B. (2004). Entrepreneurship education: Toward a model of contingency-based planning. *Academy of Management Learning and Education, 3*(3), 258–273.

Howard, M. O., McMillen, C. J., & Pollio, D. E. (2003). Teaching evidence-based practice: Toward a new paradigm for social work education. *Research on Social Work Practice, 1*(2), 234–259.

Jack, S. L., & Anderson, A. R. (2002). The effects of embeddedness on the entrepreneurial process. *Journal of Business Venturing, 17*, 467–487.

Katz, J. (2003). The chronology and intellectual trajectory of American entrepreneurship education 1876–1999. *Journal of Business Venturing, 18*(2), 283–300.

Kavanagh, M. (2014). Teacher encounters good and bad in homeless experiment. *News 13*, July 18. Retrieved from http://www.mynews13.com/content/news/cfnews13/news/article.html/content/news/articles/cfn/2014/7/18/instead_of_taking_a_.html. Accessed on February 16, 2015.

Kolb, D. A. (1984). *Experiential learning: Experience as the source of learning and development.* Englewood Cliffs, NJ: Prentice Hall.

Kouprie, M., & Visser, F. S. (2009). A framework for empathy in design: Stepping into and out of the user's life. *Journal of Engineering Design, 29*(4), 437–448.

Kuratko, D. (2005). The emergence of entrepreneurship education: Development, trends and challenges. *Entrepreneurship Theory and Practice, 29*(5), 577–597.

McLaren, K. (2013). *The art of empathy: A complete guide to life's most essential skill.* Boulder, CO: Sounds True.

Mintzberg. (1978). Patterns of strategy formation. *Management Science, 24*(9), 934–948.

Morris, M. H. (1998). *Entrepreneurial intensity: Sustainable advantages for individual, organizations and societies.* Westport, CT: Quorum.

Neck, H., & Greene, P. G. (2011). Entrepreneurship education: Known worlds and new frontiers. *Journal of Small Business Management, 49*(1), 55–70.

Neck, H. M., Greene, P. G., & Brush, C. B. (2014a). *Teaching entrepreneurship: A practice based approach.* Northampton, MA: Edward Elgar Publishing.

Neck, H. M., Greene, P. G., & Brush, C. B. (2014b). Practice-based entrepreneurship education using actionable theory. In M. Morris (Ed.), *Annals of entrepreneurship education and pedagogy.* Northampton, MA: Edward Elgar Publishing.

Norman, D. A. (1988). *The design of everyday things.* New York, NY: Basic Books.

Noyes, E., & Brush, C. (2012). Teaching entrepreneurial action: Application of creative logic. In A. C. Corbett & J. A. Katz (Eds.), *Entrepreneurial action* (pp. 253–280). Advances in Entrepreneurship and Firm Emergence and Growth. Bingley, UK: Emerald Group Publishing Limited.

Osterwalder, A., & Pigneur, Y. (2010). *Business model generation.* Hoboken, NJ: Wiley.

Preston, S. D., & Waal, F. B. M. (2002). Empathy: Its ultimate and proximate bases. *Behavioral and Brain Sciences, 25*, 1–72.

Rouse, M. (2006, June). Enhancing effective inclusive practice: Knowing, doing and believing. Keynote address delivered at the *Learning for All: Enhancing Effective Practice in Special Education Symposia*, New Zealand.

Sarasvathy, S. D. (2001). Causation and effectuation: Toward a theoretical shift from economic inevitability to entrepreneurial contingency. *Academy of Management Review, 26*(2), 243–263.

Sawyer, R. K. (2006). Explaining creativity: The science of human *innovation* (1st ed.). Oxford: Oxford University Press.

Schlesinger, L., Keifer, C., & Brown, P. (2012). *Just start: Take action, embrace uncertainty, create the future.* Cambridge, MA: Harvard Business Review Press.

Schön, D. (1983). *The reflective practitioner: How professionals think in action.* New York, NY: Basic Books.

Schön, D. (1987). *Educating the reflective practitioner.* London: Jossey-Bass.

Shane, S., & Venkataraman, S. (2000). The promise of entrepreneurship as a field of research. *Academy of Management Review, 25*, 21–226.

Stevenson, H., Roberts, M. J., & Grousebeck, H. I. (1989). *New business ventures and the entrepreneur.* Homewood, IL: Irwin.

Stone, S. J. (1995). Integrating play into the curriculum. *Childhood Education, 72*(2), 104–107.

Timmons, J. A. (1989). *The entrepreneurial mind.* Andover, MA: Brick House Publishing.

Titchener, E. (1909). *Lectures on the experimental psychology of the thought processes.* New York, NY: Macmillan.

Vesper, K. H. (1987). Entrepreneurial academics—How can we tell when the field is getting somewhere? *Journal of Small Business Management, 25*(2), 1–25.

Wasserman, S. (1992). Serious play in the classroom: How messing around can win you the Nobel prize. *Childhood Education, 68,* 133–139.

Weick, K. (1993). The collapse of sensemaking in organizations: The Mann Gulch disaster. *Administrative Science Quarterly, 38*(4), 628–652.

Weick, K. E. (1995). *Sensemaking in organizations.* Thousand Oaks, CA: Sage.

Xavier, S. R., Kelley, D., Kew, J., Herrington, M., & Vorderwülbecke, A. (2012). Global entrepreneurship monitor: 2012 global report. Global Entrepreneurship Research Association. Retrieved from www.gemconsortium.org

Zahorik, J. A. (1995). *Constructivist teaching.* Bloomington, IN: ERIC Clearinghouse.

Zahra, S., & Dess, G. (2001). Entrepreneurship as a field of research: Encouraging dialogue and debate. *Academy of Management Review, 26*(1), 8–10.

4

An Ecosystem Approach to Diversity in Management Education

Nan Langowitz and Anjali Bal

Discussions of diversity are often politically charged, evoking immense passion from scholars, students, business leaders, and popular press alike. Lawsuits and protests about affirmative action and quotas are often highlighted in the news when speaking of diversity; yet, diversity is so much more than admissions practices and hiring decisions. When it comes to enriching the classroom experience and challenging students, the impact of diversity on student learning is immense. Important discussion ensues when students consider questions of equality and access for underrepresented groups.

Business schools in particular are criticized because students may leave degree programs without the proper skills to succeed in business positions (Holland, 2009). Further, business schools have been attacked for not having enough diversity in the classroom (De Meglio, 2013; Otani, 2014). One of the key complaints by businesses has been that students are not being prepared to handle the challenges of working in a diverse setting, nor do they have the cross-cultural knowledge to be effective in a global workplace (Holland, 2009). With increasing globalization, societal integration, and current demographic trends, the workplace has become diversified in new ways (Mor Barak, 2011). It is clear that diversity strongly impacts success in business (Egan & Bendick, 2008). As the world shrinks, cultural intelligence and the ability to interact with people from diverse backgrounds are becoming imperative skills for business leaders (Park, Fables, Parker, & Nitse, 2010).

Some believe that business schools are not equipping their students to deal with the interpersonal side of business nor to be adept and effective leaders in an increasingly diverse world (Datar, Garvin, & Cullen, 2010; Holland, 2009).

Acknowledging this change in business, accrediting bodies like the Association to Advance Collegiate Schools of Business (AACSB) and the European Foundation for Management Development (EFMD) — through its EQUIS program — have added diversity education and cultural exposure as a critical aspect to accreditation (Egan & Bendick, 2008). Given the dynamic nature of education, accrediting bodies such as these have a purpose of unifying and improving the value of education across numerous colleges and universities. Diversity and cross-cultural competence are key holistic educational dimensions that both AACSB and EFMD demand from their accredited schools.

Babson has taken an ecosystem approach to enabling student learning with respect to diversity. This approach has evolved over time and, more recently, has been operationalized through the philosophy of the institution as a living/learning laboratory where student learning is interwoven inside and outside of the classroom, with program-learning goals incorporated and supported beyond formal coursework. An ecosystem approach to diversity is one where every aspect of the institution has a role in focusing on diversity. Through our educational activities inside and outside the classroom, as well as through our campus-wide initiatives, Babson focuses on modeling and developing community members' ability to effectively engage across differences through the diverse population of our community. Using this ecosystem approach, Babson creates an environment that enables graduates to develop as more effective global citizens who are open to difference. The strategic mission of Babson College includes a strong focus on diversity, recognizing its importance to building a holistic educational experience. This mission indicates that Babson is "a diverse, multicultural, and inclusive community of highly talented students, faculty, and staff characterized by respect, understanding, and appreciation of the uniqueness and value of all people" (Babson College Website/About Babson/Diversity). To this end, numerous initiatives, groups, courses, and experiences have been created to encourage students' development of a global mindset and the ability to work effectively in a diverse world.

We begin this chapter with an overview of existent literature to frame our view on diversity. Then, we detail key aspects of the ecosystem approach in the Babson community and, finally, close with some general thoughts on diversity at Babson.

What Is Diversity?

The importance of diversity is at the forefront of educational discussion. Various definitions have been offered over the years, with a now common typology of visible and invisible diversity. Visible diversity refers to observable or readily discernible characteristics such as gender, race, or some physical disabilities. Invisible diversity refers to underlying attributes such as sexual orientation, religion, education, or socioeconomic status. In short, to characterize an individual with respect to invisible diversity requires additional information beyond a visible impression (Mor Barak, 2011). Diversity is a means of indicating the level of variety in either thought or identity within a group or institution (Milliken & Martins, 1996). In addition, scholars also discuss diversity as having two major components: cognitive and identity. Cognitive diversity has to do with how people "see, categorize, and understand" the world around them (Page, 2008, p. xiv). Identity is a perceived connection to certain groups based on demography, social and personal groups, and beliefs (Randel & Jaussi, 2003). Identity communities range across visible and invisible differences — for example, gender, sexual orientation, race, ethnicity, religion, and socioeconomic status. A diverse group would be heterogeneous, made up across a range of visible and invisible differences, often with interactive effects. While cognitive diversity and identity diversity are not the same measure, they are highly correlated; that is, the means by which individuals see and understand the word is highly influenced by the communities of which they are a part and the resulting beliefs they hold (Page, 2008).

Higher education has long been touted as a location where diversity is beneficial to facilitate both learning and human development. The effects of diversity on development have been extensively studied, and there is widespread agreement that exposure to diversity at key times greatly influences social development. Early adulthood is a key time in social development and identity formation (Erikson, 1956; Gurin, Dey, Hurtado, & Gurin, 2002). Prior to early adulthood, identity and belief are largely driven by family influences (Jones, Vaterlaus, Jackson, & Morrill, 2014). Although the United States is often called a "melting pot," research indicates that high schools and elementary schools are highly homogeneous in terms of race, socioeconomics, and religion. Thus, higher education is often the first time that students experience any significant diversity. Early adulthood is a time when people start to move away from familial norms because students are freer to experiment with different social roles and beliefs (Gurin et al., 2002). In early adulthood, identity is still somewhat malleable and people are more open to trying different social roles; this period of experimentation is known as a psychosocial moratorium (Erikson, 1956; Gurin et al., 2002). While diverse environments within the classroom provide opportunities to challenge beliefs, researchers posit that the vast majority of psychosocial moratoria occur outside the classroom through interactions in residence halls and in social settings (Antonio, 1999; Gurin et al., 2002). Colleges that foster diversity in organized events nurture student development and identity formation. Institutions of higher education with diverse student bodies foster environments where students are free to experiment in this way. This experimentation leads to social development and, ultimately, identity formation.

While the effect of diversity on social development has been well substantiated, there is debate as to its value in teams and overall business success. Numerous studies indicate that the existence of diverse teams can lead to increased creativity and problem-solving abilities (Cox & Blake, 1991; Page, 2007; Watson, Kumar, & Michaelsen, 1993). In 2011, Forbes Insights conducted a study on diversity in the workplace among 321 companies and found that 85% of those surveyed believed that diversity was an important component to innovation and creativity in an organization. Conversely, some researchers contend that diversity might actually increase turnover and can lead to feelings of disunity amongst the team (Milliken & Martins, 1996). Team disunity and lack of connections among group members are often cited as reasons that heterogeneous groups are not as successful as homogeneous groups. Other researchers have found that a diverse work environment actually decreases turnover and, in fact, helps attract talented employees (Forbes, 2011). Another study indicated that a key differentiator for the success of heterogeneous groups is group members' level of training with respect to diversity and inclusion (Kochan et al., 2003). Further, numerous studies have indicated that cognitive diversity actually leads to increased problem-solving abilities, and Page (2007) likens the benefit of cognitive diversity in a team to the values of portfolio management. Groups with varying ways of looking at the world are more likely to tackle a problem from multiple angles. In other words, a team with many ways of looking at the world is more likely to effectively deal with complex situations because of the variety of perspectives and problem-solving approaches.

Numerous criticisms of business school training indicate that students from top MBA programs are entering the workforce with low levels of cultural awareness (Datar et al., 2010). These criticisms suggest that graduates are not properly trained to work with diverse teams. In response to feedback from professional organizations, business schools have begun implementing cultural awareness and diversity training into their programs (Egan & Bendick, 2008; Page, 2007). One criticism of business school approaches to increasing cultural awareness and diversity understanding is that programs often embed diversity training only in the classroom settings and that within those courses, diversity is taught through an American lens using stereotypes that are prominent within western culture (Egan & Bendick, 2008). Many who are critical of current diversity training within U.S. business schools recommend training students in a more holistic fashion so that students are encouraged to challenge their own perceptions of differences within a community.

The Babson Ecosystem

Babson College's commitment to diversity is evident in every aspect of the institution. From admissions and hiring to event programming and co-curricular activities, Babson weaves its strategic mission into every touchpoint with students in all programs and across the institution. Babson actively celebrates individuals across "cultures, countries, and capabilities" in order to enrich the experience for all members of the community (Babson College Website/About Babson/Diversity). The Babson ecosystem is created through the strategic investment of resources to attract a diverse population and to design and deliver a holistic learning environment and experience that benefits the entire community.

DIVERSE POPULATIONS

A key ingredient of any ecosystem is the membership of those within the community. Babson has made positive progress toward building a robust ecosystem approach to diversity through its focus on faculty, staff, and student population diversity.

Faculty and Staff

Babson College has diversified its faculty over the past several years. There are close to 190 full-time faculty members at Babson College, 20% of whom are professors within the liberal arts divisions. In recent years, the percent of women on the business discipline faculty has risen from 27% to 32%, and women comprise 36% of the entire full-time faculty. By contrast, the composition of staff is primarily female, with 58% comprising women staff. Staff racial and multicultural diversity have improved modestly in recent years, with a decline in Whites from 85% several years ago to 81% in 2014. Racial and multicultural diversity among faculty have similarly progressed, shifting from 87% Whites in 2010 to 83% in

2014, across 397 full- and part-time educators (Babson College Office of Diversity & Inclusion, 2014).

Undergraduate Students

Over time, Babson has been successful in developing an increasingly diverse undergraduate student population. These efforts have been supported through admission activities across the globe, financial aid to attract students of greater economic need, participation as a Posse school, and development of the Honors Program, Women's Leadership Scholars Program, and Multicultural Scholars Program, among others. Recent statistics show that the undergraduate Babson student body is made up of 47% women, 25% international students from 43 countries, 31% multicultural students, and a remarkable 29 languages spoken on campus (Babson College Website/Admission/Undergraduate/Class Profile). Babson College has an extraordinarily diverse student body, creating a dynamic learning environment and an ideal situation where a psychosocial moratorium can occur.

Graduate Students

Babson's graduate population is in many ways more diverse than the undergraduate student body. The graduate school offers an MBA degree in four formats, including two full-time programs and two programs for working professionals. Students bring an average of five years of work experience from a range of industries and functional responsibilities to the full-time classrooms, whereas working professionals have an average of six years of work experience in the evening program and nine years of average work experience in the blended online program. Similar to the undergraduate strategy, admissions and financial aid activities support the desire to attract a diverse student group. The composition of the full-time programs is highly international, ranging from 65% to 75% international students in two-year and one-year programs. Overall, MBA students speak more than 26 languages and are citizens of more than 45 countries. The racial and ethnic diversity within the U.S. graduate student population also varies, ranging from 21–25% in the working professional programs to 33–40% in the full-time programs. Similarly, while gender diversity varies by program, the Babson graduate student community is 34% female overall (Babson College Website/Admission/Graduate/Class Profile).

BABSON DIVERSITY IN ACTION

Babson's ecosystem approach to diversity leverages our living/learning laboratory philosophy. In this way, students have an opportunity to enhance their ability to engage effectively across differences through a range of educational experiences.

Undergraduate

In the undergraduate program, Babson College has embraced the idea of a holistic approach to education. Students encounter diversity both inside and outside the classroom. When students are young adults, their identities are still forming. As such, Babson focuses efforts on the idea of psychosocial moratorium and challenges students to see the world through multiple lenses. In the "From Day One" orientation activity, students are provided with the information and an opportunity to reflect in order to embrace and gain insight on their own diversity and that of others. All undergraduate students at Babson receive a Bachelor of Science in Management degree through the lens of both liberal arts and management. Three of the undergraduate program-learning goals focus on helping students better address differences that they will face in the increasingly diverse and interconnected world. These undergraduate learning objectives are:

> *Global and multicultural perspectives* – You will know the historical and cultural contexts in which you live and operate, and meet the challenges presented by a world characterized by diverse cultures and ways of knowing.

> *Ethics and social, environmental, and economic responsibility* – You are committed to continually developing ethical and professional character and abilities and making decisions based on an awareness of relevant stakeholders and an attempt to create and sustain social, environmental, and economic value.

> *Leadership and teamwork* – You understand your sense of purpose and identity and are adept at leading and functioning effectively in teams.

These three learning objectives are woven into the fabric of all classes at Babson. Additionally, specific elective courses allow students to further explore diversity issues through an academic lens. Some of the most popular courses are classes where students are stretched past their comfort zones to look at the world through someone else's eyes. Examples of these courses include: "The T in LGBTQ: An Introduction to Transgendered Studies," "Critical Race Studies," "The Personal and the Political: Gender in Modern U.S. History," and "Race and Ethnicity in Latin America."

In keeping with the living/learning laboratory approach, Babson is committed to helping students understand their own identities as well as their identities in relation to the world around them. To this end, the College encourages and supports numerous co-curricular events on campus such as Multicultural Education Week, East Meets West, and the Martin Luther King, Jr. Legacy Day, among many others. Perhaps more importantly, there are formal and informal opportunities for conversation around current events, such as civil rights concerns raised from insensitive Halloween costumes, social media activities by student groups to the Taliban shooting of Pakistani youth Malala Yousafzai in 2012, and the police shooting of Michael Brown in Ferguson, Missouri in 2014. Babson supports this work through significant training of residence hall assistants, orientation activities for all students, and the presence of a range of staff with deep expertise in diversity, international, and multicultural education. In addition, the College has a wide spectrum of faith and service activities available to all in the campus community.

This holistic education at the undergraduate level matches the developmental stage of students. Identity among undergraduates is still relatively malleable, and students may have limited exposure to those who hail from circumstances and backgrounds different from their own. The ecosystem approach of intentional diversity in the learning community, program-learning goals that target the value of understanding diversity, various co-curricular opportunities, and support to explore identity and diverse viewpoints provides a rich learning environment.

Graduate

Although students entering the graduate programs at Babson typically have had exposure to diverse groups and perspectives through work, undergraduate education, and personal experience, the College's ecosystem approach to diversity extends to its graduate school, where program-learning goals have a similar focus on understanding one's identity, developing global awareness, and valuing diverse perspectives as a key component of effective leadership and teamwork. Through a mix of core courses and electives, aspects of diversity are a key theme within the academic program. The following graduate learning objectives apply across all formats of the MBA and Masters in Management programs:

> *Self and contextual awareness*: Babson MBA graduates understand their sense of purpose, identity, and context, and use this understanding to inform their decisions.
>
> *Managing in a global environment*: Babson MBA graduates recognize and evaluate global opportunities, while incorporating cultural context and complexities associated with managing in a global environment.

Leadership and teamwork: Babson MBA graduates exercise appropriate leadership, value diverse perspectives and skills, and work collaboratively to accomplish organizational goals in a changing environment.

Across the 14-course common MBA core, these diversity-focused learning objectives are addressed at the support or depth level in 7–12 of the courses, depending on the objective.

While numerous graduate electives allow students to make further progress in aspects of their diversity thinking, one course called "Managing in a Diverse Workplace" was designed specifically to address students' ability to be effective leaders in the increasingly diverse and globalized world of organizational life. This course focuses on understanding the factors that create leaking talent pipelines. It first examines the context for the so-called war on talent and the need and opportunity to effectively diversify the talent pool and leadership pipeline. Next, the course examines the perspective of the manager, looking at how social identity impacts individuals and the choices they make for themselves and in their managerial roles. Finally, it addresses the underlying social norms and organizational barriers that may engender talent loss and considers examples of how organizations set and implement policy to attract and retain a diverse talent pool and the challenges they face in doing so. The focus throughout the course is on ways to enhance effectiveness in managing a diverse group of employees. Because the course is offered in a blended online format, it allows for participation by students across all four MBA formats, creating a diverse mix of MBA perspectives as a starting point.

Learning objectives for this course state that students will be better able to:

- Understand and identify the conceptual frameworks within which diversity issues in organizations may be viewed
- Enhance their self-awareness with respect to personal attitudes, implicit assumptions, bias, and stereotypes, and the way in which these may influence their own behavior and decision-making
- Deploy greater effectiveness at engaging in dialogue and leveraging individual differences (their own and others)
- Deploy greater multicultural awareness and cross-cultural competency
- Understand and influence the policies and practices their organizations use and the ways in which these impact employee contributions and inclusion in the workplace
- Enhance their interpersonal skills and leadership within their workplace teams

The course includes significant interactive discussion, role-play, and personal journaling so that students are enabled to explore their own personal identity as well as consider their potential impact on others with whom they work or on organizational policies they may set or implement. The final group project is to develop a case and analytic note based upon a real world example that is of particular interest to the students. Groups share their work with the entire class for feedback prior to finalizing the projects. The value of using a blended format has become apparent over time as students gain trust with each other through an initial full day face-to-face class session and then have the ability to think and reflect on discussion boards and in their personal journals without the pressure of having to contribute on the fly in the midst of a standard classroom session. The group comes back together at the end of the course to share and provide feedback on project and course learning.

In addition to the core curriculum and the specific elective described above, the graduate program also supports the development of a global mindset and the ability to manage and lead effectively within diverse teams through co-curricular activities. In a similar manner to the undergraduate program, formal and informal activities are supported that focus on understanding and valuing differences. Graduate students benefit from the staff expertise and activities across the campus, while creating their own learning events, including the Latin America Forum, the Asia Forum, religious and cultural celebrations such as Eid, Thanksgiving, Diwali, and Chinese New Year, and activities by social identity clubs such as Net Impact, Out Network, and the Babson Association of Women MBAs, among others.

Community

Across the Babson campus there has been considerable activity in support of valuing differences and the ability to live, learn, and work in a diverse community. This community-wide activity supports an ecosystem approach that benefits the student educational opportunity. Developing a strategic campus-wide approach to diversity has been championed, for example, by the American Council on Education (American Council on Education, 2013; Williams, 2013). Babson's diversity strategy has evolved over time, with the appointment of a Chief Diversity and Inclusion Officer and the establishment of a Council for Inclusiveness and Community in 2008. The Council is comprised of faculty and staff from across the institution who meet regularly to focus on key campus-wide issues, including how to create and maintain inclusive classroom experiences, how to support work in the residence halls for peer diversity mentoring, the development of a bias incident protocol, and ongoing training opportunities for staff and faculty.

In addition to the Council's work, the College supports employee resource groups such as the LGBTQ Action Group, the Elder Care Resource Group, the Muslim Connections Group, and the Parent Connection group. Initiatives of the LGBTQ Action group include Safe Zone training for any interested faculty or staff member, designed to help them support those in the LGBTQ community, as well as sponsorship of the Lavender Graduation, a ceremony designed to recognize the accomplishment of LGBTQ community members and allies at the point of graduation.

Through Babson's Glavin Office of Multicultural and International Education, numerous educational opportunities are provided for community-wide interaction, including the opportunity for faculty and staff to join an elective abroad for professional development. As a major aspect of the role, the Vice Provost for Multicultural and International Education focuses on enhancing the level of cross-cultural competence among the Babson community. This work includes leading training on global mindset and intercultural development during orientation sessions for both undergraduate and graduate students.

In addition to these tangible programmatic aspects of the community, there is the intangible aspect of the daily cross-campus dialogue spurred by faculty research and community members' interests. These conversations are sometimes officially convened, as with the "diversity matters" and "gender research" lunches scheduled twice per semester, but more often such discussions simply occur as faculty, students, and staff informally converse around research, coursework, or current events. Such discourse represents the best of an academic community and cannot be underestimated in importance toward building the capacity to engage effectively across differences. These, among other institutional dimensions in support of diversity, set an important foundational underpinning for Babson's ecosystem approach to valuing diversity in management education.

Conclusion

Babson's ecosystem approach to valuing diversity has been highly successful for students and employees alike. Students receive significant exposure to cognitive and identity diversity, both in the classroom and in the greater Babson community. At the core of Babson's commitment to increased diversity is the idea that to properly educate the next generation of business leaders, students must be able to engage in culturally diverse environments and with a range of individuals across a spectrum of differences. The approach taken at Babson has evolved over time and remains a work in progress.

Improving the achievement of successful outcomes and keeping the approach relevant and vibrant requires continuous investment of time, resources, and focus, as well as a willingness to experiment. As an institution focused on innovation and dedicated to the philosophy of higher education as a living/learning laboratory, we expect to implement further adaptations over time as our commitment to diversity in management education continues to thrive. Any sustainable ecosystem must be continually diversified, renewed, and supported.

References

American Council on Education. (2013). *A matter of excellence: A guide to strategic diversity leadership and accountability in higher education.*

Antonio, A. L. (1999). Racial diversity and friendship groups in college: What the research tells us. *Diversity Digest*, 3(4), 6−7, 16.

Babson College Office of Diversity & Inclusion. (2014, May 13). *Diversity data report* [Internal document].

Babson College Website/About Babson/Diversity. *Diversity at Babson*. Retrieved from http://www.babson.edu/about-babson/diversity/Pages/home.aspx. Accessed on November 23, 2014.

Babson College Website/Admission/Graduate/Class Profile. *Graduate Programs Class Profile*. Retrieved from http://www.babson.edu/admission/graduate/class-profile/Pages/default.aspx. Accessed on November 23, 2014.

Babson College Website/Admission/Undergraduate/Class Profile. *Undergraduate Class Profile for Class of 2018*. Retrieved from http://www.babson.edu/admission/undergraduate/classprofile/Pages/default.aspx. Accessed on November 21, 2014.

Cox, T. H., & Blake, S. (1991). Managing cultural diversity: Implications for organizational competitiveness. *The Executive*, 5(3), 45−56.

Datar, S. M., Garvin, D. A., & Cullen, P. (2010). *Rethinking the MBA: Business education at a crossroads*. Boston, MA: Harvard Business Review Press.

Di Meglio, F. (2013). B-Schools get grades for diversity efforts. *Bloomberg Business*. Retrieved from http://www.bloomberg.com/bw/articles/2013-05-14/b-schools-get-grades-for-diversity-efforts. Accessed on February 18, 2015.

Egan, M. L., & Bendick, M. (2008). Combining multicultural management and diversity into one course on cultural competence. *Academy of Management Learning and Education*, 7(3), 387−393.

Erikson, E. (1956). The problem of ego identity. *Journal of American Psychoanalytic Association*, 4, 56−121.

Forbes. (2011). Global diversity and inclusion: Fostering innovation through a diverse workforce. *Forbes Insights*. Retrieved from http://images.forbes.com/forbesinsights/StudyPDFs/Innovation_Through_Diversity.pdf. Accessed on November 22, 2014.

Gurin, P., Dey, E. L., Hurtado, S., & Gurin, G. (2002). Diversity in higher education: Theory and impact on educational outcomes. *Harvard Educational Review*, 72(3), 330−366.

Holland, K. (2009). Is it time to retrain B-Schools? *The New York Times*, March 14, 2009. Retrieved from http://www.nytimes.com/2009/03/15/business/15school.html?pagewanted=all&_r=0. Accessed on November 25, 2015.

Jones, R. M., Vaterlaus, J. M., Jackson, M. A., & Morrill, T. B. (2014). Friendship characteristics, psychosocial development, and adolescent identity formation. *Personal Relationships, 21*, 51−67.

Kochan, T., Bezrukova, K., Ely, R., Jackson, S., Joshi, A., Jehn, K., … Thomas, D. (2003). The effects of diversity on business performance: Report of the diversity research network. *Human Resource Management, 42*(1), 3−21.

Milliken, F. J., & Martins, L. L. (1996). Searching for common threads: Understanding the multiple effects of diversity in organizational groups. *Academy of Management Review, 21*(2), 402−433.

Mor Barak, M. E. (2011). *Managing diversity: Toward a globally inclusive workplace* (2nd ed.). Thousand Oaks, CA: Sage.

Otani, A. (2014). Rutgers business school accidentally hits an elusive diversity benchmark. *Bloomberg Business.* Retrieved from http://www.bloomberg.com/bw/articles/2014-10-10/more-than-half-of-new-students-at-rutgers-business-school-are-women. Accessed on February 18, 2015.

Page, S. E. (2007). Making the difference: "Applying a logic of diversity". *Academy of Management Perspectives*, (Fall), 6−20.

Page, S. E. (2008). *The difference: How the power of diversity creates better groups, firms, schools, and societies.* Princeton, NJ: Princeton University Press.

Park, J., Fables, W., Parker, K. R., & Nitse, P. S. (2010). The role of culture in business intelligence. *International Journal of Business Intelligence Research (IJBIR), 1*(3), 1−14.

Randel, A. E., & Jaussi, K. S. (2003). Functional background identity, diversity, and individual performance in cross-functional teams. *Academy of Management Journal, 46*(6), 763−774.

Watson, W. E., Kumar, K., & Michaelsen, L. K. (1993). Cultural diversity's impact on interaction process and performance: Comparing homogeneous and diverse task groups. *Academy of Management Journal, 36*(3), 590−602.

Williams, D. A. (2013). *Strategic diversity leadership: Activating change and transformation in higher education.* Sterling, VA: Stylus Publishing.

5 Destination: Intercultural Development

Amir Reza

Introduction

The increase in the numbers of participants in study abroad programs (Institute of International Education, 2014) coincides with additional resources to administer such programs, and also with a cadre of scholars who are looking more critically at the intended outcomes of study abroad and whether or not the current programmatic and academic structures are able to enhance the students' learning as intended. The past decade has seen an increase in the number of qualitative and quantitative studies critically reviewing short- and long-term study abroad through snapshots and in rare cases in longitudinal studies.

Study abroad and the development of intercultural competence of students in higher education is not a new goal. In the past decade, however, a combination of increasing internationalization of colleges and universities, the widespread articulation of international and multicultural perspectives as learning outcomes, and the greater pressure for assessment of learning outcomes has created a new environment for practitioners in the field of international education (Hammer, Bennett, & Wiseman, 2003). For decades, a predominant educational tool at the disposal of institutions of higher education has been study abroad: a program of study through which students earn credit toward their degree at their home institution. In the past, participation in the traditional "Junior year abroad" was an activity available to a small cohort of students (Hoffa & Pearson, 1997). However, today the United States has seen a steady increase in the number of students studying abroad for either a short-term or traditional semester, as well as for a year-long duration (Institute of International Education, 2014).

Proponents have argued that, through exposure to others in an immersion experience, students will develop a better understanding of themselves and others, presumably cultivating a stronger sense of humanity in all. The notion that exposure to others matters is a long-standing assumption within the field of study abroad. A review of the literature between the 1980s and 1990s reveals few critiques investigating this assumption. Rather, most of the literature from this time period is simply a review of the history of study abroad (Vande Berg, Connor-Lindton, & Paige, 2009), and largely focuses on the metrics of growth and preparation of the professionals who worked in the field (see, e.g., Gillespie, Braskamp, & Braskamp, 1999). In addition to the evaluation of programs, the focus of many articles during the mid-1990s (and earlier) is on metrics that assumed that students were gaining a great deal of knowledge while abroad (Vande Berg, Paige, & Lou, 2012a), that experiences abroad were transformative as revealed by the anecdotal evidence in the journals provided by sojourners, and that ultimately, more students studying abroad equated to more students being transformed by the experience and developing into interculturally competent global citizens.

Today, the rapid internationalization taking place at institutions of higher education (Altbach & Knight, 2007) is in part motivated by the goal of developing global-ready graduates. At the same time, "Intercultural competence development is emerging as a central focus — and outcome — of many internationalization efforts" (Deardorff & Jones, 2012, p. 283). Despite the growing support for world citizenship education, there remain a number of important questions about the role of higher education in cultivating cosmopolitanism. Study abroad is a primary means through which many U.S. higher education institutions attempt to develop intercultural competence in their students, often citing the number or percentage of students who have studied abroad as a metric for assessment of this increasingly important learning outcome. Of course study abroad has other associated learning goals such as language skills, historical and regional knowledge, career preparation, and a sense of responsibility and independence (Anderson, Lawton, Rexeisen, & Hubbard, 2006). However, does simply reporting the numbers and percentages of participants provide sufficient assessment of intercultural development? In fact, scholars in the field of study abroad and assessment have called for improved assessment of study abroad learning outcomes in order to respond to this question (Bennett, 2010; Comp & Merritt, 2010; Deardorff & Hunter, 2006; Gillespie, 2002; Rubin & Sutton, 2001; Vande Berg, 2009; Vande Berg, Paige, & Lou, 2012b).

Vande Berg et al. (2012b) argue that simply measuring the numbers and percentages of students who participate in a stint abroad is not sufficient to answer the broader question: does study abroad cultivate intercultural competence in students in the way that has traditionally been assumed? If yes, what aspects of study abroad are most impactful? If not, what are the shortcomings of study abroad in developing students? How can we accept the simple metrics of student study abroad participation as evidence that stated objectives of intercultural development are taking place?

The current literature on study abroad indicates that there are many unanswered questions and the mixed results of past studies do not provide a clear path for practitioners. As Bok (2009) has noted, "educators are still far from understanding how to develop intercultural competence" (p. x). Among the most comprehensive research studies in the past decade is the Georgetown Consortium study (Vande Berg et al., 2009). This longitudinal study has provided significant empirical evidence of study abroad intercultural competence development, but the mixed results are indicative of the many ways that study abroad is not meeting the intended intercultural learning outcome.

At a time of increased accountability and competition for resources, it is critical that institutions of higher education operationalize the learning outcome of intercultural competence by improving the metrics utilized to measure the impact of study abroad in developing students with a global mindset. Vande Berg et al. (2012a), among other scholars, argue for improved assessment of the intercultural goals of study abroad, as they are central to the claim that institutions of higher education are preparing global-ready graduates. To address the need for concrete data on the impact that study abroad participation may have on intercultural competence, this chapter will examine the intercultural sensitivity of a cohort of students who studied abroad in multiple destinations for one semester. This approach to study abroad is in some ways unique because of its multi-destination approach and the fact that it was led by the home institution faculty and staff. However, it incorporates many aspects of a traditional semester abroad program and has within it many of the features that past researchers have found to be important in intercultural development of participants. While multi-destination programs are rare, they tend to combine the short-term duration approach with a long-term overarching theme of learning objectives that relate to cultural immersion and adaptation.

The current research on intercultural development as a study abroad learning outcome indicates mixed results (Vande Berg et al., 2009). It is also apparent that conditions of study abroad vary greatly depending on a number of variables (Engle & Engle, 2003). Thus, it is important to understand which conditions cultivate intercultural competence and which ones do not. This chapter will attempt to address (in part) the call for additional assessment of study abroad learning outcomes in a unique multi-destination program that has many of the features that prior research (Vande Berg et al., 2012b) indicates as influential in fostering intercultural development.

The analysis of this program utilized pre and post levels of students' intercultural sensitivity as measured by the Intercultural Development Inventory (IDI), examination of student journals that were written throughout the semester, and student interviews focused on students' perceptions of learning linked to program features to explore the participants' intercultural competence development. The goal was to explore whether or not participation in this study abroad program influenced students' intercultural competence; and, if yes, what features of this program influenced students' intercultural competence.

Description of Program and Participants

The focus of this chapter is on a group of undergraduate students participating in a semester-long program that was led by Babson College faculty and took students to three countries (Russia, China, and India). The students participated in classroom lectures, discussion seminars, cultural excursions, and company visits in each country. The classes in each country were taught by Babson's faculty. This program's goal was to expose students to a variety of cultures, business practices, and economies, while enhancing the students' knowledge and skills to operate competently in various cultures.

The students were required to complete an application for admission to the program, which was facilitated by the international office and reviewed by faculty and administrators for admission. The students were also required to attend a half-day pre-departure orientation in May and a more extensive pre-departure orientation spanning over a week in August at the home institution.

Twenty-one of the 24 program participants agreed to participate in this study. Eleven of the participants were female and 10 were male students. Six of the students identified themselves as international students from a variety of nations; in addition, there was representation from a variety of religious (e.g., Christian, Hindu, Jew, Muslim), ethnic (e.g., African-American, Asian-American, European-American), and socioeconomic backgrounds. Five of the participants spoke only English, while the others spoke two or more languages. Eight of the students noted that they were able to speak (with varying levels of fluency) at least one of the languages (not English) of one of the host countries (China, Russia, India). Ten participants had lived abroad for six months or longer at some point in their lives, prior to the start of the program. Two participants noted that they had lived abroad, but for a duration of less than six months, while the remaining nine had never lived abroad before the program. Seven of the participants indicated that they were ethnic minorities in their home countries. Three were in their final year of undergraduate study (seniors), while the rest were in their third year (juniors).

The program of study began at the home campus in late August, followed by a four-week program in each country (China, Russia, and India). The program ended in India at the end of November. Students earned one semester's worth of credit toward their graduation requirements upon successful completion of this program.

This multi-destination program was titled BRIC and included the following five courses (titles obtained from the college's course catalog online):

1. Encounters with BRIC: Comparative Analysis in Cross-Cultural Contexts (2 credits)
2. Russia in Modernity: History, Politics, and Culture (3 credits)
3. Business Environment in Russia (4 credits)
4. Entrepreneurship and New Ventures in China (4 credits)
5. India: World Religions, Ideologies and Society (3 credits)

These courses were all taught in English by faculty from the home institution and included a variety of guest lecturers (who also taught in English) from the respective host nation. In addition to the coursework, visits to important sites and attendance in cultural activities offered learning opportunities for the students. The students did not enroll in any courses at institutions abroad; however, they were formally introduced to a small group of undergraduate students attending St. Petersburg State University (Russia), Fudan University (China), and various universities in New Delhi (India).

Table 1 provides an outline for the location and timeline of this program.

Table 1:   BRIC Program Overview.

Course	Duration	Location
Encounters with BRIC: Comparative Analysis in Cross-Cultural Contexts	August 20–November 22 Meets weekly	August – USA September – China October – Russia November – India
Entrepreneurship and New Ventures in China	August 30–September 25 Meets most weekdays	Beijing, China Shanghai, China
Business Environment in Russia	September 26–October 24 Meets weekdays	St. Petersburg, Russia Moscow, Russia
Russia in Modernity: History, Politics, and Culture	September 26–October 24 Meets weekdays	St. Petersburg, Russia Moscow, Russia
India: World Religions, Ideologies and Society	October 25–November 21 Meets thrice a week	New Delhi, India Jaipur, India

Quantitative Findings

The IDI was administered to the participants prior to the program start date and again during the final week of the program. The IDI is an instrument designed to reliably measure the stages of the Developmental Model of Intercultural Sensitivity (Bennett, 1993). The latest version of the IDI (v.3) was introduced by Hammer (2011). This version of the IDI includes five scales of measurement as outlined in Table 2.

The results of the IDI at the outset of the program indicated that most participants (12) were in the "minimization" orientation. There were two participants who began in the "denial" orientation; two who were in the "polarization orientation"; and five who were in the "acceptance" orientation. There were no participants who scored within the "adaptation" orientation. Figure 1 provides a visual representation of the pre-BRIC IDI findings:

Table 2:   IDI Scales.

Intercultural Development Continuum Orientation	Definition
Denial	An orientation that likely recognizes more observable cultural differences but may not notice deeper cultural difference and may avoid or withdraw from cultural differences.
Polarization	A judgmental orientation that views cultural differences in terms of "us" and "them." This can take the form of: • Defense – An uncritical view toward one's own cultural values and practices and an overly critical view toward other cultural values and practices. • Reversal – An overly critical orientation toward one's own cultural values and practices and an uncritical view toward other cultural values and practices.
Minimization	An orientation that highlights cultural commonality and universal values and principles that may also mask deeper recognition and appreciation of cultural differences.
Acceptance	An orientation that recognizes and appreciates patterns of cultural difference and commonality in one's own and other cultures.
Adaptation	An orientation that is capable of shifting cultural perspective and changing behavior in culturally appropriate and authentic ways.

Source: Hammer (2010).

PRE-BRIC IDI Orientations

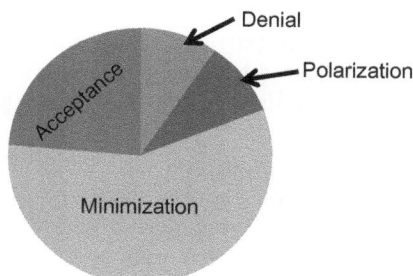

Figure 1: Pre-BRIC IDI Results. This figure illustrates the IDI orientations according to scores of the participants before the program started.

Post-BRIC IDI Orientations

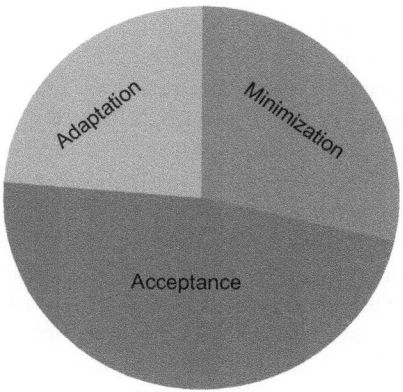

Figure 2: Post-BRIC IDI Results. This figure illustrates the IDI orientations according to scores of the participants at the end of the program.

At the end of the BRIC program, participants were asked to take the IDI again. The results indicated that most participants (10) were within the "acceptance" orientation, as compared to only five who were within this range at the start of the program. Furthermore, none scored within the "adaptation" orientation when the program started, but five scored within this range at the end of the program. The remaining six participants' post-IDI score fell within the "minimization" category. No post-IDI scores fell within the "denial" or "polarization" orientations. Figure 2 illustrates the post-IDI orientations of the group. Notably, the two lowest orientations on the developmental model cease to appear on this illustration, which is indicative of growth. In other words, while four participants began in ethnocentric stages of the Intercultural Development continuum, no participants were in these stages at the end the program, as measured by their post-IDI scores.

Table 3 provides an outline of the shift in pre-post IDI orientations in numerical terms.

The IDI provides a Developmental Orientation (DO) score which ranges from 55 to 145. The pre score of 96.35 indicates that the mean IDI DO score of the 21 participants was within the Minimization orientation. This orientation suggests that most students emphasized commonalities in their intercultural interactions, and tended to de-emphasize differences. Individuals in this orientation have a great deal of respect for the humanity of all people; however, there are shortcomings in their orientation toward cultural differences. For instance, their emphasis on similarities may mask important differences when comparing and contrasting various cultural groups. Individuals in Minimization often assume similarities based on their own cultural lens, when in fact their cultural lens may not be universal and this may lead to an ethnocentric perspective. The focus on similarities is important when considering intercultural development; however, the key is to understand similarities and difference to truly understand one's own culture in comparison with other cultures. This understanding can then lead to adaptive behavior that is appropriate and effective in intercultural interactions. The DO score of participants grew by an average of 24.45 points to 120.80 at the end of BRIC. The average post-DO score falls within the Acceptance orientation. This indicates that, on average, the participants developed their intercultural competence to an orientation that signifies a more complex understanding of cultural differences and similarities. This is indicative of an ethno-relative perspective with a significant shift toward intercultural awareness and understanding. Individuals in the Acceptance orientation are curious about and seek to understand cultural differences. They tend to show respect for and awareness of different cultural practices. This shift in awareness and the significant increase in IDI DO scores surpass the gains made by participants in other studies (e.g., Engle & Engle, 1999; Medina-Lopez-Portillo, 2004; Vande Berg et al., 2009, 2012b).

Figure 3 illustrates the change in the IDI DO score of each participant. It is apparent that all but one participant saw gains in their IDI DO score. The change in IDI DO scores ranged from −9.62 to 49.22.

Table 3:   Pre-Post IDI Orientation Frequency.

Orientation	Denial	Polarization	Minimization	Acceptance	Adaptation
Pre	2	2	12	5	0
Post	0	0	6	10	5

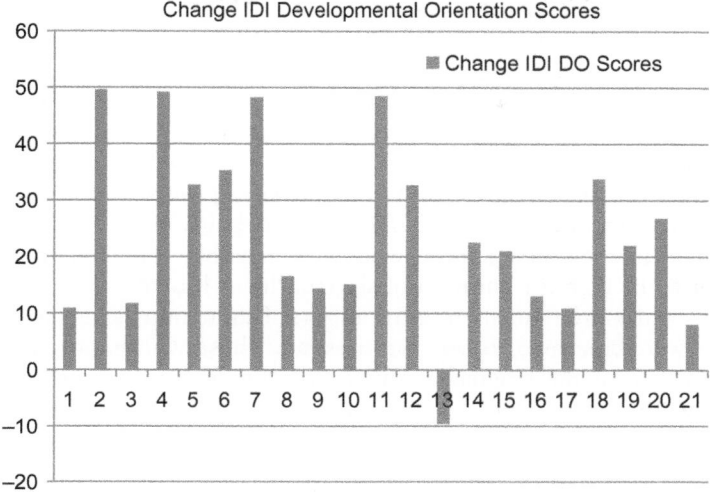

Figure 3: Change in IDI DO Scores. This figure illustrates the change in the IDI scores of the participants at the end of the program.

It is noteworthy that the increase in average IDI DO scores in this study is greater relative to the findings of past research in this area (Vande Berg et al., 2012b). It is also important to understand the increase in participants' DO score in the context of statistical analysis. The pre and post IDI DO means were compared through a Paired-Samples T-test. The Paired-Samples T-test procedure compares the two means for a single group by computing the difference between values of the two means for each case in the study. The results of the T-test indicated that average post-DO scores were statistically significantly higher than average pre-DO scores.

Another statistical procedure to compare the two means is to calculate the effect size by calculating Cohen's *d* (Cohen, 1988). This is especially relevant since the sample size in this study is relatively small (21). In other words, while statistical significance may indicate that the difference between the two means (pre and post) is not likely due to chance alone, calculating the effect size helps us determine the magnitude of the change in the means (which is possibly attributed to the intervention − BRIC). Below is the calculation of Cohen's *d* from this study:

$$d = \frac{T_2 - T_1}{SD} \text{ or } \frac{120.8 - 96.35}{14.55} = 1.68 \text{ (value of Cohen's } d)$$

In summary, among the BRIC participants ($N = 21$), there was a statistically significant difference between pre IDI DO Scores ($M = 96.35$,

SD = 15.6) and post IDI DO Scores (M = 120.8, SD = 13.5), t = 7.011, $p \leq .05$. Further, Cohen's effect size value (d = 1.68) suggests a very high practical significance.

Aside from the pre and post comparisons, IDI data was analyzed for differences in the gains made according to a number of variables. One-way Analysis of Variance (ANOVA) is a statistical technique that compares the means between groups. ANOVA was used to compare the average IDI DO score gains made by men and women in the cohort; those who indicated they had lived abroad prior to BRIC for a duration of six months or less versus those who had spent more than six months abroad; U.S. nationals versus those who were citizens of other countries; and those who indicated they spoke one of the languages (other than English) that is spoken in one of the BRIC countries (China, India, Russia) versus those who did not speak any of the languages of these countries. ANOVA results indicated that there were no statistically significant differences between the mean IDI DO score changes for these groupings. This suggests that the overall gains made along the intercultural development continuum were not necessarily dependent on these variables and that the intervention (BRIC program) developed participants consistently.

Qualitative Findings

The quantitative findings of this study suggest that the participants made significant advances in their intercultural development; however, it is unclear what features of the BRIC program were influential in their development. The following discussion and figures will summarize the results of the analysis of the qualitative data in this study. The transcripts of the semi-structured interviews and the nine journal entries of each participant were coded for features of the BRIC program that were influential in their intercultural development.

In all, there were 1482 coded segments of transcripts and journal entries that fell into 10 broad features of the BRIC program. Figure 4 displays the variety of features that were coded, along with a visual estimation of the frequency of the coding for each feature, with the largest circles representing the most frequently coded and so forth. This figure also illustrates the number of times each feature was coded in the qualitative data. Facilitated Contact with Natives, Academic, and Student Self-Initiated codes were the most prevalent in interview and journal entry data. Social, Residential, Pre-Departure, and Coaching/Mentoring were coded least frequently. Multi-Destination, Cohort, and Co-Curricular had a moderate number of codes relative to the other features of the BRIC program.

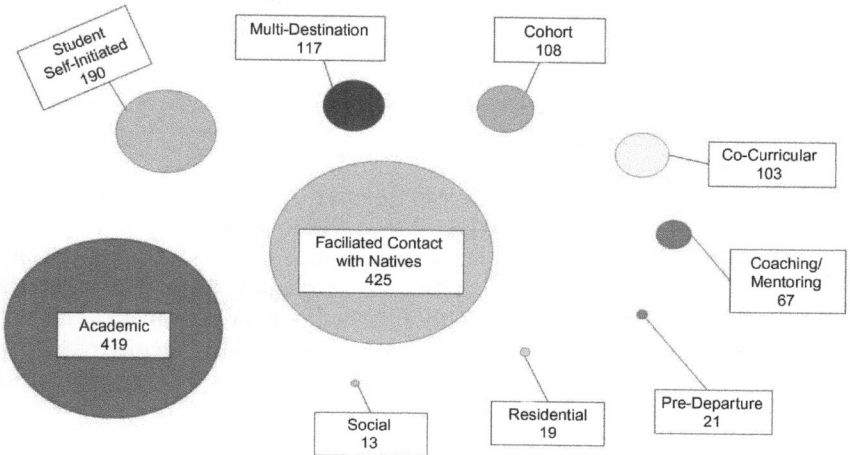

Figure 4: BRIC Feature Code Frequency. This figure illustrates the number of times each BRIC feature was coded.

Intersections of BRIC Features

Throughout the qualitative analysis, the common theme is that most of the features do not work in isolation to improve participants' intercultural competence. There are frequent explicit and implicit connections, shared in interviews and journal entries, that point to the importance of one feature supporting another. In addition, they highlight the ways in which some features negatively impact another feature, thus reducing the potential for the secondary feature. For instance, as the BRIC program prioritized Academic features in Russia by requiring two courses, resulting in additional course readings, papers, and co-curricular offerings, the remaining time that participants had to spend in independent exploration or connecting with locals, either in social or formal settings was reduced, thus negatively impacting the potential impact of that feature.

The thematic analysis of the BRIC features indicates that the Academic feature positively impacted all but one feature (Social). The BRIC program is designed as an academic program with a full course of study delivered through intensive short duration courses; therefore, it is not surprising that the Academic feature is paramount in influencing the other features. At the same time, the Academic feature was influenced by all the other features because participants were using what they learned in class since it related so directly to their context as sojourners in each of the three countries.

A number of participants commented on the intensity and focus of the subject that was being studied in each host country. They noted that when they are enrolled in a full course of study at the home institution, on any given day they may be attending classes, reading, and engaging in discussions about several subjects (often unrelated to one another). In contrast, during the BRIC program they recalled that they were focused on a particular subject (i.e., world religions) and would study, read about, engage in discussions in and out of the classroom, and complete an ethnography project that required the exploration of religion through discussions with practitioners of that faith in their home environment. This triangulation of theoretical learning through reading, faculty expertise and classroom discussion, and access to the people and context of the subject studied, helped the participants think more deeply about the subjects on a daily basis.

Another intersection of BRIC program features is the Encounters course component within the Academic feature and the Multi-Destination feature. The goal of the Encounters course was to foster attitudes and skills that enable students to adjust and adapt to various cultural contexts. The Multi-Destination approach provides a laboratory for experimentation by the participants. The common sentiment among participants was that the Encounters course provided them with tools to become observant and go beyond the cultural differences that are readily visible when one enters a new culture by exploring the nuances of behavior, communication, and beliefs. This was especially important since the IDI orientation of the majority of the cohort was within Minimization, an orientation that suggested the participants were more likely to seek out commonalities with other cultural contexts. The Encounters course encouraged them to develop curiosity for the differences, even if that meant that they would have to leave their comfort zone. The Multi-Destination feature took participants to three strikingly different regions of the globe, so that differences were apparent and the Encounters course helped the participant unpack what they were experiencing and observing.

The analysis of the participant narratives is indicative of a web of interconnected features that provided the scaffolding for students to develop empathy, recognize their own biases, challenge stereotypes and ethnocentric beliefs, and ultimately gain knowledge and skills that enabled them to communicate and behave appropriately and effectively in intercultural situations. While some of the features were formal and structured (i.e., Academic), others were minimally structured and provided opportunities for students to engage on their own terms (i.e., Residential, Facilitated Contact with Natives). This combination of formal and informal settings and required versus voluntary engagement also meant that intercultural development among the participants was uneven, as was evident in the quantitative findings of this study.

The features of Facilitated Contact with Natives, Pre-Departure Orientation, Cohort, and Coaching/Mentoring empowered the students to have greater tolerance for ambiguity by taking risks to engage with the people and environment of the host culture. Participants frequently noted that although they had traveled to various countries in the past, the expectations that were set by the BRIC program and the encouragement that they received through these features mandated that they approach the host culture with great curiosity and utmost respect. In particular, they mentioned that the group dynamics created opportunities to learn from one another (Cohort feature) and to challenge one another to abide by these attitudes. Furthermore, their faculty often role modeled and empowered them to explore with the understanding that one can make mistakes when interacting across cultures and that is part of the learning process.

Vande Berg (2007) suggests that study abroad programs that are most successful provide participants with cognitive and behavioral intercultural tools to allow them to reflect on their own learning in new and challenging environments abroad. The findings of this study indicate that the BRIC program is successful because the combination and intersections of the program features provided students with scaffolding that enabled them to compare and contrast cultures with curiosity while withholding judgment, develop in-depth knowledge of the host cultures they visited, and hone their skills of intercultural interaction. Furthermore, the program provided numerous opportunities for reflection.

Conclusion

The common theme that is evident in the literature on study abroad learning outcomes over the past 15 years is one that challenges practitioners to embrace a paradigm shift to intervene intentionally in order to ascertain that students are learning abroad, and not just by chance.

There are indeed many skeptics within the academic structure of institutions who are not convinced that study abroad is a worthwhile endeavor or that students gain the target competencies (Hoffa & DePaul, 2010). On the other hand, as Deardorff and Jones (2012) have remarked, intercultural competence development is increasingly becoming central to higher education's efforts at internationalization. The results and analysis of this study support the assertions that educators should intervene through intentional pedagogical models that develop students' intercultural competence rather than assuming they will develop simply because they are abroad.

The results of this study point to a number of implications for practice. In summary, educators must consider the combination of engagement opportunities that combine to provide a scaffolding to push students beyond their comfort zone and to genuinely engage with the local environment while they are abroad. It is clear that without the classroom and structured learning components, the independent exploration pursued by students would have been closer to tourism due to the fact that students would not have had the capacity to interpret the complexities of intercultural interactions. On the other hand, academic content may not be as effective if it was delivered to students without the opportunities for engagement with the locals in the three nations in BRIC. In other words, academics are planting seeds for further exploration, and the opportunities to put this learning to immediate use reinforce the learning and develop a continuous loop. The students referenced the ways in which the theoretical learning was important because it prepared them to understand the context of the culture, business, and social systems in each host country. They were then able to bring back to the classroom experiences that reinforced or challenged the theoretical learning and collectively reflected on the most important elements of their experience. In summary, learning across cultures is accelerated and internalized when the combination of academic offerings, facilitated contact with natives, and independent exploration works together.

The advancement of intercultural competence as a student learning outcome of higher education is an integral part of preparing citizens for the 21st century. This important goal cannot be achieved through long-held assumptions that simply sending students to another country for a period of time will result in competence. Given the importance of this learning outcome for the future of the global economy and society, Bennett (2010) suggests that we "promote systematic, intentional intercultural learning" (p. 449). This study supports Bennett's (2010) assertion that systematic intercultural learning can have profound impact, as is evidenced in the results of the BRIC program. Furthermore, the results provide educators a better understanding of the components that are most effective in students' development.

Finally, it should be noted that, although the title of this chapter presents intercultural development as a one-time destination, it is actually a complex, life-long endeavor that requires continuous learning without a particular endpoint. Those who strive to develop a global mindset understand the importance of the cycle of continuous learning, experience, and reflection.

References

Altbach, P. G., & Knight, J. (2007). The internationalization of higher education: Motivations and realities. *Journal of Studies in International Education, 11*(3–4), 290–305.

Anderson, P. H., Lawton, L., Rexeisen, R. J., & Hubbard, A. C. (2006). Short-term study abroad and intercultural sensitivity. *International Journal of Intercultural Relations, 30,* 457–469.

Bennett, M. J. (1993). Towards ethnorelativism: A developmental model of intercultural sensitivity. In R. M. Paige (Ed.), *Education for the intercultural experience* (pp. 21–71). Yarmouth, ME: Intercultural Press.

Bennett, M. J. (2010). A short conceptual history of intercultural learning in study abroad. In W. W. Hoffa & S. C. DePaul (Eds.), *A history of U.S. study abroad: 1965-present* (pp. 419–449). Carlisle, PA: Frontiers Journal, Inc.

Bok, D. (2009). Foreword. In D. K. Deardorff (Ed.), *The Sage handbook of intercultural competence* (pp. ix–x). Thousand Oaks, CA: Sage.

Cohen, J. (1988). *Statistical power analysis for the behavioral sciences* (2nd ed.). Hillsdale, NJ: Lawrence Erlbaum.

Comp, D., & Merritt, M. (2010). The development of qualitative standards and learning outcomes for study abroad. In W. W. Hoffa & S. C. DePaul (Eds.), *A history of U.S. study abroad: 1965-present* (pp. 451–489). Carlisle, PA: Frontiers Journal, Inc.

Deardorff, D. K., & Hunter, W. (2006). Educating global ready graduates. *International Educator, 15*(3), 72–83.

Deardorff, D. K., & Jones, E. (2012). Intercultural competence: An emerging focus in international higher education. In D. K. Deardorff, H. de Wit, D. Heyl, & T. Adams (Eds.), *The Sage handbook of international higher education* (pp. 283–303). Thousand Oaks, CA: Sage.

Engle, J., & Engle, L. (1999). Program intervention in the process of cultural integration: The example of French practicum. *Frontiers: The Interdisciplinary Journal of Study Abroad, 5*(Fall), 39–60.

Engle, L., & Engle, J. (2003). Study abroad levels: Toward a classification of program types. *Frontiers: The Interdisciplinary Journal of Study Abroad, 9,* 1–20.

Gillespie, J. (2002). Colleges need better ways to assess study abroad programs. *The Chronicle of Higher Education, 48*(43), B20.

Gillespie, J., Braskamp, L. A., & Braskamp, D. C. (1999). Evaluation and study abroad: Developing assessment criteria and practices to promote excellence. *Frontiers: The Interdisciplinary Journal of Study Abroad, 5*(Fall), 101–127.

Hammer, M. R. (2010). *The intercultural development inventory manual.* Berlin, MD: IDI.

Hammer, M. R. (2011). Additional cross-cultural validity testing of the intercultural development Inventory. *International Journal of Intercultural Relations, 35,* 474–487.

Hammer, M. R., Bennett, M. J., & Wiseman, R. (2003). Measuring intercultural sensitivity: The intercultural development inventory. *International Journal of Intercultural Relations, 27,* 421–443.

Hoffa, W., & Pearson, J. (1997). *NAFSA's guide to education abroad for advisers and administrators* (2nd ed.). Washington, DC: NAFSA, Association of International Educators.

Hoffa, W. W., & DePaul, S. C. (Eds.). (2010). *A history of U.S. study abroad: 1965-present*. Carlisle, PA: Frontiers Journal, Inc.

Institute of International Education. (2014). *Open doors 2014: Report on international educational exchange*. New York, NY: Author.

Medina-Lopez-Portillo, A. (2004). Intercultural learning assessment: The link between program duration and the development of intercultural sensitivity. *Frontiers, 10*(Fall), 179–199.

Rubin, D. L., & Sutton, R. (2001). Assessing student learning outcomes from study abroad. *International Educator, 10*(2), 30–31.

Vande Berg, M. (2009). Intervening in student learning abroad: A research-based inquiry. *International Education, 20*(4), S15–S27.

Vande Berg, M., Connor-Lindton, J., & Paige, R. M. (2009). The Georgetown Consortium Project. *Frontiers: The Interdisciplinary Journal of Study Abroad, 18*(Fall), 1–75.

Vande Berg, M., Paige, R. M., & Lou, K. H. (2012a). Student learning abroad: Paradigms and assumptions. In M. Vande Berg, R. M. Paige, & K. H. Lou (Eds.), *Student learning abroad: What our students are learning, what they're not, and what we can do about it* (pp. 3–28). Sterling, VA: Stylus Publishing, LLC.

Vande Berg, M., Paige, R. M., & Lou, K. H. (Eds.). (2012b). *Student learning abroad: What our students are learning, what they're not, and what we can do about it*. Sterling, VA: Stylus Publishing, LLC.

6

What's So Wrong with Student Subjects? A Brief Guide to the Ins and Outs of Using Student Subjects in Research

Richard C. Hanna and Charles Winrich

Introduction

A key challenge in conducting research is finding research participants. Not just any participants, but ones that are representative of
the phenomenon or issue that is being studied. Unfortunately, finding participants can be both time-consuming and costly and there
are many other challenges to consider along the way. In order to
conduct research efficiently and cost effectively, many researchers
use convenience samples of student subjects to support their research
activities. The cost is minimal and access is easy. Hence, two of the
most critical challenges are settled. However, the extant literature is filled
with debates and illustrations of the pros and cons of using student
subjects from both validity and ethical perspectives. While student
subject issues may never be fully resolved for most research needs, the
good news is that when it comes to educational scholarship — which
is central to many academics' research and focuses on pedagogy
and processes related to education — the best possible research participants *are* the students. In this chapter, we will present the most
common issues and propose some strategies as to how to navigate
student subjects for educational research.

Defining Educational Research

Educational research, broadly defined, consists of investigations relating to the effectiveness (i.e., impact on student outcomes) of educational programs, practices or policies (U.S. Department of Education, n.d.). Activities subsumed under educational research include the development of evaluation instruments, the evaluation of specific pedagogical strategies, or the evaluation of entire programs or curricula. In each of these cases, the use of student research subjects can inform the work. For example, in the development of an evaluation instrument, pilot testing the instrument with students helps to ensure the clarity of the questions and uniform interpretation between the research team and the student subjects. In the evaluation of a pedagogical strategy, program, or curriculum, evaluative instruments can be given to the participating students (ideally before and after the intervention) to measure any changes in their knowledge, skills, or attitudes about the subject of the class or program. Thus, the students in the various educational programs studied are the natural subjects of this research, because it is the students' achievement or attitudinal change that is the measured dependent variable in such educational studies, where the differences between the different classes, programs, or curricula represent the independent arm of the research.

WHY STUDENT SUBJECTS ARE CRITICIZED
Validity of Using Student Subjects
In academics, we often turn to using student samples because of the cost savings and availability relative to a nonstudent sample. However, there are many concerns in the extant literature toward the reliability and validity of student subjects for research purposes. In fact, the appropriateness of using student subjects in research was debated extensively throughout the 1980s in many disciplines (e.g., Calder, Phillips, & Tybout, 1981; Gordon, Slade, & Schmitt, 1986, 1987; Greenberg, 1987; Lynch, 1982) without much resolve. While there are fewer debates today, the validity of student subjects is still a subject of concern in more recent years and often questioned in the review process (e.g., Compeau, Marcolin, Kelley, & Higgins, 2012; Mortensen, Fisher, & Wines, 2012; Peterson & Merunka, 2014).

The biggest criticism of student subjects is the lack of external validity (Mortensen et al., 2012; Peterson, 2001). For example, some researchers argue that student subjects lack the real-world experiences that nonstudent subjects might possess and hence make different decisions. Peterson (2001) found student subject responses to be slightly more homogeneous than those of nonstudent subjects through a second-order meta-analysis of social science research using student subjects. Moreover, Peterson found that student subjects differed from adult subjects in approximately one out of every five relationships studied. As a result, Peterson questioned the generalizability of studies with student subjects without first replicating with nonstudents.

Other researchers question whether student subjects lack the appropriate experience or knowledge to make certain complex decisions. Abdolmohammadi and Wright (1987) compared experienced accountants to a less experienced group comprising of new employees and accounting students on their ability to compete a series of structured and unstructured tasks. They found significant differences in decisions by the two groups and were able to isolate experience as a driving factor for decision-making. They concluded that student subjects may not be appropriate as surrogates for professionals in some complex or advanced decision settings. Hughes and Gibson (1991) found similar results when comparing MBA students and professionals on strategic decision-making. Yet, while experience may be critical in certain settings, there have been some instances where experience has been shown to be a determinant. For example, Einhorn (1974) found that actual experience can lead "experts" to ignore certain cues or evidence provided, or otherwise overlook things they believe they already know, and hence perform suboptimally.

What all of these criticisms have in common is the appropriateness of the student subjects for the task at hand. In other words, for these studies, knowledge and experience were critical components for the participant in order to examine a subsequent behavior. However, not all research is focused on behavior but, instead, more focused on attitudes. Indeed, Kardes (1996) points out that we are concerned with explaining relationships between variables (i.e., relative effects) as opposed to forecasting or predicting specific behaviors (i.e., absolute effects) in most social science research. Moreover, Beltramini (1983) found that while student and adult subjects were significantly different on actual behavioral decisions, they were not significantly different in underlying psychological processes, or attitudes. Thus, for research that is focused on psychological processes rather than specific actions or decisions, college students may be qualified surrogates for most studies. Indeed, because college students are generally younger, more educated, and less experienced than the typical American consumer, they are ideal participants for research that examines relationships between variables since they are unbiased. As a result, researchers using student subjects can cleanly examine different processes and, if some characteristic is lacking, model that characteristic as a variable in the study.

The debate over the appropriateness of student subjects in broad areas of behavioral research will likely continue, and most researchers would recommend replicating studies with nonstudent subjects as confirmation (see Compeau et al., 2012). However, as noted earlier, when evaluating educational interventions, the knowledge, skill, or attitudinal change in the students is the relevant dependent variable under investigation. Thus, student subjects are uniquely appropriate in such research because it is through measuring the change in the students as a result of an educational intervention that we can judge the effectiveness of such an intervention. However, the authority of faculty over their students raises potential ethical implications for including them as subjects in a faculty-run research project.

Ethics of Using Student Subjects

While students are typically the best subjects for educational studies, such research must be held to the ethical standards appropriate for research involving human subjects. This can be a particular problem when faculty are doing research in their own classes or on their own students. Ethical protections for human subjects in research go back to post-WWII concerns about the treatment of prisoners in experiments (Smith, Cutting, & Riggs, 1991). Concerns about the treatment of human subjects in behavioral research arose from the Milgram experiments and the Stanford Prison experiment. In 1974, the U.S. Department of Health and Human Services (HHS) issued regulations for the protection of human subjects in Title 45, Part 46 of the Code of Federal Regulations (45 C.F.R. § 46). The regulations in 45 C.F.R. § 46 have been adopted by 15 federal agencies and so are now known as the "Common Rule" and were updated in 2009 (Protection of Human Subjects, 2009).

The fundamentals of the Common Rule were informed by the Belmont Report. The Belmont Report was issued by the HHS Commission for the Protection of Human Subjects of Biomedical and Behavioral Research in 1978 (HHS, 1978). The report outlined the basic ethical principles researchers should adhere to when conducting research on human subjects: respect for persons, beneficence, and justice. The report also includes a section on applications of each of the ethical principles to the practice of conducting research.

Respect for Persons

The Belmont Report begins its section on respect for persons with the following language: "Respect for persons incorporates at least two ethical convictions: first, that individuals should be treated as autonomous agents, and second, that persons with diminished autonomy are entitled to protection" (HHS, 1978). This leads to two fundamental questions for using students as research subjects. First, how can we guarantee that students are treated as autonomous agents? Second, are students deserving of protections because of diminished autonomy?

The answer to the first question is given in part by the Belmont Report itself. To respect a person requires that he/she be allowed to choose freely whether he/she participates in research or not (HHS, 1978). To be informed, potential research subjects must know that they are being asked to participate in a research project, the goals of the project, and the procedures they will be asked to complete as a part of the project. The potential research subjects must also be informed of the possible risks associated with their participation. However, simply informing the potential subjects of the research is not sufficient, they must also comprehend the information offered and then be given the option to volunteer to participate in the research without adverse consequences for refusing.

It is fairly straightforward to inform students about a research project. In general, faculty members are adept at providing information to students in a comprehensible way as well. However, the standard of voluntariness for research subjects leads directly to the second question above. Do students operate with diminished autonomy? In a situation where a faculty member recruits students in his or her own class for a research project, students might feel coerced to participate in order to please the professor, especially if extra credit is offered as an incentive to participate (Leentjens & Levenson, 2013). In terms of strict legal obligations, the 45 C.F.R. § 46 does not include a section on additional protections for students. However, faculty and institutions need to be aware that the potential for coercion, either real or perceived by the students, exists and should be minimized. Finally, many research recruitment activities are performed as part of a class, thus students might also feel peer pressure to participate in the research and feel that their privacy is being violated by disclosing to the class that they are participating in the research project.

Beneficence

The principle of Beneficence is based on the Hippocratic principle to do no harm (HHS, 1978). The Belmont Report adds the obligation to maximize the benefits and minimize the harm of research. Beneficence does not require that the subjects of research must directly benefit from the research. Beneficence does require that research subjects be exposed to a minimum potential harm and that researchers actively protect the well-being of the subjects.

Beneficence adds an ethical quandary for faculty and for institutions when they involve students as research subjects. There is an implicit contract that the institution, and each faculty member, will educate the student. When a faculty member is using his or her own students as research subjects, which relationship takes precedence, that of teacher-student or that of researcher-subject? This confusion of roles creates tension for the faculty in particular as to whether the faculty member is doing what is best for the education of the students or what is best for the successful completion of the research study (Lifchez, 1981). While some have argued that participation in research can be educationally valuable, it should be noted that participation does not imply that student subjects are given any insight into the data analysis procedures or the results of the research (Leentjens & Levenson, 2013; Smith et al., 1991).

In addition to promoting benefits for the subjects, Beneficence also requires the minimization of risk. Although both benefits and risks of a research project can be hard to quantify, the Belmont Report specifically recommends that the fullest possible consideration be given to the risks associated with participation in research. The report specifically suggests that there could be psychological, physical, legal, social, and economic risks to participants in a study. Some of these risks might be inherent in participating in the study, while others might result from the disclosure of a subject's participation. In all, the benefits and risks must be considered as broadly as possible for any research study, and procedures adopted to give the best ratio of benefit to risk.

Justice

The principle of justice relates the question of who benefits from a research study to the question of who bears the burden of a research study. The principle of justice bears special consideration for research on students. Students might be seen as a conveniently available group to study even in the event that the students might not see any particular benefit of the research. In pedagogical research, students are the natural subjects of interest; however, the biases introduced by using a captive student population could reduce the benefits of the research by limiting its generalizability. In an academic setting, some of the benefits of research also flow to the faculty conducting the research in the form of career advancement.

Strategies for Addressing Issues

The issues raised above create the potential for serious ethical issues surrounding research on students. However, this by no means should suggest that students cannot be ethically and productively used in research projects by faculty. By carefully crafting a research study, faculty can avoid the potential for ethical problems that arise from using students as subjects in the research. Possible issues that can arise and their solutions are discussed in this section and summarized in Table 1.

Table 1: Potential Issues and Strategies for Avoidance.

Potential Issue	Strategies for Avoidance
Students rewarded for participation or punished for nonparticipation	• Do not offer extra credit in a course for participation in a study. • Do not require extra work from students in a course who choose not to complete research-related tasks.
Students feel coerced by recruitment procedure	• Do not have the course instructor recruit his or her own students for a study. • Do not recruit to groups of students in a way that makes a student's participation known to other students.
Conflict between research activity and teaching activity	• Have independent investigators (i.e., not a course instructor) record any observational data from class activities. • Use anonymous identifiers on student work before evaluating the work for research aims.

The issue of coercion of students can be minimized by removing any requirement for students to participate in research. This leaves the decision to participate or not participate entirely up to the students. However, issues of coercion can still arise in nonrequired research activities. Students should neither be offered extra credit in a course nor should nonparticipating students be required to perform an alternative assignment to make up for the time spent on research activities by those students who choose to participate. While it may not always be possible, a better alternative would be to require the same work of all students and only use the work of participants for research purposes.

Assuming that a faculty member would like to use students from his or her own class in research, the potential for coercion exists in the recruitment process, both by peer pressure by recruiting in class and through pressure from having a professor for class asking for a student's participation in a research study. An alternative strategy that would reduce the pressure on students to participate would be to have an independent faculty member recruit the students in a private individual setting.

The potential conflict between being a researcher and teacher can also be reduced by adopting careful research strategies. The suggestion above to require the same activities of all students will also help to address this issue. In such a situation, the conflict between what is educationally appropriate for the student and what is required for the research project is minimized. In a setting where observations of the students will be part of the data, a second researcher should be engaged to make those observations so that the course instructor can stay focused on doing what is best for student learning. Both of these strategies will help guarantee that student participation or lack of participation in research has minimal impact on their education.

Finally, as with any research study, researchers should carefully consider exactly who the target population of a study will be. It is a basic statistical principle that one cannot generalize to a population with a sample drawn from an independent population. Therefore, if students are not part of the target population, then a justification is needed for why the research should be done with student subjects. Further, if students form only part of the target population, then the research sample should be expanded to represent the target population as a whole.

As the strategies discussed in this section suggest, educational research by faculty with their students as subjects can be done ethically. In the following two sections, we present cases in which the authors were involved in research with student subjects. We highlight the strategies used to avoid the ethical pitfalls of faculty using their own students as research subjects.

Case Study 1: Learned Ethical Attitudes

One can better understand what future practitioners will do in the field by understanding how students learn and think about certain topics. Crittenden and colleagues, in a series of papers, explore influences of unethical behavior in future business leaders (see Crittenden, Hanna, & Peterson, 2009a, 2009b; Hanna, Crittenden, & Crittenden, 2013). A survey on attitudes toward ethical and unethical behavior was distributed to undergraduate business classes from around the world with over 6000 responses collected and analyzed. Student data was collected by faculty at different schools across the world on a volunteer basis. No specific rewards were provided and students opted-in of their volition. Crittenden and colleagues used this data to better understand business students' attitudes toward ethical and unethical behavior and how these attitudes differed by culture and level of corruption in the environments where these students were being educated. For this particular research, the student subjects were the natural selection as they were representative of the future workforce and, at the time, unbiased by influences in the workplace. Moreover, since the focus was on social influence and psychological attitudes toward ethical behavior, the typical criticisms that are called out in student subjects did not apply.

Given the increase in unethical behavior in business environs and the responding emphasis on teaching ethics in business schools, the researchers wanted to better understand the influences on unethical behavior and to what extent these influences were related to the social environment. As such, examining business students before they enter the workplace (i.e., hence, unbiased) would provide the ideal lens to learn about the influence of their learning environment. Consistent with social learning theory (Bandura, 1977), Hanna et al. (2013) found that students in most cultures reported being most influenced by their role models. At the same time, attitudes toward capitalism and risk were less related with unethical behavior. In other words, if students perceived that their managers regularly engaged in unethical acts, the students were more likely to compromise their own behavior. Whether or not these same students believed in capitalism or that risk should be rewarded was not related to their attitudes toward unethical behavior. A key takeaway here is that educators need to be aware of what type of role models they present to their students. While this same finding might have been uncovered using a nonstudent sample from the workforce, there likely would have been greater noise and the potential for misattributing the influence of role model simply to the culture of business or the firm.

Case Study 2: Attitudes toward a Topic

Laprise and Winrich (2010) studied the use of Hollywood films in science class assignments. The goal was to understand student attitudes toward the class and science as a whole as a result of the particular pedagogy of watching and critiquing science fiction films. Additionally, the researchers wanted to see if students felt they learned more effectively by watching and critiquing the films. Students in the classes taught by the authors were recruited as subjects for the project. The students were surveyed about whether they felt they learned the course material better as a result of watching the films and whether they had a more positive attitude toward the course as a result of watching the film. The surveys were distributed in class during the end-of-semester course survey, so the students could complete the survey without the instructor being present. While the instructor distributed the survey and explained the research project, the implied pressure for the students to participate was removed by the instructor leaving the room while the students actually completed the survey. Students were asked not to put their names on the survey forms and leave them in the room for retrieval after class so that the instructor would not know who had or had not completed the survey. A machine-scored form was used to eliminate the possibility of recognizing handwriting.

(continued)

While it is possible that there was still peer pressure to complete the survey, the overall completion rate of the survey was 90%, so some students did feel free to skip the survey. The courses included in the study included both required and elective courses. Overall, students in elective classes reported statistically significant shifts in their attitude toward science and at least the feeling that they understood the course material better for having watched and critiqued a movie. While instructors believed that the pedagogical methods used in class were interesting and effective for their students, the only way to uncover the students' perceptions is to involve the students as research subjects. In this case, the students reported that they were not more likely to consider a career in science or science-related industries as a result of the assignment.

Conclusion

The debate over the appropriateness of using students as research subjects will likely continue. In some cases, good questions can be raised about whether students are the most appropriate subjects. In educational research though, there is little question that students are the population of interest to the researchers. However, the possibility for ethical problems arises when using students as research subjects for any type of study.

At many institutions, the Institutional Review Board (IRB) will serve to protect the faculty performing research on students from ethical quandaries and the students from potential abuses. However, by understanding the potential issues and strategies for minimizing those issues, researchers can prepare more effectively for the IRB review. The first question to ask is whether students are the appropriate target population for the research. If not, then investigators should strongly consider whether the research can be done with student subjects. If so, then consider the major pitfalls of having faculty do research on their own students and adopt strategies to avoid those issues. While these strategies do not guarantee that issues will not arise in the research study, advance planning around ethical issues with student subjects should help to ensure that the study team is prepared for such issues if they do arise.

References

Abdolmohammadi, M., & Wright, A. (1987). An examination of the effects of experience and task complexity on auditor judgments. *The Accounting Review*, 62(1), 1–13.

Bandura, A. (1977). *Social learning theory.* Englewood Cliffs, NJ: Prentice Hall.

Beltramini, R. F. (1983). Student surrogates in consumer research. *Journal of the Academy of Marketing Science, 11*(Fall), 438–443.

Calder, B. J., Phillips, L. W., & Tybout, A. M. (1981). Designing research for application. *Journal of Consumer Research, 8,* 197–207.

Compeau, D., Marcolin, B., Kelley, H., & Higgins, C. (2012). Research commentary—Generalizability of information systems research using student subjects—A reflection on our practices and recommendations for future research. *Information Systems Research, 23*(4), 1093–1109.

Crittenden, V. L., Hanna, R. C., & Peterson, R. A. (2009a). The cheating culture: A global societal phenomenon. *Business Horizons, 52*(4), 337–346.

Crittenden, V. L., Hanna, R. C., & Peterson, R. A. (2009b). Business students' attitudes toward unethical behavior: A multi-country comparison. *Marketing Letters, 20*(1), 1–14.

Einhorn, H. J. (1974). Expert judgment: Some necessary conditions and an example. *Journal of Applied Psychology, 59,* 562–571.

Gordon, M. E., Slade, L. A., & Schmitt, N. (1986). The "science of sophomore" revisited: From conjecture to empiricism. *Academy of Management Review, 11*(1), 191–207.

Gordon, M. E., Slade, L. A., & Schmitt, N. (1987). Student guinea pigs: Porcine predictors and particularistic phenomena. *Academy of Management Review, 12*(1), 160–163.

Greenberg, J. (1987). The college sophomore as guinea pig: Setting the record straight. *Academy of Management Review, 12*(1), 157–159.

Hanna, R. C., Crittenden, V. L., & Crittenden, W. F. (2013). Social learning theory: A multicultural study of influences on ethical behavior. *Journal of Marketing Education, 35*(1), 18–25.

Hughes, C. T., & Gibson, M. L. (1991). Students as surrogates for managers in a decision-making environment: An experimental study. *Journal of Management Information Systems, 8*(2), 153–166.

Kardes, F. R. (1996). In defense of experimental consumer psychology. *Journal of Consumer Psychology, 5*(3), 279–296.

Laprise, S., & Winrich, C. (2010). The impact of science fiction films on student interest in science. *Journal of College Science Teaching, 40*(2), 18–22.

Leentjens, A. F. G., & Levenson, J. L. (2013). Ethical issues concerning the recruitment of university students as research subjects. *Journal of Psychosomatic Research, 75,* 394–398.

Lifchez, R. (1981). Students as research subjects: Conflicting agendas in the classroom? *Journal of Architectural Education, 34*(3), 16–23.

Lynch, J. G. (1982). On the external validity of experiments in consumer research. *Journal of Consumer Research, 9,* 225–239.

Mortensen, T., Fisher, R., & Wines, G. (2012). Students as surrogates for practicing accountants: Further evidence. *Accounting Forum, 36,* 251–265.

Peterson, R. A. (2001). On the use of college students in social science research: Insights from a second-order meta-analysis. *Journal of Consumer Research, 28*(3), 450–461.

Peterson, R. A., & Merunka, D. A. (2014). Convenience samples of college students and research reproducibility. *Journal of Business Research, 67*(5), 1035–1041.

Protection of Human Subjects. 45 C.F.R. § 46 (2009).

Smith, D. L., Cutting, J. C., & Riggs, R. O. (1991). Use of students as research subjects: Institutional responsibility. *Research Management Review*, *5*(1), 23–34.

U.S. Department of Education. (n.d.). Institute of Education Sciences, National Center for Education Research. Retrieved from http://ies.ed.gov/ncer/aboutus/. Accessed on December 8, 2014.

U.S. Department of Health and Human Services. (1978). *The Belmont Report: Ethical principles and guidelines for the protection of human subjects of research.* Retrieved from http://www.hhs.gov/ohrp/policy/belmont.html. Accessed on November 15, 2014.

PART 2
Cross-Disciplinary Learning and Teaching

7

Developing Entrepreneurial Leaders — Integrating Entrepreneurship Education and Organizational Behavior in the First Year

Danna N. Greenberg and James Hunt[†]

Entrepreneurial Thought and Action (ET&A®) is a unique methodology developed at Babson College that helps individuals identify and pursue opportunities particularly in an environment that is increasingly unknowable and uncertain. This method integrates two distinct approaches, predictive and creation logics (Keifer, Schlesinger, & Brown, 2010). Predictive logic involves our ability to gather data, apply the appropriate concepts and then predict likely outcomes. Creation logic is rooted in the assumption that there is much in our world that is not knowable, because in essence, it hasn't happened yet. In an unknowable environment, one can't simply use existing data to predict how a new idea or opportunity will impact the world. Rather an entrepreneurial leader must learn to engage in small experiments in which they manage acceptable loss, bring others

---

[†]Please note authors are listed alphabetically. Both authors contributed equally to this chapter.

along and fail frequently as they learn from these experiments and try again. With the ET&A® methodology, one learns to cycle through act, learn, build as one moves a new idea forward (Neck, Greene, & Brush, 2014). If we are to teach this method of entrepreneurial leadership then we will need to challenge some of the underlying assumptions we have made around curriculum design as it relates to entrepreneurship education. In this chapter, we describe how we approached this challenge as we redesigned Babson's flagship course that is taken by all first year students, Foundations of Management and Entrepreneurship (FME). More specifically, we describe a novel approach to integrating entrepreneurship and organizational behavior in order to teach students how to work with and through others as they pursue new opportunities. The integration of these two disciplines has enabled us to create a pedagogy that facilitates students' skill with the ET&A® methodology and thereby their development as entrepreneurial leaders.

The benefits of integrating organizational behavior and entrepreneurship pedagogy should not be surprising given that the seminal Timmons Model of Entrepreneurship proposes that start up ventures require bringing together and balancing opportunity, resources and a team (Spinelli, Neck, & Timmons, 2006). As Rock pointed out even earlier (1987), the entrepreneurial process requires that a team be able to pivot, to change course when, as is inevitable, the nature of the product has to evolve, or more than that, a venture must respond to pressures and crises. While the lone entrepreneur is unlikely to be able to successfully navigate this process, a good team has a chance. The entrepreneurial leader's role is to balance team, opportunity and resources, in order to build the team and facilitate its development (Spinelli et al., 2006).

It is ironic and perhaps inappropriate then that entrepreneurship and organizational behavior aren't inevitably seen as being partners in entrepreneurship education. It takes significant skill to lead an effective team. The business founder must make decisions about who to bring on board, how the various members of the team will work together, how to develop and optimize team performance, all in a very diverse context. Indeed, it is well known that many founders will step down from leadership roles because they simply don't have the right skill set to lead the team (Boeker & Karichalil, 2002).

Over the past three years, FME has undergone a significant redesign in which Babson College's required course in organizational behavior, which had been taught for the past 15 years in the sophomore year, was integrated with a completely revamped first year entrepreneurship curriculum. Experiential learning is the core pedagogy of this year long business project course in which teams of 15−20 students to develop a business idea using the principles of "design thinking" (Brown, 2008), study the business feasibility of that idea to determine whether or not is in fact a business opportunity, apply for a startup loan from the College, launch and operate their business, and then close it down, donating any profits made to a not for profit community partner.

This is an intense course. It requires a level of student engagement that is challenging throughout. Just like a startup, the teams experiment and iterate. They are very likely to repeatedly face the need to rethink any and all aspects of their venture. There is far too much work for even the most ambitious student to accomplish on her own. Students learn they have to engage others and build an effective team, with all that such a task involves. As a result, students are repeatedly confronted with opportunities to challenge and grow their abilities as a team member, as a leader and as a member of a larger organization. As such, the business project presents an ideal context in which to teach organizational behavior in an experiential way.

However, the teaching of organizational behavior so early in the students' curriculum, remember this is a first year course, is pedagogically controversial. Even some Babson faculty questioned whether students would have sufficient life experience to draw on so that they could make sense of the complexities of human behavior in a work context. Interestingly, the shared assumptions that many have regarding the most appropriate time to teach undergraduate organizational behavior in the curriculum have no basis in research. The question has simply not been explored. Indeed, we were not able to find any higher education program in business that had tried to position organizational behavior so early in students' academic careers. As such, we had to engage in exactly the kind of entrepreneurial thinking that we teach: We had an idea, the idea made sense to quite a few stakeholders including former students, alumni and a variety of faculty, we launched a pilot, learned from our successes and failures, iterated, and scaled up. While it may seem simple, the risk of pursuing this pedagogical opportunity was high. Incoming students point to FME as one of the top reasons for their decision to attend Babson. Furthermore, this is a very expensive program to run that demands coordination among over 20 faculty across 14 sections of the course, academic services support, and quite a bit of the College's curricular budget. While we anticipated that we would have much to learn and make some mistakes as we launched the redesigned course, we were also aware that the basic design needed to come up with an approach that would likely work.

In this chapter, we'll tell the story of FME 2.0 as we have come to call it and illustrate what we believe are some important lessons learned in the process. We start with a short history of the course and move toward elaborating some of the factors that provoked a major redesign. Throughout, we will offer insight into the key concepts underlying the design of the pedagogy, particularly as it relates to experiential learning. We'll then provide more detail about FME 2.0 and how the integration of entrepreneurship education, organizational behavior pedagogy and the business project enhances student learning. We close by discussing some key lessons learned in the process about both pedagogy and the role of the professor, lessons that can be applied broadly in entrepreneurship education.

FME: Course History and the Need for Change

The FME course has been central to the Babson curriculum since the early 1990s. At that time, the College was engaged in a significant rethinking of the curriculum. Many business schools were doing the same in response to stakeholder feedback that while business curriculum enabled students to develop functional skills such as finance and marketing, business students were less competent at integrating concepts across disciplines and even less skilled at working with others, particularly in a team context. The pedagogical task of building actual competence in the integration of business disciplines and interpersonal effectiveness naturally points to the value of curriculum design that emphasize experiential learning, educational interventions in which students integrate academic learning with direct experience (McCarthy & Mccarthy, 2006). While experiential education was already central to many of Babson's advanced electives, this approach had not been integrated into the core curriculum in a significant way.

The design for an experiential-based entrepreneurship course drew on the work of John Miller at Bucknell University (1991). In the course Miller designed and implemented, students, working in teams, created a business. Miller had designed his course based in part on prior work by Allan Cohen (1976) in which he advocates that the most effective way to teach organizational behavior is not with cases and simulations but by structuring the classroom as an organization (Cohen, 1976). Rather than teach *about* an organizational behavior concept, this perspective draws attention to the fact that organizational dynamics also occur within the classroom itself. Leadership, teamwork, listening, influence, and other behavioral concepts are inevitably important to the effectiveness of a class. Those phenomena can be identified, discussed, and even explored through class experimentation. Students and faculty are encouraged to reflect on how their behavior in the classroom illustrates important concepts and how they can leverage the classroom experience for personal development.

Cohen, Babson's Vice-President for Academic Affairs at the time, connected with Miller and encouraged a team of faculty to build on his and Miller's work as they redesigned the undergraduate curriculum. Out of this research came the design for an experientially oriented course that went beyond the classroom as organization. In this new course, students would actually launch and run a business using seed money from the college. In order to both support and leverage this task for instructional purposes, students would be provided conceptual frameworks and tools from a variety of business disciplines including entrepreneurship and organizational behavior, but also including accounting, operations, and business law, among others.

At this time technology was also emerging as an important educational focus for business schools. Students were entering their first year with very little understanding or skills in the use of technology. To highlight the importance of information technology it was decided that it would be pedagogically appropriate to integrate an information technology and systems course into the business project. The successful outcome of the course pilot lead to a required full year business project course for all incoming students which became known as FME. Beyond the learning that occurred, FME became a central component to students' socialization into the Babson culture and into business. Stories of success, failure and stress attained the status of folk legends, shared by students, faculty, and ultimately alumni and other members of the community. With approximately 15 student businesses appearing every spring, nearly everyone in the Babson community knew about and in some way was impacted by FME.

Many of those legends highlighted just how difficult it was for student business project teams to "deal with the people issues." Stories of business project team "CEOs" effective and not so effective leadership styles were common place. Team conflicts were frequent and motivation and engagement challenges often arose that derailed the business projects. In addition, stress and time pressures meant students would often respond to interpersonal challenges in ways that were not just ineffective but at times could border on unethical. While some organizational behavior content was included in this course, it was minimal as there were many other business concepts to be covered. Furthermore, even though the faculty spent hours outside of class coaching the student teams, few of the faculty teaching FME were organizational behavior professors who had the skills and knowledge to significantly support the teams and help students develop their interpersonal skills. Over time, as the Babson student body became increasingly diverse, student teams also struggled with working with students from significantly different cultural backgrounds. While students were certainly experiencing the challenges of organizational behavior in a real world context, we were not finding that they were developing the skills and conceptual understanding of how to successfully work through these challenges.

At the same time our understanding of entrepreneurship was evolving as well (Costello, Neck, & Williams, 2011). As mentioned above, the Timmons Model of Entrepreneurship (Spinelli et al., 2006) would predict that new ventures will actually inhabit a highly uncertain and perhaps unknowable context, making elements of the process as important as the strength of the underlying business idea. The notion of a "business plan" became increasingly suspect because of its inherent predictive logic. Failure was coming to be viewed as central to a process of intentional iteration in which the entrepreneur experiences setbacks, false starts, wrong turns, and mistakes and learns from these experiences, adapts, and moves forward (Neck, 2014). As Neck points out this is not just a language change but shifting from failure to intentional iteration "allows entrepreneurs to develop the skills needed to respond to the uncertainty they face" (Neck, 2014). A central component of intentional iteration is its inherent connection with working with others. Beyond needing a team, the ET&A methodology focuses on enlisting the help of others to move forward and pivot around mistakes and challenges. As such, social capital was coming to be seen as a key factor in entrepreneurial success.

In 2012, the Undergraduate Dean commissioned several committees to review FME as part of a larger curriculum refreshment process. Interviews with students and alumni emphasized the critical role that "dealing with people issues" played in the experience of and frustrations with the course. While these experiences were debriefed in the organizational behavior course in the intermediate curriculum the following year, in which students would reflect on their FME experience and develop more effective skills for working with people, this is too little too late. Nearly all the stakeholders, an increasing number of faculty included, believe it would be more valuable to teach organizational behavior in the FME business context so students could learn effective ways of working with others from the beginning.

Our evolution in thinking about the potential fit between organizational behavior and FME coincided with a similar process of rethinking the position of our information systems and technology education for our students. As we entered the second decade of the century, students were entering college with more technological competence than had been the case in the 1990s. Not only did they typically have a good understanding of how to use desktop technologies but many also knew how to build websites and utilize social media. They no longer needed to be convinced of the importance of technology. What students were lacking was an understanding of topics such as big data, enterprise wide information systems solutions and mobile computing which are closely connected to marketing, a course normally taught later in the curriculum.

Across the curriculum, faculty were also exploring how to respond to compelling trends related to changing social values. Like many business schools, Babson was looking hard at the rising criticism of management education with regards to ethical transgression and prioritization of finance over social and environmental value (Holland, 2009; Khurana, 2007). The faculty were looking at how to redesign the pedagogy to support students' ethical development and to help student's address the role of business in addressing opportunities related to the environment and social value creation. This research resulted in the college's new focus on educating entrepreneurial leaders, individuals who engage entrepreneurial thought and action (ET&A®) and a deep understanding of self and context to create social and economic value everywhere (Greenberg, McKone-Sweet, & Wilson, 2011). FME needed to be redesigned to better align with the college's pedagogical vision.

All of these issues factored into considerations of how to rejuvenate the pedagogy of FME. Fortuitously, the redesign also allowed the faculty to change several other aspects of the course in order to better model the actual start up experience. The number of students in each section was reduced to 40 from 60 which allowed for smaller business project teams. With smaller teams, all students became more accountable for their actions and the smaller teams more accurately mirrored the experience of a new venture. At the same time, the College began to overhaul the support infrastructure for the businesses that were launched during the second semester so that students could focus more on developing their understanding of the ET&A® methodology and working with others.

None of these changes were without risk or without resistance. The ideas we were proposing also were met with some pedagogical resistance. For many the teaching of organizational behavior so early in the students' curriculum, remember this is a first year course, was controversial. The question those with this perspective raised was whether or not students had reached a level of maturity and had experienced sufficient organizational relationships to be able to comprehend the complexities of organizational behavior. However, as previously stated, such assumptions regarding the most appropriate time to teach organizational behavior in the curriculum have no basis in research. However, as folk wisdom, they do have a certain "common sense" perspective which we felt it was appropriate to consider. An alternative approach, the one taken, was to consider not whether we could teach organizational behavior under such circumstances but rather *how* we could teach it effectively.

FME 2.0: A PEDAGOGY FOR DEVELOPING ENTREPRENEURIAL LEADERS

To design FME 2.0, we had to engage in the same methodology of entrepreneurial leadership that we wanted to teach. We had an idea, we met with numerous stakeholders and brought a team along. As the team worked, the scaffolding of the course evolved till the point that we could launch a pilot. We engaged in the act, learn, build cycle of ET&A® to learn from our pilot, to iterate, and to scale up. As we continue forward, we continue to iterate as we cycle through act, learn, and build to make this course central to the development of entrepreneurial leaders.

The Deans and Chairs conference at the College re-defined the learning objectives of FME 2.0 as the following:

- Experience the nature of business as an integrated enterprise
- Practice entrepreneurial thought and action
- Identify, develop, and assess entrepreneurial opportunities that create social and economic value
- Analyze local and global context as it relates to entrepreneurial opportunities
- Explore the self, team and organization in relation to entrepreneurial leadership.

These learning goals draw heavily on the insights gained from our deeper understanding of entrepreneurial leadership as mentioned above (Greenberg et al., 2011). These were the goals with which the design committee worked.

The syllabus that was created to support these objectives follows the pictorial diagram illustrating how students' learning of these objectives follows an iterative, integrated process (see Figure 1). This figure shows how the development of a new venture is not the end goal rather it is the vehicle for teaching the aforementioned learning objectives. The x-axis shows the timing and competency development which illustrates where we are in the course and how students' conceptual understanding and skills are evolving. The y-axis points to the two elements of ET&A®, creation and prediction logic and is designed to help students understand where in the course they are more likely to develop their creation thinking and where they are more likely to develop their prediction thinking. The two upward curving lines illustrate how the entrepreneurship course content is linked with the organizational behavior content, each of which is discussed in more detail below. Course topics are rarely learned just for a "test" as they are needed and built upon as the students engage in their business projects.

The business project is the central element of this course design as the students move through three distinct phases, *explore, pursue,*

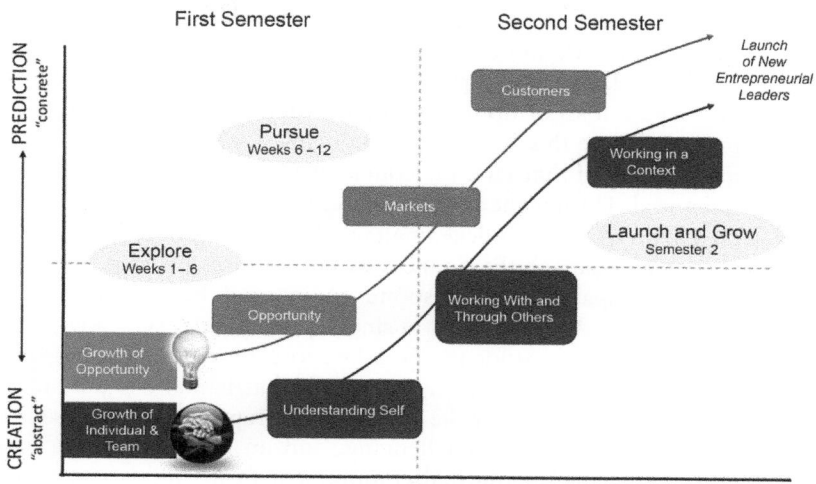

Figure 1: Developing Entrepreneurial Leaders the Babson Way. *Source*: Created by Professor Heidi Neck, Babson College, 2011, copyright © Babson College.

and *launch and grow*. The Explore phase of the business project begins with the first day of class when students are divided into four explore teams of 10 students each. In their Explore teams, the students brainstorm different ideas for a business project. Students begin by focusing first on a problem area and opportunity space as they consider solutions that would respond to that problem. Students are encouraged to focus on a wide range of potential business problems ranging from product-related to social-related and service-oriented problems. This explore stage ends with "rocket pitches" during which students have three minutes to pitch an idea that they feel has the potential to be a business opportunity. Typically, each 10-person explore team will pitch 2−3 ideas. The 40 students in the class vote on the opportunities along multiple dimensions and 5−6 opportunities are typically selected to move forward to the second phase − Pursue.

Students are redeployed across five or six Pursue teams during which time they evaluate the feasibility of their ideas. While the explore phase of the course emphasizes the use of creation logic, the pursue phase requires the use of more predictive approaches, including market research and financial analysis, to study their opportunities. In addition, each team must do a corporate social responsibility assessment to better understand the impact of their potential business on other stakeholders and the environment. This phase ends with "feasibility presentations" during which students present the feasibility of the opportunities they are considering. Two or three business project teams are then selected to go forward as business projects in the third phase, Launch and Grow.

In the launch and grow phase, 13–20 person student teams are provided a loan of up to $3000.00 to fund and launch the business project. While this is in fact a forgivable loan, and the students are quite aware of that fact, the course proceeds as though the loan was quite real. During the launch phase, the student teams will manage their loan from the college, manage the operations, sell their product or service, manage the finances of the business project, design marketing campaigns, and respond to internal human resource and team issues. Whether the business project is specifically a social enterprise or not, students are asked to explore the creation of both social and economic value. Any profit that is made is donated to a non-profit partner after the initial loan is repaid.[1] The course is fast-paced, interpersonally challenging, and an intense learning experience that demands unusual commitment from students and faculty both in and out of the classroom.

In this new course design, the curriculum integrates two disciplinary perspectives: entrepreneurship/marketing and business acumen and organizational behavior. There are two faculty who co-teach the course, one from organizational behavior and the other from entrepreneurship or a related management field. Depending on the daily focus, sessions may be led by one faculty member or both though both faculty participate in all sessions. Either way, conceptual material is taught such that it integrates with and supports students' execution of their business projects. Below, we discuss each disciplinary content in more detail.

Entrepreneurship/Marketing/Business Acumen Curriculum

The entrepreneurship/business curriculum is designed to support the students at every phase of the venture development process. In the explore phase, much of the course content centers on design thinking and creation logic (Brown, 2008). Students learn a process for identifying a problem area and considering a range of possible solutions. Design thinking is used to teach students how to brainstorm around their interests and then use observation to explore that idea in more depth. Creation logic, the testing and shaping of ideas through action, learning, and building guides this teaching.

---

[1]While we do indeed hope that most of the businesses will attain break even as it helps the economic sustainability of the course, that is not a requirement. The College underwrites the loans and student grades are in no way impacted by whether or not their project makes money!

In the explore phase, students are also introduced to two principles that remain central to the entire course — pivoting and intentional iteration. When one faces obstacles, one must learn to pivot
around them. A large wall can't be climbed over but one can find a
new way to move around that wall. Intentional iteration is what one
does when they fall off the wall. Iterating is not just trying again but
it is about assessing what one learns from one's mistakes and applying that learning to the next wall encountered. Both ideas are foundational to creation logic and both are difficult concepts for students
to conceptualize and act upon.

As the students move into the pursue phase, the entrepreneur-
ship/marketing/business acumen curriculum focuses on teaching students the tools they will need to assess the feasibility of their
business. Students learn market research, corporate social responsibility analysis, and financial analysis. While all concepts are taught
at a basic level, these are first year undergraduate students, they are
taught such that students can apply these concepts immediately.
Furthermore, the focus is not just on learning these concepts but on
learning how to integrate these analytical frameworks into an
ET&A® methodology. Students learn how to pivot based on market
research, financial research, and feasibility.

As students move into the launch phase, prediction logic
becomes more central to the course. Students are now actually running their business projects and they now learn varied financial,
sales, and marketing tools to build their businesses. The course
focuses on integrating these predictive based approaches with prior
creation approaches so that students develop a mindset of oscillating
between analysis and action. Through a year-long course in which
creation and prediction logic is reinforced and reviewed, the students
develop a strong understanding and significant skill with the
ET&A® methodology which is one of the principles of entrepreneurial leadership.

Organizational Behavior Curriculum

The organizational behavior curriculum is designed to link to the
explore, pursue, and launch phases of the business project. While
the content follows a somewhat traditional model as it moves from
the individual to the team to the organization level, it is framed in a
way that connects explicitly to entrepreneurial leadership and
ET&A®. A central principle of entrepreneurial leadership is the ability to take action based on deep understanding of self and context
(Greenberg et al., 2011). Three questions frame the principle of self
and context understanding "Who am I?," "Who do I know?," and
"What do I need to understand about the context in which I am
working?" By understanding the answers to these questions, entrepreneurial leaders are better able to pursue opportunities that create

social and economic value. Exploring these three questions is the basis for the organizational behavior curriculum.

The first section of the curriculum is focused on the theme of "Who am I?" as students learn to reflect on who they are and the skills, knowledge, and views they bring to the business project. This content focuses on traditional individual level concepts such as identity, behavioral style, values, and one's personal motivation or passion. The later in particular of course connects directly with the decisions that entrepreneurs make about how they devote their time and resources. The students must struggle with the question of "what kind of business do I want to create?"

The course then transitions to the theme of "Who do I know?" Since a central component of ET&A® is bringing others along and having them contribute in ways that enable a new venture to evolve, entrepreneurial leaders must understand how to work with and through others. To address these questions, the organizational behavior curriculum moves to the interpersonal level as students learn how to analyze and develop their personal and professional networks and learn skills for more effectively working with and through people. This component of the course introduces topics such as leadership, network relationships, managing conflict, and negotiation. The final theme of the OB curriculum covers the questions of "Where am I?" as students learn to analyze the contexts in which they are operating and how context affects their actions. Thus, this section of the course covers topics such as organizational culture, organizational design, and national culture.

Additional organizational behavior content is integrated into the course that connects to these themes but are also central to running a 13−20 person venture. Throughout the year students learn how to give and receive feedback and the importance of feedback to learning and development. Students also learn how to respond to the ebbs and flows of stress and energy management and engagement, both of themselves and of their teammates. By the end of the year, students not only understand organizational behavior at a conceptual level but they have experienced and acted upon this curriculum and seen how it connects to their own growth as entrepreneurial leadership.

FME 2.0 requires a level of student engagement that is challenging throughout, as mentioned above. It also requires a level of faculty responsiveness and teaching through complexity that is not characteristic of a more traditional course. Just like a startup, the teams experiment and iterate. They are very likely to repeatedly face the need to rethink any and all aspects of their business project. They often don't know what they are doing, yet have to jump in regardless. There are numerous and sometimes intense disagreements about the way forward, about how to make decisions, how to allocate the power to make decisions, how to delegate, how to communicate and over communicate, how to deal with widely different cultural perspectives and a range issues that a mature team of forty-year olds find daunting. Students are repeatedly confronted with opportunities to challenge and grow their abilities as a team member, as an entrepreneurial leader and as a member of a larger organization. The students themselves validate the importance of organizational behavior for themselves and the faculty on a regular basis as they often utilize learnings from organizational behavior immediately in their project teams. However, the value of organizational behavior actually extends beyond its traditional areas of leadership, teamwork and organizational functioning.

Integrating Entrepreneurship and Organizational Behavior

As the above description illustrates, integration between organizational behavior and entrepreneurship is foundational to the design of this course. This integration is executed through two key pedagogical themes. First, throughout this course, entrepreneurship and organizational behavior course content is designed to leverage the power of experiential learning (Kolb, 1976). Experiential learning is an iterative process of learning concepts, taking action based on those concepts, reflecting on the results, perhaps with the help of feedback from others, rethinking one's approach and the application of the original concepts, and taking action again. In experiential learning, all phases of the learning process are required for continued acquisition of a competency (Gruver & Miller, 2011). These principles are central to the design of every course session. In each session, students are using the business project to engage in experiential learning around a particular course topic and to link that topic back to a previous session. In this way the course moves beyond classroom as an organization (Cohen, 1976) to be organization as a classroom.

Second, both disciplinary perspectives are based on the process of ET&A® that involves *acting*, taking a small step, pausing to see what has been *learned* by doing so, and *building* that learning into the next action (Keifer, Schlesinger, & Brown, 2011). Class discussion and reflection is guided such that the learning students' experience will not be solely about their product or service, but will also involve important insights regarding who they are as individuals, what they are interested in doing, what they need to do as a team to work together more effectively and how their team relates to the larger world. The confluence of methodologies between ET&A® and organizational behavior creates powerful opportunities to integrate the two disciplines. Below, we discuss some of these integration points more fully.

As was mentioned above, the start of FME is focused on understanding "Who am I?" "Who am I?" is a fundamental component of entrepreneurial leadership and ET&A®. In the abstract, students are often lost at how individual-level organizational behavior concepts connect to the larger themes of entrepreneurial leadership and opportunity creation. In FME, we design the content to make these connections explicit. For example, the brainstorming and observation exercises students do at the start of the business/entrepreneurship curriculum connect directly to their identity, values, and even behavioral style. Students learn how important it is to pursue business projects that connect to who they are as this forms the basis for the knowledge skills, and passion they bring to the project. As students continue down the path of exploring the ideas they have brainstormed they start to see how their behavioral style influences how they think about and investigate an opportunity. Students don't just learn what their behavioral style is but they begin to understand how their behavioral style directly influences what they see as an opportunity and how they look at the challenges and potential of an opportunity. Students also begin to learn the importance of engaging with others who see an opportunity differently. While these concepts can certainly be taught to students in the abstract or in connection with a case or exercise, we find students are inherently more motivated to think critically about behavioral style and other topics related to self when they see how these concepts directly impact their business projects.

Individual level concepts such as social identity and values are also linked to other aspects of the management/entrepreneurship curriculum such that students understand how these topics inherently impact their business projects. For example, these connections are made quite explicit when market research is taught. In introducing the concept of social identity, we focus students' attention on how social identity influences our group affiliations and perspectives and lead us to feel more comfortable with some groups than others. In teaching market research, students are required to conduct focus groups and market surveys to explore new perspectives on their ideas. Students frequently invite those who are similar to them to participate in their exploration efforts rather than get input from those who are dissimilar and might have differing viewpoints. We see this tendency even when the students have defined a potential target market as being very different from them (older, in particular). This tendency discourages them from consider the many possible opportunities that may surround their core pursuit. As students check in with faculty about the progress of their market research, we draw attention to this tendency and it provides an opportunity to further discuss how social identity influences actions and decisions. This connection to social identity is enlightening for many students.

Another example of how this integration of disciplines occurs relates to the concepts of values and ethics. With this content, we see how integration between organizational behavior and entrepreneurship content also happens in a cyclical fashion as the business projects progress and challenges arise. Conceptual material regarding values and ethics is covered early in the course as these ideas are connected to the theme of "Who am I?" Yet, as the business project progresses through the year situations will arise that will call into questions students' values and ethics. Some of the issues that have arisen in the past relate to withholding critical information from the faculty, colluding on peer evaluations, and/or failing to appropriately respond to a customers' complaints about a product. When these problems arise, students are confronted with the fact that what they will do in the abstract often deviates from what they do in the moment. We utilize Gentile's (2010) *Giving Voice to Values* framework as this action-based framework enables students to learn to work with their peers to more effectively respond to value based conflicts in their business projects. New learning arises as students' experiences in the business project are connected to prior learning and through these connections more thorough comprehension of the course content arises (Reis, 2014). A key design component in the second semester is the designation of the first 30 minutes of each 90-minute session as a time for a deep dive into one of the business projects' issues and successes. This 30 minutes block enables faculty to engage the entire class in a conversation that further links conceptual knowledge with action.

The integration of the two disciplinary perspectives with the business project provide the hand-on experience that undergraduate students need to move from understanding of a topic to critical thinking about how to evaluate and take action based on that topic. For example, some of the most difficult topics to develop critical thinking about are macro topics such as organizational design. Undergraduate students often fail to grasp the ways in which organizational design influences power, culture, and coordination. They can understand this linkage at the abstract level but with limited work experience it is hard for undergraduate students to understand how organizational structure can fundamentally change people's behavior. For years, we have taught Oshry's classic simulation on tops, middles, bottoms (Oshry, 2007). Through this simulation, students receive practice and feedback around power and structure in order to develop more insightful learning related to this topic (Reis, 2014). Unfortunately, it was never quite as successful as we desired.

However, when this exercise is taught in FME, the experience is quite different. FME businesses inevitably require some sort of structure, usually some variant of a functional structure in which departments are formed to do certain kinds of work: finance, marketing, and sales for instance. Students can actually see tension arise as a result of departmental alliances as well as observe how power can be mismanaged and motivation problems arise as a result of hierarchies that they create. The Oshry simulation is real for students now as it connects to their daily lives in their business projects. When we teach this exercise, we can move into higher order learning as students critically think about the complexities of structure and synthesize and take action based on their understanding (Bloom, 1956). Based on their new understanding, students will frequently pivot and experiment in their business projects with new and different ways of organizing that create better collaboration and engagement.

Lessons Learned: Flexibility in Designing and Delivering a Course

Teaching organizational behavior in this manner is indeed challenging and complex. It is easier, simpler, less time-consuming, and less emotionally frustrating to teach a traditional syllabus that has a clear, daily plan. Yet, we believe with undergraduate students who have limited points of reference, be they first year students or seniors, it is difficult to help students reach a higher order of learning and critical thinking about organizational behavior in a traditional classroom context. To move undergraduates from simply understanding organizational behavior concepts to integrating these ideas into their actions, we believe these concepts must be integrated into lived experiences. Below, we discuss some of the ways a professor and a course must evolve to teach organizational behavior in this manner.

In this pedagogical approach, flexibility becomes central to the course and to the professor's role. First, professors must be flexible around the content that is included in an organizational behavior survey course. As was mentioned previously, this course is not designed around a traditional text-book model of individual, team, organizational level analysis. Certain course topics that some traditional organizational behavior faculty might consider essential to a survey course, such as perception biases and decision making, are not explored. Other concepts that are more likely to be taught in a human resources or management course, such as giving and receiving feedback and performance management, are integrated into this class as they are central to students' running of their business projects. As a professor, one needs to shift his or her frame of reference such that the focus is on learning a model for effectively working with and through others in an organizational context rather than memorizing the conceptual elements of such a model. Students learn to deeply and critically think about the framing of organizational behavior problems which will often provoke self-directed inquiry on their part that goes well beyond the concepts presented in the course.

Professors must also be flexible in how they teach. As the aforementioned description of FME highlights, a guiding assumption of this course is that students learn greater insight around organizational behavior topics when these topics are connected to students' experiences running their business projects. While class sessions can be designed to include such discussions, professors must be flexible to also respond to the unexpected. In the second semester of our course, we use the first half hour of each 90-minute class to discuss the business projects. We provide students with explicit questions to consider related to the course and we ask them to share with us in a structured fashion some of their ongoing successes and challenges. We then use these written and verbal updates as the basis for questions that are asked or problems that are discussed with the entire class. These are not glossy, sales presentation of the business projects rather students are taught that these are working sessions designed to provide them with new perspectives. In these discussions, faculty never know what will arise. Hence, faculty must be flexible and agile as they respond and connect new learning to old learning and show students how course concepts can guide how they solve real problems or respond to real opportunities in their business projects. Unfortunately, the 30-minute timeframe is not always long enough. Unexpected situations frequently arise that are more complex than a 30-minute session allows. Professors who are successful in this context must be willing to forgo the content of the day's syllabus to discuss and debate the challenges the students are facing. It is through these discussions that significant learning happens even if it means that one less content class is covered.

As the structure of the course changes, so does the professors' role in relationship to the students. In today's educational context, we frequently debate the role of the professor particularly as we think about the ideas of the flipped classroom (Berrett, 2012) or try to integrate the competing paradigms of "sage on the stage" versus "guide from the side" (King, 1993). Yet, a pedagogy that revolves around organization as a classroom requires that the professor move beyond even these dichotomies. In this organization based environment, the professors role is very much that of leading from behind. While learning certainly happens in the more traditional classroom paradigm that is occurring in the context of this course, more significant learning happens as the professor pays close attention to what happens outside the classroom.

Professors need to build relationships with their students so that students will raise the behavioral pain points of the business projects. Cohen (1976) suggested that in this model the organizational behavior teacher needs to recognize that he or she is in many respects a manager, crafting experiences that the students engage in that help them learn from each other, not just the professor. In the model we have created the faculty are not just managers but are mentors, coaches, and boards of advisors. The students are managing the business project and to effectively teach around the project, faculty need to be coaching students. Sometimes the role of coach can be gentle and advising, and at other times it is firm and final. In any case, faculty need to be available to support students in and out of the classroom to ensure that they are iterating as they learn from their mistakes and experiment with new ways of behaving and organizing.

Teaching in this way is exciting and invigorating but also emotionally exhausting at times. Students will make serious mistakes in how they engage with their peers. Frequently a professor feels as if they are failing as they watch students in the classroom appear to understand the material but then not integrate it into the daily running of the business project. However, professors must remember that one is not just teaching ET&A®, one is also using ET&A® to guide their pedagogical approach. Human behavior is messy and not prescribed. Students learn theories to guide their actions and then they experiment with these ideas as they learn how to work with others. When they make mistakes, they have to learn to pivot and iterate as they build more effective ways of working in an organizational context. Teaching in this way is iterative and lacks the linearity of a syllabus. Yet, at the end of the year the learning and critical thinking that students' develop makes the circuitous route worthwhile.

As one reads these challenges, one may be left wondering about one of the original questions we wrestled with in the design of this course "Can organizational behavior be taught in the first undergraduate year?" While we cannot provide empirical evidence to address this question directly, we do believe that the answer is yes based on our experiences to date. FME 2.0 was launched in a one section pilot program before being implemented across the entire first year curriculum. At the end of the pilot year, faculty explored with students the question of teaching organizational behavior in the first year. The undergraduate students felt strongly this had been a successful learning experience for them. They valued the direct, indepth exploration of the "people issues" involved in running the business project. They learned to think critically about themselves and could implement what they had learned immediately in the business project. Since that time faculty skepticism has largely abated and most express satisfaction in being able to link organizational behavior concepts with the business project. Student opinion surveys indicate a high level of satisfaction with the course, on par with and frequently greater than the previous iteration of FME. Most importantly, FME 2.0 provides the pedagogical basis for developing our students as entrepreneurial leaders.

Singh and Schick (2007) among others have raised questions regarding the relevance of organizational behavior in the business school curriculum. Do business leaders need or use what they learn in an organizational behavior course? We doubt seriously that they utilize complex theories of motivation or other concepts often taught in survey organizational behavior courses. But do they deal with "people issues?" All the time. Emphasizing the application of theory in practice we believe helps to solidify the role and value of organizational behavior. In the entrepreneurial setting, if the great team trumps the great idea, then the place of organizational behavior is assured.

Acknowledgments

The authors want to acknowledge the work of the many faculty and staff from Babson who were involved in the redesign of FME. In particular, this course is based on the work by Bob Halsey, David Hennessey, Rob Kopp, Heidi Neck, Phyllis Schlesinger, and Yasu Yamakawa, along with the authors.

References

Berrett, D. (2012, February 12). *How "Flipping" the classroom can improve the traditional lecture.* Retrieved from http://chronicle.com/article/How-Flipping-the-Classroom/130857/. Accessed on December 21, 2012.

Bloom, B. S. (Ed.). (1956). *Taxonomy of educational objectives: The classification of educational goals handbook I: Cognitive domain.* New York, NY: David McKay Company, Inc.

Boeker, W., & Karichalil, R. (2002). Entrepreneurial transitions: Factors influencing founders departure. *Academy of Management Journal, 45*(4), 818–826.

Brown, T. (2008). Design thinking. *Harvard Business Review, 65*(6), 84–92.

Cohen, A. (1976). Beyond simulation: The classroom as organization. *Journal of Management Education, 2*(1), 13–19.

Costello, C., Neck, H., & Williams, R. (2011). *Elements of the entrepreneur experience.* Wellesley, MA: Babson College, Babson Entrepreneur Experience Lab.

Gentile, M. (2010). *Giving voice to values.* New Haven, CT: Yale University Press.

Greenberg, D., McKone-Sweet, K., & Wilson, H. J. (2011). *The new entrepreneurial leader: Developing leaders who create social and economic opportunity.* San Francisco, CA: Berrett-Koehler.

Gruver, W. R., & Miller, J. A. (2011). *Teaching the unteachable?* Leadership Studies at Bucknell University. Retrieved from SSRN http://ssrn.com/abstract=1874113 or http://dx.doi.org/10.2139/ssrn.1874113

Holland, K. (2009). Is it time to retrain B-Schools. *New York Times*, March 14. Retrieved from http://www.nytimes.com/2009/03/15/business/15school.html

Keifer, C., Schlesinger, L., & Brown, P. (2010). *Action trumps everything: Creating what you want in an uncertain world.* Corte Madera, CA: Innovation Associates.

Keifer, C., Schlesinger, L., & Brown, P. (2011). *Action trumps everything: Creating what you want in an uncertain world.* Corte Madera, CA: Innovation Associates.

Khurana, R. (2007). *From higher aims to hired hands: The social transformation of American business schools and the unfulfilled promise of management as a profession.* Princeton, NJ: Princeton University Press.

King, A. (1993). From sage on the stage to guide on the side. *College Teaching, 41*(1), 30–35.

Kolb, D. (1976). Management and the learning process. *California Management Review*, XVIII, 21–32.

McCarthy, P., & Mccarthy, H. (2006). When case studies are not enough: Integrating experiential learning into business curricula. *Journal of Education for Business, 81*(4), 201–204.

Miller, J. (1991). Experiencing management a comprehensive "Hands-On" model for the undergraduate management course. *Journal of Management Education, 15*(2), 151–169.

Neck, H. (2014). Reframing failure as intentional iteration: New research on how entrepreneurs really think. *Babson Insights.* Retrieved from http://www.babson.edu/executive-education/education-educators/babson-insight/articles/pages/reframing-failure-as-intentional-iteration.aspx

Neck, H., Greene, P., & Brush, C. (2014). *Teaching entrepreneurship: A practice-based approach.* New York, NY: Edward Elger Publishing.

Oshry, B. (2007). *Seeing systems: Unlocking the mysteries of organizational life.* Oakland, CA: Berrett-Koehler.

Reis. (2014). *Tomorrow's professor Msg.#1363 learning fundamental principles, generalizations, or theories.* Retrieved from http://cgi.stanford.edu/~dept-ctl/tomprof/posting.php?ID=1363

Rock, A. (1987). Strategy vs. tactics from a venture capitalist. *Harvard Business Review, 65*(6), 64.

Singh, R., & Schick, A. (2007). Organizational behavior: Where does it fit in today's management curriculum. *Journal of Education for Business*, July/August, *82*, 349–356.

Spinelli, S., Neck, H., & Timmons, J. (2006). The Timmons model of entrepreneurship. In A. Zackarakis & S. Spinelli (Eds.), *Entrepreneurship, the engine of growth* (Vol. 2). Westport, CT: Greenwood Publishing.

8

The Business Model Canvas as a Framework for Integrating the Operations Management and Managerial Accounting Curricula

Jennifer Bailey and Benjamin Luippold

Introduction

In this chapter, we provide a review of the integrated Technology and Operations Management (TOM) and Managerial Accounting (MAC) courses offered as a part of the Babson College Sophomore Management Experience (SME). These two courses are taken after students complete their year-long Foundations of Management and Entrepreneurship (FME) course. In FME, students focus on creating, launching, and managing a new business. Critical learning objectives of the FME course include opportunity recognition, marketing research, organizational design, and business leadership (Neck & Stoddard, 2006). However, during FME, students assume that their company's business model and value chain both operate as a "black box." In contrast, during the integrated technology and operations and managerial accounting SME courses, students have the opportunity to examine the detailed building blocks of a company's operational business model and value chain. The unique aspect of the integrated SME TOM/MAC course is that students simultaneously examine the business model from the point of view of two very different, yet complementary, disciplines — operations management and managerial accounting. In so doing, students are afforded the opportunity to synthesize these two different disciplinary perspectives to attain a more holistic and comprehensive understanding of how a company works (Ducoffe, Tromley, & Tucker, 2006). Specifically, this interdisciplinary approach allows students to gain a deeper understanding of the tradeoffs, tensions, and sometimes conflicting goals which must be managed through cross-functional decision making.

Importance of Cross-Functional Decision Making for the Entrepreneurial

The importance of cross-functional decision making skills has been long recognized as a core competency required for the business undergraduate student. There have been many calls by the Association to Advance Collegiate Schools of Business (AACSB) to increase the level of integration in the undergraduate business curriculum. For example, in its 2010 report titled "Business Schools on an Innovation Mission," the AACSB specifically noted that "innovation requires more integrative thinking and integrated curricula" (AACSB, 2010, p. 25). This underscores the importance of the interdisciplinary courses that exist within the Babson curriculum, given our mission to educate entrepreneurial leaders who create great economic and social value — everywhere. This mission encompasses entrepreneurial leaders who create new business models, as well as those who innovate within established ventures to test and implement new elements of an existing business model (Bell & Ansari, 2014).

In this chapter, we demonstrate the importance and the relevance of the integration of the Operations Management and Managerial Accounting courses using the Business Model Canvas (Osterwalder & Pigneur, 2010) as a common framework (see Figure 1). The Business Model Canvas is a tool that provides a holistic picture of the interrelated factors associated with a company's ability to generate revenues and manage its costs. The key factors that determine a company's potential to generate revenues are its unique value proposition, customer segments, customer relationships, and the channels through which it delivers its products/services. These factors are reflected in sections O1, O2, O3, and O4 of the Business Model Canvas. In addition, delivering value to customers requires a company to gain access to and manage key

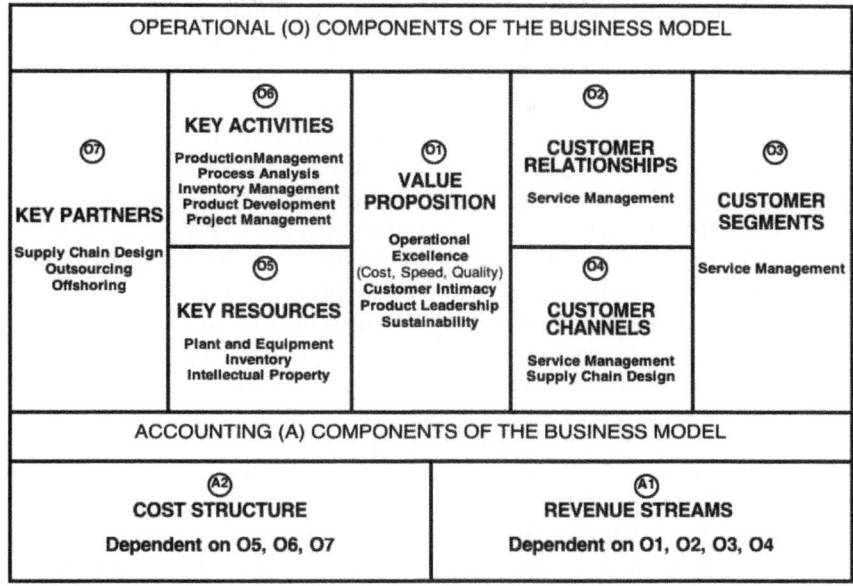

Figure 1: Business Model Canvas as a Framework for Integrated Decision Making. *Source:* Adapted from Osterwalder and Pigneur (2010).

resources, activities, and partners, which are reflected in sections O5, O6, and O7 of the Business Model Canvas, respectively.

During the TOM course, we discuss the TOM decisions and tradeoffs that a venture or company must make to create and deliver its unique value proposition to its customers. We begin by exploring the three main value proposition choices available to a company: Operational Excellence, Customer Intimacy, and Product Leadership (Treacy & Wiersema, 1993) as represented in section O1 of the Business Model Canvas. For each value proposition choice, we highlight some of the potential operational decisions that must be made in order to deliver value. We continue our discussions in the TOM course by discussing issues related to service operations management which must be considered when managing the company's customer segments, customer relationships, and the channels through which it serves its customers, as highlighted in sections O2, O3, and O4 of the Business Model framework. Section O5 (Key Resources) permits a discussion of the operational resources in which a company must invest, such as Inventory, Plant and Equipment. For section O6 (Key Activities), we focus on typical operations management activities such as Inventory Management, Production Management, Process Analysis, Project Management and Product Development activities. Finally in section O7 (Key Partners), we discuss operations management topics related to issues such as Supply Chain Management, Offshoring, and Outsourcing.

Simultaneously, during the MAC course, we expose students to the managerial accounting tools and techniques that allow them to measure and analyze the impact of various operational choices on a company's profitability. Both the revenue streams and the associated costs (see Sections A1 and A2) are impacted by decisions made in sections O1−O8, based on assumptions about the company's customer value proposition and its TOM plan. Therefore, in the MAC course, students gain insights on how to measure the effectiveness of operational decisions, including their impact on revenues, the resources they consume, and the required investment (Gupta & Galloway, 2003).

Leveraging this common Business Model framework across both courses demonstrates to students that Operations Management and Managerial Accounting are interrelated inputs to and outputs from the Business Model, which underscores the importance of cross-functional decision making. To illustrate these points, the TOM and MAC courses are integrated through a number of mechanisms including several shared cases and shared simulations (see Table 1), which are discussed by the faculty and students from the perspective of each specific discipline (Ducoffe et al., 2006; Hamilton, McFarland, & Mirchandani, 2000).

SELECTING AND DELIVERING A VALUE PROPOSITION: CHOCOMIZE CASE

One of the key elements of the Business Model is a venture's (or a company's) choice of its Value Proposition (see Figure 1, Section O1). The value proposition is a statement of a company's unique set of product and service offerings upon which it will compete within its targeted customer segments. As the students discover throughout the semester, the value proposition is the central decision that impacts all subsequent operational decisions, and it has a direct impact on both the revenue and cost structure of the venture. Hence, an early discussion of the value proposition choice sets the stage for the rest of the two courses.

To illustrate the integrated operational and financial decisions that can affect a company as it tries to develop a sustainable business model early in the life of a venture, students are introduced to a shared case on a startup company called Chocomize (Bell, 2012) at the beginning of the semester. Chocomize, an online chocolatier, has entered the market with a value proposition based on product customization. At the time of the case, the operation is a low volume, labor intensive process. However, the founders are presented with

Table 1: Integrated Class Sessions, Cases, Simulations.

Business Model Canvas	Topic	Integrated Session	TOM Learning Objectives	MAC Learning Objectives
VALUE PROPOSITION	Selecting and delivering value proposition	Chocomize case	Operational excellence (quality, time, cost); customer intimacy; product leadership. ROA analysis.	Show that managerial data supports achievement of quality, cost & time strategies. ROA analysis.
	Competing on sustainability	Sofra case	Triple bottom line. Tradeoffs between environmental issues and operational decisions. Managing closed loop supply chains and sustainable operations.	Triple bottom line. Balanced scorecard, performance measurement and strategy mapping.
KEY RESOURCES & KEY ACTIVITIES	Production and inventory management	Gazogle simulation	Process mapping, process types, process analysis, throughput time, cycle time, bottlenecks, WIP.	Impact of process choices on managerial accounting (direct materials, labor, overhead, marketing, administrative costs, cost objects, kinds of inventory).
	Product development	Payload simulation	Product development. project management. design for manufacturability. target costing. decision making under uncertainty.	Target costing, value index analysis, feature/function costing.
KEY PARTNERS	Outsourcing and offshoring	Coloplast case	Operational considerations in the make or buy decision. What processes can be outsourced? Reasons to outsource. Outsourcing and offshoring risks.	Incremental costs analysis between decision alternatives. What costs are relevant to decisions? The impact of opportunity and sunk costs.

an option to deliver a high volume order for a large European luxury retailer for the holidays. Students reflect on the implications of pursuing this opportunity by considering various concerns such as describing both the company's current and proposed value proposition, explaining what operational activities, resources and partners are required for each value proposition, and outlining the financial implications of each option.

Value Proposition and Operations Management Integrated Learning Objectives

In the TOM class, we discuss the three key value proposition choices available to a company: Operational Excellence, Product Leadership, and Customer Intimacy (Treacy & Wiersema, 1993). We describe Operational Excellence as the decision to compete on operational cost efficiency, operational speed, or reliable operational quality. We stress the importance of class sessions on Process Analysis and Quality Management as a means for understanding how to optimize cost, speed and quality when delivering goods and services. These process analysis topics are also the focus of the integrated Gazogle simulation (discussed later). We describe Product Leadership as the decision to compete on offering innovative products and services. In this discussion, we highlight the competitive advantage of having an effective and efficient Product Development process. Many of the factors related to innovation and product development are highlighted in the Payload simulation (discussed later). Finally, we describe Customer Intimacy as the decision to compete on tailoring the company's product and service offerings to niche customer segments. The shared Chocomize case serves as an illustration of the company whose value proposition is based on Customer Intimacy, and students are introduced to a business in which each customer is able to customize their individual order. Students consider the various operational decisions which are necessary to support delivering customized orders. This discussion therefore motivates the future learning objectives on Process Analysis, where students examine the importance of operational flexibility and the differences between make-to-stock and made-to-order processes.

Value Proposition and Managerial Accounting Integrated Learning Objectives

In the MAC class, we discuss the required resources to execute each of these value propositions and the potential revenues generated under each. Importantly, we also introduce the different cost drivers and cost structures that relate to the various processes, resources and assets required to execute each of the different value propositions. By simultaneously considering the operational decisions and the related revenue and cost implications, students are able to consider the degree to which a business model can sustain profitability. For example, the shared Chocomize case serves to illustrate the potential revenue benefit of selecting the Customer Intimacy value proposition. Students are directed to customize their own order on the Chocomize website and to compare the price of a customized chocolate bar with that of a standard chocolate bar.

Students are introduced to the Return on Assets (Operating Income/Assets) measure, which offers an example of the clear interdependence between operations and accounting.[1] In the introductory sessions, students examine the various operational factors which impact financial performance, as demonstrated through the ROA metric. We highlight the impact, for example, of choosing to focus on Customer Intimacy (where companies can leverage premium pricing strategies) versus choosing to focus on Low Cost/Operational Excellence. In the former, delivering customized products and orders might require higher labor costs (i.e., variable costs) which could limit a company's benefit of scaling its operations. While in the latter, in order to compensate for low-cost pricing, companies must often focus on high-volume operational strategies, which might require investing in expensive equipment or considering alternative supply chain structures which can impact operational costs and/or assets. All these points are reinforced during the introductory TOM sessions, during which we also discuss the ROA metric.

The latter conversation on pursuing a high volume, low-cost value proposition motivates later discussions on Outsourcing and Offshoring that are covered in the shared Coloplast case (discussed later in this chapter). However, importantly, we use the Coloplast case to demonstrate that cost reduction is only one factor to consider when contemplating offshoring and outsourcing options. For example, in order to deliver on their order to the luxury retailer, the Chocomize founders consider outsourcing; however, the potential outsourcing agreement requires significantly higher volumes, which is inconsistent with their current low volume, mass-customization operations and value proposition. Students are asked to consider what types of managerial accounting information would be needed as they consider the various alternatives for expanding the operation to meet the luxury retailer's order. Furthermore, students are also encouraged to consider non-financial information that could reflect the impact of operational decisions, including metrics related to employees, stakeholders, and the environment. This introduces the concept of performance measurement and the Balanced Scorecard as a means of appropriately mapping and monitoring the venture's strategic plan (Kaplan & Norton, 2007). By touching on this topic early in the semester, we stress the importance of the consideration of non-financial factors (e.g., environmental impact) that

---

[1]In MAC, we also dissect the Return on Assets measure and explain how it is a function of both Return on Sales (Operating Income/Sales) and Asset Turnover (Sales/Assets).

foreshadow later sessions on Sustainability which is covered in both TOM and MAC using the shared Sofra case.

SUSTAINABILITY VALUE PROPOSITION: SOFRA CASE

In addition to the three traditional value proposition choices available to a company which include Customer Intimacy, Operational Excellence and Product Leadership (see Figure 1, Section O1), we also extend the discussion on value propositions to consider how firms can compete on the basis on Sustainability. To illustrate the issues related to competing on sustainability, we discuss the Sofra case (Bell, Erzurumlu, & Fowler, 2010, 2013). Sofra is a large, multinational, food aggregator that primarily services corporate, education, and government clients. In the mid-2000s, Sofra started two major initiatives, one for improved sustainability and the other for increased profitability. The Bright Future Plan contained Sofra's 10 global sustainability commitments, while the Initiatives 2015 focused on site level profitability through initiatives around activity-based costing and organizational effectiveness. In North America, an Office of Sustainability and Corporate Social Responsibility (OSCSR) was created to implement the Bright Future Plan and a dedicated team (consisting mostly of Supply Chain Management personnel) was established to implement the Initiatives 2015 plan.

Sustainability and Operations Management Integrated Learning Objectives

In TOM, we begin the Sofra case discussion by linking back to the earlier discussions on value propositions. Students note that Sofra is currently pursuing the Operational Excellence value proposition. The TOM discussions then focus on organizational effectiveness strategies and operational decisions which lower cost and improve profitability, including reducing the frequency of deliveries, reducing SKUs and increasing purchasing through prime vendors. On the other hand, students will recognize that the sustainability initiatives pursued by the OSCSR called for an operational strategy that required local purchasing from a greater number of smaller suppliers (not prime vendors) and reduced offerings of non-sustainable items such as bottled water or foam products. The Supply Management Team viewed OSCSR's efforts as threats to Sofra's profitability and opposed many of its initiatives, which they considered operationally inefficient and economically irresponsible. This shared case discussion allows students to examine how sustainable choices impact both operational (Angell & Klassen, 1999) and financial performance (Caliskan, 2014) and to consider ways to simultaneously manage the two initiatives in order to achieve the profit goals and operational objectives as well as the sustainability targets.

Sustainability and Managerial Accounting Integrated Learning Objectives

The Sofra case introduces students to the concept of the Triple Bottom Line, in which companies consider not only profits but also the impact of various operational decisions on people and the planet (Caliskan, 2014). In MAC, we also use Sofra to emphasize the importance of linking effective performance measures to strategic initiatives. The case discussions allow students to recognize that, while Sofra was focused on both supply chain efficiency and sustainability, sustainability was not linked to the performance measurement system. That is, the measures used to evaluate management performance did not refer to any actions pertaining to sustainability. We discuss this case in our unit on performance measurement and the Balanced Scorecard (Kaplan & Norton, 2007). The Balanced Scorecard is a way to measure performance along four dimensions: (1) learning and growth, (2) internal processes, (3) customer, and (4) financial. The measures should tie closely to a company's strategic objectives and should be an effective indicator of whether the company is achieving its goals.

After discussing the case, students work on an assignment pertaining to Sofra where we provide them with Sofra's Balanced Scorecard and ask them to independently indicate which sustainability initiatives they expect would be carried out given the existing set of metrics. What they find is that many of the sustainability initiatives would not be executed under the current scorecard. We then assign students into small groups to compare answers. Once students have a consensus about which initiatives would receive action, they are asked to examine the scorecard as a group to determine what behaviors and actions the existing set of metrics encourage and why. Next, students discuss whether the metrics are consistent with the sustainability strategy. Finally, if students determine that the metrics do not promote sustainability actions, then they are asked to formulate practical and effective measures of sustainability.

KEY RESOURCES AND KEY ACTIVITIES: GAZOGLE PRODUCTION AND INVENTORY MANAGEMENT SIMULATION

A second area that is integrated across the TOM and MAC courses is the consideration of the management of a company's Key Resources and Key Activities (see Sections O5 and O6). In both courses, we emphasize the message that companies remain profitable through the effective use of resources and the efficient execution of activities. To that end, a core component of both courses is the coverage of how to analyze and improve the effectiveness and efficiency of the manufacturing and service processes through which companies deliver value to their customers. In the TOM course, students are exposed to operations management topics such as process flow charting, process type selection (e.g., assembly line, batch, job shop processes), process analysis, managing capacity utilization, alleviating bottlenecks, and just-in-time inventory management. At the same time, students are exposed to complementary topics in the MAC course that demonstrate the impact of operational process choices on various managerial accounting concepts such as manufacturing costs (direct materials, direct labor, and manufacturing overhead) versus nonmanufacturing costs and cost behavior (fixed and variable costs).

The Gazogle simulation (Weiss, 2006) is an experiential production management game that uses LEGOs to demonstrate to students how operations management and managerial accounting are integrated and interdependent in real production systems. The team-based simulation requires students to produce a product and meet customer demands. Teams are evaluated on total profits which are based on revenues (generated from meeting demand in a timely manner at a pre-specified quality level) net of the costs of labor, facilities, and materials. While there are many ways to adapt this exercise, at Babson, we convene students into teams containing between 10 and 13 members. Student roles for each team include 4 assemblers, 2−4 material handlers, 1−2 procurement persons, 1 production accountant, 1 customer, 1 supplier, and 1 or 2 observers. Teams compete to maximize profitability during four-minute simulation rounds by producing and delivering Gazogles (a product that is made out of LEGOs). Each round represents one month of production.

Teams incur several costs during each production month. First, teams are charged a fixed fee for every internal worker (labor resource) and a fixed occupancy cost for every table (production location) used. There is a material cost associated with the number of LEGO blocks used in the production of a Gazogle, making this cost variable to the number of units sold. Larger LEGO pieces command a marginally higher material cost than smaller ones. In addition, teams incur a fixed procurement charge every time the procurement personnel go to retrieve LEGOs from the supplier, reflecting an order setup cost. At the end of the production period, teams accrue warehousing and carrying costs for the work-in-process (WIP) inventory associated with those LEGOs that are still in production but were not delivered to the customer by the end of the round. The production accountant is responsible for collecting all the data and information that is required for reporting the monthly profits. Between rounds, teams can elect to make process improvement changes. Teams are given 15 minutes between rounds to improve the production process. Highlighting the benefits of cross-disciplinary decision making, teams leverage their managerial accounting information to identify opportunities for process improvements that can improve profitability. Improvement opportunities include reduction of the workforce, changing the layout of the production process, redesigning the product, and working with the customer and supplier to simplify the production process. Changes must be approved by a Board of Directors (the TOM and MAC faculty) and may require additional one-time or recurring charges that affect the profitability of the subsequent period(s).

Production and Inventory Management Integrated Learning Objectives

The Gazogle simulation has several learning objectives that relate to analyzing and managing operational processes. In particular, the simulation presents several opportunities for the student teams to improve their processes in order to reduce bottlenecks and improve throughput time. Early on in the simulation (especially in the first month), teams often struggle to get LEGOs procured and to the assemblers in a timely manner. In fact, given that the simulation month is only four minutes long, many teams are not able to produce any Gazogles in the first month because of the bottleneck formed at the procurement stage. In addition, the initial process layout design is inefficient because of the distance between the assembly stages, which necessitates material movers to transport material between the stages. Students are able to recognize that their supply chain lead time and assembly lead time, under the initial configuration, are unnecessarily long. Accordingly, between rounds, teams will brainstorm solutions to improve their processes by reducing bottlenecks and improving throughput times. Then, by running subsequent simulation rounds, the students are able to see what impact the changes had on their operations.

Almost always, teams will reconfigure their processes for a more fluid production line that removes the need for materials movers and requires fewer tables. It is also common to see teams reassigning workers from a non-value added position (e.g., material mover) to a more value-added job (e.g., assembler). From time to time, we also see students getting laid off when their position is deemed unnecessary.[2] Teams also like to redesign the Gazogle to require fewer LEGOS, which not only reduces the material costs but also reduces the assembly time required. Finally, we encounter changes involving working with the customer and supplier. Teams often request to co-locate with the customer to reduce the delivery time of finished

---

[2]In rare occasions, laid-off students have banded together to form their own Gazogle-producing teams. This provides a unique learning experience for these students who can form their operations from scratch without experiencing the learning-curve obstacles and legacy costs that the original teams had to endure with their inherited processes.

Gazogles. They have also requested changes with the supplier, including: (i) co-locating with the supplier to reduce procurement charges and to decrease the time it takes for materials to enter the production process or (ii) having the supplier provide sub-assembled components or kitted materials.

Production and Inventory Management and Managerial Accounting Integrated Learning Objectives

Through the shared Gazogle simulation, students get a first-hand look at how production process decisions have an impact on various managerial accounting measures and can impact profitability. For example, as previously discussed, most teams experience a bottle-neck at the procurement stage preventing them from producing many (or any) Gazogles. This allows students to experience the financial impact of the bottleneck, as it not only prevents them from producing any Gazogles but also limits their ability to generate revenue. Moreover, since many of the costs of the simulation are fixed and occur regardless of production volume (e.g., labor costs, facility costs), students also see how costs can still be relatively high, despite the low production, in the wake of these bottlenecks. Students quickly realize the benefit of maximizing production and, therefore, maximizing the use of those resources. In general, students are able to gain an understanding of the costs associated with an inefficient process.

KEY ACTIVITIES: PAYLOAD PRODUCT DEVELOPMENT SIMULATION

Another topic which is integrated across the TOM and MAC courses considers the execution of Key Activities related to the Product Development process (Section O6). In the TOM course, this entails discussion of issues related to the concept of Design for Manufacturability, where students examine the downstream impact of their product design decisions on material choices, process choices, and on their supply chain. As they discover in the MAC course, these product development decisions have a direct impact on project costs, material costs, and supply chain costs, all of which have an impact on final product costs. Moreover, they recognize that operations management and managerial accounting are also intricately linked in the execution of the product development pro-cesses and activities, as they realize how various decisions impact the quality-cost-time tradeoff during the development process.

The Payload simulation (Schmitt, Brown, & Obermiller, 2006) is an experiential product development game that is an adaptation of an egg-drop competition. During the game, teams enter a ficti-tious NASA-sponsored competition to develop and submit proto-types for a Martian landing module. Each product development team consists of five members. Student roles for each team include a NASA customer representative, a business development representative, a marketing representative, a design engineer and a manufacturing engineer. Teams are evaluated on total profits which are based on revenues from meeting performance goals (quality) minus the cost of development, which is a function of elapsed development time (speed) and the material expenses (cost). Each member of the team is given a different subset of the information related to the profit drivers, and teams must work together to fully comprehend the entire information set. This underscores the importance of cross-functional decision making in the development process.

The business development representative role is given information on the profit and revenue targets and is responsible for generating a budget for the project to meet the profit targets. Specifically, the company aims to achieve a profit margin of 10%. If the payload accurately hits the landing target, it is able to achieve revenues of between $200,000 and $2,000,000, depending on proximity to the target. The marketing representative has key information on time-to-market and development cost. For example, if the team completes development in 10 minutes (the equivalent of 10 weeks) it incurs a development cost of $10,000. Whereas, if the team completes development in 60 minutes, the development cost increases exponentially to $2,000,000. Finally, the manufacturing engineer has information related to the material costs. Teams incur fixed costs for non-discrete parts (e.g., a roll of duct tape) and variable costs for discrete parts (e.g., straws, paper clips, balloons). Additionally, there are incentives for part commonality, reflecting bulk purchasing discounts and product integration cost savings. For example, a single balloon costs $60,000 but two balloons cost $90,000.

Product Development and Operations Integrated Learning Objectives

The Payload simulation offers several illustrations of the typical operational decisions that must be made during the product development process. In the simulation, the design and manufacturing engineers, representing the operations management point of view, have four main objectives: (1) reduce development time, (2) increase part commonality, (3) make a stackable product, and (4) make a green product. The first objective, to reduce product development time, illustrates a significant conflict between the product development team and the managerial accounting objectives. While a shorter development process is more cost-effective, a greater focus on longer periods of prototyping leads to products which tend to perform better in the final competition. This debate sets the stage for later in-class discussions on effective project management strategies. The second and third objectives, to increase part commonality and make the product more stackable, demonstrate ways in which operations can positively contribute to managerial accounting objectives by designing costs out of the product. These lessons are reinforced by an in-class operations management case on IKEA in which students discuss the various strategies that IKEA used during the design process to achieve its target costs. These include: designing products to be more stackable so as to reduce shipping costs, increasing part commonality across products, and choosing suppliers early during the design process to optimize the value chain. The simulation also facilitates a conversation on issues of sustainability and innovation. The design engineer is focused on the degree to which the final design is "green" (i.e., made from recyclable materials). Students have a range of materials from which to choose including paper, wood, metal, Styrofoam cups, and plastic balloons. However, the Styrofoam cups and balloons are the most buoyant and, therefore, lead to higher performance of the payload prototype. However, these are also the least recyclable products, which presents a conflict in the manufacturing design process. Since there are long-term financial incentives to "going green," the students must grapple with the tensions between short-term operational performance and the longer-term financial benefits.

Product Development and Managerial Accounting Integrated Learning Objectives

Students are introduced to Target Costing as a strategic profit and cost management process based on the premise that, for most organizations, both the selling price for products/services and the required return to capital providers are exogenous factors determined by market conditions. That is, Target Cost = Selling Price − Profit. Therefore, the target costing process manages factors that are under an organization's control (e.g., the design of the product and the design of its value chain). As a result, management first establishes a target cost for a new product and then decomposes that target cost into cost projections for the corresponding subassemblies and individual component parts. If a "gap" exists between the target cost and cost projections, based on current designs and manufacturing capabilities, then designing costs out of the product is accomplished by analyzing the product's design, raw material requirements, value chain arrangement, cost drivers, and manufacturing processes to search for cost savings opportunities.

The Payload simulation highlights many of the target costing lessons that occur squarely at the intersection of managerial accounting and manufacturing/operations management. Through the game, students recognize that several key factors, such as revenue (price) and profit margins are exogenously determined, which highlights the importance of a target costing process. Moreover, the game allows for a discussion of how capital shortage leads to increasing pressure on cost because the product development officer needed to budget a ROS of 10% or higher.

KEY PARTNERS: COLOPLAST OUTSOURCING/OFFSHORING CASE

A final topic that is integrated across the TOM and MAC courses is the impact of a company's Key Partners on the delivery of its value proposition and on its profitability (see Section O7). In this section, students consider ways in which a company can leverage various partner relationships through offshoring and outsourcing arrangements in order to gain access to supplemental resources and expertise to execute key activities. Whereas the topic of Process Analysis discussed previously was focused on the operational challenges faced inside a specific manufacturing or service operation, this section of the course expands the view of a company by considering issues related to supply chain design and management. In determining whether to keep activities in-house or to outsource, students in the TOM course are introduced to the "Make versus Buy" decision framework. In order to choose between these alternatives, students in the MAC course are introduced to the Incremental Costs Analysis framework where they examine what costs are relevant to the outsourcing/offshoring decision, including the consideration of various opportunity costs and sunk costs.

To illustrate the concepts associated with outsourcing and off-shoring, we discuss the Coloplast case (Nielson et al., 2008) across both the TOM and MAC class sessions. As per case details, Coloplast is a Danish producer of medical care products. Its core business deals mainly with ostomy and continence care. In the early 2000s, the company faced financial challenges as the result of a healthcare reform in Germany that reduced the public reimbursement. To combat these financial pressures, Coloplast implemented a two-pillar strategy to achieve sales of nine billion Danish Krones and a profit margin of 18% through product innovation and process optimization with an emphasis of offshoring its volume production to Hungary and China. Coloplast aimed to have 20% of all revenue coming from products launched in the last four years. As a result, product development and innovation would continue in Denmark while volume production would move to Hungary. The case describes how the company arrived at its decision to make the move to Hungary. There were several cost factors that made the move to Hungary an attractive option. For example, production and labor costs in Hungary were 20% lower than Denmark, building costs were 50% lower and taxation levels in Hungary were 16% as compared to 28% in Denmark. However, as students discover, cost is not the only important consideration for Coloplast to consider, and the case allows them to examine the various operational challenges which arose during the transition. The story contains several integrated learning points that span both TOM and MAC.

Offshoring and Operations Management Integrated Learning Objectives

As a prerequisite to discussing the Coloplast case, students are required to read the paper, "Getting Offshoring Right" (Aron & Singh, 2005) which highlights the various operational issues and risk factors to consider when making an outsourcing or offshoring decision. In discussions, students must consider the impact of an outsourcing/offshoring decision on a company's ability to sustainably deliver its value proposition by maintaining control of key resources and consistently executing its key activities at a high level of quality and consistency. As an example, Coloplast's decision to outsource was mainly cost-related. However, when making decisions, it was important that the offshore location would be able to produce the product with the same level of quality and precision. In this regard, Hungary seemed like an advantageous move because not only were the wages much less expensive, but Hungary also proved to have a very technically adept workforce. However, cultural and operational differences brought challenges to Coloplast's decision to move to Hungary. In Denmark, facilities operated in a decentralized fashion, employees were afforded a large degree of autonomy and most of the operation knowledge was tacit. On the other hand, Hungarian workers were used to following precise orders and working with well-documented and highly codified production processes. This created a potential operational risk, as the lack of documentation from the Denmark location meant that the offshoring arrangement would lack clear production guidelines and metrics, which would likely result in quality-related issues (Aron & Singh, 2005).

In addition, at the conclusion of the case, it is pointed out that while the offshoring move was beneficial, there were some missed opportunities relating to the decision. Firstly, all materials in the Hungarian facility came through Coloplast Denmark. However, it was later discovered that many of the materials were initially sourced from Hungary. But instead of sending them directly to Coloplast Hungary, those materials were sent through Denmark. These discussions highlight the importance of considering the entire supply chain when making outsourcing decisions, as the move to Hungary led to Coloplast having a sub-optimal supply chain.

Offshoring and Managerial Accounting Integrated Learning Objectives

For the initial part of the MAC exercise, students can calculate cost savings in three areas: production costs, administrative costs, and costs related to building additional facilities (which are depreciated over a five-year period). In MAC, Coloplast provides us an opportunity to show the importance of a relevant/incremental cost analysis. The relevant cost analysis provides clear cost savings with the outsourcing decision. In the second part of the analysis, we address the additional unrealized cost savings had they also moved some of the sales distribution and materials procurement to Hungary.[3]

In the class prior to discussing Coloplast, we introduced the topic of relevant costing by examining the impact of decisions to add or drop a product line. In that lesson, students are taught to examine how costs differ between two decision alternatives. In particular, students are shown how to analyze costs not only on their cost behavior (i.e., fixed or variable) but also whether those costs are directly attributable to certain decision alternatives or whether those costs are common and simply allocated across business segments. In addition, we also emphasize how sunk costs should not play a role in any decision, while other hidden opportunity costs may be relevant and, therefore, should play a role.

We also developed a Coloplast assignment that takes specific information out of the case so that students can perform a structured incremental analysis. To complete this exercise, students must first understand that the decision alternative is whether the expansion will occur in Denmark or in Hungary. All of the costs related to working in Hungary are presented as a cost savings from Denmark. So, by setting up the decision alternative as described, students can first examine what the incremental costs would be had they expanded in Denmark and then make appropriate comparison to the portion of operations that would be offshored to Hungary. In particular, 81% of Coloplast's operations would be sent to Hungary, and would encompass all operations of products that are produced in volume, while the 19% related to new product innovation would remain in Denmark. As a result, the cost savings would only apply to the portion of Coloplast that is offshored to Hungary, because the remainder would stay in Denmark regardless of an offshore strategy. The Coloplast case provides a very pragmatic way to apply these relevant/incremental cost analysis concepts.

---

[3]Similar to the inefficient procurement process that was described in the TOM section, all sales to Eastern Europe were sold and distributed through Coloplast Denmark. That means the goods produced in Hungary were sent to Denmark and then distributed back to Eastern Europe.

Conclusion

Babson College's core mission is to educate the entrepreneurial leaders of tomorrow, and we believe our integrated curriculum provides our students with the versatility required in a dynamic business environment. The label "entrepreneurial leader" encompasses those who create new business models, as well as those who innovate within established ventures to test and implement new elements of an existing business model (Bell & Ansari, 2014). Therefore, our curriculum endeavors to prepare students to become successful entrepreneurial leaders who can innovate to create new business models in response to new opportunities and who can also adapt existing business models in response to the business challenges which their companies will face.

As mentioned previously, the AACSB (2010) has called upon colleges to have more integration in their business curriculum. At Babson, we have had integration in our core curriculum since the mid-1990s. Our integrated TOM and Managerial Accounting courses provide different, yet complementary, perspectives to provide a more detailed and thorough understanding of how a company works. We teach these two courses in an integrated fashion and discuss these courses following the Business Model Canvas as our framework to demonstrate the interdependence between TOM and MAC.

In this chapter, we have discussed five integrated touch points that occur throughout the semester. For each of these, students are provided an opportunity to examine the situation (e.g., case, simulation) through two different lenses and apply two different "toolsets" to addressing the problems in each. Within each integrated touch point, TOM discusses the operational perspectives of a company when delivering its value proposition to its customers, while MAC discusses the managerial accounting perspectives. This integrated approach to our curriculum provides students with a more holistic view of a business model and empowers them to incorporate multiple perspectives into their business decision making.

Acknowledgments

We would like to thank Jan Bell, Danna Greenberg, Kate McKone Sweet, Sinan Erzurumlu, Ivor Morgan, Phil Licari, Paulo Gomes, and the many others who contributed their extensive efforts in the design of the integrated curriculum components discussed. In addition, we would like to thank Steve Fuller for his comments and suggestions as well the two anonymous reviewers who provided helpful feedback on earlier drafts of the chapter.

References

AACSB International. (2010). *Business schools on an innovation mission.* Tampa, FL: AACSB International.

Angell, L. C., & Klassen, R. D. (1999). Integrating environmental issues into the mainstream: An agenda for research in operations management. *Journal of Operations Management, 17*(5), 575–598.

Aron, R., & Singh, J. V. (2005). Getting offshoring right. *Harvard Business Review, 83*(12), 135.

Bell, J. (2012). *Chocomize: Case A.* Babson College.

Bell, J., & Ansari, S. (2014). *Management accounting in an ETA environment.* Babson College.

Bell, J., Erzurumlu, S., & Fowler, H. (2010). *Sustainable supply management at Sofra.* Babson College.

Bell, J., Erzurumlu, S., & Fowler, H. (2013). Better tomorrow at Sodexo North America, *AB146.* Wellesley, MA: Babson College.

Caliskan, A. O. (2014). How accounting and accountants may contribute in sustainability? *Social Responsibility Journal, 10*(2), 4.

Ducoffe, S. J. S., Tromley, C. L., & Tucker, M. (2006). Interdisciplinary, team-taught, undergraduate business courses: The impact of integration. *Journal of Management Education, 30*(2), 276–294.

Gupta, M., & Galloway, K. (2003). Activity-based costing/management and its implications for operations management. *Technovation, 23*(2), 131–138.

Hamilton, D., McFarland, D., & Mirchandani, D. (2000). A decision model for integration across the business curriculum in the 21st century. *Journal of Management Education, 24*(1), 102–126.

Kaplan, R. S., & Norton, D. P. (2007). Using the balanced scorecard as a strategic management system. *Harvard Business Review,* (July–August).

Neck, H., & Stoddard, D. (2006). *Babson college nominates the Foundation Management Experience (FME) for USASBE's innovative entrepreneurship education course.* Babson Park, MA: Babson College.

Nielsen, B. B., Pedersen, T., & Pyndt, J. (2008). *Coloplast A/S – Organizational challenges in offshoring.* London: Ivey.

Osterwalder, A., & Pigneur, Y. (2010). *Business model generation.* Hoboken, NJ: John Wiley.

Schmitt, T. G., Brown, K. A., & Obermiller, C. (2006). Conveying cross functional product development concepts: The Payloads 9.8 Mars lander exercise. *Decision Sciences Journal of Innovative Education, 4*(2), 293–299.

Treacy, M., & Wiersema, F. (1993). Customer intimacy and other value disciplines. *Harvard Business Review, 71*(1), 84–93.

Weiss, E. (2006). The Gazogle case. *INFORMS Transactions on Education, 6*(3), 46–47.

CHAPTER

9

Marketing—ITS Integration: Developing Next-Generation Managers

Dhruv Grewal, Anne L. Roggeveen and
Ganesan Shankaranarayanan

Modern firms need employees who are marketing, techno-logically, and analytically savvy so that they can help the firms better serve their customers. Nearly every company today actively uses social and mobile media to market products and services to customers. Whether those firms engage in manufacturing or retailing, and whether their customers are consumers or other businesses, they use the Web and various forms of social media to communicate (Rapp, Bietelspacher, Grewal, & Hughes, 2013). Fortunately, today's students are also very technology savvy. They are well versed in using social, mobile, and online media and accessing these media through their smartphones, tablets, and laptops. They spend hours perusing the Internet to post on Facebook and/or Instagram, communicate with one another through e-mail, texts, and/or instant messaging, watch videos on YouTube, tweet, search, and shop online.

Accordingly, students expect that technology will be leveraged in their classrooms and used to enhance their learning experiences (McCabe & Meuter, 2011). But simply being effective in social media is not sufficient to transform students into appealing, competitive employees. Rather, modern business requires integration across functional silos, encouraging members of different departments to work together. A similar cross-functional integration is central to Babson College's value proposition and a key element stressed in our curriculum and courses.

For example, in the Sophomore Management Experience, we pair marketing with information technology and systems (ITS) to achieve strategic benefits. The pairing invokes synergies consistent with the increasing range of marketing efforts by both large and small firms that rely on the latest advances in data management and analysis, social media, mobile applications, localization, and online presence. With this combination, we can discuss topics that need to be reinforced across the two courses, starting with how data are generated through business processes, the use of data to examine business performance (including data analysis), the use of software tools to facilitate data analysis and visualization, the importance of analytic dashboards, the value of customers and customer relationship management (prospecting vs. retaining customers), and the distinct roles of social, mobile, and online channels. The integration and coverage of common topics from these multiple perspectives enhances student engagement and learning. Finally, in line with Babson's entrepreneurial thinking, the pairing emphasizes "learning by doing" through the use of interactive digital resources, immersive simulations and case discussions, hands-on activities, and real-life projects.

The marketing segment of this pairing relies strongly on digital resources to support key learning experiences, with the recognition that these resources can enhance self-learning (Dowell & Small, 2011). Key learning tools include online interactive quizzes (e.g., Connect Marketing exercises from Grewal & Levy, 2014), LearnSmart® (an adaptive study tool), a host of relevant interactive tools, and engaging videos. Class time also has been devoted to pertinent cases (e.g., Natick Shopping Mall, Jay-Z and Bing, Carpet-Pro) and exercises (e.g., designing an advertisement using an online ad development toolkit, break-even analyses). The marketing segment of the Sophomore Management Experience achieves three critical learning objectives through this integration:

1. Understand the value of data and move beyond data into understanding the actionable insights that can be gleaned from them.
2. Highlight the role of data analytics and the role of experiential simulations.
3. Acknowledge the growing role of social media and the critical importance of the marketing–ITS interface for helping businesses serve their customers.

The ITS component complements marketing by exposing students to how data are generated, collected, stored, managed, and analyzed for business decisions. By using various forms of technology — from the Web to databases to spreadsheets to data cubes to prototyping tools — the ITS component offers hands-on learning experiences that reinforce student learning. Similar to marketing, the ITS side relies on team-based experiential simulations and cases to facilitate interaction and peer learning. In addition to communicating strategies for web design and search engine optimization, the ITS course emphasizes strategies for the use of social media and Web 2.0 in the context of inbound marketing, branding, and customer relationship management. Because future business managers must be technologically self-sufficient, the ITS component supports the critical learning objectives of marketing by:

1. Providing an understanding of the cross-functional nature of business processes and the generation of transactional data and their role in business decision making.
2. Exposing students to different data manipulation and analytical tools, such as databases, data cubes, and dashboards, to move beyond data into actionable insights.
3. Describing actionable strategies for managing the Web and associated e-business, implementing social media campaigns, and using data and analytics to understand the performance of web and social media strategies.

As a result of this integrative pairing, students gain expertise, the ability to understand and apply discipline-based learning, and practice in applying lessons from one academic or functional silo to another. Such cross-functional integration produces students who will be more effective in the workforce and require significantly less training by their hiring organization, which significantly increases the return on investment of hires from Babson College.

Valuable Data, SPSS, and Actionable Insights

To be truly customer-centric, firms need to orient themselves toward both marketing and IT (Trainora, Rapp, Beitelspacher, & Schillewaert, 2011), especially if they function in an e-Marketing domain (Brodie, Winklhofer, Coviello, & Johnston, 2007). Therefore, on the marketing side of the marketing—ITS pairing, students work extensively with various types of data, aiming to achieve different insights and action plans. For example, real-world firms have realized the importance and value of collecting data and then mining that data as the resulting insights are central to developing and implementing marketing campaigns. The marketing component covers key data collection and analytical tools; the ITS component addresses pertinent data storage, access, and manipulation tools. These constantly emerging tools provide rich insights into the methods that are available to firms to leverage their existing or available data, whether to identify and attract new customers or to gain a better appreciation of the lifetime value of customers with which they already have relationships.

Early in the semester, students in the marketing component are exposed to the concept of survey-based data through a timely case study that describes the Natick Shopping Mall, the largest mall in the northeastern United States (Grewal & Motyka, 2014). In this case, students take the role of a manager of one of the stores in the mall, such that they are responsible for identifying their customers and recommending ways to appeal to the relevant customer segments. To be able to do so, students consider the role of survey data and how to analyze the data in-depth using marketing tools (e.g., SPSS[1] software) or IT tools (e.g., databases, Excel Power Pivot[2]).

The exercise requires students to review, work with, and investigate data available through the related case files in order to understand how they might initiate, develop, and conclude segmentation and product assortment decisions in the presented scenario. The case also highlights the benefits of online data collection survey tools such as Qualtrics,[3] the vast span of panel respondents available through Amazon's Mechanical Turk,[4] and IBM's sophisticated SPSS software package.

Specifically, each student is assigned a store in the mall for which he or she will serve as the retail manager. Students can access files that detail a questionnaire that has been distributed to store customers and the data gleaned from those surveys. The data are available in both Excel and SPSS. The case trains students how to use SPSS to conduct and interpret a basic descriptive analysis, together with cross-tabulations. Through a six-step procedure, students actually use the SPSS Cross-Tab tool to find their assigned store and customer segments, conduct a chi-square analysis, select

---

[1]Statistical Package for Social Sciences (SPSS) is a software package for statistical analysis widely used by market researchers, data miners, and survey experts among others.
[2]A Microsoft Business Intelligence software offering that is available as an add-on to Microsoft Excel. It offers the ability to do data summarization and cross-tabulation.
[3]Qualtrics is an online survey design software that enables online data collection and includes the ability to do market research analysis.
[4]Mechanical Turk is a crowdsourcing internet marketplace offered as a service by Amazon.

cell counts, and gather the results of the assessment. Finally, the case requires students to conduct a review of the analysis that they have performed with the software. In this review, they must determine who shops at their store, how often, and at what level. Then students integrate these details to develop recommendations. But the case also requires them to perform a final, critical step of thinking about whether their recommendations are realistic and actionable, rather than just allowing the software to spit out the results for them.

To complement this exercise, students teams in the ITS component of the Sophomore Management Experience receive a large survey data set that includes demographic data and information about purchase intentions, price points, and package sizes. Using Excel pivot tables/Power Pivot, student teams identify segments of customers and determine who will buy which package sizes and at what price. The analyses provide students with an in-depth understanding of the foundational concepts and analytics typically used to construct segments.

Using these tools, students also gain an understanding that various customer segments prefer and therefore shop at different stores, and they learn to identify which attributes the various customer segments value. Thus, the students come away with insights into the positioning edge that can be achieved by a given retail chain, along with realistic experience using a software tool that is prevalent in real-world retail practice. In this process, students learn that data are not inherently clean; rather, noise makes it difficult to identify clean segments. Thus, the exercise reinforces the need to pre-process data for analytics and gives the students a sense of both "dimensions" and "facts" — concepts introduced subsequently in discussions of data warehouses and business intelligence.

Analytics and Experiential Simulations

In the Practice Marketing simulation (http://www.mhpractice.com) developed by McGraw-Hill, students expand on their analytic and experiential insights by creating and marketing a backpack. The key lesson for this project is the recognition that the most beautiful, best, and most insightful marketing plan remains effective only for a short period of time, after which firms must use their marketing knowledge to respond to the ever-changing competitive landscape. Throughout the semester, student teams apply the ideas and tools they have learned by completing the backpack manufacturer simulation game (Figure 1). The simulation strongly reinforces the connections between classroom or textbook topics and real-world applications.

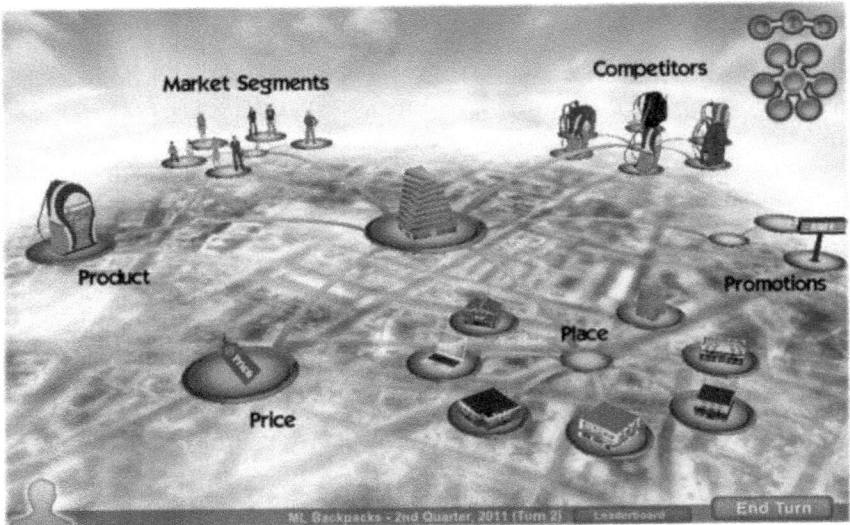

Figure 1: The Backpack Simulation Game. *Note:* Copyright McGraw-Hill Education. Reproduced with permission.

In designing a simulated backpack, one of the first steps students undertake is to examine five different market segments. They receive segment information, including size and growth rate that is critical to determining the attractiveness of each simulated customer segment. They also can access other tabs that provide information about customer demographics; purchase frequency, sales data, and customer awareness (see Figure 2).

After reviewing the available information, students must make some decisions. First, they select a primary segment to target and design the backpack to appeal to these customers. Therefore, in this step, students must leverage their knowledge of segmentation, customer needs analyses, and new product development. The simulation includes extensive details about various product attributes (e.g., shape, straps, material, colors, and features), attribute importance, attribute options, and the manufacturing costs associated with the various attribute options. In this sense, the simulation helps reinforce accounting cost elements and forces the student designers to make trade-offs in their new product development efforts (Figure 3).

The pricing decision comes next. The design of the backpack determines the variable costs associated with producing the specifically designed product. With the cost information in hand, the group must select the sale price for their backpack. In so doing, they gain a better understanding of profit margins and that this margin also depends on the channel the students choose for selling their backpack. The

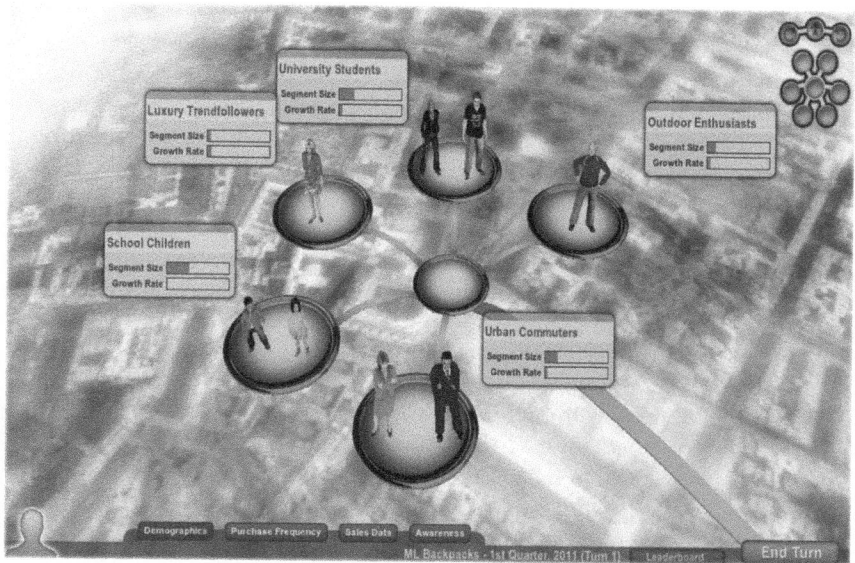

Figure 2: Key Segments and Segment Characteristics. *Note*: Copyright McGraw-Hill Education. Reproduced with permission.

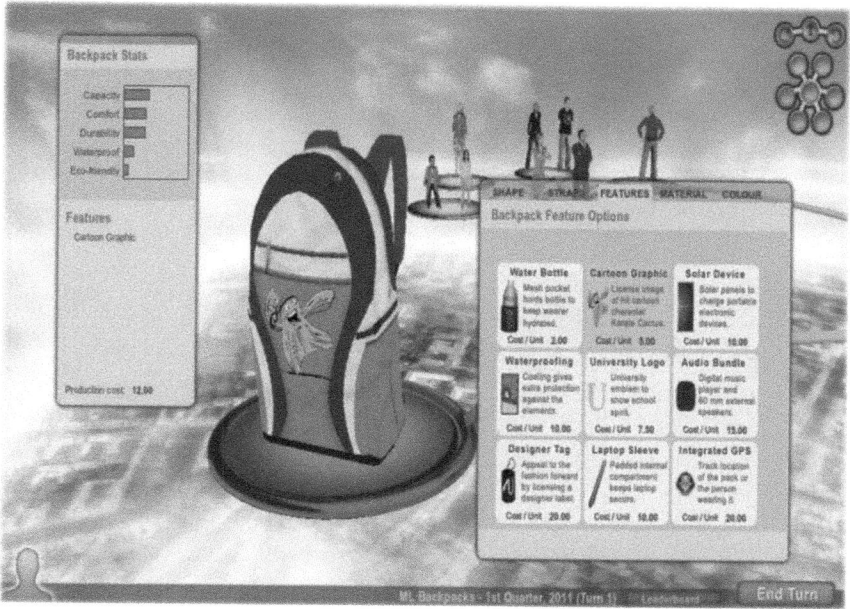

Figure 3: Designing the Backpack. *Note*: Copyright McGraw-Hill Education. Reproduced with permission.

simulation provides seven potential sales channels for the backpack (Figure 4). By analyzing this option, students come to realize that the margins would be highest through the direct channel and lowest if they sell their backpacks through high-end retailers.

Finally, groups must choose the media they will use to communicate about their product (types, cost, frequency), as well as what the message will look like (consistency, clarity, competitiveness). At this point, they have reached the end of the first round and have the opportunity to learn what their competitors (i.e., the other student groups) have done. The results of the competition depend on the performance along key marketing metrics.

Toward the end of the semester, each team prepares and delivers a presentation to summarize their choices over the five simulation rounds. The presentation must include, at the least, the scores they earned at the end of each round (which they obtain from the dashboard analytics), as well as their ultimate score at the end of all five rounds, together with a summary of their overall strategy, an accounting of the strategic changes they implemented from one quarter to the next, and the key lessons they took away from the game. These key lessons pertain to the various decision areas, including segmentation and positioning, product design, pricing, distribution channels, and promotion.

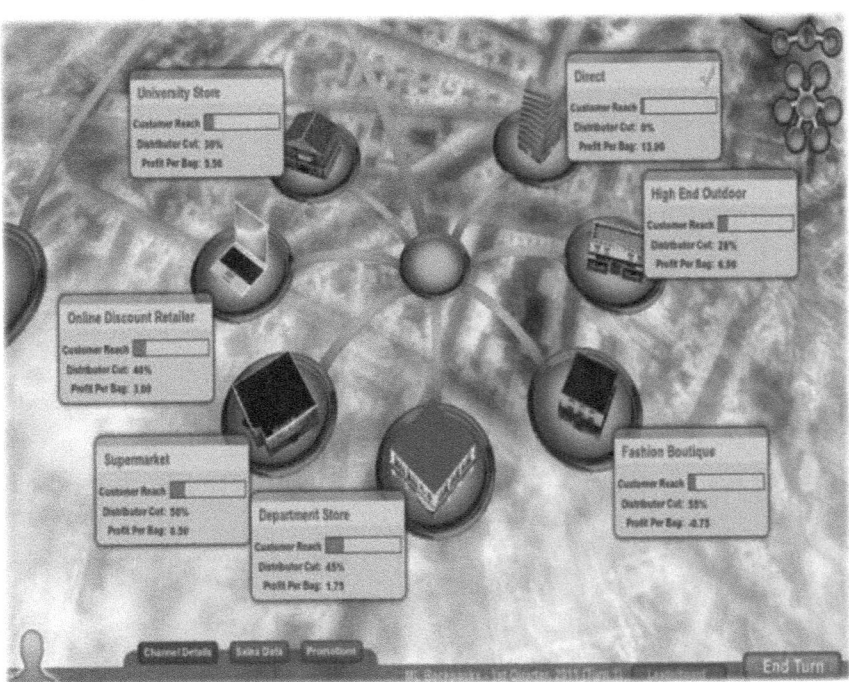

Figure 4: Which Channels to Pick? *Note*: Copyright McGraw-Hill Education. Reproduced with permission.

Beyond traditional marketing goals (e.g., revenues, units sold, market share, customer satisfaction, net profits, return on marketing investments), the backpack simulation exercise thus reinforces the importance of recognizing and comprehending competitive dynamics, understanding and interpreting profit-and-loss statements, and leveraging data analytic tools. (More details about the exercise and the review template are in Appendix A.) Accordingly, students consistently report in their evaluations and other feedback that the backpack simulation helps reinforce the content of their marketing courses, as well as the important role of marketing metrics. It provides them with insights into other core business areas as well, including accounting, professional teamwork, and communication skills.

The team-based activities in the Marketing-ITS pairing reinforce teamwork and team management skills that the students are introduced to in the first-year course, Foundations of Management and Entrepreneurship. The projects are designed so that responsibilities may be sub-divided and delegated to sub-groups within each team. Team members are encouraged to recognize the strengths of their teammates and delegate accordingly. Communication and consistent interactions are strongly encouraged to express, clarify, and reflect on not just the artifacts and ideas generated by the sub-groups but also the emotions and feelings of individuals within. While evaluating intermediate deliverables, the instructor checks in and receives comments from students on group climate and dynamics, giving the instructor an opportunity to intervene if necessary. Finally, the pairing informs students about leveraging technology to collaboratively work and deliver on the project.

Social Media: Facebook Data Analytics

As Grewal and Levy (in press) note, "Social media have revolutionized how companies communicate with, listen to, and learn from customers. Its influence is far-reaching, whether firms are selling online or in stores, providing services or products, or dealing primarily with consumers or business customers. The changes and advances in social, mobile, and online technologies have created a perfect storm, forcing firms to change how they communicate with their customers." Thus, traditional marketing practices (e.g., brick-and-mortar stores, print advertising) are being vastly augmented with the addition of social, mobile, and online media channels. To facilitate students' understanding of these digital channels as marketing tools, the marketing—ITS curriculum applies the 4E (Excite, Educate, Experience, and Engage) framework (see Figure 5):

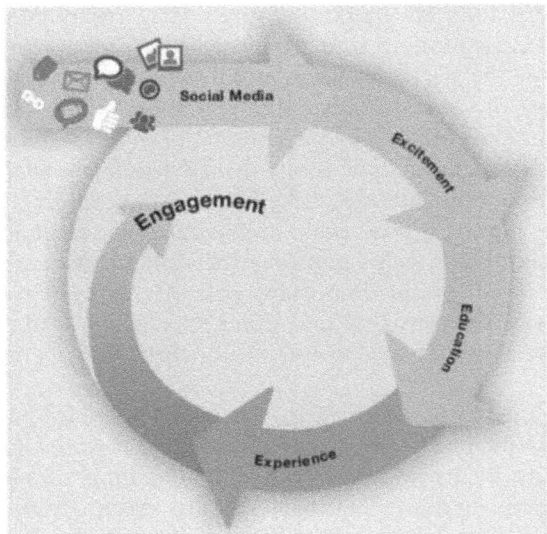

Figure 5: The 4E Framework. *Source*: Grewal and Levy (2014). *Note*: Copyright McGraw-Hill Education. Reproduced with permission.

- Excite customers with relevant offers.
- Educate them about the offering.
- Help them Experience products, whether directly or indirectly.
- Give them an opportunity to Engage with their social network.

Social media provide various ways to excite customers, including through routes that tap into existing social networks (e.g., Facebook, Pinterest, Google +). Offers issued through social media must be relevant to targeted customers, as well as grant them an explicit opportunity to take advantage of the offers through mobile devices or in person. Firms need to leverage every touch point and every opportunity to educate customers about their product value propositions − that is, the unique benefits relative to competitive offerings. By taking advantage of YouTube and video media, firms also can simulate consumption experiences. Finally, to engage the customer, firms need to grant access to social media and online/offline opportunities to develop long-term relationships with the product, as well as with the firm itself (e.g., posts, tweets, retweets, reviews).

Throughout the marketing−ITS classes, various social media tools reinforce the idea that firms can and should use the 4E framework to market their products and services. A key example is an exercise that we conduct initially in the marketing class and then reinforce in the ITS class. Specifically, students develop a Facebook fan page for a retailer. Because of its 30 percent market share, Facebook has emerged as one of the most prominent, and dominant, advertising publishers (comScore, 2011). Therefore, understanding how to market products and services on social media platforms, and especially on Facebook, is essential for future professional success. More immediately, effective social media marketing skills represent a primary criterion for recruiters on campus. By implementing these digital technologies directly in the classroom, we ensure that the students' actual experience is the central focus (Buzzard, Crittenden, Crittenden, & McCarty, 2011).

Again working in teams to continue the development of team-work skills, the students develop and launch a fan page dedicated to a well-known retailer (e.g., Sears, JCPenney, Macy's, Nordstrom, Neiman Marcus, Lord & Taylor, Abercrombie & Fitch, Banana Republic, Express, Zara). In developing their fan pages and market-ing plans, students review recent research that highlights the advan-tages and disadvantages of personalized advertisements on Facebook relative to other platforms (e.g., Aguirre, Mahr, Grewal, de Ruyter, & Wetzels, 2015). The task is to identify and post rele-vant content that will drive both organic and paid traffic to the site. Students must also carefully assess the analytics provided by Facebook, which switch on as soon as a fan page earns at least 30 likes. The Facebook analytic dashboard also provides detailed insights about how many people have visited the page, like it, actu-ally read the various posts, and enjoy particular content. In addition, the dashboard provides a snapshot of recent activity on the fan page (see Figure 6).

The lessons required to implement this project are supplemen-ted in the ITS component where students consider the design prin-ciples for websites, reinforced by hands-on activities that require them to build a website for a fictitious business using open platforms such as Yola (Yola.com) or Wix (Wix.com).[5] The task is to incorporate as many of the design principles as are applicable for their website. The evaluation of their output is based on how well the site incorporates the design principles, as well as how aesthetically and functionally pleasing the site is. Students also learn foundational concepts of search engine optimization to improve the organic placement of their sites in search engine results. They practice linking Google Analytics to their websites to

---

[5]Yola.com is a web-site builder and a web-hosting company. Wix.com is a web development platform that allows users to create websites and mobile sites.

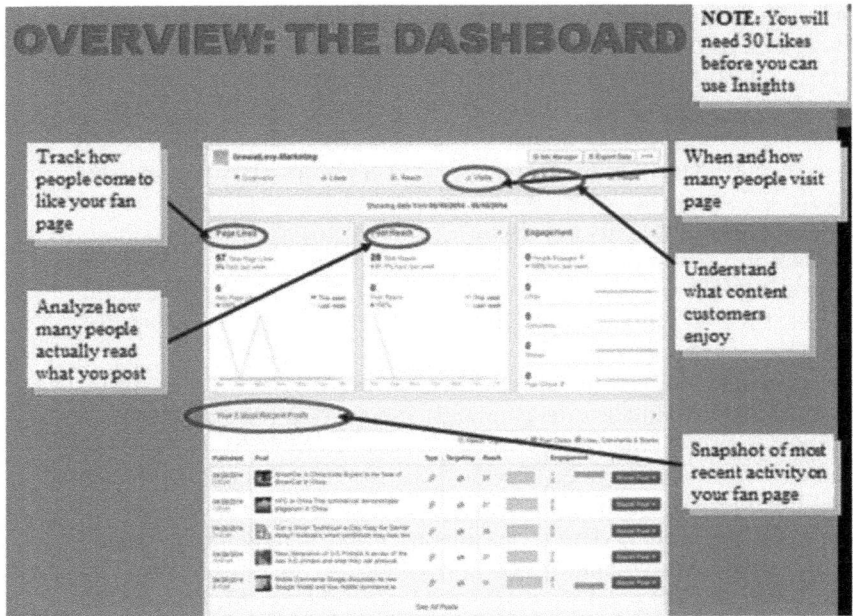

Figure 6: Facebook Analytics.

track their website's performance and traffic. Finally, students review various social media strategies that can drive traffic to their websites. In addition to the hypothetical website design, students present the data they would gather to monitor the website's performance and improve the customer experience, the social media strategy they would select to drive traffic to the site, and the metrics they would use to evaluate the performance of their social media campaigns. With this broad-based practice, students become better equipped to complete the fan page project assigned on the marketing side.

At the end of the semester, the student teams deliver a presentation to their colleagues where they must address the following questions:

- Who was the target market?
- How much traffic were you able to generate?
- What types of content did your customers find most engaging (Figure 7)?
- What are the key takeaways?
- What would you do differently in the future?

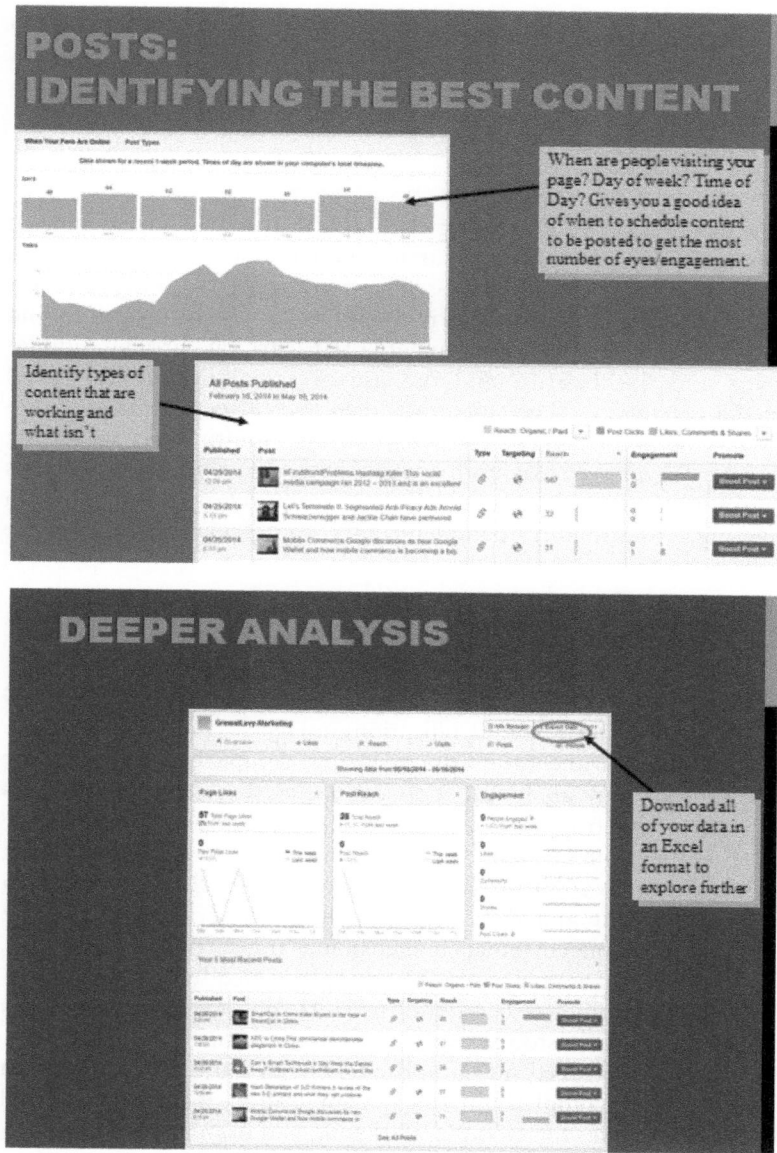

Figure 7: Post Analysis.

To answer these questions, students need to rely on relevant Facebook analytics, but they also must seek out additional analyses of relevant posts and engagement statistics. Thus students gain actual experience measuring the outcomes of their chosen efforts.

(More details and the reviewing template for this exercise are in Appendix B.)

Conclusion

The integration of marketing with ITS in the sophomore year of our undergraduate business curriculum has enabled us to reinforce both academic and industry-relevant concepts for and with students. In particular, this pairing emphasizes the role of data and insights, the importance of experiential learning through simulations and dashboards, and the use of social media and social media analytics. The integrated course also emphasizes the complements of each paired component at multiple points during course delivery. Across both components, the consistent emphasis is on the value of data and their interpretation for decision making. Additionally, complementary topics also extend to the following pairs:

- Product innovation in marketing, complemented by an understanding of the role of technology in product innovation and collaboration through the use of social media and Web 2.0 (e.g., crowdsourcing, gamification) in ITS.
- Customer segmentation in marketing, complemented by a clear sense of how analytical tools can be used to identify segments and the importance of cleaning and pre-processing data in ITS.
- Customer lifetime value and customer relationship marketing in marketing, complemented by explications of the role that data management and data management tools serve in identifying and managing customers and customer transactions in ITS.
- Market-basket analysis in ITS, complemented by students' investigations of the co-location of products and the role of analytics in improving customer experiences in marketing.
- The role of social media and alternative marketing channels in marketing, complemented by the application of social media and web strategies for inbound marketing and branding in ITS.

In sum, the pairing of Marketing and ITS produces an analytically rich course that provides students with a number of distinct takeaways that they can apply immediately in a business setting. In addition to leaving the course with actionable learning that is immediately applicable, the students leave the course engaged and understanding the important and necessary synergies between marketing and ITS in today's rapidly changing marketplace.

References

Aguirre, E. M., Mahr, D., Grewal, D., de Ruyter, K., & Wetzels, M. (2015). Unraveling the personalization paradox: The effect of information collection and trust-building on online advertisement effectiveness. *Journal of Retailing, 91*(1), 34–49.

Brodie, R. J., Winklhofer, H., Coviello, N. E., & Johnston, W. J. (2007). Is e-marketing coming of age? An examination of the penetration of e-marketing and firm performance. *Journal of Interactive Marketing, 21*(1), 2–21.

Buzzard, C., Crittenden, V. L., Crittenden, W. F., & McCarty, P. (2011). The use of digital technologies in the classroom: A teaching and learning perspective. *Journal of Marketing Education, 33*(2), 131–139.

comScore. (2011). *U.S. online display advertising market delivers 1.1 trillion impressions in Q1 2011*. May 4. Retrieved from http://www.comscore.com/Press%20Events/Press%20Releases/2011/5/U.S.Online%20Display%20Advertising%20Market%20Delivers%201.1%20Trillion%20Impressions%20inQ1%202011. Accessed on September 24, 2012.

Dowell, D. J., & Small, F. A. (2011). What is the impact of online resource materials on student self-learning strategies? *Journal of Marketing Education, 33*(2), 140–148.

Grewal, D., & Levy, M. (2014). *Marketing* (4th ed.). Burr Ridge, IL: McGraw-Hill/Irwin.

Grewal, D., & Levy, M. (in press). *Marketing* (5th ed.). Burr Ridge, IL: McGraw-Hill/Irwin.

Grewal, D., & Motyka, S. (2014). *Natick shopping mall: Segmentation exercise.* Unpublished case study, Babson College.

McCabe, D. B., & Meuter, M. L. (2011). A student view of technology in the classroom: Does it enhance the seven principles of good practice in undergraduate education? *Journal of Marketing Education, 33*(2), 149–159.

Rapp, A., Bietelspacher, L., Grewal, D., & Hughes, D. (2013). Understanding social media effects across seller, retailer, and consumer interactions. *Journal of the Academy of Marketing Science, 41*(September), 547–566.

Trainora, K. J., Rapp, A., Beitelspacher, L. S., & Schillewaert, N. (2011). Integrating information technology and marketing: An examination of the drivers and outcomes of e-marketing capability. *Industrial Marketing Management, 40*(1), 162–174.

Appendix A: Backpack Simulation

1. **Description:** The most beautiful, best-laid marketing plan is only effective for a very short period of time, after which firms must use their marketing knowledge to respond to the ever-changing competitive landscape. Throughout the semester you will apply the ideas and tools you have learned to compete in teams in a backpack manufacturer simulation game to help reinforce the connections between topics and real-world application of textbook ideas. Groups will play five quarters (five simulation rounds) and must submit their decisions by the respective dates. **It is critical that you submit your decisions by the due date.** The game automatically advances to the next quarter after the due date has passed so it is not possible to submit decisions late.

2. **Deliverables:** Teams will be required to submit four rounds of decisions in the simulation (this will be discussed in much greater detail in class). Additionally, each team will be required to prepare and deliver a 15 minute presentation with 5 minutes of Q&A. All teams will be required to present their final score (include dashboard analytics), their overall strategy and the key takeaways they learned from the game. Additionally, each team will discuss their strategy and key learnings from one of the decision areas (assigned randomly): product design, pricing, segmentation, distribution channels, promotion, or positioning.

3. **Due dates for decisions:** ___

4. **Presentation Date:** ___

5. **Grading:** Students will be graded on a scale from 0 to 100, based on:

Score at End of Simulation	25 pts
Presentation of Your Firm's Overall Strategy & Key Takeaways	50 pts
Presentation of Specific Strategy Area (assigned)	25 pts

BACKPACK SIMULATION	
Group Members	
Presentation of strategy	
Initial Scores and adjustments	
Final score/balance relative to competitors (will be worth 25%)	
Key Take-Aways	
Marketing topic presentation (25%)	
Overall preparation	
Visual aids	
Within allocated time	Start: ___ End: ___ Total Time: ____
Q&A	

Other Comments:

Appendix B: Facebook Fan Page and Analytics

1. **Description:** To be effective competitors in the modern market-place, both startups and Fortune 500 companies must be social media savvy. Social media marketing is not only an important and fast growing area in marketing, but it also offers some of the highest salaries for starting positions outside of college.

2. Working in your teams, you will be required to develop and launch a Facebook Fan Page (details discussed further in class). You will use the marketing and analytics tools taught to create postings that drive traffic to your site and engage your customers.

3. The fan page will be built by the students but the instructors need to be provided administrative access to the page. Content posted on the page should be **appropriate by Babson College's standards.** The instructors will not likely use their administrative access to change content unless it is deemed necessary. The **fan pages will be closed and taken down at the end of the semester.**

4. The Facebook fan page will be created for a retailer (____).

5. **Deliverables:** Teams will be required to prepare and deliver a 15 minute presentation with 5 minutes of Q&A. In this presentation should address the following questions:
   a. What was your fan page topic? Include screenshots.
   b. Who was your target market? What was your strategy for reaching this market? Was it effective? Why or why not?
   c. How much traffic were you able to generate? Support with analytics.
   d. What types of content did your customers find most engaging? Support with analytics.
   e. What are your key takeaways? What would you do differently in the future?

6. **Presentation Dates:** ____

7. **Other Requirements:**
   a. You must add the professor as Admins of your fan pages.
   b. All posts must meet Babson's standards, thus, no offensive material – including, but not limited to, alcohol and/or drug references and sexual images – may be posted.
   c. All fan pages must be taken down within two weeks of the last day of class.

8. Presentation Template:

Facebook Presentation	
Group Members	
Presentation of strategy	
Content/Posts	
Engagement/Likes	
Generating audience	
Marketing content	
Overall preparation	
Visual aids	
Within allocated time	Start: _____ End: _____ Total Time: _____
Q&A	

Other Comments:

10 Science Education as an Entrepreneurial Thought and Action® Methodology

Charles Winrich, Vikki L. Rodgers,
Meghan G. MacLean, David M. Blodgett
and Jodi H. Schaefer

Historically, undergraduate business majors have been disconnected from science disciplines. However, many business schools and programs are now realizing the important value of incorporating science into their curriculum (Banschbach & Letovsky, 2011; Charski, 2008; Laprise, Winrich, & Sharpe, 2008). A strong foundation in scientific literacy is increasingly recognized as important for all career paths (Heindel, 1996), and inquiry-based learning is a necessary skill that is often derived from the sciences (Smith, 2003). This is especially significant for business students because when employees misunderstand the science behind a business model, a steep decline in profits can result (Hubbard, 2005).

All Babson students are required to take four courses across the mathematics and science disciplines. Traditional single-discipline science courses, such as General Biology or Chemistry, would be of little practical value to our students because such courses tend to focus on the specific content of the discipline and build toward specialization. Since entrepreneurs in the business world rarely work within single disciplines, we have designed unique science courses with a multidisciplinary focus organized around themes of scientific investigation and discovery. This approach gives our students the opportunity to develop the skills needed to bridge the development of scientific ideas and analysis of results with real-world applications. Ultimately, students both build scientific knowledge and understand the relationship between scientific and entrepreneurial processes through our courses.

Babson College's Entrepreneurial Thought and Action® (ETA) methodology consists of three components: cognitive ambidexterity; social, environmental, economic responsibility, and sustainability (SEERS); and self and contextual awareness (Greenberg, McKone-Sweet, & Wilson, 2011). The cognitive ambidexterity component combines creativity, action, and experimentation all built on fundamental knowledge and rigorous analysis (Greenberg et al., 2011). In this context, entrepreneurship bears a close resemblance to scientific discovery and investigation. Both ETA and science stem from fundamental knowledge and are advanced through ingenuity, experimentation, and exploration. In addition, each has rigorous analyses applied to results of an experiment that guide the next round of ideas and experiments. Science also contributes fundamentally to the SEERS component of ETA in terms of understanding nature, our role in it, and defining sustainable practices. This chapter describes the development of an undergraduate science curriculum for Babson College where the value of scientific education for business students is emphasized and the parallels between scientific investigation and ETA are described.

Scientific Literacy for Entrepreneurs

Scientific literacy emphasizes the interplay between scientific knowledge and societal concerns (Hurd, 1958). The importance of developing a scientifically literate populace is vital for effective decision making and economic competitiveness (Committee on Science, Engineering, and Public Policy, 2007; Hurd, 1958). Considering that future business leaders and entrepreneurs are studying at Babson, scientific literacy has helped shape the development of the science curriculum.

Knowledge produced by scientific investigations will continue to grow over the course of our students' lives. On a large scale, science is divided into increasingly specialized sub-disciplines (Hurd, 1998) and new interdisciplinary fields of inquiry make our focus on the core skills of critical thinking and understanding the scientific process more applicable to the future needs of our students. Our curriculum mirrors Hurd's (1958) suggestion to emphasize methods over specific content so that science courses can be grounded in timeless principles.

The core science courses offered at Babson combine content from multiple science disciplines centered around a particular real-world problem, challenge, or idea. This allows students to analyze problems and solutions, rather than focus solely on textbook information. Such a thematic focus for science courses is not without precedent. Hofstein and Yager (1982) argue for such an organization of science courses, DeBoer (1991, 2000) includes examples of previous curricula organized along such lines, and Bruner (1960) also emphasizes sophistication of ideas over content. Our focus on the application and practicality of science in our students' everyday lives, with particular attention to applications in the current business environment, makes our courses unique.

Overview of the Science Curriculum

The science group's ambition is to educate and inspire students to think critically about our natural world. As future leaders in the global marketplace, business students must be able to analytically question their surroundings to identify new and innovative solutions for the issues affecting our society. There is no shortage of global issues that can be used to construct courses for our curriculum. The courses described below reflect our current and planned offerings and should be taken as just a few examples of how course design and implementation can occur in our framework.

The current science curriculum offers both foundation and intermediate science courses. First we discuss the foundation courses which are designed to introduce students to broad range of scientific thought with an emphasis on the development of scientific knowledge. The reason for this is twofold: (1) understanding the production of scientific knowledge is fundamentally important for understanding any scientific conclusion and (2) in order to be informed and effective consumers of scientific knowledge, students need to think critically about the rigor of the scientific investigation and the potential uncertainties arising from the development of that knowledge. The intermediate courses then build on these foundation courses and are designed to have a greater emphasis on evaluation of the contextual self-awareness, cultural, and business aspects of investigation and the potential solutions of that investigation. The intermediate courses are described in detail later in the chapter and will show how they further explore the SEERS and cognitive ambidexterity components of ETA.

FOUNDATION SCIENCE

In the foundation courses, the methodology of science — and experimentation in particular — plays a central role. Experimental designs are discussed so that students are able to see how properly designed experiments contribute to the growth of scientific knowledge and how improperly designed experiments can lead to faulty conclusions. Theoretical models are used in scientific research and their applications are discussed so that students have the chance to see the real-world applications of the discipline. Models are discussed in the sense that they are simpler systems than the natural world, and thus yield useful but potentially limited information. These particular epistemological principles are used to introduce points for critical examination of scientific results. Students gain practical experience with experimental design, data collection, data analysis, and rigorous interpretation of results through laboratory activities.

The current foundation courses and descriptions are the following:

- Astronomy — humans have been inquiring about the history and nature of the Earth and the universe for thousands of years. This course builds on that tradition of inquiry while addressing the philosophical and practical difficulties involved in studying remote parts of the universe. The course crosses at least three different scientific disciplines and extends the discussion of the tools needed to study the universe to using those tools can be used to study and manage the Earth's resources.
- Sustainable Energy Solutions — the current world energy crisis has environmental and societal impacts, particularly in the demand and consequences of electrical energy generation and inequity in distribution. The students discuss potential technological solutions as well as identify areas of uncertainty in future energy generation. The ethical issues and business applications associated with energy creation and distribution are also discussed to enhance social responsibility and integrative thinking.
- Electronics — automated control systems can both reduce individual energy demands and create more possibilities for incorporating renewable energy into the electrical power grid. Electronics combines the study of electricity grids with foundational understanding of semiconductors and computers to explore such systems uses with utility scale (>100 MW generating capacity) wind and solar installations and small-scale installations such as those on individual homes. The economic and environmental benefits of these changes are also discussed.
- Human Biotechnology (under development) — Biotechnology connects the genetic and chemical makeup of living organisms (biology) to using the products these living organisms produce to provide beneficial solutions to society (Tang & Zhao, 2009). Biotechnology connects basic biology to practical applications that the food industry, the future of personalized medicine, and

genetic testing all use to create small start-ups and large corporations.

Hands-on Laboratory Investigations

All of the core science courses include a significant laboratory component. These laboratory sections directly link the concepts discussed in classroom lectures with hands-on experiments that highlight techniques, thought processes, and the significance of individual results to our collective understanding of a scientific concept. Furthermore, gaining the ability to interpret self-generated results by using specialized pieces of equipment links the significance of an experimental finding with applications related to daily life on both personal and professional levels. Through these laboratory exercises, the students cycle through the processes of investigation, analysis, and conclusions, another parallel to the ETA cycle for entrepreneurship. In this section, we describe three approaches to laboratory investigations both in and out of the physical laboratory space.

Science often relies upon active demonstrations to determine if an observation can be explained by hypothesis-driven experimentation (Blosser, 1990). Sometimes the subject matter is microscopic or not visible to the naked eye (e.g., genes, viruses, wireless signaling, greenhouse gases). Other topics are macroscopic and possibly overwhelming in scale (e.g., climate change, disease outbreaks, cloud computing). By exploring these concepts through inquiry-based laboratory experiments, we connect the discussion points with student experience.

Students have expressed interest in understanding how different technologies present in the lab are connected to solving larger problems. In the foundation Biotechnology course, we capitalize on this interest by running labs that actually use machines like a 3D printer or thermal cycler to provide hands-on experience and the opportunity to actually answer scientific questions, rather than just following a standard protocol (Halford, 2013). Some of the biotechnology labs show how the microscopic molecules associated with infectious disease, genetically modified organisms, drug discovery, and genetic inheritance can all be visualized in a hypothesis-driven manner and linked to a product, marketing campaign, controversial technology, or industrial strategy that solve a human problem (Eheman, 2012; Gerngross, 2012; Halford, 2013).

For much of 2014, mainstream news discussed the Ebola outbreak, antibiotic resistance, state ballots about food labeling and genetic engineering, the expense and time constraints on drug discovery, and genetic testing. Our labs specifically allow the students to see the strengths and limitations of current biotechnology approaches and provide insight into why these topics are relevant for their daily lives on both personal and business education levels. One lab investigates microscopic molecules that teach lessons in epidemiology, immunology, disease detection, and diagnosis. Students exchange "bodily fluids" which simulates the way that a communicable disease spreads in a small community, like a college where norovirus can quickly spread (Castello, 2009), or more globally like the current Ebola outbreak or recent H1N1 flu pandemic. By recording their sharing partners, providing all of the data regarding who shared with whom and using an immunoassay to see who tested positive for the specific disease, the students can trace back to identify the person who first brought the disease to their community (patient zero). This lesson accomplishes three major objectives: (1) students learn how diseases are detected by screening for specific molecules called antibodies that uniquely report the presence of a disease specific protein, (2) students experience how disease spreads, and (3) students look at real-world applications for this assay, which is especially important given Centers for Disease Control and Prevention protocol (2014) and mandatory quarantine discussions on state and national levels (Drazen et al., 2014). This connection between disease outbreaks and disease detection shows how scientists visualize the invisible (Carnegie Mellon University in Qatar, 2011).

One of the most controversial biotechnology topics today concerns the presence of genetically modified (GM) crops in our food supply and consumers' right to know regarding their presence (American Association for the Advancement of Science, 2012; Kamle & Ali, 2013; Priest et al., 2013). In the GM lab, students bring in their favorite snack (e.g., Pepperidge Farms Goldfish), predict whether their food item will contain GM ingredients based upon the marketing used to create the label, and then determine whether or not the product is actually made with GM crops. This lesson introduces a fundamental biotechnology technique, polymerase chain reaction (PCR) that allows students to study the concept of genetic engineering in a very real way. Screening for the presence of GM crops in everyday foods shows that food cannot be identified as GM just by looking at it and its packaging, which highlights the controversy. We also ask students if they support GM food production and relate it to the real-world problem of being able to sustain our ever-growing population with current resources, a question that requires the exploration of multiple viewpoints from business, ecological, and humanitarian perspectives.

This application-based learning style shows how broad scientific conclusions are drawn by investigating the most intricate details and improves students' scientific literacy by critically analyzing scientific methodologies and creating scientific knowledge (Gormally, Brickman, Hallar, & Armstrong, 2009).

Exploring Product Prototyping

In the foundation Electronics class, groups of 2–4 students work together over the course of the semester to develop a prototype of a device that could be incorporated into a smart home. This project fits within the overall theme of the course by continuing the discussion of smart grid technologies to a more personal scale, and by applying the idea of computer control to an existing system. The student groups are given an Arduino Uno microcontroller board as the basis for their project. The groups have access to many different sensor modules for input, and lights, motors, and speakers for output. The deliverables associated with the project are a final report on the development of their project, a presentation/demonstration of their prototype, and a blog with a minimum of one entry per lab session that was spent on the project.

Class exercises introduce the students to the Arduino programming environment, the connection of devices to the input/output (I/O) ports on the board, and the construction of auxiliary circuits to connect to the I/O ports. At the conclusion of these exercises, the students have the basic skills necessary to start researching and building their own prototypes. The Arduino platform was chosen for this project because there is an online Arduino community which allows the students opportunities for research and support as independent learners throughout the project.

The first task that students complete for the project is to define the data they will collect. To assist the students with this part of the process, a list of available Arduino-compatible sensors is distributed. The students choose which sensor or sensors they wish to use and in what context they would use the sensor. For example, one group built a device to shut off the water supply when frozen pipes were detected and another built a thermostatically controlled fan. After choosing the sensor, the students had four full lab periods to build their project, spaced over approximately two-thirds of the semester. Some groups also elected to take their Arduino board home between labs to make additional progress.

This project directly supports the development of the students' scientific literacy, with a particular focus on experimentation. Although the hardware comes with instructions, the students need to build the circuitry to wire the sensors and output devices into the Arduino. The students need to test their sensors under different conditions to find the best triggering value for action based on the sensor input. Students end up developing their own series of experiments over the course of the project, complete with designing the experiment, collecting and analyzing the data, and deciding whether they have sufficient information to continue or whether another test is warranted.

A final paper on the project summarizes the progress made and knowledge gained over a series of experiments. In total, the project is also an exercise in applied entrepreneurship. The students create products and then have to decide what data they need to collect to move their prototype forward, collect that data, and decide what the results mean for how they should move forward. In the final paper, they make a hypothetical recommendation for their business as to whether they would want to move forward with the project or if the project is not worth further investment of resources.

Exploring Energy Limitations

In Sustainable Energy Solutions, students critically analyze how and why our current energy creation and distribution system is in place, discuss many of the challenges of using that system, explore some possible solutions with current technology, and identify fields open for creative entrepreneurship. The course focuses on the science and applied technologies of current energy production, including the current use of fossil fuels and alternative energy sources. Each energy source is evaluated for both its benefits and drawbacks, as well as the potential for future success.

Many students feel disconnected from the energy crisis and see it as an issue only for those with limited access to energy. Even when students understand that the energy crisis is a global concern, they often believe that there is nothing that can be done to change the way energy is produced and consumed without negatively impacting our quality of life. Some students also believe viable technology does not exist that can improve the sustainability of our energy use. In order to motivate the students to take ownership of their own energy use on campus, as well as to explore how current technology can help reduce Babson's reliance on electricity generated using fossil fuels, the students complete a semester-long project designing a system that will deliver enough power to one of Babson's dormitories to meet the demand of the dormitory without the use of a conventional electrical grid. In collaboration with the Facilities Department, students are given the monthly energy use of the Van Winkle dormitory on campus and work in groups to evaluate the data. They then use their knowledge from class to suggest the technologies they think are best to meet the energy demand of the dormitory. Since the students have explored the science and technology behind current energy sources (renewable and non-renewable) in class, they are able to critically analyze the practicality of each source for use at the dormitory, including a computation of the ability of each potential energy source to generate the necessary electricity.

Students evaluate their own personal energy use (using a kill-a-watt meter) to model the energy use of the "average Babson student." This model is then used to predict how energy is consumed in Van Winkle given the number of students living in the dorm. This exercise gives the students the opportunity to use scientific methodology to gather and interpret data on energy use by students. The critical analysis of how energy demand could be reduced at the dormitory without impacting the enjoyment of the space further connects the students to the global energy crises and provides opportunity to reflect on their own personal energy use. One example of this outcome is seen after experimenting with the energy consumption of three different light bulbs in the laboratory; students were astonished to learn how much power can be saved in a month simply by switching from incandescent to LED bulbs in their dorm.

Armed with their knowledge about how energy is used in Van Winkle, students critically analyze the different options for energy savings within the dormitory, current energy sources, and proposed different methods for how to provide enough power to the dormitory to keep it off of Babson's electricity grid. Their proposals are presented in four different phases. First, draft proposals are provided with initial thoughts on how to analyze the Van Winkle dorm and which energy sources are most feasible. The groups then present their ideas to other groups for peer evaluation. A final written proposal is then submitted with their overall suggestions as well as the mathematical justification for their energy source choices. This semester-long project culminates in a presentation of their proposal of how to power Van Winkle to the Babson community, including Facilities and Sustainability Office representatives. Groups often suggest using a portfolio of different energy sources, usually including some form of solar photovoltaic (PV) cells as an economically viable renewable energy source for the building. The implementation of the solar PV cells suggestions have ranged anywhere from the more traditional roof-mounted system to a parking-lot solar cover that would be wired to the dormitory. Other proposals have included a variety of passive solar techniques to lower heating costs, small geothermal heating plants, and even forming a student group to re-open the biodiesel generation plant on campus and using the yellow grease from the Babson's cafeteria to create biodiesel to use as heating oil for the building.

Overall, students become excited and motivated by the idea of improving their own lives and the campus environment when they are personally invested in their own energy consumption. Throughout the completion of this project, students learn to ask more meaningful questions about energy solutions compared to the classroom setting. Students were able to practice and improve their critical thinking skills through evaluating the benefits and drawbacks of alternative energy sources, and then apply their knowledge directly to a real-world, local issue.

INTERMEDIATE SCIENCE

The intermediate courses build on the knowledge and sophistication of students from the foundation courses. These courses offer a greater emphasis on evaluating the societal or business aspects of the problems and proposed solutions. Students apply their knowledge of scientific processes and critical thinking skills from the foundation course to consider questions of law and public policy and the trade-offs inherent in adopting particular technologies. The intermediate courses also include laboratory activities so students can further develop their analytical skills with data.

The current intermediate courses offered and the course descriptions are:

- Case Studies in Forensic Science – explores the application of science to crime scene investigations. Each scenario brings a different discussion to the classroom and can cover topics such as crime molecules, blood spatter pattern analysis, toxicology, law, and DNA evidence. Students take scientific analysis, apply it to real situations, and critically question results. Milestone legal cases in the acceptance of scientific evidence in the US courts are also discussed.
- Case Studies in Ecological Management – explores the ecological impact of economic production, more sustainable solutions, and ecosystem conservation. The course focuses on developing sustainable resource management options for the future as our demand for resources and ecosystem services increases but our supply and quality decreases.
- Case Studies in Biomedical Science – rooted in the application of translational research, this course explores the development and commercialization of diagnostic and therapeutic medical technologies.

A Case Studies Approach to Science

The intermediate science courses offer students the opportunity to continue developing scientific literacy by building their critical thinking skills about scientific concepts. Since the development of these skills begins in the foundation courses, any foundation course can be used as a prerequisite for any intermediate course. Each intermediate course emphasizes the application of scientific knowledge to address current global societal problems along with the analysis of technological solutions for business application. Because these courses are not traditional courses, classic science textbooks are not used. The topics covered would require a large number of different textbooks; instead, relevant readings from current popular science articles (e.g., *Scientific American*, *National Geographic*, *New*

Scientist), governmental and non-governmental organization research reports (e.g., Environmental Protection Agency, World Resource Institute), and public audience-based scientific journals (e.g., *BioScience, Issues in Ecology*, commentary in *Nature*) are compiled as the required readings. In addition, these courses integrate case studies as a pedagogical approach.

The philosophy behind the case study approach is to associate knowledge directly with action, similar to a professional education (Boehrer, 1995). The case method allows students to immediately apply, synthesize, and challenge concepts to address higher-order cognitive skills (Bloom, 1956). Although business and law classes have long relied on case studies as an approach to teaching and engaged learning, this method was seldom used in undergraduate science courses until relatively recently (Herreid, 1994).

In previous class activities and projects, we have found that Babson students respond well when a business teaching style or familiar activity is utilized in a non-business discipline (Laprise, Philips, Rodgers, & Winrich, 2011; Lester & Rodgers, 2012; Rodgers, 2014). As compared to lecture style, case study cooperative learning has been found to promote greater learning and longer retention of verbal, mathematical, and physical skills (Johnson & Johnson, 1993). Case studies also motivate students to learn the material by providing a specific challenge, forcing students to practice applying theory and using evidence, and encouraging students to discover the limitations to theory (Velenchik, 1995); all of which are important skills in science. In addition students claim to enjoy the experience, become more articulate and engaged, and have better attitudes toward the subject material (Herreid, 2007; Johnson & Johnson, 1993). This last point is particularly important for our courses as we strive to both educate and interest our students in science as a process that is relevant for their future in business.

Ecological Cases

Case Studies in Ecological Management investigates vital natural resources and ecosystem services for human survival and the unequal distribution of global supply and demand. There is a strong emphasis on the impact of economic production in extracting resources from nature and generating waste. At each step, sustainability-based solutions for product design, supply chain management, and waste generation are discussed.

The case studies in this course serve as specific examples of either natural resource disasters/problems or innovative business solutions for sustainability. The individual cases are chosen to represent different geographic regions, which provides a global and multicultural perspective (one of Babson's learning goals) and specifically appeals to our diverse student body, 31% of whom are multicultural

Table 1:   A Sample of Case Study Topics and Geographic Regions Included.

Subject of Case Study	Geographic Region or Company
Ecosystem services – pollination of coffee	Costa Rica
Air pollution and health concerns	Beijing, China
Drought and agricultural exports	California and China connection
Fisheries and marine protected areas	India, Russia, Mexico, Ecuador, Norway
Ore mining acid pollution	Papua New Guinea and South Africa
Deforestation	Brazil
Plastics in ocean	Pacific islands
Bioplastic	NatureWorks company[a]
Life cycle analysis	Haworth, Pangea Organics, IDEO companies[a]
Biomimicry	Regen Energy company[a]
Ecological restoration	Indonesia, Florida, Wyoming

[a]Company profiles.

and 25% who are international (Babson College, 2014). Table 1 shows the subject material and the associated geographic regions or specific companies involved in some of the cases used in the course.

Some of the cases used in this class are traditionally written science cases, such as those available through the National Center for Case Study Teaching in Science (http://sciencecases.lib.buffalo.edu/cs/) or the National Socio-Environmental Synthesis Center (http://www.sesync.org/publications), but others are simply news stories, podcasts, or business profiles with included discussion points for analysis in class. Utilizing newspaper articles as case studies has been documented as successful in motivating and enhancing the analytical skills of students in economics courses (Becker, 1998). Including these non-traditional case studies allows students to see course material application in a variety of media formats and to make connections to relevant stories or events they may encounter outside of class. The case analyses take a number of forms, which helps to keep students engaged throughout the semester. Some case activities involve entire class discussions, others require small groups to agree and propose solutions, some utilize electronic personal response systems or "clickers," and others involve role playing.

As an example, a recent NPR podcast on water-intensive crops being grown in California and then exported to China was used as a case study to discuss freshwater scarcity and droughts. Students are required to listen to the seven minute podcast before coming to class. For this case, the class was immediately split into groups of four. They were given a series of questions to discuss, analyze, and solve. Each group was also given a large tabletop easel pad with paper and markers to sketch out their ideas to present to the rest of the class. The first question asks students to formulate what the problem is and why it exists. The second question requires students to connect the case to previous concepts we have discussed in class, such as the Tragedy of the Commons, irrigation for industrialized agriculture, and future impacts of climate change. The final question asks each group to create and then evaluate two different potential solutions to the problem and include an analysis of how each affects the environment, economy, and society. Students work with their groups for roughly 15 minutes with guidance from the professor as needed. Each group then selects one student to report out on what they developed. Often times this reporting out then generates further discussion between different groups on what the most appropriate strategies are and why the problem exists.

Conclusions

The multidisciplinary design of Babson College's science courses offer business students the chance to take scientific knowledge and relate it directly to both societal issues and how business can contribute to solving such problems. The focus of our courses is on the development of scientific knowledge for two reasons: (1) understanding the production of knowledge is an underlying skill for life-long learning and (2) the scientific process mirrors the entrepreneurial process.

Students practice the experimental cycle in science: ask questions, collect data related to those questions, evaluate the data to reach conclusions, and ask new questions to continue moving forward in understanding. This makes science courses an ideal context to learn ETA, in which students need to ask questions, collect data related to those questions, reach conclusions based on the data, and decide what the next course of action should be in the development of an entrepreneurial venture.

The course designs and their emphasis on the applicability of science in our business students' lives make our science courses at Babson unique. Our curriculum improves the scientific literacy of our students and engages them in new ways of addressing scientific knowledge. We emphasize teaching the scientific process and improving critical thinking in our students, which directly benefits their education, particularly in conjunction with ETA. Our science curriculum parallels the definition of ETA in that it "addresses the real-world problems of business and society, while at the same time evolving our methods and advancing our programs. We shape the leaders our world needs most: those with strong functional knowledge and the skills and vision to navigate change, accommodate ambiguity, surmount complexity, and motivate teams in a common purpose to create economic and social value."

References

American Association for the Advancement of Science. (2012). *Statement by the AAAS board of directors on labeling of genetically modified foods.* Retrieved from http://www.aaas.org/sites/default/files/AAAS_GM_statement.pdf

Babson College. (2014). *Undergraduate class profile for the class of 2018.* Retrieved from http://www.babson.edu/admission/undergraduate/class-profile/Pages/default.aspx

Banschbach, V. S., & Letovsky, R. (2011). Teaming environmental biology and business administration seniors on "Green" enterprise plans at Saint Michael's College, Colchester, VT. *Journal of Environmental Studies and Sciences, 1*(3), 215–222.

Becker, W. (1998). Engaging students in quantitative analysis with short case examples from the academic and popular press. *American Economic Review Papers and Proceedings, 88,* 480–486.

Bloom, B. S. (1956). *Taxonomy of educational objectives, handbook I: The cognitive domain.* New York, NY: David McKay Co Inc.

Blosser, P. E. (1990). The role of the laboratory in science education. *Research Matters – to the Science Teacher,* No. 9001.

Boehrer, J. (1995). *How to teach a case. Joh F. Kennedy School of Government Case Program.* Cambridge, MA: Harvard University.

Bruner, J. S. (1960). *The process of education.* Cambridge, MA: Harvard University Press.

Carnegie Mellon University in Qatar. (2011). *Students simulate disease outbreak at Qatar outreach program.* Retrieved from http://www.cmu.edu/bio/news/2011/qatar_outreach.html

Castello, C. (2009). *Babson college closed due to norovirus cases.* Retrieved from http://www.boston.com/news/local/massachusetts/articles/2009/03/29/babson_college_closed_due_to_norovirus_cases/

Centers for Disease Control and Prevention. (2014). *Detailed hospital checklist for Ebola preparedness.* Retrieved from http://www.cdc.gov/vhf/ebola/pdf/hospital-checklist-ebola-preparedness.pdf

Charski, M. (2008). Business schools teach environmental studies. *U.S. News and World report.* Retrieved from http://www.usnews.com/education/articles/2008/03/26/business-schools-teach-environmental-studies

Committee on Science, Engineering, and Public Policy. (2007). *Rising above the gathering storm: Energizing and employing America for a brighter economic future.* Washington, DC: The National Academies Press.

DeBoer, G. E. (1991). *A history of ideas in science education: Implications for practice.* New York, NY: Teachers College Press.

DeBoer, G. E. (2000). Scientific literacy: Another look at its historical and contemporary meanings and its relationship to science education reform. *Journal of Research in Science Teaching, 37,* 582–601.

Drazen, J., Kanapathipillai, R., Campion, E., Rubin, E., Hammer, S., Morrissey, S., & Baden, L. (2014). Ebola and quarantine. *New England Journal of Medicine, 371*, 2029–2030.

Eheman, K. E. (2012). Planning for the exit. *Nature Biotechnology, 30*(2), 132–134.

Gerngross, T. (2012). It's the problem, stupid! *Nature Biotechnology, 30*, 742–744.

Gormally, C., Brickman, P., Hallar, B., & Armstrong, N. (2009). Effects of inquiry-based learning on students' science literacy skills and confidence. *International Journal for the Scholarship of Teaching and Learning, 3*(2), Article 16.

Greenberg, D., McKone-Sweet, K., & Wilson, H. J. (2011). *The new entrepreneurial leader: Developing leaders who shape social and economic opportunity.* San Francisco, CA: Berrett-Koehler Publishers.

Halford, B. (2013). Lab lessons for reluctant chemists. *Chemical and Engineering News, 91*(19), 46–47.

Heindel, N. D. (1996). Science careers in a new era [Book review]. *Chemical and Engineering News, 74*(26), 80–81.

Herreid, C. F. (1994). Case studies in science-a novel method of science education. *Journal of College Science Teaching, 23*, 221–229.

Herreid, C. F. (2007). Chicken little, Paul Revere, and Winston Churchill look at science literacy. In *Start with a story: The case study method of teaching college science.* Arlington, VA: National Science Teachers Association Press.

Hofstein, A., & Yager, R. E. (1982). Societal issues as organizers for science education in the '80s. *School Science and Mathematics, 82*, 539–547.

Hubbard, K. A. (2005). Help wanted: Science manager. *PLOS Biology, 3*(1), e32.

Hurd, P. D. (1958). Scientific literacy: Its meaning for American schools. *Educational Leadership, 16*, 13–16.

Hurd, P. D. (1998). Scientific literacy: New minds for a changing world. *Science Education, 82*, 407–416.

Johnson, D. W., & Johnson, R. T. (1993). Cooperative learning: Where we have been, where we are going. *Cooperative Learning and Teaching Newsletter, 3*(2), 6–9.

Kamle, S., & Ali, S. (2013). Genetically modified crops: Detection strategies and biosafety issues. *Gene, 522*(2), 123–132.

Laprise, S., Philips, J., Rodgers, V., & Winrich, C. (2011). Practice-oriented science education for business students. *The International Journal of Science in Society, 2*(3), 235–242.

Laprise, S., Winrich, C., & Sharpe, N. R. (2008). Business students should learn more about science. *Chronicle of Higher Education, 54*(36), A35.

Lester, T., & Rodgers, V. (2011). Beyond green: Encouraging students to create a simultaneity of positive SEERS outcomes. *The New Entrepreneurial Leader* (pp. 94–112). San Francisco, CA: Berrett-Koehler Publishers.

Lester, T., & Rodgers, V. L. (2012). Teaching a cross disciplinary environmental science, policy and culture course on Costa Rica's ecotourism to business students. *Journal of Environmental Studies and Sciences, 2*(3), 234–238.

Martin, R. (2009). *The opposable mind: Winning through integrative thinking* (p. 224). Boston, MA: Harvard Business School Publishing.

Miller, A. (1981). Integrative thinking as a goal of environmental education. *The Journal of Environmental Education, 12*(4), 3–8.

Priest, S. H., Valenti, J. M., Logan, R. A., Rogers, C. L., Dunwoody, S., Griffin, R. J., … Steinke, J. (2013). AAAS position on GM foods could backfire. *Science, 339*(6121), 756–756.

Rodgers, V. L. (2014). Pitching environmental science to business majors: Engaging students in renewable energy choices. *Journal of College Science Teaching, 43*(5), 28–32.

Smith, G. F. (2003). Beyond critical thinking and decision making: Teaching business students how to think. *Journal of Management Education, 27*(1), 24–51.

Tang, W. L., & Zhao, H. (2009). Industrial biotechnology: Tools and applications. *Biotechnology Journal, 4*(12), 1725–1739.

Velenchik, A. D. (1995). The case method as a strategy for teaching policy analysis to undergraduates. *Journal of Economic Education, 26*, 29–38.

11

Leading Entrepreneurial Action Project (LEAP): A Project-Based Course Integrating Three Disciplines

Sebastian K. Fixson,
Danna N. Greenberg and
Andrew Zacharakis

What does a recent graduate with a humanities degree do for employment? How about the engineer who has developed a new product idea in the lab, but doesn't know where to go with it? What about the fine arts student who doesn't know how to manage the business aspects of their performing or creative arts practice? Or the recent business degree graduate who has deep knowledge of a discipline, like accounting or marketing, but needs a jumpstart to master skills of leadership and problem-solving? Without work experience these new graduates are not qualified to enter a traditional MBA program. Yet, without greater understanding of management many of these students are not prepared to enter the work world. Caught in this dilemma, it is not surprising that as many as 44% of recent graduates are underemployed[1] (Abel, Deitz, & Su, 2014).

To support the learning needs of these less-experienced students, Babson has recently launched a masters of science in management in entrepreneurial leadership (MS EL). This program is specifically designed for the recent college graduate who wants to expand their understanding of business fundamentals, such as finance, accounting, and marketing. Students learn a unique approach to these traditional business disciplines as they learn to utilize an entrepreneurial mindset in all business areas. Experiential learning, personal development, and traditional case pedagogy are all central to helping students develop a combination of foundational business knowledge and entrepreneurial leadership skills.

One of the unique pedagogical elements of this program is a year-long interdisciplinary, project-based course, Leading Entrepreneurial Action Project (LEAP). In this course, students learn in the context of a simulated work environment as they spend two semesters working in a six-person team to create a product or service moving from exploring an opportunity space to idea generation to design to inception to launch. The faculty form these six-person teams prior to the start of the semester based on shared career interests. Having a shared career interests helps team members be more engaged throughout challenging project. Beyond career interests, the teams are also balanced for gender and domestic/international origin. The end goal is that each team will create a product or service that is ready to launch by the time the students earn their degree. In this way, students not only learn the business basics but they also can now demonstrate to a potential employer their ability to move an idea to execution. Beyond that, they develop their expertise as entrepreneurial leaders as they learn how to engage an entrepreneurial mindset and how to pursue an idea based on a deep understanding of self and context. In this chapter, we will detail the course and how it fits into the MS EL program.

Babson's New Masters of Science in Management in Entrepreneurial Leadership Program

Rapid changes in technology, work, and society in recent years have put an increasing focus on how to prepare students, or in fact

---

[1]Underemployment is defined here as working in a job that does not require a bachelor's degree of any type.

anyone, for a world and jobs that do not exist yet. Most put a premium on the ability to navigate uncertain environments and on the importance of being able to design one's own learning in these circumstances. For example, Wagner (2012) identifies cultures of innovation based on collaboration, interdisciplinary problem-solving, and intrinsic motivation as key aspects of future innovators. Similar arguments are coming from academics (Gardner, 2006) and popular authors (Pink, 2006). Precisely to focus on helping students to develop the capacity and skills to take initiative in a business context, the new MS EL program combines business fundamentals with applied entrepreneurial learning (see Figure 1 for an overview).

Utilizing the full length of the program, LEAP forms an ongoing backbone for the curriculum. It also serves as a lab context for the material and content the students learn in the other nine courses (marketing, operations, data analysis, IT, financial accounting, managerial accounting, finance, strategy, and economics) that comprise the program. A substantial portion of what the students take away from these courses can be directly applied to their LEAP projects.

The LEAP curriculum is enhanced by a substantial co-curricular program. In addition to LEAP, individual development that includes personal and career planning, accompanies the program for the entire length of the program in the form of the individual leadership

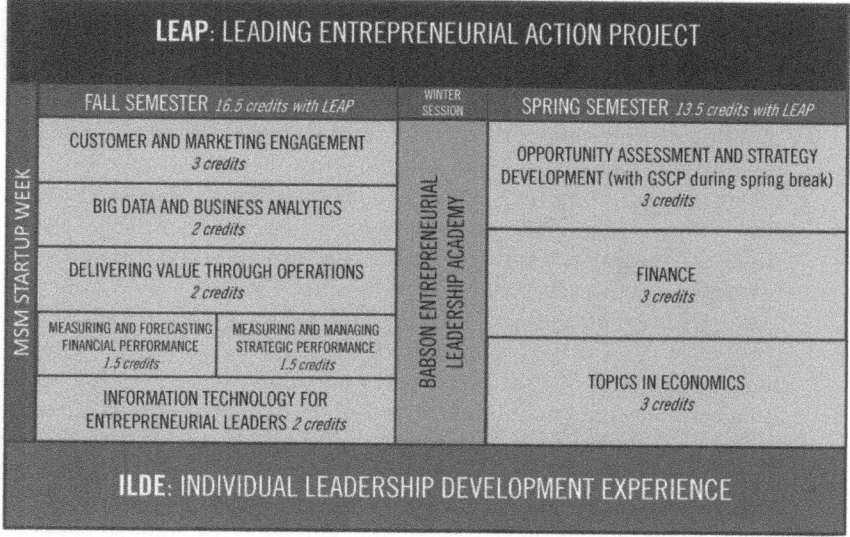

Figure 1: Program Design for Babson's Master in Management in Entrepreneurial Leadership.

development experience (ILDE). This work begins before the students even arrive on campus as students begin to connect with a Babson career counselor. Finally, to further support the development of students' leadership skills, the MS EL program involves the students in two additional experiences. In one, they serve as teachers of entrepreneurship in a lower socioeconomic context unfamiliar to most of them and, in the other one, they serve as consultants on a business problem in a country outside of the United States.

LEAP: LEADING ENTREPRENEURIAL ACTION PROJECT

To embody Babson's entrepreneurial spirit and to recognize its place in the MS EL curriculum, the LEAP course reflects an action-oriented curriculum that couples conceptual learning with practice. It moves students from the classroom to the design lab. It fosters ideation, primary and secondary research skills, presentation abilities, teamwork, design capabilities, and an entrepreneurial spirit that will serve graduates whether they choose to launch their own business or work for established company. After completing the class, students will have a prototype and launch plan ready to take to the marketplace. Specifically, those interested in pursuing their own business will have achieved significant milestones of going through several prototypes, testing them in the marketplace and having a detailed launch plan to start executing on the next steps, such as identifying vendors, seeking capital and so forth. Students who choose not to pursue the project as a business will have a portfolio, including prototypes, to distinguish themselves from others as they enter the competitive workforce.

To achieve this goal, LEAP is a multidisciplinary course combining design, entrepreneurship, and organizational behavior. It is team taught with professors from each of those disciplines who not only facilitate traditional learning but coach groups as they go through the entire process. The interdisciplinary nature is strategic. Design focuses on ideation, gathering customer and market data, and rapid prototyping. Entrepreneurship brings the skills of analyzing and testing idea feasibility, identifying and securing important resource providers (e.g., investors) and partners (e.g., vendors and mentors), and presenting and selling the opportunity to important stakeholders. Organizational behavior helps students understand who they are and what they can bring to a team, an organization, and as entrepreneurial leaders. As the students work on their projects, the nature of the challenges they encounter varies over time and sometimes contains elements from the different disciplines simultaneously. Just as in the real-world problems seldom come compartmentalized by discipline, the integrated nature of the course

Figure 2: Highly Integrated Nature of LEAP.

enables students to develop a better response to the multifaceted nature of the problem they are facing. In addition, by having multiple faculty members from different disciplines engaging in a discussion of a single problem from different angles, students learn to integrate different, and sometimes contradictory, viewpoints in their search for solutions. As a result, LEAP is not divided into disciplinary segments, but rather exhibits a course design that highly integrates the three disciplines (Figure 2).

The key vehicle for the learning in LEAP is the team project that progresses from nothing at the start of the year as students begin by identifying an interesting and relevant opportunity; then engage in user research, concept generation, prototyping, business model development and testing, to more prototyping; and finally culminating after nine months into a launch plan. The project provides a mechanism through which students own their work as they progress forward as well as move through detours via iterations and pivots. Many of these detours lead to entirely new goals and completely different businesses than the students first envisioned.

THE DISCIPLINARY BASIS OF LEAP
Design
The word "Design" carries different meanings for different people, ranging from the idea that everything that humans purposefully create constitutes "designing" as Simon (1996) articulated almost half a century ago to various narrow definitions of design professions such as graphic design, industrial design, engineering design, etc. Recently, the term design thinking has been used to convey the idea of porting the way of working used by designers to non-designers (Brown, 2008; Cross, 2011; Lockwood, 2009; Martin, 2009).

The increasing importance that both existing organizations and start-ups place on the tools and mindset of design thinking can be seen by the attention and resources they dedicate to design. Some companies hire designers into important leadership positions. For example, medical equipment and supply company Johnson and Johnson recently hired as its first corporate-wide Chief Design Officer a designer of technology products such as iPhone and iPad cases; automobile manufacturer Toyota put its design chief to head its Lexus brand; and venture capital company Khosla Ventures hired the former head of Google's user interaction team as design partner. In other instances, companies spend substantial amount of resources to train their employees in design thinking. For example, the multinational technology and consulting company IBM opened a new Design Studio in Austin, TX, with the goal of hiring 1000 designers in the next few years and to convert the over 400,000 IBM employees to design thinking. Similarly, Indian software company Infosys recently announced that 30,000 of its staff will be trained in design thinking.

Various definitions of design thinking have emerged in recent years, varying mostly in granularity of the process description and sometimes in the labels being attached. Most of them align, however, on three major sets of activities as part of design thinking. The first set of activities, user research, includes all activities to actually develop a deep and detailed understanding of what the problem or opportunity really is. The second set of activities, ideation, is concerned with generating and finding relevant solution options. Finally, the third set of activities, prototyping, focuses on using quick and inexpensive techniques to learn about challenges and potential of a subset of ideas.

The increasing rates of uncertainty that today's businesses and entrepreneurs are facing makes it imperative to include design elements into business education (Fixson & Read, 2012). At Babson, design has been introduced at multiple places in the curriculum (core and electives) across all programs (undergraduate, graduate, and executive education). In our new MS EL program, design is a core element in the year long LEAP course, together with entrepreneurship and organizational behavior.

The user research activities encompass a substantial portion of the first semester. In their teams, which have been formed around the students' interests, students are asked to identify a problem they consider interesting and relevant. In addition to secondary research, students engage in in-depth qualitative research using ethnography techniques such as interviews and observations. Following individual homework exercises to apply these methods, class discussions, and in-class mock exercises, we ask the students to engage in these activities for their team projects. During this work a link to organizational behavior becomes obvious as most students are unaware how their own biases can get in the way of empathically understanding the needs of others. In LEAP, we address this challenge with built-in reflection assignments as well as faculty coaching. The raw data from the teams' user research is then synthesized and mined for insights, using design tools such as personas and journeymaps. The status of the projects is reviewed by faculty in bi-weekly studio-style pin-ups which are requests for the teams to lay out their work visually (more details on pin-ups below).

Once the teams have developed a crisp problem/opportunity statement with associated target user definition, we guide them in creating a portfolio of possible solutions. Conceptual instruction of various idea generation techniques and mechanisms is followed by the students themselves engaging in these very activities for their projects within their teams. To enforce the connection to entrepreneurship, we ask the teams to present a subset of their ideas in the form of rocket pitches (see more detail on this teaching tool below). The rocket pitch supports multiple goals: (i) it forces students to craft a three-minute pitch of an idea, (ii) it starts the development of the habit to shape a pitch through repeated presentations, and (iii) it asks each team to ensure that its set of presentations collectively exhibit a broad search of the solution space. This is an important lesson, as the tendency to like one's own and early ideas is a human shortcoming in developing novel solutions (Liedtka, 2014). This aspect also provides another link to organizational behavior, as idea preferences often trigger strong team dynamics that can become very dysfunctional if not addressed quickly.

The third set of activities in design focuses on prototyping in its various forms. The goal is to learn both techniques and mindset to engage in early and simple idea testing in order to eliminate those ideas that are built on faulty assumptions and alter and reshape other concepts to improve their market fit. In the early days, these prototyping activities should be quick and inexpensive and focus on unearthing unarticulated assumptions and fatal flaws. Later, prototyping activities involve more sophisticated models and prototypes, and a more scientific approach of testing. Students learn the tools and techniques to design both the prototyping (process) and the prototype (artifact) and immediately apply the learning in their own projects. Particularly beneficial for the construction of prototypes is access to tools and materials of a workshop, something that our newly established Design Zone 125 provides. In fact, the Design Zone supports various design activities, such as synthesizing information into personas and journeymaps or team-level brainstorming in its own way (more details on this aspect are described in Fixson, Seidel, and Bailey, 2015, this volume). Testing concepts through prototyping provides additional linkages to entrepreneurship (e.g., increasingly detailed consideration of business models and options and constraints for financing) and organizational behavior (e.g., failure tolerance varies across individuals, thus affecting team performance). In fact, research shows that the ability of teams to appropriately debate their own process to determine which activity to conduct next based on the to-date understanding has a strong influence on team performance, especially in the early phase of a project (Seidel & Fixson, 2013).

Entrepreneurship

At Babson, we define entrepreneurship as the process of transforming ideas into opportunity, thereby creating both economic and social value for the entrepreneur and others. Thus, our definition incorporates key elements of design and organizational behavior. As noted above, design is the process of taking an idea and creating a manifestation of that idea into a product or service. This is the core of value creation. A product delivers value to the customer who in turn willingly exchanges money for that product. As that exchange occurs, value is passed through the company to its various stakeholders, such as employees, vendors, etc.

The pedagogical goals are to convey the concepts of Entrepreneurial Thought and Action (ET&A®), the overarching framework of a Babson education (Kiefer, Schlesinger, & Brown, 2010). Specifically, we want our graduates to understand the unique resources that they bring to any organization (Sarasvathy, 2001). These resources are based on three questions: (1) Who they are? (2) Who they know? and (3) What they know? These are the resources that the individual brings to any opportunity they pursue. We then focus on the ET&A® methodology for launching a business.

ET&A® is an iterative combination of the predictive and creaction logics (Kiefer et al., 2010). The predictive logic is what the traditional business and entrepreneurship curriculum teaches. With predictive logic, students collect information, analyze that information and then follow a plan to reach a goal. The predictive logic is embodied in the 40-page business plan that is often central to most entrepreneurship courses. The predictive logic is valuable but limited. It presumes that the environment is stable and that all the information is readily available to make valid assumption on which to launch a business. Unfortunately, real life is not that clean. ET&A® suggests that entrepreneurs break down that predictive planning process into more digestible pieces; the essence of cre-action or what Bygrave and Zacharakis (2014) label escalating "market tests." Specifically, ET&A® emphasizes action early and often. Successful entrepreneurs do not THINK (write a 40-page business plan) and then ACT (launch the business), instead they follow a rapid iteration process between thinking and action, a cre-action logic. Cre-action is about understanding your current resources, creating some element of the business and then acting on that element within in the marketplace, a "market test" mentality.

Students follow a "market test" mentality bringing their idea to the marketplace quickly and then adjusting based upon what the market tells them (Bygrave & Zacharakis, 2014). Specifically, we advocate an iterative four-step cycle. First, the entrepreneur does a bit of **planning**. Every business is built upon assumptions or more appropriately, the entrepreneur's hypotheses on how the idea will translate into reality. Just as the scientific process illustrates that not all hypotheses prove out, the same is true for entrepreneurs. Therefore, it is imperative that entrepreneurs not invest all their time and money into a huge business before validating all the underlying hypotheses. Second, entrepreneurs should run a small scale, low cost **experiment** in the marketplace to validate a few of the key assumptions. Third, entrepreneurs **learn** by comparing their expected and actual outcomes. The final step is to **reshape** the business idea and then do the four steps over and over again. After each iteration, the entrepreneur has validated more assumptions, thereby reducing risk and can now run more expensive experiments. The market test mentality is simulated throughout LEAP by activities, assignments and deliverables (such as the pin-ups), ethnographic interactions, rocket pitches, and other activities highlighted throughout this chapter.

Organizational Behavior

Organizational behavior recognizes that an organization is made up of individuals. To function effectively and thereby create social and economic value, people need to understand who they are, how to work effectively with and through others, and how to work across different contexts. In this way, individual organizational members can grow and develop while also contributing to the organization's goals. In the LEAP course, the organizational behavior curriculum is designed in such a way that it plays a supporting role to design and entrepreneurship. Yet, it is in this supporting role that the value of organizational behavior becomes central. Below, we describe the primary ways in which the organizational behavior curriculum is structured such that it integrates with the evolution of the business project.

As students begin the LEAP course, most of their project work is centered on design thinking. Students are learning to engage in user research to understand a problem from the users' perspective and ideation as they brainstorm possible solutions. Relative to the entrepreneurship curriculum, students are very much centered on understanding who they are and how who they are connects to the ideas they are generating. As such, the organizational behavior curriculum is designed to support students' learning of these key elements of being an entrepreneurial leader. Through experiential exercises and conceptual framing, students begin to understand how their values, their behavioral style, and their identity affects how they see the world and how they frame opportunities. More importantly, they begin to uncover the significant biases that underlie their perceptions and judgments. As they work in their design team, students see the strengths and limitations of their cognitive biases and how to balance their biases by relying on their teammates' perspectives. Similarly, students learn how their sense of self can lead to biased understanding of the end user. As we seek to deepen students understanding of emotional intelligence and action inquiry, students learn how to engage in more open observation and exploration of the experiences of the end user. These organizational behavior principles take center stage as students see how they enable them to develop a more nuanced understanding of their opportunity space.

As the LEAP course revolves around a team-based project, developing skill and critical thinking around teamwork and leadership is also core to the organizational behavior curriculum. Nothing incites students' interest more than real-world experience, and the advantage of the LEAP design project is our students experience the same challenges any project team faces. Conceptual ideas around group development, group decision-making, and conflict resolution are not just practiced through experiential exercises and case discussion. These concepts are acted upon as students face new and unexpected problems in their LEAP groups. Whether it be cross-cultural communication, lack of forming as a team, or groupthink, all of the typical team issues arise in these high-pressured, uncertain LEAP projects. As these issues arise, students also learn to consider why team members may vary in their engagement in the team. Through discussions of topics such as social loafing, motivation, and values, students become more empathetic and responsive to students with diverse interests and backgrounds and how this responsiveness improve a team's effectiveness. While this conceptual material is discussed in specific class sessions, the organizational behavior professor also introduces these concepts as she consults to the teams throughout the life of the project. Students' critical thinking around these topics deepens as they begin to experiment with different ways of organizing and leading to create a better team environment.

Through their work in their teams, students also learn different models of leadership. In these teams, there are no formally appointed leaders. Rather informal leaders emerge in the groups with different students taking on different leadership responsibilities such as task leaders and social leaders. In this way, students experience the difference between role assignments and true leadership.

The third theme of the curriculum relates to context. One of the principles of entrepreneurial leadership is an understanding of self and context. To work effectively and pursue an opportunity, entrepreneurial leaders do not just understand who they are and who they know, they also appreciate and respond to the context in with they are working (Greenberg, McKone-Sweet, & Wilson, 2011). Just as students begin to understand how individual level factors can bias their perception, they also learn how context can similarly shape and influence their perspective. Context is looked at from a number of dimensions including culture, structure, and climate and at more macro-levels of industry evolution, economy, and government. As students move forward on their business projects from feasibility analysis to launch plan, they learn to pay attention to the intricate and subtle influence that context can have on their proposed venture. They begin to understand how context can influence the feasibility of an idea and of a team.

In this way, students develop their understanding and skill with all facets of organizational behavior. As they begin their business projects, they experience how an understanding of who they are is central to the development of the ideas they pursue. They learn how empathy and engagement with others is as important to their work in their teams as it is to their understanding of their end user. They hone their skills and understanding of how to work effectively in a team and as a leader. Finally, they learn how the macro-organizational world influences their pursuit of a new opportunity. In an organizational behavior class with students who have limited work experience, faculty often struggle to help students become motivated to learn organizational behavior as these students frequently question the relevance and value of the topics (Burke & Moore, 2003). Yet, when organizational behavior is taught such that it supports the evolution of a business project and is connected to design and entrepreneurship, students not only see the value in the discipline, they become motivated to engage deeper with the content as they see the impact organizational behavior has on their lives, their teams, and their effectiveness.

Innovative Pedagogical Tools in This Project-Based Course

To effectively teach in an interdisciplinary, project-based course, one must engage pedagogical tools that are somewhat distinct from traditional courses and disciplines. Because of the iterative nature of this class and the learning that occurs through the project, we had to devise pedagogical tools that would enable us to more frequently check in with the teams and provide them real time feedback. While some professors might do this outside of the classroom in office hours, we wanted students to learn how to dialogue around the challenges and successes they were experiencing in order to help them move forward now. Our goal is for students to learn to move their projects forward as well as learn a process for moving projects forward in the future. As such, we integrated opportunities for feedback and dialogue into the course sessions. Below, we overview four of the pedagogical approaches we engage to do this.

PIN-UPS

What we call *pin-ups* are occasions to check in on the team's project progress; they are in effect design reviews. The term "pin-up" is borrowed from the art school world where art students pin up their work to a wall for review by the instructor. For several reasons, the pin-ups we use have a particular form. First, in contrast to art school students, most business school students are not used to presenting their work visually or using graphics and other illustration techniques. However, working visually is integral to the design process, and pin-ups that force the teams to visually display their work serve as a repeated signal to the students of the importance of this mode of work. Second, our design reviews are purposefully designed differently from sales-pitch type presentations. While the latter is a critical skill in front of superiors and investors (students learn this in our rocket pitches), our design reviews are modeled as a collaborative exercise in which faculty engages the students in a conversation to probe for weak points or unexamined assumptions. The goal of these reviews is not to test for performance, but to help develop the projects and by doing so, help develop the students as designers of novel solutions. This less formal, albeit not less rigorous, style of review also allows the introduction of non-financial evaluation considerations, emphasizing the role of a more comprehensive evaluation perspective we espouse at Babson as social, environmental, and economic responsibility and sustainability (SEERS).

ROCKET PITCH

The *rocket pitch* is an early market test. Students present their current product/service idea in three minutes, distilling their idea down to its purest essence. The three-minute pitch is invaluable for gaining early feedback and nurturing potential partners. In that three minutes, students convey three or four important aspects about their product/service. First, the presenters identify the problem/need that they are seeking to address. It is critical that they create a hook that draws in the audience. For example, if you are developing a solution for obesity, do not state that people are fatter than ever, hook the audience. That hook might be that over 78 million Americans, one third of the population, are obese, leading to almost $150 billion in annual medical expenses (CDC, 2014 http://www.cdc.gov/obesity/

data/adult.html). These startling stats capture attention. Second, talk about your product/service and how it addresses the problem. Third, explain how your product/service has a competitive edge in the marketplace. Finally, exclaim your call to action which basically means getting the audience to take some action to engage with you after your presentation. A call to action may be to ask for an expert to join the team. In the obesity example, the call to action might be to find a nutritionist to join the team. The rocket pitch gets students interacting with others and fits the cre-action logic of ETA.

LAUNCH AND GROW PLAN

The *Launch and Grow Plan* is the culmination of the yearlong LEAP course. It incorporates all the learning shaping that has occurred throughout the year as manifested in the product or service prototype that the students have developed. Moreover, it details a path forward for those students who wish to build a business around the idea. Specifically, it lays out a timeline of detailed activities that the students need to pursue to move the project forward. Instead of the traditional business plan, the deliverable is in the form of a detailed presentation with slides that include (as a handout) detailed citations and explanations within in the notes section of the plan.

FEEDBACK AND REFLECTION

Beyond teaching students how to assess and obtain feedback on their ongoing projects, we also focus on developing student skills in giving and receiving interpersonal feedback and reflecting on their own personal development as an entrepreneurial leader. As teams have become more central to education and management education in particular, self and peer evaluation has increased as a method for creating better teamwork experiences (Gueldenzoph & May, 2002). Peer evaluation has been found to lead to greater satisfaction, less social loafing, and higher perceived fairness of grades (Aggarwal & O'Brien, 2008; Chapman & van Auken, 2001). Yet, we were interested in using peer feedback not for evaluation but for developmental purposes. We wanted to provide students with a mechanism by which they could learn to solicit and reflect on feedback to propel their continual development as entrepreneurial leaders. In today's organizations where feedback and evaluation often occurs less frequently, it becomes even more of an imperative that individuals have the skills to manage their own development.

To help students learn a process of feedback and reflection, we began by teaching core conceptual material around this topic. Framed in the lens of positive organizational behavior (Cameorn,

Dutton, & Quinn, 2003), we teach students how feedback is not just about evaluation but rather is an opportunity for self-improvement. Through a series of exercises, students learn how to give developmental feedback and how to receive feedback (Stone & Heen, 2014). Effective leadership is dependent on an individual's ability to actively seek out feedback and through this course students become skilled at seeking and responding to feedback early in their careers.

This conceptual material provides the basis for extensive peer feedback in the business project teams. Following the first major deliverable, the rocket pitch presentations, students have the opportunity to anonymously give one another developmental feedback. This specific set of feedback is not used to evaluate the students, it is used to support the student's development. Relying on extensive research by Ohland and colleagues (2012), an anonymous on-line instrument was developed that enables all team members to provide quantitative feedback on five key dimensions of team behavior: contributing to the team's work, interacting with teammates, keeping the team on track, work quality, and related knowledge and skills. Beyond these dimensions, students also provide qualitative feedback to one another on what they should start, stop, and continue doing to support the team's work. A custom report is then produced for each team member in which all feedback remains anonymous.

This report is just the start of the feedback process. Students are also taught to reflect more deeply about feedback through the use of two pedagogical interventions. First, each project team is encouraged to have a session in which they openly discuss their feedback and receive further clarification. Teams are encouraged to create a process by which each team member has an opportunity to talk about the feedback they received, to ask for clarification, and to get support on ways they can continue to develop. Ground rules are established (limiting defensiveness, not asking who said what, and being open to difficult conversations) so that an environment is created that enables students to deeply, honestly, and openly reflect on their feedback. For some students, they also need to reflect individually on this feedback in order to fully comprehend and respond to it. Therefore, students in the course are asked to write a self-reflection paper in which they incorporate various forms of feedback that they have received to explore how they need to further develop as entrepreneurial leader. A central aspect of these reflection papers is the peer feedback and the peer feedback discussions. Students often learn to confront blind spots and be honest about who they are. The confidential aspect of the paper brings out this honest self-reflection. The combination of peer feedback and reflection also teaches students a model for personal development that they can carry forward into their work careers.

Conclusion

LEAP is not an easy course to design or teach. The pedagogy of the course is not centered in any one discipline nor is it centered in a traditional business school pedagogy. It requires adaptation and adjustment as the faculty learn to balance the teaching methods of each discipline while maintaining a unified curriculum for the students. Yet, the integration that is the center of this course is the only way to realistically teach students about the complex work world they will enter. Students finish the course not only with a deep understanding of the conceptual foundation behind design, entrepreneurship, and organizational behavior, but they leave the course with skills and experiences that provide the basis for their work careers. The projects they complete become the basis for a portfolio that enables them to more successfully present the skills and knowledge they have developed during the course. More importantly, the learning that occurs in these project teams becomes the basis for life-long team-based learning and self-development.

References

Abel, J. R., Deitz, R., & Su, Y. (2014). Are recent college graduates finding good jobs? *Current Issues in Economics and Finance.* 20(1), 1−8. Retrieved from http://www.ny.frb.org/research/current_issues/ci20-1.pdf

Aggarwal, P., & O'Brien, C. L. (2008). Social loafing on group projects structural antecedents and effect on student satisfaction. *Journal of Marketing Education, 30,* 255−264.

Brown, T. (2008). Design thinking. *Harvard Business Review, 86*(6), 85−92.

Burke, L. A., & Moore, E. (2003). A perennial dilemma in OB education: Engaging the traditional student. *Academy of Management Learning and Education, 2*(1), 37−52.

Bygrave, W. D., & Zacharakis, A. (2014). *Entrepreneurship* (3rd ed.). Hoboken, NJ: Wiley.

Cameorn, K., Dutton, J., & Quinn, R. E. (Eds.). (2003). *Positive organizational scholarship: Foundations of a new discipline.* San Francisco, CA: Berrett-Koehler Publishers.

CDC. (2014). Retrieved from http://www.cdc.gov/obesity/data/adult.html. Accessed on June 22, 2015.

Chapman, K. J., & Van Auken, S. (2001). Creating positive group project experiences: An examination of the role of the instructor on students' perceptions of group projects. *Journal of Marketing Education, 23*(2), 117−127.

Cross, N. (2011). *Design thinking.* Oxford: Berg.

Fixson, S. K., & Read, J. M. (2012). Creating innovation leaders: Why we need to blend business and design education. *Design Management Review, 23*(4), 4−12.

Fixson, S. K., Seidel, V. P., & Bailey, J. (2015). Creating space for innovation: The role of a "design zone" within a business school. In V. L. Crittenden, N. Karst, & R. Slegers (Eds.), *Evolving entrepreneurial education: Innovation in the Babson classroom.* Bingley, UK: Emerald Group Publishing Limited. doi:10.1111/jpim.12163

Gardner, H. (2006). *Five minds for the future*. Boston, MA: Harvard Business Press.

Greenberg, D., McKone-Sweet, K., & Wilson, H. J. (2011). *The new entrepreneurial leader*. San Francisco, CA: Berrett-Koehler Publishers.

Gueldenzoph, L. E., & May, G. L. (2002). Collaborative peer evaluation: Best practices for group members assessments. *Business and Professional Communication Quarterly, 65*(1), 9−20.

Kiefer, C. F., Schlesinger, L. A., & Brown, P. B. (2010). Action trumps everything: Creating what you want in an uncertain world: Innovation Associates.

Liedtka, J. (2014). Linking design thinking with innovation outcomes through cognitive bias reduction. *Journal of Product Innovation Management*.

Lockwood, T. (Ed.). (2009). *Design thinking: Integrating innovation, customer experience, and brand value*. New York, NY: Allworth Press. Original edition.

Martin, R. (2009). *The design of business: Why design thinking is the next competitive advantage*. Boston, MA: Harvard Business School Press.

Ohland, M. W., Loughry, M. L., Woehr, D. J., Bullard, L. G., Felder, R. M., Finelli, C. J., … Schmucker, D. G. (2012). The comprehensive assessment of team member effectiveness: Development of a behaviorally anchored rating scale for self- and peer evaluation. *Academy of Management Learning and Education, 11*(4), 609−630.

Pink, D. H. (2006). *A whole new mind − Why right-brainers will rule the future*. New York, NY: Riverhead Books.

Sarasvathy, S. D. (2001). Causation and effectuation: Toward a theoretical shift from economic inevitability to entrepreneurial contingency. *Academy of Management Review, 26*(2), 243−263.

Seidel, V. P., & Fixson, S. K. (2013). Adopting design thinking in novice multidisciplinary teams: The application and limits of design methods and reflexive practices. *Journal of Product Innovation Management, 30*(S1), 19−33.

Simon, H. A. (1996). *The sciences of the artificial* (3rd ed.). Cambridge, MA: MIT Press.

Stone, D., & Heen, S. (2014). *Thanks for the feedback: The science and art of receiving feedback well*. New York, NY: Viking.

Wagner, T. (2012). *Creating innovators − The making of young people who will change the world*. New York, NY: Simon & Schuster.

12 Global Film Across the Curriculum: Narrative Imagination and Pedagogical Innovation

Julie Levinson and
Virginia Rademacher

B abson's Global Film Series is an expression and an extension of the college's pedagogical principles. Those principles are reflected in a curriculum that finds common cause in students' business and liberal arts courses: to educate leaders who will create both economic and social value and will be conversant with a range of complex global and ethical concerns. As public gatherings of members of the college community, the screenings transcend the usual way that feature films are taught outside the realm of film studies – as narratives to be mined for moments that are directly pertinent to the topic of a given course. Our mission is broader and more ambitious than simply integrating movie screenings into classroom activities. Through contextual presentation and curricular integration of the films, the series engenders cross-disciplinary collaborations and creative pedagogies that challenge the compartmentalization of courses into different disciplines. The film series offerings, along with concomitant discussions and classroom exercises, place Babson in the vanguard of integrated business and humanities education.

Film Pedagogy

Although the discipline of films studies was not widely taught in universities until the 1960s, commercial feature films have been used in American college classrooms at least since the early years of the sound era in the 1930s (Polan, 2007; Smoodin, 2011). The notion of film culture as a valid pedagogical component was part of the progressive education movement and the general embrace of modernity that held sway in the United States during the first half of the twentieth century (Smoodin). There are many accounts of how theatrical movies have been adopted and repurposed for pedagogical purposes. In *Scenes of Instruction: The Beginnings of the U.S. Study of Film*, Dana B. Polan constructs a historiography of the discipline of film history, detailing how the emergence of academic courses in film helped to legitimize the notion of the cinema as worthy of serious study. The edited volume *Inventing Film Studies* (Grieveson & Wasson, 2008) further elucidates how an array of institutions beyond academia fostered a wide cultural acquaintance with and acceptance of movies as pedagogically useful texts. The book's contributors examine how, alongside academic institutions, cultural milieus including museums, film societies, and national film institutes "coalesced to provide forms of exhibition and reception alternative to the dominance of commercial forms and institutions; each had its own unique relationship to a larger civic vision for cinema and to cultural networks and social imperatives distinct from Hollywood" (Grieveson & Wasson, 2008, p. xx). The aptly titled *Useful Cinema* extends the consideration of movies as cultural artifacts by detailing how film exhibition in such non-theatrical, non-commercial venues as community halls, factories, and libraries positioned certain types of cinema (e.g., industrial, health, and training films) as purposefully utilitarian and didactic (Acland & Wasson, 2011).

Many of the early efforts to incorporate movies into college classrooms saw film pedagogy as a focused effort to mine narrative movies for particular subject matter that could then be applied instrumentally to a particular disciplinary focus or social purpose (Acland & Wasson, 2011). This idea of bringing films into the classroom for their direct utility to a given topic is at the center of much of the scholarly literature on film pedagogy beyond the discipline of film studies. There are numerous accounts that document the use of movies to teach topics in such disciplines as management, political science, business ethics, marketing, sociology, and history. For example, in one such discipline-focused endeavor, *Dead Poets Society* (Weir, 1989) is used to teach principles of management and organizational behavior (Serey, 1992). A broad list of titles including *The Fog of War* (Morris, 2003), *Hotel Rwanda* (George, 2004), *The Killing Fields* (Joffé, 1984), *The Godfather* (Coppola, 1972), *and Pulp Fiction* (Tarantino, 1994) are among the motley collection of films used to teach international relations (Engert & Spencer, 2009). Writer David Mamet's business-focused screenplay for *Glengarry Glen Ross* (Foley, 1992) and his suspense drama *House of Games* (Mamet, 1987) lend themselves to instruction in business ethics (Berger & Pratt, 1998). This utilitarian model of film pedagogy cherry-picks pertinent scenes and elements from the films' narratives in order to foster a discussion of their direct application to the subject at hand. In using films as, in effect, business cases, such courses tend to analyze through a single lens, thereby privileging a narrow reading of the film based on its relevance and applicability to a given topic.

The archives of the *Journal of Management Education* list dozens of articles describing experiments with deploying movies as auxiliary texts which augment the customary curricular delivery of management principles and approaches. Occasionally, professors go beyond simply integrating movies into classroom settings and preexisting syllabi to design entire courses around film texts: indeed, to use the films in lieu of conventional written texts. Gerald Smith describes one such course in organizational behavior (OB) in which he uses feature films as the primary texts for — and the organizing principle of — his class (Smith, 2009). This approach to building a syllabus around movies engages students in scenarios that allow them to directly apply and contextualize the OB theoretical models that they are learning. Such an approach avoids positioning film analysis as an occasional enjoyable alternative to the quotidian agenda of the classroom, but it still views film pedagogy as a process of homing in on those scenes or subtexts directly related to the discipline at hand and analyzing them for their immediate applicability to the course outline. This utilitarian ethos, while a valid mode of instruction, limits and undervalues the ways in which feature films can encourage students to go beyond a narrow, discipline-based, narrative-focused analysis of movies. It misses the pedagogical opportunity to view films through a prism of diverse, and sometimes competing, analytical perspectives and contexts: to understand the cinema as a complex discourse informed by its hybrid status as, at once, visual sign system, narrative art form, cultural artifact, and industrial product. By reducing the discussion of movies to pertinent plot points, it neglects a broader consideration of how films create meaning affectively and rhetorically.

Babson's Series as a Distinctive Film Pedagogy

As faculty at Babson College and co-directors of Babson's ongoing Global Film Series, we approach the challenge of repurposing an affective medium for educational purposes with a more holistic pedagogical model. We seek to expand the reach and applicability of film screenings by positioning them as a shared resource. Our public presentation of films, to which the entire college community is invited, moves the movies out of individual classrooms and into a public space to participate in "shared pleasures," in film historian Douglas Gomery's evocative phrase (Gomery, 1992). Attendance at the public screenings by students from a variety of courses and faculty with an array of disciplinary expertise creates a discursive crossroads where different spheres of knowledge and points of reference confront and enrich one another. The act of gathering together for a film is a shared experience, unlike the necessarily more individual activity of reading a text; movies are mobilizing, engaging, and immediate in ways that a written text cannot be. Perhaps most importantly, film can make complicated, challenging topics more accessible and tractable for discussion and analysis both in and out of the classroom.

Many college faculty use film in their courses only within the disciplinary confines of a specific topic rather than in an integrated fashion. With Babson's public screenings, faculty across varying disciplines can incorporate the same film, but from differing disciplinary perspectives. To help faculty broaden their purview, we develop pedagogical materials that integrate global film across management and liberal arts disciplines, and that support the use of film as a concerted mode for faculty and students to explore, collaborate, and address ethical and global concerns. The movies are augmented by pre- and post-film discussions led by an invited subject expert. They are also often preceded and succeeded by individual classroom work related to the topics, settings, and subtexts of the film.

Integration of Liberal Arts and Business Courses

The pedagogical philosophies that inform and inspire Babson's public film screenings are rooted in the college's curriculum rationale and design. Unlike many undergraduate business programs, Babson's does not dispense with its liberal arts requirements in the first two years so that students can get on with what is putatively their more useful vocational training. Instead, liberal arts and management courses are purposefully interwoven throughout the four years. The three-tiered, competency-based curriculum design — comprising foundation, intermediate, and advanced courses — is built on the conviction that all courses are invested in creating not just skilled professionals but also thoughtful and informed citizens of the world who have been exposed to a range of texts and contexts, challenges and possibilities. Babson's integrated curriculum aims to foster habits of mind that will serve students well both within and beyond their professional ventures.

Babson faculty members have worked assiduously over the years to articulate the precise underpinnings of such grandiose goals. In 2004, Professor of English Elizabeth Goldberg and Professor of Management Danna Greenberg wrote an article wryly titled, "What's a Cultural Studies Curriculum Doing in a College Like This?" (Goldberg & Greenberg, 2004). There, they discuss how the hybrid mode of inquiry known as cultural studies has been used by some courses at Babson to encourage students to explore the ways in which individual identities, aspirations, and actions are situated within and constructed by cultural practices and institutions. Among other things, a cultural studies approach locates cultural artifacts at the nexus of historical, economic, ideological, and social forces, thereby validating the products and practices of popular culture, including film, as worthy of serious consideration. By encouraging close readings of cultural texts (and, for that matter, by significantly broadening the sense of what constitutes a text), a curriculum that includes cultural studies encourages students to perform evidentiary analyses of a range of materials and to think about the contingent nature and ethical implications of individual or group actions. Such pedagogy contributes to Babson's vision of higher education — a vision that entails not simply imparting information that is directly applicable to vocational pursuits but also teaching students how to interrogate all information rigorously, analytically, and with an eye toward creative ways of applying it.

We also draw inspiration from the pedagogical aims of a White Paper written by a group of Babson faculty members, titled "Themes for Educating the Next Generation of Babson Students: Self and Contextual Awareness, SEERS, and Complementary Analytical Approaches to Thought and Action" (Greenberg et al., 2009). Babson's three overlapping themes strive to combine the humanistic abilities of critical thinking and imagining with management education to "challenge, create, and change the ways individuals address social and economic problems in society," to "tackle seemingly intractable problems, and "to examine issues from multiple perspectives" (Greenberg et al., 2009, p. 3). The three integrative pedagogical approaches — Self and Contextual

Awareness, Social, Environmental, and Economic Responsibility (SEERS), and Analytical Approaches to Thought and Action – intend to "provide students with the tools to better understand themselves as well as social and ethical contexts" (Greenberg et al., 2009, p. 3). Emphasizing heterogeneity of thought, history, and experience in the global sphere, Babson's White Paper centers on educating students who are contextually self-aware – "cognizant of how their perspective relates to the diversity of views, perspectives, and backgrounds that exist in the world" (Greenberg et al., 2009, p. 3). Babson's concept of SEERS considers issues beyond profit maximization to engage with more complex understandings of the relationship between social, economic, and environmental value. And lastly, "Analytical Approaches to Thought and Action" depend greatly on the kind of active, creative engagement that we associate with the concept of "narrative imagination" as described below (Nussbaum, 2009). Challenging assumptions requires looking at things from differing perspectives than one's own; creative innovation similarly builds from considering divergent opinions and possibilities.

While designing a film series that would be responsive to internally-generated pedagogical and curricular philosophies, we were also mindful of the work of many scholars who have written broadly about the purposes and practices of higher education. Foremost among those who shaped our programming is philosopher Martha Nussbaum, whose writings on education are widely, and justly, cited as central to the ongoing public discourse about the place of the humanities in contemporary education. In "Education for Profit, Education for Freedom" Nussbaum outlines the risks of defining education in "low-level, utilitarian terms," or what we have earlier referred to as a purely "instrumental" approach (Nussbaum, 2009, p. 6). As she argues, this emphasis on basic, marketable skills "neglects the humanistic abilities of critical thinking and imagining that are so crucial if education is really to promote human development" (Nussbaum, 2009, p. 6). She identifies three values that are essential to responsible global citizenship and that also have particular salience for our initiative. These are (1) critical thinking (2) understanding the multiple histories and heterogeneity of our world, and (3) "narrative imagination" – that is, the ability to "think what it might be like to be in the shoes of a person different from oneself, to be an intelligent reader of that person's story" (Nussbaum, 2009, p. 12).

So, how does a global film series address these pedagogical goals? As Nussbaum has observed, "Entertainment is crucial to the ability of the arts to offer perception and hope" and arts programming creates "a venue for exploring difficult issues without crippling anxiety" (Nussbaum, 2009, p. 13). Movies, arguably the most powerful affective art form, are ideal vehicles for cultivating students' narrative imaginations and for exploring complex issues and fostering meaningful discourse in a shared space. Accordingly, prominent education philosopher and critical theorist Douglas Kellner has promoted the pedagogical value of "multiple literacies" and the importance of teaching critical skills about how to understand and use "media as modes of self-expression and social activism" (Kellner, 2000, p. 203). Kellner refutes the "traditionalist" or "protectionist" view of college curricula which place popular media such as feature films as outside the academic realm (Kellner, 2000, p. 203). We might extend this same limited view to business education, which has not typically included film and other art forms as part of its pedagogy. Yet, we argue for this pedagogical hybridity. Rather than seeing film audiences as passive viewers or mere spectators, we want to prepare citizens and future business leaders to perceive their own participation and responsibility in the creation and reception of meaning through images and other forms of representation. Notably, Kellner points to the role of media literacy not only in "teaching students to be critical of media representations and discourses" but also to the role that "critical media literacy" can play in "motivating more competitive participation in the creation and analysis of media as instruments of social expression and change. [...] developing skills that will empower citizens and will make them more motivated and competent participants in social life" (Kellner, p. 203).

Ethics and International Film across the Curriculum

Since the adoption of SEERS principles at Babson, we have put particular emphasis on selecting films and speakers that highlight the ethical dimensions of the narratives. As a parallel activity, we embarked on an initiative titled "Ethics and International Film Across the Curriculum" which aims to help faculty learn how to incorporate movies into their courses as a way of teaching ethics. "Ethics and International Film across the Curriculum" constitutes part of a broader effort to strengthen undergraduate education in both business and the liberal arts by using the power of film to explore ethical questions and to create interdisciplinary conversations. The teaching of business ethics and of global responsibility has too often been cordoned off within undergraduate business education from more fundamental questions of responsible leadership, citizenship, and humanity. Ethics and social responsibility are frequently taught in business courses as individual modules or as discrete sections of a course. By segmenting business ethics from other aspects of ethical and social responsibility, questions of ethics become instrumental: What do I do in this *specific case*? "Ethics and International Film Across the Curriculum" differs from other models we have studied not only in its application of international film as a means to integrate business and liberal arts approaches to knotty ethical questions, but also in the extension of these conversations to a more *global* view – in both scope and perspective – of the teaching and practice of film and ethical decision making.

While many schools have international film series, and many business schools incorporate business ethics, these efforts often fall short precisely because they are not fully integrated into the pedagogical or curricular aims of the school, but are treated as discrete, self-contained units. Moreover, even business school methodologies that seem at least superficially aligned with our approach through their incorporation of feature films as modes to examine ethical questions still reflect many of the same limitations that we have seen in other business school models. For example, in "Teaching Business Ethics Through Popular Feature Films: An Experiential Approach," the authors Edward O'Boyle and Luca Sandoná contend that we should teach "business ethics" to business and economics students because of the "critical thinking skills needed to function more effectively in the global marketplace and the workplace" (O'Boyle & Sandona, 2014, p. 330). Yet, how are business ethics or the critical skills needed for making ethical decisions in business different than the skills that any professional would need? That any decision maker or leader would need? This narrowness of focus underscores another issue common to the incorporation of popular films in business curricula. To the extent that such films are included, the focus is almost exclusively on how the thematic content connects directly to specific contextual or business examples. For example, O'Boyle and Sandoná make no mention of how a film raises broader questions that extend beyond the specific situation to explore many different types of decisions. In effect, the authors' approach is still narrow and instrumental, rather than global in its vision.

Moreover, the authors contend that "[w]e do not argue that passive viewing of a film is superior to the more active reading of a book" (O'Boyle & Sandona, 2014, p. 331). Our viewpoint, one reinforced through Babson's global film initiative, is that film viewing – done thoughtfully – is not passive. Rather, the series is a vehicle that acknowledges the very real and powerful role of visual media and the need for actively engaging with these materials. It is all the more important because visual media are so ubiquitous in our lives, and even more so in the lives of our students; we need to help them develop the critical skills necessary to respond thoughtfully to these representations and to examine film from a wide range of perspectives.

Finally, O'Boyle and Sandoná conclude that feature films have two advantages in teaching business ethics. First, the authors claim that "films more nearly mimic real life than case studies because in a culture dominated by electronic media human beings are more influenced by what they see and hear than what they read" (O'Boyle & Sandona, 2014, p. 331). Second, films require students to sort out many ethical questions that would otherwise be defined for them in a case study (O'Boyle & Sandona, 2014, p. 331). While we welcome the idea that the use of film can provide a more open framework for engaging with challenging issues, we question the view that the thematic content of films should necessarily mimic real-life business situations or ethical conflicts. Our intentions are quite frequently just the opposite. We don't see the films we select as mimicking the students' own realities or their aspirational professional contexts, but as a way of drawing them into other spaces of "narrative imagination" that enrich their capacities to address a wide range of uncharted and yet challenging situations. As Babson's White Paper describes with respect to SEERS: "To create an ethical student is to create a student who is aware of a wide range of possibilities, explanations, and implications of actions *beyond her immediate context*" (Greenberg et al., 2009, p. 15). The best films for ethical and global engagement, then, are ones that allow us to teach and learn from one another across disciplines and to stretch the confines of our own experiences.

Methodology and Design

There are six key ingredients for making Babson's film series a successful pedagogy:

- Film programming that is responsive to the syllabi of several courses
- Training of professors in how to effectively use films as classroom texts
- Pre-assignments in classes so students are prepared for what they will see
- At the screening, pre-film introduction and post-film discussion with an invited expert
- Post-event assignments that integrate the film with other course material
- Buy-in from appropriate co-curricular groups.

By paying careful attention to all six components, we ensure that these screenings are not just one-off events but are woven into the fabric of curricular and co-curricular agendas.

In programming the film series, we first look at course offerings for the upcoming semester. Babson students' course load is split fairly evenly between management and liberal arts disciplines. We strive to find a broad range of courses — running the gamut from such fields as management, marketing, economics, and entrepreneurship to political science, history, literature, anthropology and sociology — that might link to and make use of the films that we have in mind and that will yield a genuinely cross-disciplinary discourse. Given Babson's commitment to enhancing our students' global perspectives and ethical thinking, we aim for films that foster broad international exposure and deep engagement with ethical challenges and conundrums. Among the international films that we have screened in recent years are *A Separation* (Farhadi, 2011 — Iran), *No* (Larraín, 2012 — Chile), *The Act of Killing* (Oppenheimer, 2012 — Cambodia), *The Lunchbox* (Batra, 2013 — India), *The Class* (Cantet, 2008 — France), *Raise the Red Lantern* (Yimou, 1991 — China), and *The Secret in Their Eyes* (Campanella, 2009 — Argentina). We have programmed American films as well, particularly documentaries that broach provocative ethical and social justice issues, including *Gasland II* (Fox, 2013), *The Queen of Versailles*, and *Trouble the Water* (Deal & Lessin, 2008). With each selected film, we hope for resonance with a broad array of courses and scholarly disciplines, so as to inspire a wide-ranging, free-wheeling discussion among varied constituencies and perspectives.

Once the programming is in place, we contact faculty whom we think may be interested in incorporating the series' films into their syllabi. Often, professors are uncertain about how to use films as texts, particularly if the linkages with their courses are not immediately obvious. In those cases, we reach out to small groups of interested faculty, offering both suggestions for how the film might dovetail with their syllabi and written materials that give background information and pedagogical possibilities (see Appendix A). Throughout the process, we are mindful of the curricular principles and pedagogical philosophies outlined above. What follows are a few specific instances of how we have integrated those principles and philosophies into the Global Film Series.

Using Global Film to Address SEERS

The theme of Social, Environmental, and Economic Responsibility and Sustainability (SEERS) in Babson's White Paper seeks to prepare our students to "think and act in ways that reflect and respect our interdependent world. [...] Responsibility builds on this, prompting us to ask questions about rights and justice and who has a role in ensuring rights and justice to whom." (Greenberg et al., 2009, pp. 17, 18). The discussions surrounding our screening of *Gasland, Part II*, which involved students and faculty from courses in sustainability, environmental science, management, economics, and others, provide an example of how this type of critical engagement has taken place within our Global Film Series. This film has been described both as a convincing indictment of the environmental and human dangers of fracking and as misleading and polemical, "leaving questions, large and small that can nag at you" (*New York Times*, 5 July 2013). While the *New York Times'* Mike Hale argues that "it's hard to take issue with Mr. Fox's resigned conclusion that economic and political forces will soon spread fracking around the world, no matter how harmful critics say it may be to the environment and our health," he also questions: "Would it have been a bad idea to include at least one interview with a homeowner who professes to *support* drilling? Did the dog with the missing leg somehow lose the limb because of fracking, as a dramatic cut would have us believe?" (*NYT*). Yet, it is exactly this type of shared critical distillation of complex, and perhaps seemingly intractable, issues that makes our use of global film so powerful. Such a wide-ranging interdisciplinary format actively supports the "more complex understanding of the relationship between social, economic, and environmental value creation and the inherent tensions and potential synergies that exist among the three" that the pedagogical aims of Babson's White Paper concept of SEERS underscores, not to mention the contextual ability to grapple with "complex issues from different viewpoints" (Greenberg, et al., 2009, p. 12).

The post-film discussion in this instance was led by an environmental economist who was able to invite all sorts of challenging questions regarding how we incorporate environmental risk and issues of sustainability in the cost and pricing of expendable energy resources. Moreover, among the audience were students from such energy-rich countries as Qatar and Venezuela, as well as students and faculty from China, who discussed the human costs of pollution that rapid development has created. The conversation veered to renewable energy generation and the challenges posed by the relative absence of reliable delivery systems. Had this film been shown only in an individual course, the discussion would have decidedly been focused within a single discipline, and most likely narrowed even further to the specific topic and readings the faculty member had planned to cover for that day. Yet, some of the most productive aspects of the conversations in the Global Film Series have been the cross-disciplinary sharing and generation of ideas in ways that then productively carry over into subsequent conversations across varied courses and other facets of campus life. Since students often have difficulty understanding the pertinence of what they are learning beyond the confines of a particular course, these conversations are vivid demonstrations of how any topic and any rhetorical presentation can be viewed through prismatic disciplinary lenses.

Some professors use the public discussion as a jumping-off point for their own application of the film to their syllabus. Depending on the focus of the course, any given film can serve as a launchpad for varied "readings." For instance, for *Gasland II*, the professor of an Environmental Technology class asked students to consider how the issues raised by the film related to their study of the social and environmental impact of hydraulic fracking and how the film addressed larger questions of environmental injustice. In a documentary film course, the professor focused less on the specific topic of the film and more on the ethical and representational issues that arose from the filmmakers' decisions. We purposefully program films that will allow for divergent approaches from and applications to a variety of disciplines.

Using Global Film to Address Cross-Disciplinary Connections among Business and Humanities Disciplines

The Chilean film *No* is another example of how we have used film as a mode for building cross-disciplinary conversations. *No* is ostensibly about the historic political campaign in Chile to oust the dictator Augusto Pinochet, but it can also be understood as a film that raises compelling questions about the slippage between product-based marketing and political advertising as a prompt for social change. In order to capitalize on the diverse ways to consider this film from both business and humanities perspectives, we worked with Marketing faculty to discuss ways that they might incorporate the film into their courses, and with the student-run Babson Marketing Club to promote the event. Peter Kornbluh, Director of the National Security Archives Chile Documentation Project and a key figure in unearthing many confidential documents regarding U.S. involvement in supporting the Pinochet regime, traveled from Washington, DC to introduce the film and to lead a post-film discussion. The audience for the screening included students and faculty from history, political science, marketing and economics courses as well as other interested members of the Babson community. Having an audience that crosses disciplines and finding compelling speakers with the expertise to help attendees think in creative ways about the films is central to the aims of our film series. Rather than simply screening films, we are interested in creating events that engage a diverse population, in fostering dialogues that further refute the idea of film viewing as passive, and that have a variety of pedagogical possibilities. As an example, this film served as the basis for an assignment in an undergraduate course called "After the Dictator" which focuses on post-dictatorship transitions. The assignment, entitled "How Don Draper Toppled a Dictator," called upon the students to consider both marketing and political approaches to analyze the strategies employed in the commercials for the "yes" or the "no" campaigns represented cinematically in *No* (see Appendix B).

Another salient example of the way that cross-disciplinary conversations have deepened the pedagogical range of the film series was our screening and discussion of the documentary film, *The Queen of Versailles*. With this film, we were able to bring Keri Putnam, Executive Director of the Sundance Institute, to introduce the film and lead the discussion. The film itself poses all sorts of intriguing questions, since when the filming began the project was initially about building "the largest house in America," and when the filming ended it had become about the emblematic loss of this dream, alongside the foreclosure crisis that faced many Americans when the housing bubble burst. We were also able to connect the presentation of the film to Putnam's experience at Sundance and her professional trajectory more broadly. How do independent filmmakers find financing for their projects? How do independent, artistically worthy films become commercially successful? How can our students combine their interests in the arts with sustainable business careers? The post-film discussion, then, opened the conversation not only to what had happened in the film, or to how it was made, but to the business of film in its many dimensions.

Similarly, both the Iranian film *A Separation* and the Indian film *The Lunchbox* generated powerful cross-disciplinary discussions. *A Separation* is about an Iranian couple whose marriage is falling apart. The woman wants permission to leave the country in order to create a better life for their daughter; the man does not want his wife and daughter to leave, as he has an ailing father that he needs to take care of, and therefore cannot relocate with them. Its subtexts are rich in ideas about social dynamics and power relations, and the Babson screening of the film was an example of how specific thematic content can be extended to broader ethical questions. Although the setting and situation is remote from most of our students' lives, they will almost certainly be in situations of difficult negotiations, in which both parties believe themselves to have reasonable claims, and for which there is no ready compromise.

In preparation for the screening of this film, we contacted Management faculty who teach courses in negotiations in order to provide suggestions for how the film might serve to introduce students to the subtleties and strategies of successful negotiations.

We also provided them with questions that they could use in the classroom or for written assignments related to the film (see Appendix A). Although those professors were initially skeptical of the film's pertinence to their courses, after a robust discussion among faculty from a variety of disciplinary backgrounds, they had several ideas about how to make the connection between the film's narrative and the situations that students might confront in their professional lives. In this case, bringing *A Separation* to campus not only enriched the students' experience; it also served as a professional development opportunity for faculty in their joint effort to find multiple meanings in and uses for a common text. *A Separation* inspired the sort of collegial conversations that happens too rarely for faculty ensconced in their own departments and disciplines.

Much in the same way, when we screened *The Lunchbox,* the conversations extended beyond the film's individual content to business and ethical dimensions that were of interest to diverse disciplines. *The Lunchbox* is a love story between two lonely individuals: a set-in-his-ways widower and a dissatisfied housewife. What brings them together, albeit only "virtually" (through letters and food), is the dabbawalla lunch delivery system. The film's representation of the highly successful dabbawalla system, an industry so well-executed that it has been the focus of a Harvard Business School case study and an exemplar of successful customer service techniques for FedEx, was also important to our choice of the film. At the same time, rather than simply focus on these business-oriented elements through clips or through case examples, as many business programs have done in their incorporation of *The Lunchbox*, we sought to show how the cultural dimensions revealed in the film are central to understanding both the human story and the business structure that it presents.

Using Global Film to Address Self and Contextual Awareness

As we have underscored, the pedagogical intentions for the Babson Global Film series draw in part from Babson's White Paper, including the themes of self and contextual awareness within an ethical framework: "A pedagogy designed to educate entrepreneurial thinkers in all facets of society should provide students with tools to better understand themselves as well as social and ethical contexts. [...] While students need to understand their own subjective, self-referential thinking, they must also develop the ability to move beyond their own individual perspective. Such thinking inhibits the students' ability to understand the perspective of another culture and to understand complex issues from diverse viewpoints" (Greenberg et al., 2009, p. 3, 12).

One example of a very successful film series event that grappled with challenging issues of both ethics and contextual awareness was our screening of *The Act of Killing*. While many documentary films focus on the victims of genocide or other forms of violence, this film concentrates on the torturers' self-conscious "reveal" of their own stories. Moreover, rather than just re-telling what happened, the film compels the former torturers to re-enact their mass killings in whatever cinematic genres they wish, including classic Hollywood crime scenes and lavish musical numbers. As noted in Babson's White Paper, "In courses in every discipline, faculty contend with issues of subjectivity and context. [...] The challenge for faculty is not only to present such opportunities to our students, but to help them surmount the initial discomfort that arises when they are placed in situations that reveal unsuspected biases or that undercut the certainty of some long held and perhaps unrecognized assumptions" (Greenberg et al., 2009, p. 13). What greater discomfort, what greater challenge, could there be than in trying to unravel the sources of this kind of violence and the explanation for how these killers could even seem to revel in its telling? Moreover, as with other films we include in the series, the film's narrative topic — the brutality of Indonesia's dictatorship and its legacy — was not something that was directly being covered in many undergraduate classes, just as most of those who attended the screening of *No* weren't necessarily studying Latin American dictatorships. But, the broader ethical quandaries that these films raised provoked robust discussions in a wide range of courses. What is the legal responsibility to the victims? What is the importance of acknowledging a crime, even if justice or punishment is no longer feasible? Is reconciliation possible without the admission of guilt, just by telling the story? How do people live among their perpetrators, or those who have done them harm, without wanting to do the same? Are we wrong to continue to do business with countries who violate human rights or who refuse to acknowledge injustices, or do disengagement or embargoes or boycotts harm their citizens more by isolating them politically and economically? The "humanistic abilities of critical thinking and imagining" (Nussbaum, 2009, p. 8) needed to thoughtfully examine these questions and to tolerate their ambiguity are likewise essential to the broad pedagogical and "human development" aims of Babson's White Paper: "Having a stronger, clearer sense of their perspective and an ability to think critically using others also allows students the opportunity to more fully understand and commit to their own ideas and values. [...] The ability to understand the full complexities of a situation, including the tensions and ambiguities that may be inherent in it, and to understand the full effects of one's actions on others helps one to make the most ethical choices possible, even in a situation where there is much ethical uncertainty" (Greenberg et. al., 2009, pp. 13, 15).

Conclusion

With Babson's Global Film Series, we have sought to create cross-disciplinary conversations, to encourage new pedagogies through film study, to explore ethical questions that move beyond narrow disciplinary or situational parameters, and to create a shared space for our students to explore their own thinking and that of cultures and experiences far removed from their own. With our programming of this series and the pedagogical materials we have developed to support it, we have drawn from the themes of Babson's White Paper, as well as from the ideas of scholars such as Martha Nussbaum and Douglas Kellner, who laud the power of interdisciplinary synergies among business and humanities disciplines, among traditional literature and new literacies — all in the effort to create new spaces for teaching and learning that enrich our own thinking and that of our students. Martha Nussbaum has argued that "[i]f we do not insist on the crucial importance of humanities and the arts, they will drop away because they don't make money. They only do what is more precious: the humanities and the arts make a world that is worth living in, people who are able see other human beings as equals, and nations that are able to overcome fear and suspicion in favor of sympathetic and reasoned debate" (Nussbaum, 2009, p. 13). We believe that business education needs this perspective, and that film is an excellent forum for supporting this integration.

References

Acland, C., & Wasson, H. (Eds.). (2011). *Useful cinema*. Durham, NC: Duke University Press.

Berger, J., & Pratt, C. B. (1998 December). Teaching business-communication ethics with controversial films. *Journal of Business Ethics, 17*(16), 1817–1823.

Engert, S., & Spencer, A. (2009). International relations at the movies: Teaching and learning about international politics through film. *Perspectives, 17*(1), 83–103.

Goldberg, E., & Greenberg, D. (2004). What's a cultural studies curriculum doing in a college like this? *Liberal Education, 90*(3), 16–25.

Gomery, D. (1992). *Shared pleasures: A history of movie presentation in the United States*. Madison, WI: University of Wisconsin Press.

Greenberg, D. N., McKone-Sweet, K., Chase, D., Crosina, L., DeCastro, J., Deets, S., ... Yellin, J. (2009). *Themes for educating the next generation of Babson students:*

Self and contextual awareness, SEERS, and complementary analytical approaches to thought and action. Babson College white paper, Wellesley, MA.

Grieveson, L., & Wasson, H. (Eds.). (2008). *Inventing film studies.* Durham, NC: Duke University Press.

Kellner, D. (2000). Multiple literacies and critical pedagogies: New paradigms. *Revolutionary pedagogies, cultural politics, instituting education and the discourse of theory.* New York, NY: Routledge.

Nussbaum, M. (2009). Education for profit, education for freedom. *Liberal Education, 95*(3), 6–13.

O'Boyle, E. J., & Sandona, L. (2014). Teaching business ethics through popular feature films: An experiential approach. *Journal of Business Ethics, 121*(3), 329–340.

Polan, D. B. (2007). *Scenes of instruction: The beginnings of the U.S. study of film.* Berkeley, CA: University of California.

Serey, T. (1992). Carpe diem: Lessons about life and management from dead poets society. *Journal of Management Education, 16*(1), 375–381.

Smith, G. W. (2009). Using feature films as the primary instructional medium to teach organizational behavior. *Journal Management Education, 33*(August), 462–489.

Smoodin, E. (2011). What a power for education!: The cinema and sites of learning in the 1930s. In C. R. Acland & H. Wasson (Eds.), *Useful cinema.* Durham, NC: Duke University Press.

Appendix A: Teaching Materials for Faculty in Varied Disciplines

A1 ETHICS AND INTERNATIONAL FILM ACROSS THE CURRICULUM

Film Title: *A Separation*

Country: Iran

Director: Asghar Farhadi

Year: 2011

Principal Characters: Simin (Leila Hatami), Nader (Peyman Moaadi), Termeh (Sarina Farhadi), Hojjat (Shahab Hosseini), Razieh (Sareh Bayat), Nader's father (Ali Asghar Shahbazi)

Summary: A married couple is faced with a difficult decision — to improve the life of their child by moving to another country or to stay in Iran and look after a deteriorating parent who has Alzheimer's disease. As they interact with other Iranians and with state institutions, their personal situation becomes increasingly complicated and their marriage becomes strained to the breaking point. Beyond being compelling story about individual lives, *A Separation* is a rich and resonant contemplation of personal ethics and social power.

Discussion Questions

- How do personal problems intersect with social institutions? How do civil law, religious law, and individual conscience collide in the film?
- How is social class presented in the film? What tensions are revealed between those of different classes and education levels?
- How is power vested in individuals and institutions? To what extent do these characters have power to decide their own fate? In what ways is their power to determine their lives limited by state power? How is the philosophical distinction between individual free will and social determinism conveyed?
- The film is full of delicate negotiations between individuals. Life seems to be a serial transaction. Cite some of the points of negotiation. How are these worked out (or

not)? Is it possible to be fair to everyone in these negotiations?

- With whom do our dramatic sympathies lie? Does this shift during the film?

- A contrast is set up between the main adults in the film (who tend not to get along with one another) and the children (who bond in spite of their differences). What is the director implying with this contrast?

- Who is right? What does our answer to that question tell us about our own values? About those of the film's director?

- There are several points in the film where characters do not act ethically but, instead, lie or manipulate to protect their own self-interest. Are these actions justified? How do we fell when even Termeh lies to protect her father?

- How is the legal system depicted in the film? To what extent is it dispassionate and fair-minded?

- Who is the moral center of the story? Can any character lay claim to the moral high ground?

- The film suggests that human equilibrium and well-being is very fragile and can change quickly. What, if anything, does it offer in terms of social stability and hope?

- Consider the camera set-up and duration of the first and last shots of the film. Why did the director choose to present the opening and closing action in this way? How does that choice position the audience vis-à-vis the characters? What does the last shot suggest about the future?

SOME IDEAS FOR CLASSROOM USE

- Have students choose one of the many negotiations that take place in the film. Analyze how each character jockeys for position and power in presenting his/her case. Then speculate how the negotiation might have been conducted more fairly and effectively. Students can role-play the characters and work to negotiate towards a more equitable outcome.

- Ask students about their own country's social and legal institutions. To what extent are they benevolent and fair-minded? Ask for examples showing how does one's social station enhances or limits social justice and legal rights.

- This film offers a rare glimpse behind the headlines into the daily lives of Iranians. What commonalities can students cite with these characters? In what ways does the film surprise us with its characterizations and depiction of quotidian existence in Tehran?

Additional Resources:

Interviews with the director:

http://www.emanuellevy.com/interview/a-separation-interview-with-the-director-asghar-farhadi/

http://www.ifc.com/fix/2012/01/asghar-faradi-interview-a-separation

http://www.avclub.com/articles/asghar-farhadi,67055/

http://www.ropeofsilicon.com/interview-asghar-farhadi-separation/

A2 ETHICS AND INTERNATIONAL FILM ACROSS THE CURRICULUM

Film Title: *The Queen of Versailles*

Country: the United States

Director: Lauren Greenfield

Year: 2012

Genre: Documentary

Principal Cast: Jackie and David Siegel (as themselves)

Summary: Screened on the opening night of the 2012 Sundance film festival, the film won an award for best director, and has since become one of the most watched documentaries of 2012. The film follows the real-life boom and bust story of time-share mogul David Siegel and his wife, Jackie, as they aspire to build the largest single family home in America — a 90,000 square foot mansion modeled after the Palace of Versailles. Rather than a simple critique, the film compels us to examine the Siegels' experience as emblematic of broader fissures in contemporary America where, like the Siegels, many of us continue to buy into the promise of a powerful American dream shaped by wealth.

Discussion Questions

- Director Lauren Greenfield has said of the film, "It was the same [old] story about the American dream, but really about the flaws as much as the virtues of that dream, as well as about the mistakes that were made because of the economic crisis." What is this vision of the American dream? How does the Siegels' story reflect or revise the American dream, in your view?

- Greenfield has quoted Jackie as saying, "Our story is like so many other people's, but on a bigger level and with bigger proportions." To what extent is Greenfield successful in depicting the Siegels' struggles as essentially no different (except on a bigger scale) from those of the tens of thousands of individuals who faced similar consequences from the economic crisis?

- What changes do we see in Jackie and David as their economic situation deteriorates during the film's making? With whom (if anyone) do our dramatic sympathies lie? Does this change throughout the film?

- Who has the power in Jackie and David's relationship, as depicted in the film? How does each try to wield power or to influence the other? Who wins — if anyone?

- By 2010, the time-share market had dried up because so many buyers had overextended themselves on their unit mortgages. Even as the Siegels' credit situation deteriorates, David refuses to sell his other obsession, a $600 million high-end time-share complex on the Las Vegas strip that he'd personally financed through loans. David Siegel has said, "We need to learn to live within our means; we need to get back to reality. I was using cheap money to buy big buildings and I thought it would go on forever, and when they took away the money, I was like, Whoa." To what extent are David Siegel's comments convincing? Is this a morality tale?

- Is Greenfield right when she argues that the story "in a sense has a happy ending, because you see what's really important to them [the Siegels]?" Do you have the sense that the Siegels learned from their experience? On a broader level, has America learned the lessons of the

(continued)

economic crisis? Have American values been in some way redefined? If so, how?

- Greenfield and Jackie are both quoted as saying they became friends during the filming of the movie, and Jackie has appeared at various promotional events for the film, despite the fact that David filed a lawsuit against Greenfield for defamation. Do you believe that Greenfield's friendship with Jackie is real? What ethical questions might be posed by this personal relationship with the subject? What advantages and disadvantages might it create in the creation of a documentary?

- Is reality TV "real?" Is it "documentary?" What makes a documentary credible in your view? How would you categorize *Queen of Versailles*? Why?

- What did you think of the ending of the film? Why might Greenfield have chosen to end the film this way? If you would have ended the film differently, what changes would you have made?

- Postscript: Since the conclusion of filming, the Siegels have since resumed construction of their Versailles-scale mansion. Do you read the film any differently in light of this knowledge?

SOME IDEAS FOR CLASSROOM USE

- Have students write the boom and bust story of Westgate Resorts as a business case. Then, have the students present the case and potential approaches to saving the company. Finally, look at what actions David Siegel has actually taken to repair the company. Analyze these decisions and their outcome.

- Ask students to analyze specific scenes from an earlier and later section of the film. From whose perspective is the story being told? How is the camera telling the story? How does the change in the Siegels' experience come across visually, along with the narrative? This could be a written assignment, or an in-class analysis/presentation. How does the film explore issues of social class? Of gender and power?

- For Business Law: Have students research what happens legally to a time share corporation (and its owners of its units) when it files for bankruptcy. See: http://online.wsj.com/article/SB124701522076409321.html. Research the example of Consolidated Enterprises and have students provide a summary and analysis of the ethical issues involved.

- For Negotiations: Have students analyze the ethical issues in David Siegel's defamation lawsuit against Lauren Greenfield. Why did the judge rule in favor of Greenfield? Divide students into different groups in charge of representing Greenfield or Siegel, and have them negotiate for their client to reach a settlement.

Additional Resources:

http://harvardmagazine.com/2012/11/the-queen-of-versailles

http://nymag.com/news/intelligencer/encounter/jackie-siegel-2013-5/

NPR interview:

http://www.npr.org/2012/07/20/157060920/in-new-documentary-our-economic-fall-writ-large

Wall Street Journal — Story Behind the Making of *The Queen of Versailles*

http://live.wsj.com/video/the-story-behind-queen-of-versailles/D72C3357-FB5B-4894-A39B-084CF5EF0A5A.html#!D72C3357-FB5B-4894-A39B-084CF5EF0A5A

Appendix B: Sample Post-Screening Classroom Assignment

CVA 2458 After the Dictator (Fall 2013)

Cultural Analysis Assignment: "How Don Draper Toppled a Dictator"

Drawing from the film *No* as an example, you will analyze the political strategies of the Opposition (No), the Pinochet campaign (Sí/Yes) *or* the uses of marketing strategies employed by either side (contesting/upholding) in **another authoritarian regime/case** you find of interest.

You may take the role of opposition strategist or of political consultant working for the authoritarian regime to analyze issues of brand management, potential opposition, how effectively the message is controlled, and questions of ethics. You will share your results as part of a "speed dating" exercise in class [designated date]. **Your assignment is due by class that day – and you should submit it online prior to class** *and bring a copy to class*. We will spend 20-30 minutes of that class sharing these projects and then the remainder of the time on the final group projects.

Your analysis (of approximately 2–3 pages double-spaced (12 pt font), no more!) should address **one of the following**:

- An in-depth look at a particular ad concentrating on its overall approach (content, creative strategy, type of ad, audience etc.) from the *perspective of* **EITHER** *the* consultant FOR the candidate OR the opposition (critiquing it) – that is, how would you attack it?
- A comparison among advertising approaches (e.g., Yes (Chile) versus No (Chile)
- Using another case/country example – Analysis of a **specific** *political campaign image or visual strategy* that you can relate to the background of the youth movements we read about in *The Dictator's Learning Curve*. This strategy could be to contest a particular youth vote or to leverage it.
- A *storyboard* analysis of one of a particular political advertisement/campaign images. This would involve breaking down the ad into various images and analyzing them individually, along with their function as part of a whole. So, the *Daisy ad*, for example, can be broken down into the various images in the power point we looked at. What is the intent of each of these images? What strategies are being used? And how to they fit – in relation to one another – to the overall message? You would apply this same type of analysis to a different example.

Sample Resources:

Chile: NO
- http://www.youtube.com/watch?v=l9QR1f-UnEo (No)

Chile Sí (YES):
- http://www.youtube.com/watch?v=egz62fcs1Fw (Si)

*See documents attached with translations ...

Russia: Nashi
- http://www.youtube.com/watch?v=-5L5I_7r2lA (nashi)

Venezuela:
- Nicholas Maduro (pro-Chavez legacy): http://www.now-thisnews.com/news/hugo-chavez-heaven-hanging-out-che/
- Chavez: Ultra Beta campaign:
- http://www.youtube.com/watch?v=Ks7lRqEEioA
- http://articles.chicagotribune.com/2012-09-23/news/sns-rt-us-venezuela-election-ghettobre88m01f-20120922_1_governor-henrique-capriles-youth-vote-petare

Egypt ("We are all Khaled Said") (social media)
- http://www.nytimes.com/2012/02/19/books/review/how-an-egyptian-revolution-began-on-facebook.html
- http://www.nytimes.com/2011/02/06/world/middleeast/06face.html?pagewanted=all (We are all Khaled Said)

Discussion Questions

I've provided some sample questions here. You do NOT need to answer all of these (by any means – please don't!) but these may be helpful as you decide what to explore. No matter what, your essay should address the first 3:

1. What does this advertisement/campaign strategy aim to achieve? What is its overall message?
2. What choice does the advertisement/strategy offer?
3. How effective is the message managed/conveyed? How ethically?

Then, depending upon your focus ....

CONTENT:

What happens in it? (Is there a plot or storyline? What is it?)

(continued)

Can you identify an overall theme? (hope, failure, happiness, accusation, etc.)

What type of ad would you characterize it as? (from the typology in class, and negative/positive)

What assertions does it make?

How is the candidate portrayed?

Who is *in* the ad? What does this suggest?

What sort of emotional response does the ad try to create?

What attributes or characteristics are associated with the candidate?

What policies are associated with the candidate?

Does the ad concentrate on the candidate or the opponent?

What is the general tone of the advertisement? What mood does it create? Does this shift? If so, where in the ad? How does it do this?

AUDIENCE

Who is the ad's intended audience? How does this shape the ad?

What is the age, gender, economic level etc of the audience?

How is likely to pay attention or be influenced by this ad?

CREATIVE ASPECTS

How does the ad use audio?

Does the ad use music, voice, voice-over, or sound effects? To what effect?

How many speakers are in the ad? Are they male or female? What does this suggest?

How many shots are used? Are successive shots visually or thematically connected? How?

What kinds of images are juxtaposed?

Are there close-ups? Medium shots? Long shots?

Does it make use of particular lighting or color schemes? (predominance of certain colors, for example, or absence of colors?)

What sort of camera angles are used, and to what effect?

13 Creating Space for Innovation: The Role of a "Design Zone" within a Business School

Sebastian K. Fixson, Victor P. Seidel and Jennifer Bailey

Introduction

Space matters! The physical space in which individuals work matters for both efficacy and efficiency, and it has long been known that smart workspace design can improve the way in which individuals communicate and coordinate their efforts (Allen, 1977). But what about the effect of physical space on students in their efforts for learning how to innovate? The physical spaces in which we teach may not always be aligned with what is required for our pedagogical approach, and our objective in this chapter is to explore the design of learning spaces in the context of teaching and learning the innovation process.

Helping students develop the skills and capacity to innovate is one of the important tasks of higher education today (Wagner, 2012). Recently, experiential approaches to learning to innovate have been the focus of course development in business, engineering, and design schools (Fixson, 2009). In such an experiential approach, learning the innovation process combines an awareness of the methods used as well as the exercise of the practices of innovating. Delivering educational offerings that cover the innovation process goes beyond designing individual courses, requiring consideration of the entire curriculum (Seidel, Marion, & Fixson, 2014) and, we will argue, the physical space in which such courses are provided.

In order to effectively develop courses and curricula, we must first understand what actually happens when individuals innovate. Parsing the innovation process into specific activities allows recognition of how these activities differ from each other along a number of dimensions, such as skills to be learned and emotional states required. For example, some activities demand paying attention with all of one's senses to empathically understand motivations and behaviors of target customers; other activities require the quiet and thoughtful search for patterns in disparate data; and still other activities require high-energy bursts of collaboration in small teams.

Helping students to learn the range of innovation activities requires an educator to pay careful attention to such things as the creation of effective interdisciplinary teams, the best way to employ problem-based learning, how to promote effective iteration by students, and the appropriate use of physical space (Fixson & Read, 2012). This last element, appropriate physical space, is the focus of this chapter. We begin with a brief review of the history of learning spaces in business education, we proceed to link innovation activities and requirements for an appropriate design and innovation space, we discuss the effects that teaching in these new spaces has on the role of the teacher, and we close with reporting on our own experiences with a newly created innovation space, the "Design Zone" at Babson College.

A History of Learning Spaces for Business Education

The design of a course or a curriculum is not only the design of lecture topics, homework assignments, and exams, it is also the selection of the physical space in which learning takes place. Business schools often started from within existing departments or schools, such as the Wharton School's founding in 1881 as part of the main faculty of Arts and Sciences or the Harvard Business School's establishment out of the department of Economics, using temporary space in existing teaching halls. Stand-alone business schools also typically drew upon the conventional classroom designs of the time. The main pedagogical focus of business education was on the provision of lectures, using the traditional classroom space which was well-suited to the approach of a professor on a high stage in good view of a room of students who themselves were not intended to interact with one another.

In contrast to the lecture format, the case study method was a novel approach to business education, involving a more discursive and participatory format. At the Harvard Business School, leading up to the move to a new campus in 1925, architecture professor Charles W. Killam and architecture student Harry Korslund sketched out designs for classrooms that would support the new case method of teaching (Cruikshank, 1987). This was the first very deliberate design of a space for business education, and the history of the experience there notes that it was an iterative process to arrive at the style that has diffused so widely today. For example, the Harvard Business School Centennial history (Harvard Business School, 2014) notes that early case classrooms used small desks attached to the arm of each chair, making it difficult to spread out reading material and making it impractical to use a later ubiquitous design feature of case classrooms which was that of name cards. In the earliest case classrooms, professors sat elevated behind a curtained barricade at the front of the classroom, prohibiting the more interactive case teaching style common today. Incremental adjustments to the case classroom design were made in the 1950s, including the development of a full-sized mock-up to be evaluated by students and faculty for sight-lines, comfort, and acoustics. The design criteria of a case study classroom are contrasted to the lecture classroom in Table 1.

There have been different experiments in other spaces for business education as well. The use of small seminar rooms has featured in higher education in a variety of contexts. At Babson College in the 1940s, small seminar rooms were outfitted to function as example boardrooms (as shown in Figure 1), simulating the space that graduates might find themselves in later in their careers (Murlkern, 1995). The use of seminar rooms as a complement to larger lecture and case classrooms has figured to differing degrees over the decades. For example, a broader use of seminar rooms has been part of a recent curriculum redesign at Stanford, in conjunction with constructing a new campus for the business school that more than doubled the number of such rooms. In this case, the change in physical space requirements was done in response to a shift to provide more personal interaction than had been possible with larger lecture rooms.

Design spaces are the most recent initiative in thinking about how physical space and pedagogical objectives are intertwined. As we outline in Table 1, a focus on a design space corresponds with a focus on appropriate areas for experiential learning, which is often team-based rather than individual, and in which the teacher needs to interact much more closely than in lecture or case based approaches. The focus of this form of learning space is on a team of students as the unit of analysis and, in many ways, the development of design

Table 1: Overview of Learning Spaces for Business Education.

	Lecture Classroom	Case Study Classroom	Seminar Room	Design Spaces
Decade of main introduction	1880	1920	1940	2000
Pedagogical focus	Lectures	Case study discussion	Small group discussion	Experiential learning
Space design objectives: teacher's role	Visibility of professor and his or her broadcast surfaces important	Visibility of professor and his or her broadcast surfaces important	Facilitator of discussion important	Interaction of professor with individuals and teams important
Space design objectives: learner's role	No interaction assumed	Interaction among large number of individual students	Interaction among small number of individual students	Interaction among student teams important. Space directly supports varied experiential learning activities
Examples	Wharton: Lecture theaters, 1880s	Harvard: Allston campus move, 1925. Babson: Campus renewal, 1950s	Babson: Boardroom format, 1949. Stanford: Seminar focus, 2007	Stanford: d. school, 2004. Harvard: iLab, 2011. Babson: Design Zone, 2014

Figure 1: A 1949 Babson Classroom Used to Simulate Boardroom Discussion. *Photo*: Murlkern (1995).

spaces is similar to the use of team-based laboratory work common in the sciences and engineering. Recent interesting design spaces with a campus-wide approach have been the d.school at Stanford and the iLab at Harvard. Both have been efforts at providing a large space for campus-wide programs. As we will discuss, the Babson "Design Zone" has been an effort specifically tailored to bringing a design space for teaching innovation right at the heart of a business school.

Our brief review of the history of learning spaces in business education shows how a range of spaces have been appropriate to meet the needs of a certain pedagogical dimension. This layering of new types of spaces has given both teachers and students a wider variety of physical spaces in which to interact based on the learning objectives of a given class. The learning space with which business schools are most newly experimenting is the design space, and we next turn our attention to a more detailed analysis of the range of activities that occur in an innovation project, and how each activity requires a different set of ingredients.

Teaching and Learning the Innovation Process

Various innovation process descriptions have emerged over the years. An important strand of these descriptions originated in thoughts about design as a process that humans use to generate and test alternatives (Simon, 1996). With the emergence of computers and a new need to focus on human-computer interaction, an explicit focus on the user of the design outcome was added (Norman & Draper, 1986). Recent innovation process descriptions still contain these elements of user focus and iteration, often brought under the label of "design thinking." For example, IDEO's CEO Tim Brown frames the design and innovation process as three overlapping spaces of inspiration, ideation, and implementation (Brown, 2008). A leader in promoting design thinking, Stanford's d-school labels five modes of its process as evaluate, define, ideate, prototype, and test. While these descriptions of the innovation process differ in the granularity of their process decomposition and their labeling of individual components, almost all design-focused methods include three broad sets of activities, which we term needsfinding, ideation, and prototyping (Seidel & Fixson, 2013). It is important to note that these sets of activities are not necessarily done within a specific temporal sequence, as they can occur repeatedly throughout an innovation project.

In performing needfinding activities, the project team tries to deeply understand the nature of an innovation problem, including whether a problem as initially formulated is actually the right problem to work on. Taking a human-centered perspective, the team tries to understand the motivation behind the need, learn about context in which the user is embedded, and search for insights for new and better solutions. Once the problem or innovation opportunity can be clearly articulated, a set of ideation activities is concerned with generating possible solution options. Various tools and techniques generally aim at generating a solution pool that is both large and diverse. A third set of activities, under the banner of prototyping, focuses on moving from a large number of solution options to a smaller number for consideration as the final innovation. This set of activities includes the testing, selection, combining, and re-shaping of solution ideas. While these sets of activities are presented sequentially, in practice there is considerable iteration and overlap among them.

These design-focused activities are central to the front-end of any innovation process, but there are additional elements of learning the innovation process that fall outside this realm. For example, learning specific design-for-manufacturing techniques or the steps in fabricating complex prototypes can also be important aspects in implementing an innovation that are not necessarily included in an innovation course adopting a design thinking approach.

MATCHING INNOVATION ACTIVITIES AND PHYSICAL SPACES

Although innovation work clearly requires the acquisition of design methods and techniques, innovating is not an activity that can be performed by exclusively following a pre-defined formula. It is important to recognize that innovation inherently involves drawing from an appropriate mindset as well (Liedtka, 2014). These mindsets, in turn, are impacted by the physical environment that humans experience when engaging in design activities (Thoring, Luippold, & Mueller, 2012).

Acknowledging these strong linkages between the skills, mindsets, and physical environment to achieve high performance in innovation activities (Doorley & Witthoft, 2012), leads us to investigate in greater detail the actual spatial requirements for each of the activities sorted under the headings needsfinding, ideation, and prototyping. Below we will discuss for each innovation activity the skills to be learned, the mindset required, and how a certain form of physical space supports each activity.

Needsfinding Activities

Needsfinding includes three major types of activities: User research, secondary research, and synthesis (Table 2). User research consists

Table 2:   Needsfinding Activities and Their Supporting Conditions.

Major Activities	Skills to be Learned	Appropriate Mindset	How Environment Supports the Activity and Learning
User research (primary research)	Interviewing, observing, and self-experiencing	Empathic, curious	Location (short distance between workspace and users/stakeholders)
Secondary research	Searching for, analyzing, and compiling relevant information	Analytic	Connectivity (Internet connection and access to data bases); limited distractions
Synthesizing, searching for insights	Recognizing patterns, forming associations	Imaginative, creative, contemplative	Vertical work surfaces critical (allow viewing large amount of various data simultaneously)
			Capability to share dynamic materials (e.g., video)

of interviewing and observing users and other important stakeholders, as well as possibly putting oneself in the user's experience. The appropriate mindset for this activity is empathic and curious. The tools needed by students are appropriate "recording" mechanisms such as pen and paper, a voice recorder for audio, and cameras for photos and videos. As a consequence, the physical environment that often serves best for the data collection portion of user research is the user's own environment; depending on the project this could be, for instance, his home, her work, or a public space. The design space itself does not play a large role in this activity, except for how the location of the space is proximate to the users under study. However, the ability to lend audio or video recording technology to students for such ethnographic work can be helpful.

A second activity is in performing secondary research, such as collecting information about markets, industries, competitors, regulations, and intellectual property. This work requires a more analytic mindset. As a consequence the environment should provide connectivity to relevant data and, thus, computer access and workspace for the team is the main support required.

The third major activity in needsfinding, synthesizing, builds on the output of first two activities. Once both primary research and secondary research have generated sufficient amount of interesting and relevant data, the next task is to mine this data for new insights. The innovation teams search for hitherto unnoticed patterns and relationships, forming associations among otherwise disconnected data elements. This activity requires both an imaginative, creative, and contemplative mindset, as the task is to imagine unarticulated needs and to interpret ambiguities. This work often includes construction of data-visualization tools such as "personas" (representations of a typical user) and "journey maps" (representations of a customer experience). The physical space that best supports this activity enables the innovation team to view many different pieces of heterogeneous information simultaneously. This requirement, also observed in "war rooms" and "command centers," is best accommodated by providing lots of vertical work surfaces such as whiteboards and pin boards, allowing students to spreading out data such as quotes, diagrams, tables, figures, and photos. Ideally, the space also includes the possibility to review dynamic data such as audio and video files through advanced projection systems.

Ideation Activities

The ideal starting point for ideation activities is a well-defined problem or opportunity statement that includes any important constraints. The first set of ideation activities, idea generation, is divergent in nature; it strives to generate quickly large quantities of solution options, ideally exhibiting a large diversity. To achieve this goal, the activities are themselves guided and constrained (Table 3). For example, to avoid group think and ensure diverse input, an innovation team can start by all members individually generating ideas by themselves and then merging all ideas into an idea pool.

Table 3:   Ideation Activities and Their Supporting Conditions.

Major Activities	Skills to be Learned	Appropriate Mindset	How Environment Supports the Activity and Learning
Idea generation (individual)	Accessing own creativity	Imaginative, optimistic, inquisitive	Space that allows stimuli but avoids distractions
			Tools and space to rapidly sketch out emerging ideas should be readily available
Idea generation (team-based)	Collaborative creative work	Imaginative, optimistic, energetic, and tolerant	Space that allows upright body posture to engage body and mind for entire team (e.g., high tables/bar stools)
			Vertical work surfaces to display developing ideas quickly and for all team members to see
Idea shaping	Stretching/relaxing of elements of raw ideas to improve idea quality	Imaginative, optimistic, reflective	Vertical work surfaces that allow spatial positioning of ideas to display relative risk/ potential

This activity is best supported by an environment that provides stimuli for the task but otherwise avoids distraction. Tools that allow quick recording and display of individual ideas, such as paper and pencils, should be readily available. If, on the other hand, the goal is to take advantage of collective idea development where individuals build upon each other's ideas, then a group brainstorming can be the right activity. For such team-based idea generation activity, the best environments support the required attitudes of being imaginative, optimistic, energetic, and tolerant. The ideal space for this activity encourages an upright body posture and movement to increase energy levels, for example by using high tables and bar stools. The physical space should also provide sufficient vertical work surface for the quick display of sketches of emerging ideas for all team members to see during the activity.

The second ideation activity aims at shaping ideas to improve their fit with the identified need. This involves re-shaping their degree of novelty, making them more useful through feature elimination or combination or even merging ideas. Idea shaping requires a mix of imaginative, optimistic, and reflective mindsets, ideally supported by large wall areas that allow relative spatial positioning of ideas to stimulate stretching, or relaxing, elements of the ideas.

Prototyping Activities

Prototyping activities focus on reducing uncertainty, including tools to sift through many possible ideas and learn about which ones will work. As we illustrate in Table 4, it is helpful to split the range of prototyping activities into two groups.

In the early stages, prototyping is aimed not at validating any particular idea but instead at learning about the potential of certain

Table 4: Prototyping Activities and Their Supporting Conditions.

Major Activities	Skills to be Learned	Appropriate Mindset	How Environment Supports the Activity and Learning
Early prototyping	Intuition, attention to unanticipated/ interesting outcomes	Curious, creative, imaginative, observant, failure tolerant	Provides access to tools and materials to allow quick design and construction of simple prototypes
			Enables fast iterations
Later prototyping	Hypothesis formulation	Attention to detail, precision, experimental perspective	Provides vertical work surfaces to develop, design, and plan experiments
	Design and execution of experiments to test hypotheses		Provides access to tools and materials to design and construct prototypes for experiments

concepts. The relevant skills to be learned for this activity are the ability to reduce a concept to one of its core elements, construct rough prototypes which mimic only the dimension of interest, and put them "out there" to see how users react. Successful early prototyping is driven by curiosity and creativity paired with attentive observation and a high tolerance for unexpected outcomes, some of which might be termed "failures" in some people's minds. Spaces that appropriately support this process provide access to materials and tools to quickly mock up prototypes and allow repeating this process quickly to increase the learning velocity.

After the initial explorative prototyping has produced some promising concepts, later prototyping requires a rather scientific approach to problem-solving and testing. Hypotheses need to be articulated, testing procedures defined, prototypes built, and experiments conducted. This form of prototyping requires more attention to detail and a more rigorous attitude. The physical space to support this activity needs to provide the option to layout testing plans and procedures, similar to a small project on its own. Of course, access to tools, materials, and actual workshop space remains as critical for this later form of prototyping as it was for the earlier form.

The Babson College "Design Zone"

We had the opportunity here at Babson College to create a design space that would serve several courses in product design, innovation, and entrepreneurship. Current course offerings span both the undergraduate and graduate student populations and include: (i) an undergraduate integrated product design course co-taught by faculty from Babson College, Olin College of Engineering, and Massachusetts College of Art and Design; (ii) an undergraduate course on affordable design and entrepreneurship co-taught by faculty from Babson College and Olin College of Engineering; (iii) an undergraduate course on social entrepreneurship; (iv) a graduate product design course; and (v) a year-long graduate design and entrepreneurship action project-based course. Product design and innovation had been taught at Babson for many years but prior efforts used a fairly generic project meeting room as the main space for such classes, consisting of a set of several conference tables and rolling desk chairs as the main space for such classes.

In the spring and summer of 2014, we had the opportunity to design a classroom for teaching design and innovation from scratch, which became known as the "Design Zone." In advance of specifying the criteria for the novel classroom, we visited and consulted with colleagues at the Stanford d.school on their experience running and experimenting with a large campus-wide design space (c.f. Doorley & Witthoft, 2012). From this insight and with a consideration of the innovation activities and classes we would run at Babson within the space available right at the heart of a business school, we developed a list of features we needed our design space to have. There were three primary modes the design space had to support:

1. Collaborative creative mode: To support both generative and associative work by teams.
2. Presentation mode: For lectures and presentations.
3. Workshop mode: To enable building physical prototypes.

The Babson Design Zone was to be built directly within a business school for the use of business students and with a primary focus on coursework. Beyond courses, the Design Zone was planned to serve as independent workspace for students and as space for events on campus and to support a culture of experiential learning on campus. The location of the Design Zone was to be in the center of the graduate school and to feature a boundary defined by glass windows and glass doors, enabling others to easily see the work underway inside. Because we would have to be able to use the design space with multiple courses, two additional requirements became very important:

- Flexibility: The space needed to be flexible in that room configurations could be easily changed, both between modes within a course, and between courses.
- Storage: We needed space to store project materials when the space was used by other courses. An important criterion here was that storing and re-deploying project work should be easy and quick.

The resulting Design Zone is pictured in Figure 2, and it has many features that distinguish it from a typical meeting room for project work. The space features concrete floors to make things easier to move and to exhibit a less polished and sensitive impression than carpet. High tables and bar stools encourage an active body posture. All tables and moveable whiteboards are on wheels to allow quick reconfiguration of the room. Almost all walls are covered with whiteboards or pin-boards to serve as vertical work surfaces, and the room also includes two types of moveable whiteboards, Z-racks that can be quickly deployed and T-walls that are sturdier. The T-walls feature hooks such that removable whiteboards can be hung on them for each class; in this way, student design teams can customize their work environment even if the space is used by others. One corner of the design room serves as material

Figure 2:   The Babson Design Zone.

and tool storage place; student and project materials are stored in a separate hallway outside the Design Zone. Figure 3 shows the schematic layout of the Design Zone.

EXPERIENCES WITH THE DESIGN ZONE

We have now had many experiences in making use of a design space, and we have come to reflect on the opportunities and challenges that such a space presents to instructors. There are many positive aspects to having a purpose-build design space. First, we generally find that through the use of raised work surfaces and high stools, students tend to take a more active physical stance within the classroom which also translates to a higher energy dynamic within the space when compared with a traditional lecture or case study classroom. An example of students engaged in some ideation work is given in Figure 4. Second, the space enables the instructor to walk up to close proximity to each student − there are no middle seats far from an instructor's reach − and so a more personal connection can be made with any student, not just those sitting in the front row of a classroom. In Figure 5 we show an example of a student prototyping exercise. As instructors who like to get to know our students well, we have found this ability to hone in on each and every student to be a positive experience. Due to its flexibility, the Design Zone can also be configured in a presentation mode for end-of-semester project presentations (Figure 6) or for small group design reviews (Figure 7).

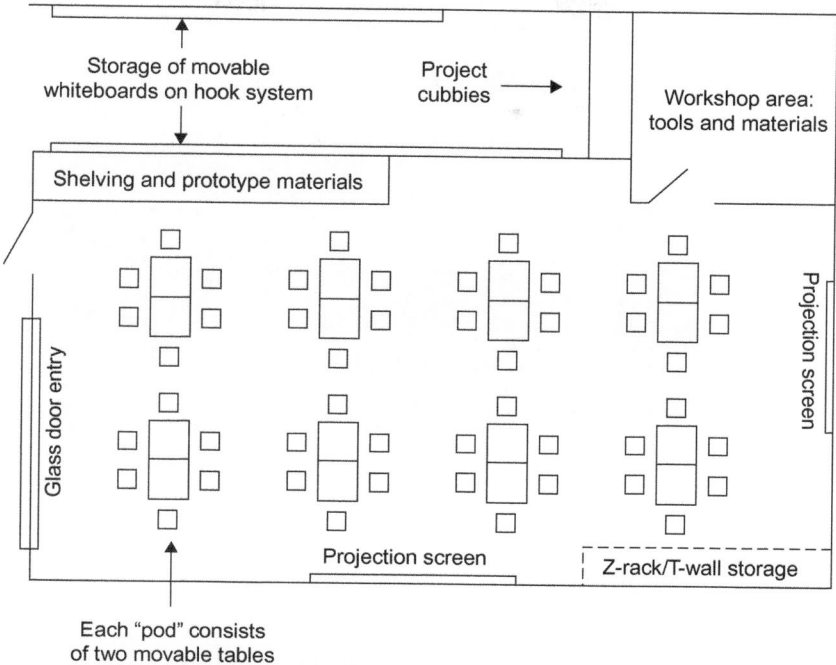

Storage of movable whiteboards on hook system

Project cubbies

Workshop area: tools and materials

Shelving and prototype materials

Glass door entry

Projection screen

Projection screen

Z-rack/T-wall storage

Each "pod" consists of two movable tables and six high stools

Figure 3: Schematic Layout of the Design Zone.

Figure 4: Idea Shaping Work in the Design Zone.

Figure 5:   Prototyping Work in the Design Zone.

Figure 6:   Presentations in the Design Zone.

There have also been some challenges in teaching in the Design Zone when compared with more traditional classroom settings. The first challenge is one of set-up and clean-up time. No matter how diligent students attempt to be, there are always myriad items to attend to in such an active room setting: tables to be realigned, post-it notes to be stocked, whiteboards to be erased, Z-racks to be repositioned, and workshop safety waivers to be filed. We estimate that it often takes an average of 20 minutes extra per class session to

Figure 7: Small Group Design Review in the Design Zone.

set-up before and/or clean-up after a session, and this is faculty time that is taken away from other items. Second, while a flat-floored design space is ideal for project work, the sight-lines are often a challenge for broadcasting information and it can be hard to engage students at the back of a class during presentations as they need to peer over a sea of heads level to theirs. The challenge of presenting material has meant that, as instructors, we have had to rethink the balance of material to be presented to students in the Design Zone, at times necessitating the booking of a traditional case study classroom for long presentations.

Another important observation is the way in which the design space impacts the role of the faculty member. As the learning objectives evolve from teaching routine problem-solving to teaching skills for innovation, the pedagogical role of the teacher is simultaneously evolving. Importantly, the teacher's role changes from one of command-and-control knowledge transfer to one of collaborative knowledge co-creation. In some sense, the teacher implicitly becomes a member of the student team. Lee (2009) refers the role of the design faculty as moving from "instructor" to "guide" to "collaborator." In our experience, all of the design space attributes that facilitate various innovation activities undertaken by students are equally important in facilitating this new faculty role. For example, an open and flexible layout allows the teacher to move freely among teams and to quickly use moveable chairs to join a team's table when necessary. On the other hand, faculty trained in, and used to, lecture- or case-based teaching formats might take some time to get used to this different teaching format. In our experience, switching between a space such as the Design Zone and more traditional classrooms, often in the same day, presents its own cognitive demands.

Design Spaces as Career Preparation

We have described the importance of design spaces in the process of learning the activities underlying the innovation process, but the importance of design spaces also extends to career preparation. Our pedagogical objective at Babson is to prepare our students as future entrepreneurial leaders who will create value, by imagining and designing new products, services, businesses, and industries. We suggest that students can be trained to utilize user-oriented design thinking and design methodologies to approach business problems by expanding the definition of the "user" to include not only customers, but also retailers, suppliers, partners, and other stakeholders in the value chain. Their tasks as future managers and employees will be identifying unmet needs in the marketplace and conceptualizing novel solutions to address those needs. This requires that students develop, through experiential learning, the design-oriented skills and capabilities to explore the unknown, deal with complexity, act under uncertainty, and work collaboratively to co-create with stakeholders, while iteratively prototyping and experimenting with evolving ideas.

We propose that the experience acquired in a design space serves as preparation for the kinds of open-ended problems, creative activities, and collaborative workspaces that these students will encounter as they enter the workforce. Even if students do not proceed to a position where they are doing day-to-day design work, the mere ability to know how best to use and navigate a design space is becoming ever more relevant. Increasingly, graduates of business schools may find themselves working within design spaces at innovative organizations, such as Google Ventures (Knapp, 2014). Furthermore, even more traditional corporations such as Procter & Gamble, Canadian Tire, and Home Depot are adopting the use of design spaces for innovation activities where collaborative, multidisciplinary teams can propose creative solutions to their most challenging problems. For example, Procter & Gamble initiated its Clay Street project in 2004, serving as a dedicated design space in an offsite loft-style location. Motorola's Razr was developed in a dedicated design space, Motocity. Just as students in the 1940s were prepared to work within a mock Boardroom setting, today's students can be provided an opportunity to exercise the skills and capabilities associated with design spaces that are ever more prevalent. Moreover, even if students are hired at companies that are not equipped with these spaces, as result of their exposure to the design space, students may be able to advocate for appropriate design and innovation space within their workplace, given their educational experience.

Conclusion

Design spaces will, increasingly, become part of both our pedagogical toolkit and our business landscape, and we as faculty members within business schools have an opportunity to consider how best to provide the appropriate environment for our students to make use of such space. Our experience at Babson College with the Design Zone has shown us how well a thoughtfully designed physical environment can mesh with our goals as innovation educators. Our specific design was tied to our own physical and curricular environment, and different schools will want to consider how best to design for their own requirements. Matching the activities expected in a design space with the physical requirements will increase the chances of creating welcoming space for innovation.

References

Allen, T. J. (1977). *Managing the flow of technology.* Cambridge, MA: MIT Press.

Brown, T. (2008). Design thinking. *Harvard Business Review,* 86(6), 85–92.

Cruikshank, J. L. (1987). *A delicate experiment: The Harvard business school 1908–1945.* Boston, MA: Harvard Business Review Press.

Doorley, S., & Witthoft, S. (2012). *Make space — How to set the stage of creative collaboration.* Hoboken, NJ: Wiley.

Fixson, S. K. (2009). Teaching innovation through interdisciplinary courses and programmes in product design and development: An analysis at sixteen U.S. schools. *Creativity and Innovation Management,* 18(3), 199–208. doi:10.1111/j.1467-8691.2009.00523.x

Fixson, S. K., & Read, J. M. (2012). Creating innovation leaders: Why we need to blend business and design education. *Design Management Review,* 23(4), 4–12.

Harvard Business School. (2014). *Institutional memory: A centennial history of Harvard business school.* Retrieved from http://institutionalmemory.hbs.edu

Knapp, J. (2014). Why your team needs a war room — And how to set one up. *Fast Company.* Retrieved from http://www.fastcodesign.com/3028471/google-ventures-your-design-team-needs-a-war-room-heres-how-to-set-one-up. Accessed on December 4, 2014.

Lee, N. (2009). Project methods as the vehicle for learning in undergraduate design education: A typology. *Design Studies,* 30(5), 541–560.

Liedtka, J. (2014). Linking design thinking with innovation outcomes through cognitive bias reduction. *Journal of Product Innovation Management.* Epub ahead of print, March 25. doi:10.1111/jpim.12163

Murlkern, J. R. (1995). *Continuity and change: Babson College, 1919–1994.* Babson Park, MA: Babson College History — Book 1.

Norman, D. A., & Draper, S. W. (1986). *User centered system design: New perspective on human-computer interaction*. Boca Raton, FL: CRC Press.

Seidel, V. P., & Fixson, S. K. (2013). Adopting design thinking in novice multidisciplinary teams: The application and limits of design methods and reflexive practices. *Journal of Product Innovation Management, 30*(S1), 19–33.

Seidel, V. P., Marion, T. J., & Fixson, S. K. (2014). *Teaching and learning the innovation process: A framework for curriculum design*. Working Paper. Babson College.

Simon, H. A. (1996). *The sciences of the artificial* (3rd ed.). Cambridge, MA: MIT Press.

Thoring, K., Luippold, C., & Mueller, R. M. (2012). Creative space in design education: A typology of spatial functions. *Proceedings of the International Conference on Engineering and Product Design Education (E&PDE)* (pp. 475–480). Artesis University College, Antwerp, Belgium.

Wagner, T. (2012). *Creating innovators — The making of young people who will change the world*. New York, NY: Simon & Schuster.

14 Welcome to the Babson MBA: Sustaining Curriculum Integration with the TechMark Business Simulation

Paul R. Joseph and Peter R. Wilson

Introduction

Babson College completely transformed its MBA curriculum and differentiated itself in the business school marketplace with the launch of its "new" curriculum in the fall of 1993 (Zolner, 1999). Most notably, the Babson MBA program "adopted a team-based teaching approach ... (and) shifted from a discipline-based to an interdisciplinary orientation" (Zolner, 1999). Further, the program was rapidly becoming recognized as the world's leading graduate school for teaching Entrepreneurship, beginning its 21-year streak as the #1 Ranked MBA program for Entrepreneurship, according to *U.S. News and World Report,* in 1994.

Critical to Babson's success was the development and delivery of deeply integrated "streams" of first year classes – multi-disciplinary modules consisting of traditional business subjects that were taught in an integrated fashion where context mattered as much as the content. In addition to the new curriculum format,

Babson also introduced engaging student onboarding and culture-building activities during the early weeks of each MBA program.[1]

Among Babson's most enduring "Signature Learning Experiences" (SLEs) is the TechMark business simulation event. Created by Babson professor Dr. Robert Eng in the early 1980s, TechMark was first integrated into the Babson MBA curriculum in the fall of 1989 (Zolner, 1999). However, it wasn't until the introduction of the Blended Learning MBA program in 2003 and its subsequent inclusion of TechMark in its Orientation Week programming that many of Babson's faculty began to more fully understand the role and relevance of TechMark to individual and student team performance. Further, by emphasizing a multidisciplinary, system-level perspective, TechMark reaffirms the importance of developing the mindset of a business generalist to foster "entrepreneurial thinking and acting."

What Is TechMark?

Simply speaking, TechMark can be described as a business simulation, a "pedagogy that brings decision making to the forefront of strategy instruction" (Kachra & Schnietz, 2008). The "TechMark world" is a fictitious business environment where students work in teams as the managers of several global manufacturing companies. Despite incredible time pressure, ambiguous information, dynamic market conditions, and the "real world" stress of learning how to work together as a team of colleagues whom have only recently met, each team is accountable to its Board of Directors (both their fictional board and the program faculty) for improving the performance of their TechMark companies.

The measures of success are defined and presented at the beginning of each TechMark event by the program faculty. Traditionally, Babson's MBA Orientation exercises have assessed the performance

---

[1]At the time, Babson offered three different MBA program options: a traditional, Full-Time Two-year MBA program; an intensive, Full-Time One-Year MBA program; and a Part-Time, Evening MBA program. Babson launched the Blended Learning MBA program in 2003 under its former name, "Fast Track MBA" (Babson). It should be noted that orientation programming decisions for each of the four MBA programs have been made by their respective program and faculty directors. As such, the adoption of TechMark as an Orientation SLE has varied by program: the Two-Year MBA has employed TechMark for most of the 25 consecutive years since it was first introduced by Professor Eng in 1989; the Blended Learning MBA first adopted the simulation in 2004; and the Part-Time/Evening MBA adopted TechMark in 2012.

of each team based on a combination of metrics which might vary from program to program. For example, a "typical" iteration might measure team success based on achieving a target Stock Price, Gross Margin Percent, Revenue Growth Percent, Inventory-to-Asset Ratio, and Debt-to-Asset Ratio. Often the faculty will include peer-evaluations and team-based performance assessments as a reflective exercise and to serve as a launch point for the students' subsequent classes in group dynamics and organizational behavior.

During each round of TechMark, where one "round" is defined as one business quarter, student teams must, interpret, analyze, and respond to business information that is provided to them from the TechMark Administrator (typically the lead faculty or a TechMark facilitator). Realistic decision support tools, such as financial statements (e.g., Balance Sheet, Income Statement, etc.), product positioning maps, and market research reports are provided to each TechMark team for their analysis and subsequent decision-making.

The TechMark "product" consists of a software application and associated print and/or electronic materials, which can include a printed student manual for each individual participant, sets of printed decision books and wall charts for each TechMark team to consult in its breakout room, and electronic files such as pre-recorded lectures, online data-entry forms, and decision support tools. By design, the TechMark software application remains entirely faculty-facing rather than employing a video game-like graphical user interface (GUI) for the students to access; TechMark participants are essentially engaged in a data-driven role-play, and the faculty are able to adapt the experience both from within the exercise and through their presentation materials.

According to its creator, Dr. Robert Eng:

> TechMark should not be positioned as a simulation; it's better described as a "platform for teaching." We use a coaching-based model rather than a traditional lecture-, computer based training- (CBT-), or gaming-based approach. At first glance, the delivery and "storyline" of TechMark appear to be similar to many of the supply chain and global marketing management simulation products available today — products like Markstrat (by StratX) or Business Fundamentals (by CapSim). They each model a global supply chain environment, with several competing companies selling products in multiple geographic markets. What sets TechMark apart is the teaching, and the instructor's capacity to design lessons around any business topic and to engage with individuals and groups of students when they are at their most teachable moments — during real-time decision making and after receiving and interpreting

the results of their decisions in an evolving context. TechMark is just an engine. What matters most is how the programs built around that engine are defined and delivered.

In the words of one current Babson MBA student, "(TechMark is an) excellent way to meet members of the class, start building relationships, as well as get a 50,000 foot view of concepts that will be taught throughout the (MBA) program."[2]

Not Simply Simulation-Based Teaching

It is widely accepted that "a well-designed simulation can potentially impart both theory and practice" (Salas, Wildman, & Piccolo, 2009), and Babson's faculty has a long history of developing and employing effective simulations and experiential exercises in their courses. What differentiates TechMark from simulations used by faculty in their core or elective courses is that the Orientation event is designed to *bridge* theory and practice. The purpose of using TechMark in this case is not to teach per se, but to create a learning environment from within which students can discover linkages across multiple business topics, exercise their ability to learn and make decisions as teams, and anticipate and engage in the MBA curriculum with better contextual awareness. TechMark and program faculty facilitate the students' discovery process, but it is impossible to provide anything but a rudimentary coverage of core curriculum content given the time constraints and disparity of knowledge and experience among members of the incoming class.

Also, unlike most business simulations that feature a "student versus- computer" style of play or where students merely engage concurrently but not directly with their classmates, the TechMark software runs in the background while it is the student teams that are the protagonists in this exercise. Further, this model enhances the faculty's ability to meaningfully engage with the students during their group decision-making processes, making observations of individuals and group dynamics while providing near real-time feedback during the subsequent TechMark debrief and Learning Group development module. According to Dr. Allan Cohen, Professor of Management and an expert in Leadership and Organizational Behavior, "Not all simulations work as well as this one; often the fixed formulas on which results are based feel increasingly artificial to students. The dynamics of TechMark, however, and the ability of

---

[2]Source: Evening MBA Orientation Survey Results – Fall 2013.

the instructor to introduce variations during play, preserve the sense of 'reality', and keep students fully engaged."

Despite two major MBA curriculum changes, the pressure to continually innovate business education, and the propensity of students to "find" hints and solutions for many assignments either online or from those who have preceded, the TechMark experience has successfully adapted to various MBA program delivery formats and remains a vital and flexible teaching tool for the faculty. To illustrate an example, we will focus specifically on TechMark's role in the Blended Learning MBA which, to date, has employed the highest degree of faculty collaboration and integration around TechMark. We will share our perspectives both as contributors to the delivery of TechMark during Orientation, as well as while subsequently working with our students during the MBA program. We will also share observations from our colleagues who have lectured and coached during the TechMark exercise. Finally, we will provide examples of how the Blended Learning Group (BLG) — technologists and instructional design specialists within Babson's Information Technology and Services Division (ITSD) — integrated content from, and built exercises around, TechMark to help students learn how to use the various online resources for the technology-intensive, blended format MBA program.

The Blended Learning MBA and TechMark

The Blended Learning MBA program poses special challenges when trying to create a sense of community and shared purpose for its incoming classes that are not found in more traditional daytime/full-time MBA programs. These challenges occur due to the fact that the program targets working professionals with significant work experience[3] who opt for the blended format of the program in order to be able to complete the degree in a timely manner (21 months) without having to quit their jobs and return to school full time.

The blended format consists of a series of seven-week "mini-semesters" in which students take two courses at a time. The courses take place almost entirely online and include a two-day, on-site ("face-to-face") weekend during which the students come to campus to spend two days in a more traditional class setting. Given that the students spend the vast majority of their time working online, away from campus and physically separated from each

---

[3] Average length of work experience for recent classes has ranged from 9 to 14 years.

other, it became necessary to create a significant learning experience at the beginning of the program that would help to jump start the bonding process between and among the students.

Each incoming class starts their MBA program by attending a (typically) five-day, on-site "Orientation Week" which includes a variety of activities designed to familiarize the students with the program, curriculum, and instructional technology. This week also provides an opportunity to create experiences that will help the cohort bond with each other and with the student Learning Groups to which they are assigned prior to the start of the program. One of the most effective learning experiences in this regard has been the TechMark simulation, which serves the MBA program in a number of ways.

One of TechMark's most important contributions is to provide an interactive, engaging exercise that allows the students to work in their pre-assigned Learning Groups. While most, if not all, of our MBA students have had experience working in groups, having to complete graded course assignments in a group is not as familiar to our students and can create significant stress on the group and its members. Thus, it becomes important to give the students an opportunity to work within their Learning Group while they are together so they can assess the strengths and weaknesses of their group processes before classes start. According to one student, "… (the) TechMark sessions really increased post session dialogue among cohort members."[4]

If significant problems do occur, they can be addressed quickly with specific resources provided by the program. What might be a much bigger issue for a group during the online portion of the program is often handled easily during the simulation. Ultimately, this helps each group get off to a much stronger start once classes begin.

The Academic Impact of an Orientation Week "Activity"

The primary purpose of Orientation Week is to onboard the incoming members of each MBA class. Creating and managing the week's agenda is within the purview of the Program Management office, working together with the Blended Learning Faculty Director and program faculty. In addition to TechMark, the calendar holds a mix of introductory activities and extra-curricular classes (e.g., a workshop in accounting basics and various classes designed to facilitate their individual and team-based learning throughout the program), ITSD information sessions, and several social activities. The

---

[4]Source: Blended MBA Orientation Survey Results − Fall 2014.

weekends with the students dividing into their respective class cohorts and attending the first of their MBA curricular classes. Once the students leave campus, they will work exclusively online for six weeks before returning for their next "face-to-face" class.

While TechMark had been historically viewed as an Orientation Week "activity," its relevance and value to the curriculum and to the students has increased over the years, particularly since it was added to the Blended MBA Orientation schedule. According to Dr. Janelle Shubert, Coordinator for Learning Groups for the Babson Blended Learning MBA:

> The TechMark exercise has become an integral, essential feature of launching the Blended Learning MBA Program. Early in the Orientation week before the TechMark exercise is launched, there are two sessions that begin laying the groundwork for successful group learning throughout the MBA program: "My Story," an exercise which helps the students begin the process of getting to know one another and really see and hear the kinds of experiences and expertise that each of them brings to the program and "The Essentials of Successful Learning Groups," which helps them continue this exploration and begin creating shared aspirations for their joint work, norms, and the beginnings of work processes.

> But, we recognized that, as stand-alone sessions, these were too abstract, too "academic" and too disconnected from the complex realities they were going to experience working together. It was only when we created a design that fully integrated these dimensions and made TechMark the centerpiece for "test-driving" their learning about one another, and about group dynamics, that the real power emerged. In real-time the students begin to really see, feel and see the consequences of the myriad elements of working together: assumptions about what the task is, who has and who shares expertise, who talks and who listens, how decisions get made, how disagreements are surfaced and managed.

> The anchoring experience of TechMark and the real-time debrief[5] of that experience gives them the "data" they need

---

[5] A typical debrief would have student teams spend 20–30 minutes in their breakout rooms reflecting on their TechMark experiences and then return to the plenary room having prepared answers to the following questions: *What worked well and helped you be successful? What will you need to work on, moving forward into Blended Learning assignments? What do you need to focus on individually? What do you need to focus on collectively?*

to take those initial hours of working together and create a solid blueprint, a Learning Group Charter, for their ongoing work in the MBA program.

TechMark is the quintessential "living case" that creates a common frame of reference for every incoming member of the MBA class. It also provides important, real-time, "in-the-moment" opportunities for the faculty and program managers to begin the process of observation, feedback and coaching which are hallmarks of the Babson MBA program.

Pedagogy

Given the simulated world experience and the "real world" experiences of TechMark, the exercise aligns well with the six Learning Goals of the Babson MBA,[6] which include: Entrepreneurial Thinking and Acting, Social, Environmental, and Economic Responsibility, Managing in a Global Environment, Self and Contextual Awareness, Functional Depth with Integrative Ability, and Leadership and Teamwork. Some examples of this alignment are as follows:

The TechMark simulated environment:

- *Fosters entrepreneurial thinking and action* by providing incomplete and ambiguous market data from which student teams must define their "go to market" strategies and commit to pursuing markets without any competitive intelligence. They must act like true entrepreneurs by deciding to invest hard dollars into R&D and building new manufacturing capacity ahead of knowing if they will even achieve a competitively advantageous breakthrough with their product designs;
- *Promotes social and economic responsibility* by rewarding teams that commit early to manufacturing their products in emerging market economies, thus creating local jobs, improving the local standard of living, and having a stabilizing effect on politics in the region. Specifically, teams gain, and retain, more market share from more loyal, local customers; and
- Challenges students to analyze opportunities and *manage global operations* across widely varying geographical markets and with evolving customer requirements.

---

[6]*Source*: http://www.babson.edu/Academics/graduate/mba/Pages/default.aspx

In the "real world" classroom, the TechMark exercise:

- *Creates self-awareness* by highlighting the value of knowledge and skills that individuals may not yet possess (or may not feel completely comfortable demonstrating among their new colleagues) and providing opportunities to reflect on the impact of these gaps;
- *Creates contextual awareness* by emphasizing the linkages among multiple business disciplines while stressing the critical differences between relative performance and absolute performance measures;
- Stresses the criticality of *balancing functional depth with the ability to integrate facts* to assess new business opportunities, define strategy and make decisions; and
- *Encourages leaders* to emerge from the initially unstructured and unguided breakout sessions and *identifies effective teamwork* through facilitated reflection and debrief on successful (and unsuccessful) group process during plenary sessions.

Impact of TechMark Experience in the MBA Program

In addition to the team-building aspects of TechMark, the simulation serves an important role as an integrating experience across a number of the functional areas that comprise the core curriculum of the Blended MBA program. Additionally, because "most issues facing business leaders are, in the final analysis, questions of judgment" (Bennis & O'Toole, 2005), the simulation requires most decisions to be made under ambiguous circumstances and with imperfect data. TechMark draws on virtually all the functional areas of the core including accounting, finance, marketing, operations, and human resources. Students have to make decisions in all these areas and they quickly begin to appreciate the contribution each functional area makes, how they are linked, and how they must be integrated in order to successfully execute a company's strategy.

From a program perspective, we have been able to leverage this aspect of TechMark to bring into the simulation many of the faculty who will be later teaching the core. Faculty typically can deliver a quick tutorial that not only helps the students in the simulation but also whets their appetites for what they will see in their core course. This creates anticipation and excitement as students start to get a feel for both the content they will be learning and the quality of the instruction they will be receiving. Integration across the curriculum is further enhanced when these same faculty teach their core courses and can reflect back on the TechMark simulation to illustrate key concepts in their class.

ACCOUNTING

During TechMark, students must understand how their decisions impact key performance metrics such as "return on assets" and "return on equity." This has created the opportunity for our Accounting faculty to make a "guest appearance" during the simulation and to provide "free consulting" to the students on how to identify the key drivers of their team's performance in the simulation. While this has an obvious benefit in terms of the simulation, it also provides a very useful experience to draw upon when teaching performance measures during the core course on financial reporting. A key learning goal of that course is getting the students to understand the linkage between a firm's business model and operating decisions and its financial statements. Being able to relate back to the TechMark simulation gives the students a quick and effective reference and enhances their understanding of this important concept.

ORGANIZATIONAL BEHAVIOR AND ENTREPRENEURIAL LEADERSHIP

Dr. Allan Cohen shared the following observations about his students in the MBA curriculum:

> As a faculty member teaching one of the first MBA courses (Creating and Leading Effective Organizations), I have been very appreciative of the impact of TechMark. First of all, it is intensely engaging for students, so that from the beginning they see the benefits of personal investment and classroom interaction. Second, the design allows students with no particular background in any functional discipline to learn as they go, absorbing many basic concepts, vocabulary and the notion of trade-offs required for general management. A more recent development has been the addition of time for teams to discuss their group process while making the repeated decisions required, so that the investment generated by the competition among teams has a payoff in perceiving the connection between good processes and high outcomes. Teams that do not utilize the talents of all members, fail to listen to quieter members, are not open to examining their assumptions and learning from each round of experience, do not manage time well, or engage in fruitless power struggles rather than constructive conflict, tend not to get good business results. Learning this experientially

rather than just through case discussion or readings has a powerful impact on subsequent behavior.

MARKETING

On many occasions during both the first year core Marketing course or in second year electives, faculty have challenged students to "recall back in TechMark ..." key lessons, such as the devastating impact of failing to capture market share when launching a new company or product, or the impact of a simple, but powerful graphic, such as a product positioning map, to sell internal constituents on the need to make investments in R&D or new product development. Better yet, the students themselves will often volunteer information during a case discussion that relates details of a homework assignment to a lesson learned during TechMark. For example, while analyzing the pricing strategy of Electronic Arts' release of a new video game title, one student astutely connected the gaming company's need to "keep its gross margins up" to the poor performance of his Learning Group's TechMark team more than a year earlier ("We lost a lot of money!"). It is clear that many students' memories of TechMark remain fresh long after their Orientation exercise, and that "scar tissue" becomes a valuable frame of reference for the core faculty and students alike.

INFORMATION TECHNOLOGY AND SERVICES DIVISION (ITSD)/ BLENDED LEARNING GROUP (BLG)

On occasion, the BLG staff has used content relating to TechMark as digital artifacts and/or exercises that they've referenced during their own Orientation Week activities. For example, one year, to demonstrate how the students could use the various collaboration technologies for sharing information and making decisions as a distributed work group, BLG and TechMark faculty developed multiple pieces of vital TechMark information and created recorded presentations, blog entries, discussion thread comments, and so forth. Each Learning Group member was assigned to one particular technology resource (e.g., "read the blog") and then all members would later attend "Google Hangout" or Skype session to share their pieces of information with the entire team. The benefits from this individual, online research and the virtual collaboration were twofold — first, these teams would begin the TechMark exercise with a better understanding of how to navigate the "TechMark world" more effectively and second, they would become more fluent with the technology employed by the Blended Learning MBA program.

APPRECIATION OF THE "INTANGIBLES"

In addition to the pedagogical goals TechMark helps to achieve, it also promotes many of the key "intangibles" of the Blended MBA program. Because TechMark is a business simulation, it requires the students to draw on their work experience to a significant degree. When this happens, the diversity of the cohort in terms of background, experience, and expertise is quickly revealed to everyone in the class. Immediately, students start to realize the wealth of resources that are available in the class and the incredible opportunity this creates. Thus, in a very natural way, TechMark is able to illustrate to the students one of the most valuable aspects of the program — the quality and diversity of their cohort.

VALIDATING THE EXPERIENCE

For the past few years, student satisfaction surveys have been employed to gather feedback on each element of the various MBA Orientation Weeks, including the students' perceived value of the TechMark exercise. Further, there has been ample anecdotal evidence tying students' subsequent, in-class performances to their experiences with TechMark. To date, we have not formally surveyed students further removed from their Orientation experiences to determine TechMark's impact on fostering entrepreneurial learners throughout the MBA program. Such a study would provide further evidence of the teaching tool's continuing effectiveness. We might also consider running TechMark (or a related experiential exercise) later in the curriculum to assess how students approach the challenge differently and to validate the benefits outlined in the previous section.

Promoting Entrepreneurial Thinking and Acting

We have already described the multidisciplinary nature of the TechMark learning environment and its emphasis on contextual awareness and demonstration of the linkages across business disciplines. Another example of linkages to fostering an entrepreneurial mindset frequently exists within the plenary lectures, when students are encouraged to relate their TechMark experiences as "turnaround management teams" (or, entrepreneurial thinkers) to those of "real world" startup entrepreneurs.

One such plenary lecture examines the business life cycle, and contrasts the "early" stage of a business with its "maturity/decline" stage. Students are encouraged to draw parallels between their TechMark companies, which must transform themselves by pursuing new opportunities in new markets to avoid decline, with a new business that might be going to market for the very first time. This reinforces the point that "entrepreneurial actions are a 'fundamental behavior of firms by which they move into new markets, seize new customer, and/or combine (existing) resources in new ways'" (Smith & De Gregorio, 2000; Ireland, Hitt, Camp, & Sexton, 2001, p. 50). Students quickly realize that there are many commonalities from both ends of the business life cycle among companies facing growth challenges. In addition to presenting theory, faculty might also engage students that are currently employed by startups and/or mature companies to provide "real world" context to the class discussion.

Conclusion

One of the keys to delivering a world-class MBA program is creating memorable and valuable learning experiences for the students. The TechMark simulation is one of those experiences delivered in the MBA Orientation Week. It helps to integrate the curriculum, allows students to bond with their Learning Groups and with the cohort as a whole, and naturally highlights two of the most valuable aspects of the Babson MBA program — the quality of the faculty and the student cohort. The TechMark pedagogy provides students with a highly social, and visceral, learning experience that serves to remind them that clarity and peer engagement are critical to building consensus and effectively leading in any organization. Finally, by emphasizing a systems-level perspective and taking a multidisciplinary, generalist approach to assessing opportunities and developing and executing a strategy, TechMark promotes entrepreneurial thinking and acting.

References

Bennis, W., & O'Toole, J. (2005). How business schools lost their way. *Harvard Business Review, 83*(5), 96−105.

Ireland, R. D., Hitt, M. A., Camp, S. M., & Sexton, D. L. (2001). Integrating entrepreneurship and strategic management actions to create firm wealth. *The Academy of Management Executive (1993−2005), 15*(1), Creating Wealth in Organizations, 49−63.

Kachra, A., & Schnietz, K. (2008). The Capstone strategy course: What might real integration look like? *Journal of Management Education, 32*, 476.

Salas, E., Wildman, J. L., & Piccolo, R. F. (2009). Using simulation-based training to enhance management education. *Academy of Management Learning & Education, 8*(4), 559−573.

Zolner, J. P. (1999). *Curriculum change at Babson College (A)*. Harvard Education Publishing Group.

APPENDIX

DETAILED DESCRIPTION OF THE TECHMARK SIMULATION

The execution of TechMark is straightforward. Faculty employ a combination of plenary session lectures and team breakout sessions, alternating between presenting cohort-wide debriefs and lectures and circulating among the TechMark team breakout rooms to observe group dynamics, answer questions about TechMark or related academic subject matter, and provide coaching to those individuals or groups most in need of guidance. The delivery of TechMark follows the following, basic flow, which is repeated for each of the 5–7 decision rounds typically involved in an Orientation Week TechMark event:

Step 1. Students assemble in the plenary room where information is presented to TechMark teams, including financial performance highlights and a general market intelligence report. In addition to TechMark-specific information, faculty might use this opportunity to provide a brief lecture on a specific business topic (e.g., analyzing competitors' strategic intent, managing cash flow, or cost-volume-profit analysis, to name some examples).

Step 2. Teams receive printed copies of their financial results and competitive market information, and move to their breakout rooms.

Step 3. Teams analyze the data, create and/or assess their strategies, and make decisions about the "next" business period. Typical decisions might include, for example, pricing their TechMark products; setting the R&D budget; relocating their manufacturing plant; hiring new salespeople; shipping new products to geographically dispersed warehouses; etc.

Step 4. Teams submit their decisions via online form. Additionally, each team must also fill out a paper decision form. We impress upon them that the paper copy is to provide a backup copy in case their online decisions "get lost" in transit; however, the another goal is to create a redundant process that requires teammates to share information with each other and also demands accurate and clear transcription of the online data. The latter can cause significant stress and occasionally results in the realization that not all team members were in agreement about the group's final submission (teachable moments, indeed)!

Step 5. TechMark faculty and administrative support process the decisions in the TechMark software application. The output takes the form of revised financial and market data, including: a product positioning map; individual team financial reports (Income Statement, Balance Sheet, statement of inventory, etc.), and a market research report that aggregates customer requirements and publicly facing competitor information. While the TechMark faculty works behind the scenes, students are either in a "break" period or return to the plenary room for a lecture by Babson MBA faculty on a topic related to the current TechMark stage or an upcoming program class.

Dr. Eng describes the optimal TechMark learning environment as one of "contrived spontaneity." This phrase captures the essence of the TechMark pedagogy — one that creates an equally entertaining and empowering classroom, where students are encouraged to discover knowledge, exchange ideas, experiment and challenge their assumptions, but one where the faculty also maintains absolute control over the pace and depth of the class's discoveries at all times. This is accomplished by techniques such as asking or redirecting questions, or occasionally by providing factual, but not necessarily complete, answers to students' questions. Students choosing the lazy path — avoiding the readings and opportunities to learn from, and interact with, their peers and the TechMark content — are more often confounded than rewarded by TechMark faculty. Managing the pace of "peeling the onion" is also critically important to successfully building up toward the climactic delivery of the final TechMark results in the final plenary session.

15

Spreading Entrepreneurial Thinking and Skills Online: Lessons from Creating a MOOC Called "Lead Like an Entrepreneur"

Allan R. Cohen

Introduction

A very recent phenomenon, massive open online courses (MOOCs), have attracted millions of (nonpaying) students and considerable controversy about whether such courses can provide quality education (Hollands & Tirthali, 2014). With Babson interested in spreading globally its knowledge of how to teach entrepreneurship, we decided to try a few short MOOCs to learn about the creation of materials that might be offered to institutions in emerging countries, along with faculty training on how to teach interactively. This chapter examines the experience from the first such offering, but putting the evaluation in context first requires some personal and organizational history.

Experiential Tradition in Organizational Behavior

Organizational behavior has a long history of lending itself to experiential, team-centered classroom activities. I came to Babson in

1982, already a lead author of a textbook, *Effective Behavior in Organizations* (Cohen, Fink, Gadon, & Willits, 2001), designed around two major innovations: the classroom as organization (Cohen, 1976) and teaching cases experientially (Gadon, 1976). We conceptualized that the course subject matter, including leadership, teams, interpersonal relations, intergroup activity, and organizational change, could apply to the classroom as we organized it. Students discussed cases in teams, with (elected) team leaders accountable for the performance of their teams, producing team papers and presentations along with individual papers, assessing team member performance, and so on. In addition, we structured the classroom case discussions in ways that produced some of the same behavioral dilemmas present in the cases, so that students would experience parallel issues. Students were to read the text material as well as prepare the case before class, so that most of the discussion involved struggling with case issues that had no correct answer.

The major reason we wrote the text (and cases) was to reduce classroom time introducing research findings and concepts, allowing the focus to be on complex discussions, utilizing concepts when appropriate. Contemporary flipped classrooms work on exactly those premises, where lectures are recorded and then classroom time utilized for hands-on learning activities.[1] We also expected students through role plays and discussions to learn about their own behavior and its consequences in organizational settings, wrestle to apply the course concepts and go beyond them to determine workable solutions they could live with, then practice resolutions.

Entrepreneurship at Babson a Separate Discipline: The Launching of Curriculum Integration

In 1982, entrepreneurship was considered a separate subject matter at Babson College. I assumed that it provided a particular perspective on the behavioral material and skills I was trying to help students learn, compatible but not requiring any special attention from me. Instead, considerable collective faculty energy over the next several years went into figuring out how to create a more integrated curriculum. After many slow, painful discussions, we no longer

---

[1]Martin (2012). Flipped classroom term attributed to Koller (2011).

taught a complete standalone organizational behavior class. We partnered with managerial accounting and operations management.

We all grappled with how to teach in a way that closely matched the reality that issues in organizational life arise as complex, messy, and ambiguous problems that do not lend themselves to being seen or resolved only from single discipline points of view. We had to search for or create cases and simulations with multiple and integrated perspectives. We also crafted relationships with our colleagues from other disciplines that carried on long after any particular common course experience. Relationships across disciplines allowed for easier curriculum innovations, usually problematic for business school faculties. The resulting, generally positive, working environment is, regrettably, rare among university faculties. The benefits have continued over many years.

TEACHING LEADERSHIP

In the early 1980s, I joined with David Bradford of Stanford Graduate Business School to conduct a series of non-credit leadership workshops for managers. Our work led to materials and designs for teaching leadership and, eventually, to several books on leadership and influence that captured what we were learning from working closely with managers struggling to improve their leadership skills (Bradford & Cohen, 1984, 1998; Cohen & Bradford, 1990, 2005, 2012). We created similar elective courses on leadership and influence at our institutions, adapting cases and experiential exercises we had developed jointly from working with managers and readings from our books, as well as leadership materials, cases, and readings from others. Over the years, we shared materials and ideas back and forth, continuing to develop highly chosen electives and executive education courses at both institutions. Keeping with Babson's collaborative spirit, I made these materials available to numerous colleagues, several of whom at various times also taught the leadership elective course. Some of the materials we had developed for the leadership elective were eventually incorporated into our core courses (Cohen & Bradford, 1989).[2]

We never thought of leadership as separate from the actual work that leaders do — strategy, marketing, finance, operations, and so on — but we took those as given, the ground on which leadership had to be exercised. We focused on setting and articulating a tangible vision, building a shared responsibility leadership team, and

---

[2]For example, Monica Ashley case series, now updated as "Monica Ashley at Energy Plus," Babson Case Collection; Nettie Seabrooks case series; Cohen and Bradford (1989).

creating mutual influence. In our view, a core leadership problem across organizations and cultures was that people in formal leadership roles made heroic assumptions about being responsible for everything, obligated to know everything (or pretend to) and in control of everything. This problem served us well as the basis for the creation of educational experiences challenging conventional leadership beliefs.

THE ADVENT OF BLENDED LEARNING

In the late 1990s, many colleges and universities began to experiment with various forms of distance learning. Like many others, Babson's early attempts started from the premise – or hope – that it would be possible to prepare PowerPoint presentations or video lectures that could be used repeatedly to convey core content and possibly sold to other institutions. The impulse came from a desire to drive down the costs of higher education and to make available high quality presentations from outstanding faculty members. This model of education proved to be naïve because (i) it was far too narrow a concept of what education really is, (ii) to create engaging reusable content was quite expensive given technologies existing at the time, (iii) students did not always stick with the work, and (iv) faculty got little satisfaction from this way of teaching. A few institutions managed to achieve scale and make some variation of this kind of education work, but a number of early ventures folded, as did one created as a Babson for-profit spinoff.

In around 2000, a new opportunity, however, stimulated by the work of the spinoff arose for Babson. Intel Corporation was looking for a partner to offer an MBA program delivered partly on site in Silicon Valley, Phoenix, Portland, and at the campus of the educational provider and partly online. There was a great deal of ambivalence among faculty about whether we could make this model into a high-quality educational experience. But, it was seen as worth pursuing as a funded way to learn more about how to deliver this kind of blended program and as a possible prestige boost to our brand for being selected by Intel. Probably partly because other high quality schools were nervous about so much innovation, we won the contract. A design team created the curriculum, mostly duplicating our required MBA courses, though requiring fewer electives for the degree to accommodate that students had extensive work experience and during the program would acquire even more.

We put a *considerable amount of effort* into creating, training, giving feedback, and support to heterogeneous student work teams that met in person about half of the time and the rest virtually, to complete team assignments as the basis for further discussion. We have widespread agreement on our faculty that teaching management has to be a contact sport, with considerable interaction and joint responsibility in order to produce maximum learning about working effectively in organizations.

We quickly discovered that some of our working assumptions were incorrect. We thought that online sessions would be good for transmitting course content, with meaningful, complex discussions reserved for the face-to-face classes on weekends every four to six weeks. It turned out that some asynchronous online threaded discussions were at least as rich as regular classroom discussions because the students were able to make thoughtful comments to each other and bring their work experiences to enrich case discussions. Additionally, sometimes straightforward content learning was very challenging without being face-to-face with other students and the instructor in the classroom. This was especially true where quantitative tools and concepts had to be mastered by those not so quantitative in background. The supportive in-class atmosphere was necessary to help people even be willing to ask questions or to know which ones to ask.

Contrary to our fears, the participants from Intel were extremely enthusiastic about the blended program, appreciating that they could still be working full-time while taking it. They liked the chance to work with employees from other functions and disciplines and valued courses with faculty who really cared about teaching and about them as people. Many quickly put what they learned to work, either in improved performance or in new jobs at Intel. After a few years, however, Intel suggested that there would be even more learning if we opened the program to people from other companies. In that way the blended MBA program, called "fast-track MBA" was born in 2004 (the name of the program was changed recently to "Blended MBA"). We pitched the program at students with at least seven to 10 years of work experience and found that there was an audience of experienced working students for this not-quite-an-executive program model of MBA education. For the most part, students were enthusiastic, although a high percentage voiced some variation of "I would love to have all the classes be face-to-face because I really enjoy being together with the faculty and other students; of course if they were I couldn't be in the program."

Having about half of class time online proved to be a challenge for faculty. In the first several years, the technology was quite cumbersome and required an enormous amount of advanced, detailed planning to create the material and sequence of discussion questions to manage engaging discussions. To simulate more of a regular classroom, we also did occasional videoconferencing classes, which came closer to replicating a live class, but we limited the number because the program had been sold as largely asynchronous, from anywhere, anytime. Even when we did a synchronous video class, each student could be in front of his or her laptop anywhere watching and participating.[3] This technology, while relatively convenient, is not as easy or satisfying as video classes where all the participants are in the same room using telepresence.

Some Faculty Opt Out

We discovered that even quite good teachers had a steep learning curve in this program, and some faculty refused to participate after the first time or two. They found it hard to get to know students individually (although it certainly was possible) and missed being in the center of the action managing discussion. In my view, many skilled faculty members were masterful conductors of discussions in person but did not find it satisfying trying to steer discussions remotely and asynchronously. For many, "conductor/mentor from the center" is more satisfying than "guide from the side." (Only a few of our faculty teach almost exclusively as "sage on the stage," lecturing most of the time).

Over the past 10 or 12 years, a cadre of faculty got more and more comfortable with this model and found that it could lead to highly successful learning and, at the very least, sufficient satisfaction from the faculty side. Teaching students who work at responsible job levels can be challenging; students will test an idea within days after discussing it in class and let the faculty and fellow students know what works and what does not. In my view, this is genuinely pleasurable and stimulating but can be threatening for faulty used to being authorities in control.

No Pure MOOCs

Many of us concluded that we would never want to do a pure online course. Although the blended model was not quite the same as full-time face-to-face, there was enough personal interaction between faculty and students and among students to keep most participants fully engaged. They were getting to know each other and building ongoing connections similar to those built by full-time MBA students. We scoffed at the very low completion rates of students elsewhere in pure online courses and took pride in having been early pioneers of blended learning, which other good schools slowly discovered. Additionally, we took enormous pride in numerous external rankings that rated our teaching as outstanding.

---

[3]Currently we use WebEx for these video classes, which seems to be most reliable, though not entirely satisfying for creating free-flowing discussions.

Really Betting on Entrepreneurship

In the meantime, Babson, a relatively small independent college not part of a large university, was externally rated year after year as number one in teaching entrepreneurship, both graduate and undergraduate.[4] Despite our relatively modest resources, we continued to get very high external ratings. While satisfying, this made us collectively very nervous. Other schools with far greater endowments and resources climbed on the entrepreneurship bandwagon and for years, we talked about other areas we should try to specialize in just in case we lost our number one rating.

A new president in 2005, Len Schlesinger, initiated a new round of strategic planning. As a result of the process, he concluded that if we were short on resources to protect our entrepreneurship ranking, we would probably never have enough resources to get to the top in any other discipline, despite existing pockets of excellence in several fields. Therefore, we should work to leverage our lead in entrepreneurship. He noted that no other school could truly focus on it, since almost every institution is decentralized, with departmental and discipline control of the curriculum, so that no one discipline could be selected as central. However, with effort, we could infuse an already innovative institution with entrepreneurial thinking, cutting across all disciplines and administrative activities. Out of that effort, one tactical objective was to spread what we came to call "entrepreneurial thought and action" to academic institutions around the world. A division called Babson Global was created to seek ways to do that. This new unit went through many variations and plans for how to transform business education, especially in developing countries. Former provost Shahid Ansari became CEO, and one idea that emerged was to create a full curriculum for a Master's degree in entrepreneurial management, develop the necessary materials, and build a consortium of interested universities and train their faculty to run interactive discussions as part of degree programs offered by those universities.

THE EXPERIMENT IN MOOCS TO HELP SPREAD ENTREPRENEURIAL THINKING

Because such an undertaking would involve distance learning in many ways, a handful of faculty was recruited to experiment with short MOOCs designed and run with very large numbers — 1000s

---

[4]*U.S. News & World Report*, Undergraduate #1 Entrepreneurship 1995, 1996, and 1999–2014, the only years for this ranking. Graduate #1 Entrepreneurship 1994–2014.

at a time — and minimal instructor interaction with individual students. The materials developed for these short courses could possibly be reused in the creation of full courses taught by faculty in developing country partner institutions.

The first MOOCs invented, now called cMOOCs or Connectivity MOOCs, assumed that learning happened best among connected learners working on problems and had a relatively high degree of connectivity with little conventional "teaching" during the course. They devalued closed-ended teaching, called "behaviorist, ... where there are right and wrong answers, facts or procedures that must be learned, or students lack higher level cognitive processing skills," as inadequate for teaching "higher order skills of critical thinking, creative thinking, and original thinking, the very skills that are needed in a knowledge-based society" (Rodriguez, 2013). But probably to spread learning widely and earn eventual fees, as well as enhance the brands of certain universities (Hollands & Tirthali, 2014),[5] a different model burgeoned. Some faculty at places like Stanford, Harvard, and MIT agreed to put their courses (now called xMOOCs or Extended MOOCs) online, for free. Most pedagogy in these MOOCs was conventional lecture delivered by video, with testing and the occasional application. It allowed for self-pacing and repetition until content was mastered. This method was more suitable for content transmission to large numbers of students (Parr, 2013; Rodriguez, 2013).[6] As skeptical as I was about whether it would be possible to create a quality educational experience in this format — highly interactive, team and project-based, participative, requiring analysis and thinking, not just content mastery — it was intriguing. Most of the learning would be stimulated student to student, with little faculty interaction. The idea of reaching thousands of students at once was certainly tempting, if only we could create significant interaction and reflection.

---

[5]The main goals for offering or using MOOC's are
Extending the reach of the institution and access to education, building and maintaining brand, improving economics by lowering costs or increasing revenues, improving educational outcomes for both MOOC participants and on-campus students, innovation in teaching and learning, and conducting research on teaching and learning (Hollands & Tirthali, 2014).
[6]"Moocs today ... are quite different from the ones that Stephen [Downes] and I developed [in 2008]. Our goal was to encourage the development of learners through open and transparent learning, where the process of knowledge generation was iterative — improving on the ideas of other learners and generating new knowledge through continual ... improvement. Most Moocs today are more didactic." George Siemens, widely credited with being the first to offer a course called a MOOC, in Parr (2013).

Having accumulated a great deal of experience teaching in our blended programs, I was willing to try.

Fortunately, Babson Global agreed to test a new platform developed by NovoEd to create the possibility of highly interactive virtual teamwork in a MOOC, which reinforced what we were trying to do. It was another startup out of Stanford, created in reaction to others designed for information dissemination by MOOCs. The initial faculty all agreed that we were unlikely to ever offer MOOCs for credit (Terwiesch & Ulrich, 2014),[7] but the experiment would give some experience with creating what I came to think of as the equivalent of an interactive textbook, complete with a teacher's manual and appropriate teacher development activities. After all, I had done the low-tech version of this when writing a textbook with a 500-page teacher's manual in the early 1970s and conducting many sessions at the Organizational Behavior Teaching Conferences over the years that were analogous to faculty development.

ADAPTING LEADERSHIP COURSE TO ENTREPRENEURIAL LEADERSHIP

Another intriguing aspect was the suggestion to reframe my usual leadership and influence approach to fit entrepreneurial leadership. On the face of it, a great deal of what we at Babson (and Stanford) did in the leadership course was totally appropriate for entrepreneurial leaders, but there were things to incorporate and adapt around opportunity/innovation obsession, rapid experimentation, willingness to fail and learn from it, etc. Since my leadership course work with David Bradford had been such a strong partnership, I asked if he would like to join in the effort for Babson. An educational innovator at heart, even though we were not being paid, he could not resist. It turned out to be hard work. We now estimate that we put 800 hours total into design and delivery.

We agreed that the core topics would build off typical leadership issues but with focus on those necessary to solve unfulfilled needs in everything from startup entrepreneurial ventures to established larger organizations. These topics included creating and articulating a vision for what might be possible, building a collaborative team to execute the work, and creating mutual influence relationships where people could push and support each other and resolve conflict. Our influence without authority model and concepts

---

[7] It is entirely possible that decisions about whether or not to ever offer MOOCs are shortsighted. A provocative report by two professors at Wharton raises interesting strategic possibilities that emanate from use of some of the technology being used in such courses, although they really talk mostly about content transmission. See Terwiesch and Ulrich (2014).

were particularly appropriate for entrepreneurial initiative, in or out of existing organizations. The reframing involved building in what entrepreneurial leaders do: look for unmet needs, try small experiments to learn, quickly modify action as results come in, and decide on affordable loss so it would be possible to quickly end experiments as well as modify them.

How would it be possible to create meaningful discussions with little faculty intervention? Could we get students to engage with each other? Would they just share ignorance? Would anyone dig in and work hard when there were no admission restrictions, fees, grades or credit? Could we create interesting content input to use in tackling resolution of cases or exercises? Could we incorporate material from actual entrepreneurial leaders?

Content Creation and Challenges

In some ways, though time-consuming, content creation was the easiest part of the process. Having already developed a great deal of the content in workshops and courses, we already had many informal lecturettes, utilizing PowerPoints, about concepts and frameworks for leadership action. These served as tools for learners to grapple with organizational and people challenges. We decided that we would videotape us delivering the material as a pair, partly because it would be more fun to do it that way and partly because we thought we might be able to model a kind of shared leadership consistent with the concept of leadership we were teaching.

We quickly learned that conventional wisdom for MOOCs is that students will not watch videos longer than about 10 minutes (Guo, Kim, & Rubin, 2014),[8] which is shorter than we occasionally directly lectured in classes or workshops. This meant we had to design our presentations to happen in much shorter bursts. It turned out that many were two to three minutes, although for a couple of core presentations, we went as high as 11 or 12 minutes. We concluded after one round of teaching the MOOC that we needed to break even these by our standard modest lengths, into shorter videos no longer than three minutes. This was especially painful because conventional wisdom also was that we cannot expect students to do lengthy readings, which had been the method by which we often tried to transmit complicated concepts. It is challenging to think about how to give just enough idea, theory, or concept to stimulate discussions applying the ideas to situations provided by us or brought by the students.

---

[8]How video production affects student engagement: an empirical study of MOOC videos (Guo et al., 2014).

Ironically, for all the good intentions about creating access for people all over the world no matter what their educational backgrounds, recent research suggests that most people who take and complete MOOCs already have college degrees (Ezekiel, 2013).

It is not clear whether such participants prefer very short videos and little reading when taking an online course or did not do much in-depth study while obtaining their college degrees. Another challenge, stimulating to us, was how either to reframe our existing leadership and influence material or create new material that would enlarge it to emphasize the entrepreneurial aspects of leadership. For a while we thought that firsthand testimonial from entrepreneurs would be important, and we started by filming several discussions with an entrepreneur, one of which we incorporated in an early class, but realized that we did not want to overemphasize startup entrepreneurs.

It was tempting to include a lot of material on particular aspects of creating startups, ranging from learning comfort with ambiguity, getting to be good at perpetually spotting opportunities, devising quick experiments for learning, managing risk, and so on. But as we thought it through and realized the limitations on length of the course, we had to remind ourselves that we were not teaching a basic course on entrepreneurship or startup entrepreneurship, but one focused on entrepreneurial leadership wherever it occurred. We ended up incorporating short reminders of the entrepreneurial mindset called Entrepreneurial Thought and Action® at Babson but not separate sessions on that.

It is not exactly unusual to have to wrestle with boundary questions when working with colleagues or ideas from other disciplines. Nevertheless, I feel that over-attention to establishing where one discipline ends and another begins is a sure way to kill creativity and make it difficult to create courses that better fit with actual complexity in the world. That does not preclude deciding what to leave to colleagues, but as a convenience not as impermeable high walls. For example, we pointed out early in our course that we would not teach about how to decide whether an opportunity is economically viable or desirable, even though that is clearly a part of entrepreneurial leadership effectiveness. That skill is well addressed elsewhere.

In addition, we had to create new short videos to fill in what normally would happen easily in class, such as instructions for activities, brief reminders of where we had been or where we were going, and so on. Of course, some of that also had to be accessible in written form. Again, this took effort but was not extraordinarily difficult, except for the need to think deliberately and in advance about what could have been mostly spontaneous in a face-to-face course. Online teaching that involves more than just running live video classes that replicate the in-person lecture room calls for an astounding level of detailed planning in order to have material ready, assignments and discussion questions clearly sequenced in advance, and so on. For an experienced instructor used to being able to improvise with students on the fly (and in my case, not being an instinctively detail-oriented person), this requisite planning was a major challenge. It can also be painful because we know that some of the best teaching happens when listening carefully to what is on student minds and deciding to pursue the unexpected because of its potential for deep and gripping learning. In blended learning, that spontaneity is still mostly possible, but difficult in a MOOC.

Part of what was so time-consuming was figuring out how to set up or modify many interactive exercises or discussions among students so that they would learn directly from each other. This ranged from simple discussion questions about learner experiences to analyzing video "problem interactions" we had created previously. Anticipating what kind of questions to ask, assignments to give, and sequences of conceptual input interspersed with activity are hard to determine in the abstract. Getting it right probably would take several rounds of running a course, looking at results, and tinkering. For people like us who are preoccupied with how to create meaningful interactive, higher-order learning, it is deeply stimulating as well as frustrating, especially the first time.

In addition to the assignments, we created over 30 short video "inputs" by spending two days in an empty classroom set up for professional video capture. Because we were both comfortable in front of the camera, at most it required two "takes" per segment to get it satisfactory, occasionally with editing to combine parts of both takes. The best part of the process was unanticipated. We had been planning to use two video cases we had made previously – a reasonably high level manager trying to influence his boss and getting considerable pushback and a manager trying to give feedback to positively influence a defensive subordinate. When we originally made the video cases some years ago, we had attempted to create examples of good ways to do it but, for a variety of reasons, had never been able to come up with anything very satisfactory. The "after" examples always seemed stilted.

When we were shooting videos for the MOOC, we found that there was some time left at the end of the last day so decided to try demonstration role-plays where we would become the characters in the cases and try to show good options for how to influence one another. The results were so good that we have now used these video demonstrations in regular courses and executive workshops and have ended up with very useful, previously elusive teaching material.

In addition, we had one other bonus from use of video. One of the assignments we planned to give was for students in the MOOC to pick someone to whom to give constructive behavioral feedback, using concepts and tools we had taught. Our partner at NovoEd, the delightful and savvy Anne Trumbore, suggested that we make it optional for students to video and post their actual influence attempt. We were skeptical that anyone would do it but thought it would be wonderful if anyone responded. Of the 628 people who completed the assignment, only one person actually videotaped and posted giving feedback to her subordinate.

The video proved to be classic, in that she did almost everything we had taught about tying desired new behavior to the subordinate's goals, but gave her subordinate almost no chance to respond to anything that she said and forced agreement. One of the other students who looked at the video and responded did a splendid job of pointing this out in a supportive way. It struck me that the videotaped session could make excellent teaching material as a case in its own right. In an act of great generosity, the woman who had posted it agreed to make it available. In turn, I made it available to Babson colleagues. One just recently used it successfully in a regular course and has distributed her teaching notes to all of our colleagues. Collaboration lives.

Reliance on Student to Student Teaching and Learning

As mentioned earlier in this chapter, I use student discussion as a major part of the teaching-learning experience. The more experienced students are, the more they will have to teach each other, but organizing and offering a MOOC takes this notion to an extreme level. With upwards of 1000 students responding to questions or assignments, it is impossible to manage the discussion in the usual way or to even read most of the student comments. We decided not to give grades or credits, which made it somewhat easier to accept this loss of control. At best, we could scan and sample.

Surprisingly, a few really strong contributors jumped out, and we engaged in interesting dialogue with them as well as encouraged them in their responses to other students. That probably served more to let participating students know that at least occasionally there was a human being looking at what they did. It was a big relief that some of the student-to-student interaction was sophisticated, for example, in the feedback provided to the woman who posted her feedback video, and expressed as well if not better than I would have. The open access to the MOOC allowed for participation of some people who were better qualified than otherwise would have matriculated, although there were certainly also some who could not do appropriate level work. Similarly, a recent study of two high enrollment business strategy courses, using sophisticated network analysis, found that there was a widespread interconnection among participants but that meaningful interaction – and presumably peer to peer learning – was not so common (Gillani, Yasseri, Eynon, & Hjorth, 2014).

That students participated from around the world, with varied levels of knowledge of English, complicated this interaction. Nevertheless, having everything written down or recorded with video content supplemented by (automatically translated) subtitles probably made it easier for some people to go back over course content than would have been the case in an all face-to-face program. The highly varied and international course population contributed to at least one dramatic episode. NovoEd advised us that to combat dramatic drop-off in completion rates we should begin with an easy assignment so people could get used to participating. Accordingly, our first assignment was to post the name, and if possible a photo, of a leader whom the learner admired along with several words about why. In no time, there were hundreds of examples of leaders from all over the world, an impressive and exciting display.

The next day an older, experienced participant in Scotland complained about the post of another learner, from Africa, who named Hitler as the leader he most admired with the five words: Charisma, Motivator, Organizer, Convincer, and Strategist. The Scot said that this was totally inappropriate and the post should be taken down. There were several other comments criticizing the post. We were clear about what we would do if something similar happened in a face-to-face class – treat it as a teachable moment and discuss both the meaning of leadership and issues of open discussion – but at first puzzled about what might be appropriate in this exclusively online course. I ultimately wrote the following response:

> Folks, we see the suggestion to delete this leader choice. As strongly as we believe that Hitler employed his skills for evil ends, it goes against the spirit of an academic course to prevent anyone from voicing his opinion. But this MOOC is built on the idea of student interaction and feedback, and we trust that you will respond, as several of you already have, with your reactions.

> There is no doubt that like almost any kind of tools, leadership skills and techniques can be used for good and noble ends (see the number of choices for Gandhi, Mother Teresa and so on), but can also be used, at least for a while, for evil or inhuman purposes. Did Hitler have a certain kind of vision and get people to follow it? It would be hard to argue otherwise. Do we admire him for it? I don't think most people do because he did so much harm to so many people.

You will notice that we have already emphasized that we do not believe in the effectiveness of heroic leadership, where one person is responsible for everything, controls everything, and is believed to have all the answers. It is a tendency to beware of and to pay attention to, even when the leader's intentions are positive. It is all the more dangerous when the leader has evil in mind.

One more point probably worth mentioning. The news is filled with the attempts of many countries to control the content of the Internet when those in charge do not like what is being said. Would you really rather have some central individual — in this case the instructor(s) — controlling all content, or allowing everyone in the course to have say, and trusting that the process will sort out what is reliable and sensible from what is not?

The protesting participant responded by saying how disappointed he was in the instructors, never an easy comment to swallow, and for a couple of days we worried about losing everybody. But the subsequent comments from learners were supportive, and even the one who had raised it stuck with the rest of the course. This interaction was potent stuff for a presumably mass, impersonal course! But the audience chose itself.

Approximately 13,850 "signed up" for the course, only 1630 (12%) looked at the video of the course overview (apparently typical), 868 then posted a picture of an admired leader, between 3 and 400 participated in early activities, and 168 people completed all assignments. If we compare those who stuck with it to those who originally registered, it is only a very small percentage (.01%) but a quite high percentage (5.17%) of those who got involved early on (Trumbore, 2014).[9] While we hoped to transform the leadership practice of everyone who originally looked at the course, we know that even in the United States a fair amount of what we teach is counter to common management practice and organizational culture and that is even truer in many other countries. We know that we have to think of it as playing the odds, attracting lots of interest and trying to get a healthy percentage engaged enough to truly examine and ultimately change their leadership behavior. Of course there are multiple motivations besides wanting to obtain directly applicable knowledge for taking a look at a MOOC, such as wanting to get course credit or even a certificate of completion, curiosity about the nature of the subject matter, the offering institution, the pedagogy

---

[9]This is the proper metric according to our NovoEd colleague, Anne Trumbore, (2014).

used, and even for the sheer pleasure of learning. When the marginal cost of adding students approaches zero, the elite university standard of making it difficult to get in may become irrelevant (Daniel, 2012). Some of this is beginning to sort out.

As already mentioned, we wanted the students to work in virtual teams. Learning to work effectively in a team is a core entrepreneurial leadership skill, despite the mythology of entrepreneurs being lone geniuses working against the tide (Cooney & Bygrave, 1997). We worried about forming teams in an efficient and useful way. It turned out that NovoEd had the technology built in to allow people with something in common to find each other. Students completed a profile that included work experience, first language, geographical location, education, and so on. They could then sort by any of these criteria for mutual interest or some basis for likelihood of working together. We wondered how this would work. Remarkably, students reasonably rapidly found each other. Sometimes it was because one person had a strong vision of an organization he or she wanted to start or a project requiring collaboration. We asked students to select an unfilled need, whether or not they actually intended to do something about it and then use it to apply course concepts throughout. Quite a few teams used existing or intended projects, and they probably got the most out of the course.

An interesting feature of doing the MOOC is measuring most everything, providing the possibility of considerable instructor feedback. We could tell how many participants did every single activity, how many completed all the assignments, watched what percentage of the videos, started or completed the videos, and so on. Our NovoEd advisor pointed out that the instructor could behave like an entrepreneurial leader, devising many tests and experiments to quickly find out what worked. This methodology is quite different from the usual academic style and pace, and we barely scratched the surface of our own personal learning in this one experience. But the set-up creates rich possibilities that could ultimately have a deep effect on how we teach and on the overall academic world.

I particularly appreciated this new possibility for testing and rapid feedback about teaching choices and of many of the learning issues described above. This possibility reaffirmed my belief in Babson's commitment to Entrepreneurial Thought and Action®, both because I could see the benefits of operating that way and because I was able to reaffirm the collaborative spirit among our faculty. It also has turned out that the material we created, with modifications and expansion into the equivalent of the full leadership course we teach in the degree programs can very likely be the basis of a course in partner institutions around the world. We would still do a manual and online teacher development to support the live classroom instructors at other partner institutions, but that is also a pleasurable activity. If the MOOC truly extended our reach, personally and as an institution, it will have made the sweat equity we donated worth it.

Conclusions

Although not anything about the experience of designing and delivering a MOOC has altered my view that, in its pure online form, it is not ready to replace face-to-face education for credit, there were numerous lessons for helping to spread entrepreneurship education and for amplifying current pedagogical practice. These include:

- The preparation and delivery of a MOOC that achieves more than would just lecturing and assigning readings is not a task to be undertaken lightly. It requires many hours and detailed planning, usually far in advance of typical course preparation. Do not do it if you are not prepared to spend sufficient time. As a colleague jokes, "this activity is carried out by professionals; do not try it at home."
- It is possible to devise online techniques that engage students in meaningful interaction and higher-order learning. Team projects, especially those that are field-based, offer enormous potential for interaction and engagement.
- Some portion of instructor intervention can be made more systematic and routinized in a way that encourages useful peer observation and feedback. For example, forms to guide peer to peer observation and feedback can lead not only to useful feedback but also serve to reinforce learning of concepts by both the observer and observed. The greater the experience of the participants, the richer their feedback is likely to be. But even novices can learn to apply concepts to interpret the activities generated by other participants.
- Methods that depend on a great deal of peer-to-peer interaction and feedback lessen the in-course control of the faculty member, decreasing centrality and visibility. More of the control resides in the course design and prepared materials, diminishing personal interaction. Some students will have difficulty learning without the sense of personal connection to faculty members, although periodic interventions and comments to individuals can offset the problem. Blended courses, where face-to-face classes are mixed with online MOOC-like material, can optimize both efficiency and effectiveness.
- The other side of lessened faculty control is greater student independence. Many faculty members profess that they want to help

students learn to learn, and there is considerable potential for that in these methods.

- Despite my belief that higher education ought to be focused primarily on higher order thinking, analysis and synthesis, there will be some content in almost every course that needs to be transmitted. Apart from facts, there are concepts, and theories, frameworks and dilemmas to be mastered in order to do the more applied, higher order work; there is a great potential benefit from having the material prerecorded so that students who want to can go over it repeatedly at their own pace. (Some Babson faculty members in face-to-face courses have been videotaping live classes in order to enable students who want to review the sessions — lectures and discussion — the opportunity to do so and early responses have been positive.)
- MOOCs and other online courses using appropriate platforms/ software allow for massive data collection and experimentation, enabling a much faster innovation cycle. Ideas can be readily tested, such as what kinds of questions elicit the best student responses, which form of charts or diagrams are viewed longest and retained best, which of several possible versions of instructions create the fewest questions back to the instructor and the best responses, and so on. The many pressures on higher education for cost reduction and demonstrated learning effectiveness can be addressed using the kind of experimentation possible with some proportion of online learning built into our educational efforts.

References

Bradford, D. L., & Cohen, A. R. (1984). *Managing for excellence: The guide to developing high performance in contemporary organizations.* New York, NY: Wiley.

Bradford, D. L., & Cohen, A. R. (1998). Power up. *Transforming organizations through shared leadership.* New York, NY: Wiley.

Cohen, A. R. (1976). Beyond simulation: The classroom as organization. *Journal of Management Education, 2*(1), 13–19.

Cohen, A. R., & Bradford, D. L. (1989). Influence without authority: The use of alliances, exchanges and reciprocity to accomplish work. *Organizational Dynamics,* (Winter), *17*(3), 5–17.

Cohen, A. R., & Bradford, D. L. (1990). *Influence without authority* (2nd ed.). Wiley.

Cohen, A. R., & Bradford, D. L. (2005). *Influence without authority.* New York, NY: Wiley.

Cohen, A. R., & Bradford, D. L. (2012). *Influencing up.* Wiley.

Cohen, A. R., Fink, S. L., Gadon, H., & Willits, R. D. (2001). *Effective behavior in organizations: Learning from the interplay of cases, concepts and student experience.* (1976, 2nd ed.; 1980, 3rd ed.; 1984, 4th ed.;1988, 5th ed.; 1992, 6th ed.; 1995, 7th ed. (McGraw-Hill Irwin). R.D. Homewood, IL: Irwin, Inc.

Cooney, T. M., & Bygrave, W. D. (1997). The evolution of structure and strategy in fast-growth firms founded by entrepreneurial teams. Working Paper presented at the Babson Entrepreneurship Conference.

Daniel, J. (2012). Making sense of MOOCs: Musings in a maze of myth, paradox and possibility. *Journal of Interactive Media in Education*. Retrieved from http://jime.open.ac.uk/2012/18

Ezekiel, E. J. (2013). Online education: MOOCs taken by educated few. *Nature, 503,* 342.

Gadon, H. (1976). Teaching cases experientially. *Journal of Management Education,* 2(1), 20–24.

Gillani, N., Yasseri, T., Eynon, R., & Hjorth, I. (2014). Structural limitations of learning in a crowd: Communication; vulnerability and information diffusion in MOOCs. *Scientific Reports, 4,* 6447.

Guo, P. J., Kim, J., & Rubin, R. (2014). *L@S '14 Proceedings of the first ACM conference on Learning @ scale conference* (pp. 41–50).

Hollands, F. M., & Tirthali, D. (2014). *MOOCs: Expectations and reality.* Full report. New York, NY: Center for Benefit-Cost Studies of Education, Teachers College, Columbia University.

Koller, D. (2011). Death knell for the lecture: Technology as a passport to personalized education. *New York Times*, December 5.

Martin, F. G. (2012). Will massive open online courses change how we teach? *Communications of the ACM, 55*(8), 26–28.

Parr, C. (2013 October). MOOC creators criticise courses' lack of creativity, *THE*: 17.

Rodriguez, O. (2013 January–March). The concept of openness behind c and x-MOOCs. (Massive Open Online Courses). *Open Praxis, 5*(1), 67–73.

Terwiesch, C., & Ulrich, K. T. (2014). Will video kill the classroom star? The threat and opportunity of massively open online course for full-time MBA programs. Mack Institute for Technological Innovation at the Wharton School, University of Pennsylvania, Philadelphia.

Trumbore, A. (2014). Rules of online engagement: Strategies to increase online engagement at scale. *Change, 46*(4), 38–45.

PART 3
Pedagogical Innovation for Entrepreneurial Thought & Action® and Self & Contextual Awareness

16

Innovation and Experimentation: Taking Risks, Learning from Failures, and Moving Forward

Anne L. Roggeveen

When the term innovation is heard, people generally think of disruptive innovators such as Jeff Bezos or Steve Jobs. However, not all innovations are radical innovations. Innovation can also be incremental such as making improvements to existing products or processes. Consider Google Instant which populates search results while the user types the query. This tool did not radically change how the user conducted the search or the results that Google produced. Rather it improved the user experience by making it faster and more efficient by providing instant feedback. Innovation can and should happen every day. Organizations such as Proctor and Gamble consider innovation to be the norm by making it part of their everyday business (Wynett, 2002).

Natural innovators possessing five key skills – questioning, observing, networking, experimenting, and associating (Dyer, Gregersen, & Christensen, 2011). The basic premise is that the activities undertaken opens your mind to new ideas and perspectives. Questioning the *status quo*, allows you to consider new possibilities. Observing small details may suggest new ways of doing things. Networking with a wide variety of people in different situations, opens you to considering new perspectives. Experimenting allows you try new experiences and test new ideas. Finally, associational thinking allows you to draw connections between these seemingly unrelated perspectives and ideas making you an innovative thinker. Although some people naturally possess all five of those skills, for others many of those skills can be learned (Dyer et al., 2011).

Some companies are natural incubators for innovative thinking. These learning organizations offer supportive learning environments, concrete learning processes and practices, and leadership that reinforces learning (Garvin, Edmonson, & Gino, 2008). The supportive learning environment allows for the psychological safety of employees (Edmondson, 2005) so that they feel safe challenging others, asking naïve questions, taking risks and exploring the unknown, as well as admitting and learning from failures (Garvin et al., 2008). The concrete learning processes involves generating, collecting, interpreting, and disseminating information; experimenting with new offerings; gathering market intelligence; identifying and solving problems; as well as developing employees skills (Garvin et al., 2008). Finally leadership that reinforces learning is where the leaders engage in active questioning and listening; are willing to consider alternative viewpoints; and signal the importance of understanding the problem, transferring knowledge, and reflecting on learnings (Garvin et al., 2008).

Whether innovation resides in a person or an organization, at the heart of creating novel and useful ideas lies experimentation. Some experiments will succeed and others will not; but failure is learning in itself. In fact, Jeff Bezos, Amazon founder has said "Experiments are key to innovation because they rarely turn out as you expect, and you learn so much" (Dyer et al., 2011, p. 136). Experimentation, the idea of testing something and learning from that experience, can be considered from multiple perspectives: exploring new interests, activities or other types of experiences; taking things apart either physically or intellectually; testing ideas through pilots, prototypes, or computer simulations; or manipulating independent variables and measuring dependent variables (Dyer et al., 2011; Shadish, Cook, & Campbell, 2002, Thomke, 2002). Whatever, perspective is taken, an experiment involves a test-and-learn approach allowing ideas to prove themselves.

Building from this backdrop, I developed an Innovation and Experimentation course to encourage students to become innovative thinkers, encouraging them to take personal risks, ask questions, try new things, learn from experiences, and to iterate. The course, taught both at an undergraduate and MBA level, follows the McKinsey influencer model as a method of providing students the tools and knowledge to innovate and experiment, but also the desire to do so. The course provides students a culture akin to a learning organization. In addition to providing psychological safety for the students, it provides concrete learning processes that focus on what creative ideas are, and provides tools to aid the students in the creation of new ideas. Recognizing that to be successful, these creative ideas must be transformed into tangible results, the course also provides tools to get feedback on the creative idea developed in order to determine if it has market potential, and then to appropriately design, execute, and rigorously analyze experiments to test the idea.

In this article, the course structure is described. This structure is organized around taking risks, creating innovative ideas, experiments, real world examples, and a hands-on project. The article concludes with the author's reflections on having taught the course and her learnings from that process.

Course Structure

TAKING RISKS

A fundamental premise of being innovative is to take risks. Innovators are curious, passionate, and interested people who love to ask questions, devour new information, seek insights, enjoy being stimulated, and take advantage of opportunities. They have a growth mindset (Dweck, 2006). When Farenheit 212, an innovation consulting company, interviews people they look for cues that someone is an innovator by examining if they enjoy traveling, have lived in other countries, are omnivorous eaters, constructive critics, and readers (Farenheit 212, 2014). These cues indicate that the person is open to new experiences.

To encourage students to be open-minded and encourage experimentation in themselves, students are asked to try something new, take something apart, or build a prototype. The students reflect upon that experience in a short paper and discuss their experiences in class. Their activities are simple, but their learnings great. Activities range from eating fish for the first time, trying out for the intramural soccer team, auditioning for a musical, taking apart a computer mouse, and building (or trying to build) a flip-up dorm bed. The students are surprised at how such a simple assignment opens them up to trying a new experience and how much they learn from the experience when they are forced to reflect on it. Some enjoy what they try, others do not, but all are proud of going through the experience and realizing that trying something new is not so risky. We also discuss how a growth mindset can encourage a person to step outside his/her comfort zone, being more open to feedback as well as open to failures (Dweck, 2006).

Risk taking is easier in environments that provide psychological safety. Psychological safety is based on the belief that a group or organization will not hold a person's failures against him/her

(Edmondson, 2005). Without this people are likely to be cognizant of risks of failure and less likely to try new things. Of course, some reasons for failure are blameworthy (e.g., deviance, inattention, lack of ability) while others are praiseworthy (e.g., hypothesis testing, exploratory testing; Edmondson, 2011). To create a culture that embraces trying new things, the culture must allow and even celebrate people who take risks, regardless of whether that risk succeeds or fails. The important thing is to learn from experience. Michael Dell, CEO of Dell Computers, describes that to be innovative "we do our best to make sure that people aren't afraid of the possibility of failure" (Dell, 2002).

To create a culture in the classroom that provides psychological safety, students are encouraged to get to know each other on a personal level. This is done in several ways. One, in the opening of the course students introduce themselves by describing something new they did or learned in the past month. Two, each class begins with a discussion of anything related to innovation or experimentation that the students have encountered during the week. Students describe something interesting they have read, experiences they have had or things they have observed. The class can then ask questions, make comments, or reflect on how it connects to something they have experienced. The goal is multifold – to get people comfortable talking with others in the class, to allow the freedom of unplanned discussion in the class, to practice questioning, perspective taking, and observing. Third, the students work in two different groups on projects. For the first project, students are assigned to the groups in an effort that they get to know, work with, and trust a variety of people in the class; not just those they have known previously. For the second project, students can choose their groups.

Once the psychological safety of the classroom is established, students are required to take risks by leading the class in different pre-assigned topics with a group that has been selected for them. The expectation is that students will put forth their best effort to effectively and engagingly lead the class. Because they recognize that all students will eventually have to lead the class and will be dependent on the active participation of the others in the class, it creates a psychological safety net and fosters a circle of trust. Further, because these topics are selected to develop the skills of both the presenting students and the other students in the class, it is part of a concrete learning process. Another way this is done is by having students present multiple times during the semester and receive feedback on how their semester long project can be changed or improved. This process also allows students to experience both being active leaders on their own projects considering different viewpoints, as well as experience providing feedback and observing how other project teams react to feedback and alternative viewpoints. With this overall culture established in the first several classes, and then reinforced throughout the semester, it provides a setting for innovative thinking and experimentation. The students have autonomy, but with a supportive structure surrounding them. The next portion of the course then focuses on generating innovative ideas.

CREATING INNOVATIVE IDEAS

A creative idea is one that is both original and useful. But for many the question is how to come up with a creative idea. In the class we discuss methods for creating these new ideas. This includes design thinking (Brown, 2008), templates of innovation (Goldenberg, Horowitz, Levav, & Mazursky, 2003), ethnographic storytelling (Cavla, Beers, & Arnould, 2014), design for delight (Martin, 2011) and an integrative process for idea generation (Sinfield, Gustafson, & Hindo, 2014). Design thinking, in very simplified terms, revolves around recognition of a problem and/or opportunity (inspiration), generating, developing and testing ideas that may lead to a solution (ideation), and implementing the idea (Brown, 2008). Templates of innovation include subtraction, division, multiplication, task unification, attribute dependencies, and contradiction (Boyd & Goldenberg, 2013). Ethnography is the act of studying people in their natural environments. Ethnographic storytelling is relating of findings after observing those people (Cavla et al., 2014). Design for Delight is a process used at Intuit that allows managers to identify consumer pain points through direct field research, brainstorm about how to reduce them and quickly prototype solutions (Martin, 2011). The integrative process for idea generation put forward by Sinfield et al. (2014) is a seven-step process designed to help managers understand problems deeply, generate tangible ideas for solutions, and translate those ideas into actions.

To bring these concepts to life for students, a variety of methods are used including assigning them readings and discussing them in class, having them watch videos, and using exercises to apply some of the innovation templates to actual products or services. In fact, with graduate students, the student groups are responsible for teaching the innovation templates to the class. This challenges them to go beyond simply relaying the readings to creating exercises that the class can actually do to apply the principles. The goal is to the have students internalize the concepts. Finally, the students draw from these concepts when actually developing an innovative idea for their course project. To further cement what they have done, when presenting their innovation, students are asked to describe and reflect on the process they used to arrive at the end result. Students must also get feedback on their innovative idea from consumers to determine if there is market potential for this idea, and is worth proceeding forward with. If not, they are tasked to go back to the drawing board until they find an idea which does have market potential. After that, we move forward to further developing and testing the idea.

EXPERIMENTS

One of the best ways to determine the success of a product is to actually experimentally test it in the marketplace. Of course, there are ethical considerations which must be taken into account. To ensure that students consider the ethical implications of experimenting, a student debate is used. The debate teams are provided with some with background material discussing ethical issues that can surface if consumers are not aware they are being experimented on, as well as the value of information that can be learned from experiments. In addition, students are encouraged to do further research to support their position. The rest of the class observes and after the debate reflects on the points.

To shift the class into more scientific thinking about testing their ideas, two articles are assigned which focus on smart business experiments (Anderson & Simester, 2011; Davenport, 2009). Again to ensure that the articles are not only read, but internalized, student groups are made responsible for leading the class in exercises related to the readings. The approaches that student groups have taken varies substantially; the commonality is a creative engaging approach.

I then run an experiment with the class as a way to demonstrate and discuss hypotheses, the design, execution, and analysis of a test. For example, to test the endowment effect (Kahneman, Knetsch, & Thaler, 1990), it is hypothesized that students will prefer to keep what they already have rather than switching to another option. To test this, the class is randomized and assigned to a test group and a control group in separate locations. Each member of the experimental group receives five M&Ms which they hold in front of them, but do not eat. After a five minute delay the experimental group is then given the choice of trading in those five M&Ms to receive three donut holes. The control group is immediately given the choice of five M&Ms or three donut holes. The experimental group and the control group are then compared to determine if there is a difference in how many people chose the donut holes. This in-class demonstration serves as a basis to discuss randomization, experimental group, control group, independent variable, dependent variables, and the procedure for executing the experiment. It also allows for a discussion of any issues which arise during the implementation of it which might affect the results.

The course then transitions to discussing research problems, hypotheses and the importance of iternative, systematic testing.

Prior to our discussion, the students create blades for a milk-box windmill. They are provided with a variety of material, a limited time, and the challenge to create the strongest blades that will lift the most weight. They can test each iteration with a fan and refine it if needed. We then reflect on this experience when discussing approaching a problem in a systematic fashion and having clear hypotheses that are testable.

The next phase of the experiments section focuses on the more traditional tenants of experimental design: understanding causality, independent variables, dependent variables, experimental design, and internal/external validity. While more lecture oriented, there are class exercises and discussion. The importance of the stimuli used to manipulate the independent variables, the clarity of the dependent variable, and reliability of measures are discussed in detail. The students also learned how to create experiments using Qualtrics, collect data using Mturk, and analyze experimental data using SPSS. A workshop approach is used for this component of the class where the technique is demonstrated while the students follow along simultaneously on their computers. Individual help is then provided to any students requiring it, while other students are applying the new knowledge in further exercises designed to cement their understanding. After this section, the content is broadened to examine real world experiments. Transitioning to this area, Google Experiments is introduced, demonstrating how easy it is to run an experiment with actual webpages.

REAL WORLD EXAMPLES

There are many ways that students can be exposed to real world examples of the concepts included in the course. In addition to discussing innovations or experiments they have encountered during the week at the beginning of each class, we also include a variety of cases and guest speakers. The case method is one excellent method developing critical thinking skills around the topics (McEwen, 1994). As such we use cases about experiments done at Bank of America (Thomke, 2002), Ohio Arts Company (Farris, Venkatesan, & Moon, 2012; Moon, Venkatesan, & Farris, 2012), and ICA Supermarkets (Hill, Roggeveen, Grewal, & Nordfält, 2015). Guest speakers also present examples of how they are using innovation and experimentation in their current work.

It is critical for students to leave the course having applied the theories they have learned to practical applications. This engrains the experience in students by bringing the learning to life. Running throughout the entire semester is a group project which allows for this action learning (Smith & Peters, 1997). It moves students through the educational objectives of knowledge, comprehension, application, analysis, synthesis, and evaluation (Bloom, Englehard, Furst, Hill, & Krathwohl, 1956). Students must first create an innovative idea using some of the methods discussed, reflect on how they arrived at that idea, and test the idea to ensure it has legs. They present this to the class. Next, they must propose two experiments to test this idea further. The students again present it to the class, and receive directed feedback on what works and what needs to be changed about the design. This allows not only that student group to learn from the feedback, but also all the students in the class. Finally, the students must conduct the two experiments, analyze the data using SPSS, and draw conclusions. Again this is presented to the class. Along with each of the presentations, a write up describing the process, outcomes, and learnings is expected. The purpose of the write-up is that the act of writing often forces the students to think in a different way than simply giving a presentation. The project encourages students to think critically, ask questions, and drill down not only on their own projects but also on those of their classmates. Encouraging and applying this critical thinking throughout the course is a cornerstone of their learning. It increases student responsibility for learning and pushes students to deeper levels of analysis.

Course Reflections

The course follows the McKinsey influencer model as a method of providing students the tools and knowledge to innovate and experiment, but also the desire to do so. The course focuses both on the individual and the organization (the class). By beginning the course focusing around trying new things and action oriented activities, it builds an understanding of what needs to be done and the commitment to do so. The course then provides a range of tools to develop the skills and capacities for the student to become innovative and be able to run experiments. The course is also designed to align the students in their desire and willingness to take risks and test ideas. By seeing that everyone in the class is taking risks and testing new ideas, they are more likely to do it themselves. Finally, I model the ideas of innovation and experimentation throughout the course. I tell the students at the outset that they are enrolled in a course about innovation and experimentation, and that they will be partners with me in this experience. Some things will work, some will not, but we will learn from our mistakes and move forward. The students and I all innovate, take risks, learn and move forward.

The course builds from the motto that "an educator can open the door, but students must enter by themselves." By having the students become partners in this course, it encourages them to learn and internalize many of the course objectives. Of course, making the students partners is risky if there is no framework to structure the learning. It is important to strike a balance between directing the students and coaching the students. By giving them guidelines, but not definitive structure, it allows them to innovate and experiment. It also allows them to take risks and learn not only from their own experiences, but from observing and providing feedback to others. Of course, there are some aspects of the course where this is more possible (e.g., discussing articles, cases) and other aspects where the students need to be directed (e.g., experimental design, SPSS).

At the conclusion of the course, the aim is to have students feel comfortable taking risks, trying new things, asking questions, observing and being innovative in their thinking. It is also to leave them with a skillset that will allow them to run experiments. Students who understand these concepts can then be more effective at running business experiments in the future. They will be able to complete the checklist for running a business experiment identified by Thomke and Manzi (2014). The checklist involves being clear on the purpose of the experiment, getting buy-in for the experiment, understanding the feasibility of conducting the experiment, as well as being able to discuss the reliability and value of the results.

References

Anderson, E. T., & Simester, D. (2011). A step-by-step guide to smart business experiments. *Harvard Business Review, 89*(3), 98–105.

Bloom, B. S., Englehard, M. D., Furst, E. J., Hill, W. H., & Krathwohl, D. R. (1956). Taxonomy of educational objectives, *handbook 1: Cognitive domain.* New York, NY: David McKay Company.

Boyd, D., & Goldenberg, J. (2013). *Inside the box: A proven system of creativity for breakthrough results.* New York, NY: Simon & Schuster.

Brown, T. (2008). Design thinking. *Harvard Business Review, 86*(6), 85–95.

Cavla, J., Beers, R., & Arnould, E. (2014). Stories that deliver business insights. *MIT Sloan Management Review,* (Winter), 55–62.

Davenport, T. H. (2009). How to design smart business experiments. *Harvard Business Review, 87*(2), 68–76.

Dell, M. (2002). Inspiring innovation – Don't fear failure. *Harvard Business Review, 80*(8), 39–49.

Dweck, C. (2006). *Mindset: The new psychology of success.* New York, NY: Random House.

Dyer, J., Gregersen, H., & Christensen, C. M. (2011). *The innovator's DNA: Mastering the five skills of disruptive innovators.* Boston, MA: Harvard Business Review Press.

Edmondson, A. (2005). Promoting experimentation for organizational learn: The mixed effects of inconsistency. *Rotman Magazine,* (Winter), 20–23.

Edmondson, A. (2011). Strategies for learning from failure. *Harvard Business Review, 89*(4), 48–55. 137.

Farenheit 212. (2014). *How to hire innovators.* Retrieved from http://www.fahrenheit-212.com/how-to-hire-innovators/

Farris, P. W., Venkatesan, R., & Moon, D. (2012). *Transformation of marketing at the Ohio arts company (B).* Charlottesville, VA: University of Virginia Darden School Foundation.

Garvin, D. A., Edmonson, A. C., & Gino, F. (2008). Is yours a learning organization? *Harvard Business Review, 86*(3), 109–116.

Goldenberg, J., Horowitz, R., Levav, A., & Mazursky, D. (2003). Finding your innovation sweet spot. *Harvard Business Review, 81*(3), 120–129.

Hill, K., Roggeveen, A. L., Grewal, D., & Nordfält, J. (2015). *ICA: Changing the supermarket business, one screen at a time.* Babson Park, MA: Babson Worldwide, A Special Case Collection.

Kahneman, D., Knetsch, J. L., & Thaler, R. (1990). Experimental tests of the endowment effect and the coase theorem. *Journal of Political Economy, 98*(December), 1325–1348.

Martin, R. L. (2011). The innovation catalysts. *Harvard Business Review, 89*(6), 82–87.

McEwen, B. C. (1994). Teaching critical thinking skills in business education. *Journal of Education for Business,* (November/December), 99–103.

Moon, D., Venkatesan, R., & Farris, P. W. (2012). *Transformation of marketing at the Ohio arts company (A).* Charlottesville, VA: University of Virginia Darden School Foundation.

Shadish, W. R., Cook, T. D., & Campbell, D. T. (2002). *Experimental and quasi-experimental designs for generalized causal inference.* Boston, MA: Houghton-Mifflin Company.

Sinfield, J. V., Gusafason, T., & Hindo, B. (2014). The discipline of creativity. *MIT Sloan Management Review,* (Winter), 24–26.

Smith, P. A. C., & Peters, V. J. (1997). Action learning worth a closer look. *Ivey Business Quarterly,* (Autumn), 63–67.

Thomke, S. H. (2002). *Bank of America case.* Boston, MA: Harvard Business School Publishing.

Thomke, S. H., & Manzi, J. (2014). The discipline of business experimentation. *Harvard Business Review, 92*(12), 70–79.

Wynett, C. (2002). Inspiring innovation – Make it the norm. *Harvard Business Review, 80*(8), 39–49.

17

Using Transformative Learning Theory to Develop a Course in Sustainable Entrepreneurship

Bradley George

Introduction

In a global economy with rising population and economic growth, environmental impacts and social justice are becoming increasingly important to today's business leaders. Environmental problems, resource shortages, and social inequality all call into question our ability to continue to meet the needs of a growing population using our current solutions. In addition, customers are increasingly demanding that companies consider human rights, social justice, and environmental issues in their operations. We have seen cases where problems at suppliers for companies like WalMart, Apple, or Nike have led to customer action and damage to brands as companies are increasingly being held accountable to a wider variety of stakeholders. This has led businesses to reexamine the definitions of organizational performance and competitive advantage in terms of social and ecological sustainability (King, 2010; Ross, 2010).

The importance and magnitude of this sea change can be illustrated by the fact that over 7000 firms in 145 countries have joined the UN Global Compact since its founding in 2000, representing a commitment by firms to align their operations and strategies to 10 principles in the areas of human rights, labor, the environment, and corruption. In the United States, this movement has also led to the creation of a new legal entity, called a Benefit Corporation, in multiple states in the United States. This legislation generally addresses three major provisions: (1) a corporate purpose to create a material positive impact on society and the environment; (2) expanded fiduciary duties of directors which require consideration of nonfinancial interests; and (3) an obligation to report on its overall social and environmental performance as assessed against a comprehensive, credible, independent, and transparent third-party standard (Clark, 2012).

This situation suggests that not only is sustainability a critical topic for future business leaders, but that these leaders need to develop and implement solutions that are likely to be radically different from those we have today. For that reason, we believe that integrating sustainability and entrepreneurship is critical for the next generation of business creators and managers. At the same time, this represents significant challenges for the educator. Some of these include the newness of the topic to higher business education (Erskine & Johnson, 2012), its complexity (Wiek, Withycombe, Redman, & Mills, 2011), and the fact that it represents a significant departure from business as usual (Kearins & Springett, 2003). The latter of these is further complicated by the fact that it is often easy to accept the business and industry structures we are familiar with as models that can be improved and give little thought to whether they may be fundamentally flawed. However, we are quickly realizing that our current solutions are inadequate for meeting the increasing population and resource demands from the developing world. This means that conceptualizing new, truly sustainable businesses may require students to critically analyze and challenge fundamental assumptions they have about how these problems can and should be solved. Many students may not even realize the assumptions they have that influence their frame of reference and subsequent consideration of alternative solutions. Understanding these inherent assumptions is a critical first step in being able to challenge them and develop the truly novel solutions that are needed.

Traditionally, sustainability education has often assumed that a lack of awareness and knowledge about environmental impacts lead to negative behaviors and, as a result, most programs use the "information/attitude/behavior" model (Uzzell & Räthzel, 2009, p. 341) in attempting to effect behavioral change (Chen & Martin, 2015). However, some researchers have suggested that these programs do not yield long-term impact (Dwyer, Leeming, Cobern, Porter, & Jackson, 1993) or are simply not effective (Kollmuss & Agyeman, 2002; Staats, Harland, & Wilke, 2004). This approach is similar to addressing the lower levels of Bloom's taxonomy by focusing on knowledge and comprehension. Yet, the higher levels of the taxonomy, those of synthesis and evaluation, are where this knowledge is combined in new ways and is the realm of sustainable entrepreneurship.

Each of these issues suggest that we should consider alternative pedagogical approaches that enable students to recognize, critique and modify the assumptions that underlie their current frames of reference. In this chapter, I will describe how I utilized transformative learning theory (Mezirow, 1991) to develop a course in sustainable entrepreneurship that attempts to address these issues. I will start with a discussion of Bloom's taxonomy and transformative learning theory. That will be followed by a description of the course and assignments to show how these attempt to provide students with a series of learning experiences that allows them to discover their own assumptions and bring about changes in student's frames of reference that will better equip them to develop novel, sustainable, and responsible businesses in the future.

Bloom's Taxonomy and Transformational Learning

Bloom's taxonomy of educational objectives suggests that students pass through different levels of cognition — knowledge, comprehension, application, analysis, synthesis, and evaluation (Bloom, Englehart, Furst, Hill, & Krathwohl, 1956). It is often suggested that students move through these levels sequentially, with each representing higher order cognitive processes, suggesting that mastery of knowledge and comprehension should be achieved in order to progress to higher orders such as synthesis or evaluation. However, as noted by Marzano and Kendall (2007), this idea is one of the most common criticisms of the taxonomy. The levels of the taxonomy were differentiated based on the degree of difficulty rather than strictly sequential dependence. In fact, this shortcoming was implicitly recognized by Bloom and his colleagues when they noted that, "It is probably more defensible educationally to consider analysis as an aid to fuller comprehension (a lower class level) or as a prelude to an evaluation of the material" (p. 144). In this case, a higher level (analysis) informs a lower level (comprehension) and that the synthesis level could be bypassed in moving from analysis to evaluation.

While it may be debatable whether students must pass through each of these levels before progressing to the next, the taxonomy has found great use in course design (Betts, 2008; Christopher, Thomas, & Tallent-Runnels, 2004; Seung-Youn & Stepich, 2003). The idea of progressive levels of learning coincides with what is often thought of as traditional education where a lecturer delivers content in an effort to provide knowledge and we use exams or assignments that provide students an opportunity to illustrate their comprehension, application, and analysis. However, most educators today understand that universities are no longer the sole (or even primary) repository of information and that our role is changing to provide more focus on the higher levels of the taxonomy. As suggested by Betts (2008), class time should focus on the middle levels of application and analysis, with the lower levels being addressed through readings (knowledge and comprehension) and the students incorporating higher levels (synthesis and evaluation) through projects and assignments. For instructors, this means that the real challenge is in developing and designing projects that enable these higher levels of learning.

Bloom's taxonomy is useful in developing course objectives and understanding the types of learning, but it is less helpful in showing us how to accomplish these objectives. Additionally, many of the issues noted previously with respect to the challenges in teaching sustainability can be traced back to student's existing world views, which cannot be changed simply by introducing new knowledge. This is where we can turn to transformative learning theory (Cranton, 1994, 1996; Mezirow, 1991, 1996, 1997). Originally developed for adult learning, transformative learning is the process of changing a student's frame of reference (Mezirow, 1997). Frames of reference are composed of habits of mind and points of view and form the structure of assumptions that students use to understand their experiences (Mezirow, 1997). Habits of mind are abstract, habitual ways of thinking, feeling, and acting that are influenced by assumptions and are articulated in a specific point of view (Mezirow, 1997). A relevant example of a habit of mind for this discussion is that of anthropocentrism, the predisposition to regard other species as inferior to humans. However, unlike points of view, we cannot try on another person's habit of mind and appropriate it. Transformative learning theory suggests that students transform their frames of reference through critical reflection on the assumptions upon which their habits of mind and points of view are based (Mezirow, 1991, 1997).

At its core, transformative learning theory suggests that through some event, an individual becomes aware of holding a particular point of view or underlying assumption. If the individual changes this belief by critically examining it and considering alternatives, they will transform some aspect of their worldview (Cranton, 2002). While noting that no teaching method can guarantee transformation, Cranton (2002) outlines the following strategies:

- Creating an activating event that exposes students to viewpoints that may be different from their own
- Getting students to recognize and articulate assumptions

- Provide students with the opportunity to question their assumptions and encourage critical self-reflection with respect to their frames of reference
- Creating a safe environment in which students can try on different points of view (such as role plays)
- Engaging in discourse
- Setting the stage and providing an opportunity for a revision of assumptions and perspectives
- Providing students with the opportunity to act on their revised assumptions and perspectives.

In each of these cases the student is at the heart of the strategy. Transformation takes place within the student and it falls on the educator who wishes to change frames of reference to design projects and curriculum that force students to recognize and be critical of their own assumptions and the instructor is a facilitator of this process rather than a subject matter expert imparting knowledge on the students and students learn through a process of discovery (Mezirow, 1997).

In the following sections I will discuss how I have used these principles to develop what I call discovery-based learning for a course in environmental and sustainable entrepreneurship in an effort to facilitate the understanding and challenging of key assumptions that are critical to developing solutions to some of our most pressing problems. I will start with an overview of the course and its objectives and then discuss various exercises and assignments that are used in an effort to effect this change.

Course Overview and Objectives

The course is an undergraduate elective entitled "Environmental and Sustainable Entrepreneurship". All students at Babson College graduate with a Bachelor of Science degree in business. Students may choose to graduate with a concentration in a particular subject area such as Entrepreneurship or Finance, but a declared concentration is not required providing students with a relatively large degree of freedom in their curriculum, particularly in their Junior and Senior years. While the course does count toward a concentration in Entrepreneurship as well as toward a concentration in Sustainability, there are no specific course pre-requisites other than the fact that students need to be in their third or fourth year. This is due to the fact that Babson has a very integrated series of courses during student's first two years which introduces them to a number of basic business topics principles that provide a common foundation and understanding for the material in the course. To date, 49%

of the students that have taken the course have declared concentrations in Entrepreneurship.

The course gives students an overview of environmental issues and current technologies as well as what it means to be a sustainable business. At Babson College, we believe that a sustainable business is not only one that considers its environmental impact, but also its larger societal impact including issues such as human rights and social justice. The central focus of the course is on two key issues for aspiring entrepreneurs. The first is to look at ways in which students can develop new solutions to existing environmental problems. The second is to examine what it means to create a "sustainable" business, regardless of the nature of the business. The course meets 14 times (once per week) for 3 hours and 20 minutes and uses a seminar format rather than lecture. While the course has been taught in more typical two day/week structure, I have found that this limits the depth of discussion, which is critical for effective transformation learning.

Given that a key goal of the course is to affect change in the student's frame of reference, or the assumptions students have regarding business and sustainability that influence their thinking, the objectives of the course are intentionally not grounded in specific, quantifiable skills. While this makes assessment more difficult, the fundamental thought is that these issues require novel trains of thought that fundamentally change the way in which our organizations operate. As such, the objectives of the course focus on improving understanding in particular areas, which is demonstrated through various assignments.

1. Students will have a basic understanding and vocabulary of the environmental and sustainable business space
2. Students will be able to better identify and evaluate potential opportunities that can help solve some of the pressing environmental problems we face
3. Students will better understand how businesses and organizations impact the environment and society and be able to identify opportunities to improve the environmental and/or sustainable performance of any organization.

Inherent in each of these is a fourth objective, which is to assist students to better understand and challenge their implicit assumptions about how businesses and industries need to operate.

The course covers a range of topics and presents students with information, facts and frameworks, but the focus here will be on aspects of the course specifically designed to address some of the unique issues associated with this topic. To this end, I use the principles of transformative learning theory to develop what I refer to as "discovery-based learning" in which students become aware of, or "discover," their existing assumptions through participation in particular exercises and completion of assignments. This allows the students to then examine and explore these assumptions in classroom discussions, setting the stage for challenging these assumptions, exploring alternatives and developing new frames of reference.

Discovery-Based Learning in the Classroom

While the course is structured around presenting some facts and frameworks in a lecture format, much of the work addressing the knowledge aspect of Bloom's taxonomy is handled through outside reading with class time focused on discussions to improve comprehension and application of the material. The challenge here is to present exercises and questions that will challenge student's preconceptions on the topic in order for them to recognize the current assumptions they hold regarding that topic. For example, many of the environmental problems we face are connected to human behavior (Chen & Martin, 2015; Steg & Vlek, 2009; Vlek & Steg, 2007) and students often have assumptions regarding the drivers of these behaviors which then influences where they look for solutions. Oftentimes students come into the course believing that many of our current problems are the result of ignorance, apathy, selfishness, or even bad intentions on the part of people and businesses. As an illustration, here are some of the student's responses to being asked what they feel are the primary causes of the current environmental problems facing the world at the beginning of the class:

> "Ignorance, apathy, and entitlement on the part of producers and consumers throughout the world's history."

> "Big businesses and lack of education. Big businesses lobby excessively to get votes in their favor which usually go against environmental protection because of their bottom line — money. In my opinion, they have zero ethics and are the evil people of today's world due to their giant contribution to the trashing of our earth."

> "Ignorance. I believe education is the solution to so many things, sometimes people don't know that what they are doing is wrong or that it has such a great impact on the environment."

> "There are many causes to the world's current environmental problems; however, the main one is probably irresponsibility."

"Human ignorance, stupidity, and greed."

"The lack of concern in people, greed in companies and not caring about what can happen because maybe it will not affect us."

Given this situation, an exercise was developed that would result in students exhibiting the exact behavior of which they are so critical. In this case, the students are then run through a series of exercises in the form of a game (see appendix) that illustrate different characteristics of natural systems and human behavior. Once we have completed the exercises, I illustrate those ties and we discuss why they behaved in the way they did. In many cases, students find that they behaved in exactly the same way that people have over time and they begin to understand that much of the behavior is rational in light of the conditions people have been faced with. Of particular interest is the last game in which all students compete. The game is designed such that if everyone cooperates rather than acting in their own best interest, everyone wins. When this is tied back to people's behavior where their family's survival is at stake rather than simply a relatively meaningless grade, the students often begin to analyze and question their initial assumptions. Additionally, this can lead to a productive discussion in which students can begin to develop alternative solutions to problems that may not have previously occurred to them. For example, if someone is cutting down the rainforest in order to create grazing or farm land because they to feed their family, a solution may be to create a local business that provides employment opportunities and removes the need to cut down the forest.

Another key aspect of developing sustainable businesses is recognizing that in many cases they need to be fundamentally different from existing business structures. A common assumption among students is that being more sustainable or environmentally friendly will cost more. This not only limits the market for their solutions, but usually treats sustainability as an "add-on." In other words, the business will utilize many of the same models and processes as existing solutions, but do them more efficiently or with more environmentally friendly materials. One student wrote that the primary cause of the problems we face was due to "*high profitability of unsustainable and cheap practices*," illustrating the assumption that sustainable business practices are more cost effective.

One way in which this is addressed is to ask students to come to class prepared to discuss how they would create an automobile company that never sells a car. There is often significant resistance to this idea and students try to cite numerous reasons why certain things could not be done. However, through a process of questioning their rationale and discussion within the class regarding alternatives, they soon come to realize that many of their assumptions about the problems with this type of model are based in the fundamental aspects of a unit sales revenue model. Once a car becomes a revenue producing asset for as long as it can functionally operate, it results in significant changes to design, manufacturing, and material selection and might even represent a more profitable business model (recognizing the key issue of initial capital requirements). This discussion allows students to not only begin to recognize and articulate their assumptions, per Cranton's (2002) suggestions but, when coupled with a later assignment in which they develop multiple revenue models for a given business concept and examine its impact on sustainability and profitability, it also allows them to potentially revise their assumptions and take some theoretical action on those revisions.

These are just two examples of ways in which to incorporate aspects of transformative learning theory into the classroom discussion. The key is to identify areas where students are likely to have assumptions related to the challenges and develop ways in which they will eventually express these and start to analyze them. At the end of the day, the goal is to offer students a new perspective and an ability to recognize their assumptions in preparation for challenging those assumptions in an effort to develop novel solutions to our most pressing problems.

Discovery-Based Learning through Assignments

Another way in which to incorporate the principles of transformative learning theory is through student assignments. In these cases, assignments are designed such that in the process of completing them, students uncover information or viewpoints that are different from those they started with, prompting them to begin to rethink their prior assumptions. The assignments take on a variety of forms, but in each case students are exposed to a variety of perspectives which they must confront and critically analyze. In this way they not only become more aware of their own assumptions and viewpoints, but are given the opportunity to discover and reflect on alternative views.

ISSUE DEBATES

One of the most direct ways of doing this is through a series of classroom debates. As noted, students often enter the classroom with a set of assumptions and views on a variety of issues. A simple and easy way to get them to begin to question these is by having them debate a topic. The key to this assignment is that students are assigned a topic, but not a position. On the day of their debate they are randomly assigned their position for the debate. This requires them to thoroughly research both sides of the topic and often results in them discovering new information and viewpoints that they had previously not been exposed to. I have learned that in order for this to be the most effective, students should be told to role play and debate as though they were someone from that particular camp rather than using what they may or may not believe in the argument. This provides a safe environment for them to try out a new point of view as recommended by Cranton (2002). In addition, it relieves the psychological burden of attempting to effectively argue for a position they don't believe or agree with. Topics are chosen to ensure sufficient information is available on both sides and have included issues such as nuclear energy, hydraulic fracturing, corporate farming, fishing quotas, and active population control.

INDUSTRY/SECTOR PRESENTATIONS

As I noted in the introduction, another challenge in this space is that many of the significant opportunities and areas most in need of attention are the industries and infrastructures in the developing world where population growth is the largest and there will be increasing demands for improved standards of living. Our current systems are incapable of meeting the needs of this growing population using our current methods. However, students often have a difficult time imagining a fundamentally different structure from everything they have seen. There is often an implicit assumption that industries have evolved in an logical manner and that the way in which needs are met in the developed world are, for the most part, the best way we know how to meet those needs. The first step in helping students to think more creatively is to help them understand the constraints they are placing on their thinking and to critically examine them.

To this end, students are assigned to a group and are asked to research the history and operation of a particular industry or sector. These are intentionally broad and include "sectors" such as water treatment, electricity production, solid waste management, etc. Students are expected to graphically depict the basic operational structure of the sector in the developed world (i.e., the basics of HOW it works) on one or two slides to ensure a high level, fundamental view of the sector. They are then asked to research and present the historical evolution of the sector, focusing on key decisions that influenced the final structure and the reasons behind these. In doing this research they begin to discover that industry structures they take for granted often developed due to constraints that no longer exist. Students are asked to illustrate how the information enlightens us as to potential opportunities – particularly in the developing world by understanding where they are in the evolutionary path of the industry and how they could potentially follow a different path going forward. This project allows students to become aware of their implicit assumptions, but challenge them in a less threatening way by understanding that there was a rationale at some point in time for these decisions. They are then able to begin to examine alternative structures via a "clean slate" in the developing world where the infrastructure may not have been built yet. As a result of this exercise, students often become more willing to question many of the basic structures they have taken for granted, which is the first step in developing radically novel solutions.

BOOK REFLECTION

Another way in which the course attempts to expose students to different viewpoints and provide opportunities for critical self-reflection is through a book reflection assignment. In this case, students are required to choose a book from a pre-approved list and write a reflection paper. In order to encourage students to begin making the connections between different views and their application to their futures as business leaders, most of the books are intentionally not business books. The books used for this assignment are chosen such that they represent a range of views in relation to causes and/or solutions to environmental or social problems. It is also important to assure the students that the books are chosen because they provide an interesting perspective and that the instructor does not necessarily agree with them (something that is explicitly stated in the assignment). This gives the students more freedom to critique the view and express their own thoughts rather than trying to write to fit what they feel is the professor's view. Listed below is a sample of some of the books that have been used in the course.

- *Ishmael* by Daniel Quinn
- *The Conundrum* by David Owen
- *Eaarth* by Bill McKibben
- *The End of Growth* by Richard Heinberg
- *The Great Disruption* by Paul Gilding
- *The Last Hours of Ancient Sunlight* by Thom Hartmann
- *The Green Collar Economy* by Van Jones

The paper is designed to make students examine their own views in relation to the author's view and defend their position either for or against the author's arguments rather than simply report what the author's stance on the issue was. This not only exposes them to alternative views but also helps them to better recognize their own personal views, which is a key first step in the critical self-reflection of transformation learning (Cranton, 2002). Sample questions for the paper typically include the following:

- Describe your interpretation of the author's primary arguments/positions as it relates to the issue of sustainability and environmental problems/issues
- What is your reaction to their arguments? Do you agree or disagree and why?
- How has this book influenced your thinking or views on sustainability?

Occasionally students have asked to use books that are not on the instructor's list for this assignment. Because the books are specifically chosen to represent different and thought-provoking viewpoints, these requests are generally denied unless the instructor is familiar with the book in question and feels that it is appropriate. This is done not only to ensure that the book is a good fit for the assignment, but also because a class period is used to discuss, compare and contrast the various author's arguments in order for the rest of the class to gain exposure to additional perspectives, making it even more important to choose books that will yield effective discussion. To further facilitate the student's exposure to these alternative arguments, the number of students that can choose any one book is generally limited to five or fewer, depending on the class size.

NEW VENTURE SUSTAINABILITY ANALYSIS

Business schools have faced criticism for prescribing a profit-driven, materialistic worldview in which everything plays a secondary role to profit maximization and shareholder value (Ghoshal, 2005; Giacalone & Thompson, 2006; Lourenço, 2013; Mitroff, 2004). Ghoshal (2005) suggests that this can be traced back to the fact that many of our management theories are rooted in economic theory in which actors are focused on self-interest and Giacalone and Thompson (2006) argue that this results in business schools promoting what they refer to as an organization-centered worldview which places all decisions in a purely economic context and further implies that the accumulation of wealth is the pinnacle of the values hierarchy.

While this may promote economic growth, Gioia (2002) notes that "for all the good that economic perspective do, they nonetheless emphasize a view of the world in dollars, profits, returns, etc., which de-emphasizes other ways in which we might conceptualize the responsibilities of business" (p. 143). As noted previously, at Babson we believe that a sustainable business is not only one that considers its environmental impact, but also its larger societal impact. The final project in the class is designed to help students better understand the connection between a business and the greater society. In doing so, they will gain an increased appreciation for how their future business decisions affect the environment, their community, and the world. Additionally, the assignment gives the students to utilize lessons from the semester to develop alternative solutions that reduce any negative impacts of their business.

In order to make the assignment as meaningful as possible, students are allowed to work on any venture idea of their choosing. This also has the impact of illustrating that sustainability is important across all types of businesses. They are also allowed to work alone or in groups. The issues they must address are designed to increase their awareness of the ways in which their business interacts with the social and natural environment, give them an opportunity to examine alternatives, and to critically assess their options. The projects are developed throughout the second half of the semester in a learn-do environment in which some class time is taken each day to discuss the application of course material to their projects and students have an opportunity to work on the project and present their progress to the class for critique and discussion.

The first part of the assignment is focused on engaging students in challenging their initial assumptions about how their business should operate. As noted earlier in this chapter, a discussion is held around the idea of challenging existing business models using the automotive industry as an example to show that it may be possible to develop more sustainable and environmentally friendly businesses by utilizing different revenue models. Students are then asked to apply this principle to their own idea by determining how their business might change under different models and examining how this might affect the profitability and sustainability of the business.

The rest of the assignment is designed to broaden the student's understanding of the impact of their business and their own business decisions. Throughout the semester students are introduced to life cycle analysis (LCA) and systems thinking and a major part of the project is to apply these concepts to their own venture idea. Students are asked to map their processes in a manner similar to an LCA and identify all the points and ways in which their business has an impact on the environment and society from cradle to grave. This includes not only impacts from their own operations, but from their suppliers, customer usage, and disposal. While this is a daunting task, the focus is not on completeness of the final model, but on creating awareness of how their future decisions potentially have global consequences for people and the planet.

Students are then asked to suggest ways in which their impact could be minimized and, given what they have discovered, make an initial subjective assessment of the environmental and social sustainability of the venture, and whether it is something that should be pursued. In the process of developing and completing the project, students gain a better understanding of the significant reach of their decisions as business leaders and their responsibilities beyond merely profitability. Furthermore, but they are better able to appreciate how it is often easier to design for sustainability on the frontend rather than try to make changes later once they see the number and magnitude of interconnections between their business and the world.

Student Reflection and Course Evaluation

The course has been taught four times with a series of modifications that have led to the structure described here. Objective evaluation of the effectiveness of the course is admittedly difficult for multiple reasons. First, much of the learning is focused on producing future entrepreneurs and business leaders that behave in a more environmentally and socially responsible way. This obviously can involve a significant time lag when dealing with undergraduate students. In addition, transformational learning is about changing a student's internal frame of reference, which is difficult to accurately measure. However, we can look to student comments on their course surveys to see if they are in line with the goals of the course. In that respect, the course has proven to be successful in achieving some of these objectives. Samples of these comments include the following:

> "Taught us how to think about things differently: Always question!"

> "The in-class discussions involving everyone were very often very productive. I got a lot from those discussions."

> "Enlightening with regard to framing many of the world's problems and why they exist."

> "It's a great class and a very important way we all need to think."

> "Forces you to think from the sustainable point of view. Really promoted learning and focuses on some of the harsh realities that we are facing."

"Forces you to change your perspective on business and sustainability – great!"

"New paths and idea making in venture creation need to be implemented. Many of these topics first and foremost require a mindset change."

"Great learning strategy about how to look at situations from a different perspective and how externalities and sustainability influences business."

"The content of the course is invaluable and something that every student at Babson should be exposed to."

"Book reflections, debates in class and group projects are all great ways of getting students to learn about the subjects/topics involved."

Comments such as these suggest that students are, indeed, reexamining and changing their frames of reference and we hold out hope that we will see longer term results in the form more sustainable businesses being created by students that have taken this course.

Conclusion

Teaching sustainability in the context of entrepreneurship has a number of challenges that involve getting students to recognize, question, and consider alternatives to their current assumptions and viewpoints. If we believe that the world requires truly novel and different ways of solving problems and meeting society's needs, this will require a different way of thinking and seeing the world. I believe that this can be accomplished through the application of transformative learning theory to course development in this area. If, rather than viewing assignments as ways in which students can illustrate their learning or mastery of a particular subject matter, we instead approach them as events through which students become aware of their assumptions and have an opportunity to examine them in relation to alternatives, we are able to lay the groundwork for what is needed to transform the student's worldview (Cranton, 2002). While I realize that awareness and examination of assumptions will, in no way, guarantee a change in an individual's viewpoint, I believe that without this awareness no change is possible.

In designing the course described in this chapter I have tried to focus on what I felt were key inherent assumptions that students were likely to have that may prevent them from considering entirely new solutions. While the assignments are specific, I aspire to instill in the students a broader understanding of issues such as the importance of history and path dependence on industry structures so that they begin to question other systems they once considered as given. Assignments such as the debates force students to confront views that they may disagree with and they often find that in their research, the picture may not be as clear as they originally thought. For some students this can be disturbing, but it serves to remind them again to question their currently held views and the value in seeking out alternative perspectives.

Finally, when we consider Bloom's taxonomy in relation to the need to create new solutions, it becomes clear that the lower levels of educational objectives are inadequate. Knowledge and comprehension are based on "what is" rather than what "could be." And, while they are an important foundation, I would argue that our time is better spent focusing on how we provide students the means to spend more of their time in the higher (i.e., more difficult) levels of the taxonomy — those of synthesis and evaluation, for this is where new combinations can form. In the case of the course I have described here, I have attempted to do this by providing projects that enable students to apply their learning to actual concepts in which they have a strong interest.

To date this approach at Babson College has shown promise in achieving the types of change in student thinking that is desired in preparing students to tackle these challenges. While I do not intend to suggest that the examples and assignments described here are the ultimate solution, it is hoped that they provide an example that other instructors can use with respect to how transformational theory can be used in developing curriculum and assignments in developing similar courses. In some ways, this is difficult and risky for us as educators. Changing a student's views and way of thinking is not easily measured or tested, which increases the challenges of assessment. Additionally, the potential rewards may be years or even decades in the future if we are successful. However, I for one feel that the potential reward is worth the effort.

> The aim of education should be to teach us rather how to think, than what to think — rather to improve our minds, so as to enable us to think for ourselves, than to load the memory with thoughts of other men.
>
> Bill Beattie

References

Betts, S. C. (2008). Teaching and assessing basic concepts to advanced applications: Using Bloom's taxonomy to inform graduate course design. *Academy of Educational Leadership Journal*, 12(3), 99–106.

Bloom, B. S., Englehart, M. D., Furst, E. J., Hill, W. H., & Krathwohl, D. R. (1956). *Taxonomy of educational objectives. Handbook 1: Cognitive domain.* New York, NY: David McKay.

Chen, J. C., & Martin, A. R. (2015). Role-play simulations as a transformative methodology in environmental education. *Journal of Transformative Education, 13*(1), 85–102.

Christopher, M. M., Thomas, J. A., & Tallent-Runnels, M. K. (2004). Raising the bar: Encouraging high level thinking in online discussion forums. *Roeper Review, 26*(3), 166–171.

Clark, W. H., Jr. (2012). *The need and rationale for the Benefit Corporation: Why it is the legal form that best addresses the needs of social entrepreneurs, investors, and, ultimately, the public.* White paper. Retrieved from http://benefitcorp.net/for-attorneys/benefit-corp-white-paper

Cranton, P. (1994). *Understanding and promoting transformative learning: A guide for educators of adults.* The Jossey-Bass Higher and Adult Education Series. San Francisco, CA: Jossey-Bass Publishers, Inc.

Cranton, P. (1996). *Professional development as transformative learning. New perspectives for teachers of adults.* The Jossey-Bass Higher and Adult Education Series. San Francisco, CA: Jossey-Bass Publishers, Inc.

Cranton, P. (2002). Teaching for transformation. *New Directions for Adult & Continuing Education, 2002*(93), 63.

Dwyer, W. O., Leeming, F. C., Cobern, M. K., Porter, B. E., & Jackson, J. M. (1993). Critical review of behavioral interventions to preserve the environment: Research since 1980. *Environment and Behavior, 25,* 275–321.

Erskine, L., & Johnson, S. D. (2012). Effective learning approaches for sustainability: A student perspective. *Journal of Education for Business, 87*(4), 198–205.

Ghoshal, S. (2005). Bad management theories are destroying good management practices. *Academy of Management Learning & Education, 4*(1), 75–91.

Giacalone, R. A., & Thompson, K. R. (2006). Business ethics and social responsibility education: Shifting the worldview. *Academy of Management Learning & Education, 5*(3), 266–277. doi:10.5465/AMLE.2006.22697016

Gioia, D. A. (2002). Business education's role in the crisis of corporate confidence. *Academy of Management, 16,* 142–144.

Kearins, K., & Springett, D. (2003). Educating for sustainability: Developing critical skills. *Journal of Management Education, 27*(2), 188–204.

King, J. (2010). 100 best places to work in IT. *Computerworld,* June 21, 26–58.

Kollmuss, A., & Agyeman, J. (2002). Mind the gap: Why do people act environmentally and what are the barriers to pro-environmental behavior? *Environmental Education Research, 8,* 239–260.

Lourenço, F. (2013). To challenge the world view or to flow with it? Teaching sustainable development in business schools. *Business Ethics: A European Review, 22*(3), 292–307.

Marzano, R. J., & Kendall, J. S. (2007). *The new taxonomy of educational objectives* (2nd ed.). Thousand Oaks, CA: Corwin Press.

Mezirow, J. (1991). *Transformative Dimensions of Adult Learning.*

Mezirow, J. (1996). Toward a learning theory of adult literacy. *Adult Basic Education, 6*(3), 115.

Mezirow, J. (1997). Transformative learning: Theory to practice. *New Directions for Adult & Continuing Education, 1997*(74), 5.

Mitroff, I. I. (2004). An open letter to the deans and the faculties of American business schools, editorial. *Journal of Business Ethics, 54*(2), 185–189.

Ross, L. (2010). Accounting for sustainability. *Financial Management, 1*, 31–32.

Seung-Youn, C., & Stepich, D. (2003). Applying the "congruence" principle of Bloom's taxonomy to designing online instruction. *Quarterly Review of Distance Education, 4*(3), 317–330.

Staats, H., Harland, P., & Wilke, H. A. M. (2004). Effecting durable change: A team approach to improve environmental behavior in the household. *Environment and Behavior, 36*, 341–367.

Steg, L., & Vlek, C. (2009). Encouraging pro-environmental behaviour: An integrative review and research agenda. *Journal of Environmental Psychology, 29*, 300–317.

Uzzell, D., & Räthzel, N. (2009). Transforming environmental psychology. *Journal of Environmental Psychology, 29*, 340–350.

Vlek, C., & Steg, L. (2007). Human behavior and environmental sustainability: Problems, driving forces and research topics. *Journal of Social Issues, 63*, 1–19.

Wiek, A., Withycombe, L., Redman, C., & Mills, S. B. (2011). Moving forward on competence in sustainability research and problem solving. *Environment, 53*(2), 3–13.

Appendix

RESOURCE UTILIZATION GAME

Objectives: To give students a better understanding of how the planet came to be in the environmental condition it is in by reflecting on drivers of their own behavior and to understand some of the complexities involved in solving the problems, but that need to be considered.

1. Illustrate effects of short-term versus long-term view on renewable resources
2. Illustrate effects of perceived "unlimited" supply on behavior
3. Illustrate the effects of competition on behavior
4. Illustrate the effects of uncertainty and nonlinearity
5. Illustrate the effects of survival.

Background: Students often feel as though environmental problems are caused by bad people or people behaving badly. While this is sometimes the case, oftentimes it can be due to basic human behavior and motivations and a lack of understanding of the impact of that behavior rather than intentionality. Playing this game allows the students to examine their own behavior and how different circumstances affect that behavior so that they have a better understanding of the issues that need to be addressed in creating a sustainable world.

Game: When resources are seen as unlimited and "free" you will use as much as you can to benefit yourself. The environment renews the supply faster than you can use it so there is no threat of depletion.

Put 10 chocolate kisses on the table. Choose a student to play with the following rules:

1. You can pick up one kiss at a time and return it to your desk
2. I will add one kiss every second unless there are only 2 remaining, then I will stop adding
3. You have 15 seconds to get as many as possible.

Record the number the student collected and the number remaining.

What was your strategy? (most likely to move as quickly as possible to get as many as possible). Why? Were you concerned about running out? (most likely not — resources perceived as unlimited in the timeframe concerned and they are added faster than you can retrieve them). How would you improve your score? (most likely find a way to do it faster — similar to focus on manufacturing efficiency and productivity). This situation is similar to the situation in North America in 1700 or 1800s.

What if resources were used faster than they were replenished? Choose a second student to play with the following rule change:

1. I will add one kiss every 5 seconds unless there only 2 remaining, then I will stop adding

Record the number the student collected and the number remaining

What was your strategy? (most likely didn't change) Why? (Resources are still sufficient for the duration of the game)

Ask the class if anyone would do something different and why.

Long-Term versus Short-Term Perspective

Choose another student to play. The rules are the same, but the game now lasts 1 minute.

Record the number the student collected and the number remaining.

What was your strategy? How did it differ from the previous rounds and why? (Resources are no longer sufficient for the duration of the game, so usage must be managed). Use this to illustrate the effects of short-term versus long-term thinking in terms of natural resource usage.

Effects of Competition

Now choose three students to play. The game is back to 15 seconds with the previous rules. The student with the most gets bonus participation points.

Record the number each student collected and the number remaining.

What was their strategy? Why? The idea here is to show that people often act in their own best interest — relate this to Adam Smith's "invisible hand" — why doesn't this work? Introduces the concept of competition into the picture. How would you improve your score? (requires cooperation).

Nonlinearity and Uncertainty

Choose another student. New rule:

1. Once the number of kisses gets below a certain number (don't tell them the number), I start taking away kisses.

What was their strategy? Why? The point here is to illustrate that many environmental problems are nonlinear and collapse can be sudden. Tie this into collapse of the cod market and general historical societal collapse — we know this happens and has happened repeatedly — what do we do about it?

Survival

Finally, all students play. Start with $2x - 6$ ($x =$ number of students). Same rules as previously except this time any student with fewer than 2 gets an "F" in participation for the day. The game will last 30 seconds. Give the students time to think (and discuss, if they choose).

There will be exactly enough for 2 each if they do not deplete the resources too soon such that I continue to add one every 5 seconds. The only way for all students to pass is for them to cooperate and agree that no one takes more than two. Second, in order for all to pass they must deplete all the resources. Do people that depend on natural resources to survive care about the long-term sustainability of the system?

18 Becoming Entrepreneurial: Constructing an Entrepreneurial Identity in Elective Entrepreneurship Courses

Candida Brush and Mary Gale

Introduction

A common starting point for an entrepreneurship course is to "name a successful entrepreneur." Who comes to mind? What was the first name you thought of? Was it Bill Gates? Steve Jobs? Or how about Richard Branson? Larry Page and Sergey Brin? It usually takes the mention of 6–10 names before a woman entrepreneur is named — and, often more names before a social entrepreneur is remembered. Why is this the case? For most students, the tendency is to ascribe the characteristics of successful entrepreneurs as male heroic figures, who single-handedly invent the idea of the business, take big risks, and aggressively grow their ventures to achieve economic wealth (Ahl, 2006; Gupta, Goktan, & Gunay, 2014). The perception of entrepreneurs as traditionally male, independent and risk-takers is mostly a myth, which is perpetuated by the media, our teaching cases, classroom materials, and in general conversation (Bird & Brush, 2002). This stereotype may fit some entrepreneurs but not all.

More specifically, current literature shows that there are differences among entrepreneurs, traditional, women, and social, in terms of goals and objectives, motivations, social capital or networks, sector of business, and outcomes. Traditional entrepreneurs are thought of in the ideal as those who brilliantly conceive of a new technology innovation, capture a large market, take a company public, and make millions of dollars. These entrepreneurs are financially motivated, take big risks, have networks that are male-dominated, and start businesses in traditional product/market sectors hoping to generate jobs and personal wealth (Aldrich, Reese, & Dubini, 1989; Allen, Elam, Langowitz, & Dean, 2008; Bruderl & Priesendorfer, 1998; Davidsson, Delmar, & Gartner, 2003; Fairlie & Robb, 2009; Kirzner, 1973; Manolova, Brush, Edelman, & Shaver, 2012; Schumpeter, 1935; Shane & Venkataraman, 2000).

Research also shows that women entrepreneurs are more often inspired by both financial and innovation motives and are more likely to have hybrid goals for their businesses (Manolova et al., 2012). Similarly, women tend to have heterogeneous networks comprised both males and females (Aldrich et al., 1989; Fischer & Reuber, 2007). While women do start businesses in all sectors, they are more prevalent in consumer and personal services (Fairlie & Robb, 2009). Finally, women entrepreneurs are more likely to seek a variety of performance outcomes, both social and economic (Allen et al., 2008; Carter & Allen, 1997; Jennings & Brush, 2013).

Similarly, the profile of the social entrepreneur is also different from the traditional entrepreneur. Social entrepreneurs are often focused on a social mission and operate businesses in multiple corporate forms, including for profit, nonprofit, or numerous hybrid models (Hechavarria, Ingram, Justo, & Terjesen, 2012; Meyskens, Brush, & Allen, 2011). Social entrepreneurs are motivated by a passion to change the system, to solve a social problem, and to create an organization or business (either for profit or nonprofit) that permits the creation of social value (Dees & Anderson, 2003; Mair & Marti, 2006; Meyskens, 2010; Neck, Brush, & Allen, 2009). Social entrepreneurs rely on efficient social networks, typically based on high social capital (Mair & Noboa, 2006). Social entrepreneurs seek outcomes different from the more narrow traditional financial performance, instead pursuing both direct and indirect economic, social, and environmental outcomes (Haugh, 2006; Robinson, 2006; Seelos, Ganly, & Mair, 2006). In sum, as shown in Table 1, research shows that traditional, social, and women entrepreneurs do differ across a variety of dimensions.

For students aspiring to be entrepreneurs, clearly some will pursue the idea of the traditional entrepreneur, with clear goals of profit, tight efficient networks, and dreams of wealth creation. But not all students may see themselves in this traditional role. This may have the effect of creating obstacles or a lack of confidence in their ability

Table 1:   Comparison of Entrepreneurial Dimensions.

Dimensions	Traditional Entrepreneur	Woman Entrepreneur	Social Entrepreneur
Goals and objectives	Profit, efficiency (Bruderl & Preisendorfer, 1998; Kirzner, 1973; Schumpeter, 1935)	Hybrid goals – profit and social (Carter & Allen, 1997; Harding, 2006; Jennings & Brush, 2013; Manolova et al., 2012)	Social mission, social change, for profit, and nonprofit (Dees & Anderson, 2003; Mair & Marti, 2006; Meyskens, 2010)
Motivations	Financial success (Davidsson et al., 2003; Manolova et al., 2012)	Self-realization, recognition, innovation, and financial success (Jennings & Brush, 2013; Manolova et al., 2012)	Variety of motives (Haugh, 2005)
Social capital	Financial networks; male-dominated (Aldrich et al., 1989)	Mixed male/female networks (Fischer & Reuber, 2007; Orser & Eliott, 2015)	Social/political/mixed affiliations (Seelos et al., 2006)
Sector	Traditional product/market (Allen et al., 2008; Fairlie & Robb, 2009)	Consumer service, personal services (Allen et al., 2008; Fairlie & Robb, 2009)	Social sector markets (Robinson, 2006)
Success metrics	Job and wealth creation (Shane & Venkataraman, 2000)	Social and economic outcomes (Hechavarria et al., 2012; Meyskens et al., 2011)	Social value creation; solving a social; or environmental problem (Mair & Marti, 2006; Neck et al., 2009)

to succeed as a traditional entrepreneur (Xavier, Kelley, Kew, Herrington, & Vorderwülbecke, 2012). In fact, perceptions about role model entrepreneurs are linked to an individual's intention to act as an entrepreneur (Arenius & Minniti, 2005). When the perceptions are hard to imagine because of the success criteria, this may create perceived obstacles in the process. For some aspiring entrepreneurs who are female, or others who wish to solve a social problem or create a new nonprofit organization, the gap between the traditional entrepreneurial role and desires may present an even greater challenge (Kelley, Brush, Greene, & Litovsky, 2012; Robinson, 2006).

Most students at colleges and universities enter elective entrepreneurship courses with expectations of learning more about what it means to be entrepreneurial in a particular context or role. The contexts can vary from a family enterprise to a less developed country to an inner city to a rural location. The roles in which they may envision their entrepreneurial experience also may be widely different as some may see themselves as a small business owner, woman entrepreneur, franchise owner, family entrepreneur, or social entrepreneur. In other cases the role identity of the traditional entrepreneur may conflict with a student's self-concept or his/her social identity, which may result in a lack of confidence or even create a fear of taking action.

Drawing from Social Identity Theory, Identity Theory, and Self-Concept Theory, we develop a framework that reflects how students develop their entrepreneurial identity using Entrepreneurial Thought & Action® (ET&A) pedagogies. We consider two specific course examples, social entrepreneurship and women's entrepreneurship to show how identity transformation among students takes place through a course experience when they desire to pursue roles other than traditional entrepreneurship. The remainder of this chapter provides a brief overview of identity theories and then offers examples of how pedagogies are used to help students construct their identities in elective entrepreneurship courses.

Theoretical Background

The process of becoming entrepreneurial is also a process of identity construction (Gannon, 2011). Identity construction is a process of navigating one's personal, relational, and social/historical contexts as one becomes an entrepreneur. Entrepreneurial identities emerge and evolve over time, and in the case of students in a class, this is referred to as student identity transformation (Keeling, 2004). During their educational experience, be they undergraduate or graduate, students' identities are shaped through many experiences and activities. Theories of identity encompass three basic aspects:

a. Self-Concept Theory proposes that a person's global identity is an integrated system combining a person's individual characteristics, values, beliefs and traits (Markus & Nurius, 1986). Self-concept can evolve and individuals can have more than one sense of their self- concept (i.e., vegetarian, thrifty, socially responsible). Self-concept evolves over time from childhood to adulthood as people have experiences and move through life. People tend to move towards identities they aspire to and away from self-concepts they fear (Erez & Earley, 1993).

b. Social Identity Theory focuses on social identities, which are memberships in groups based on demographic characteristics (race, gender, age) or affiliations (political parties or religious denominations) (Tajfel, 1982). Social identities can change when an individual moves in or out of different groups (i.e., move from one religion to another, or from one association to another). Social identities can be perceived positively or negatively in relation to one or another group (Hogg, Terry, & White, 1995) stemming from their gender, race and group affiliations (i.e., female, sorority member, Presbyterian).

c. Identity Theory focuses primarily on role-based identities, for instance, manager, father, or entrepreneur (Hogg et al., 1995; Stryker, 1987). Individuals can move from one to another identity (e.g., bachelor to husband or manager to entrepreneur) as they gain competencies and make decisions about relationships and engagements. People tend to enact their roles in ways that are deemed socially appropriate, and they try to meet social norms and expectations for different role behaviors. There is also a tendency to draw comparisons between a person's individual identity and those of others depending on situational contexts.

Identity Theory posits that collective identity might be both category and role-based (e.g., a woman entrepreneur or African-American student). At different times or in different situations, one identity might be more salient than another; for example a student identity might be more salient in a classroom, while the wife identity might be more salient at home or other context (Ashforth, 2000). Other aspects of collective identity are related to how an individual might perceive his or her own group or how he/she perceives other's assessment of this group.

Entrepreneurial Thought and Action®: A Creative Approach

Babson College is particularly interested in how students learn to think and act entrepreneurially. Babson College enrolls 2100 undergraduate students and about 1100 graduate students (MBA and MSM). Entrepreneurial Thought & Action® (ET&A) is a core concept underlying the required curriculum and 100% of students take a required course that covers basic aspects of ET&A (Schlesinger, Kiefer, & Brown, 2012). ET&A is comprised both causal (predictive) and effectual (creative) reasoning that is applied to various entrepreneurial settings (Neck, Greene, & Brush, 2014; Sarasvathy, 2001). Predictive or causal logic is consistent with planned strategy approaches (Chandler, DeTienne, McKelvie, & Mumford, 2011).

Given the deep roots of entrepreneurship as a discipline in Economics and more recently Strategic Management, most approaches to entrepreneurship education emphasize the identification and evaluation of the entrepreneurial opportunity by specifying the feasibility, attractiveness, and particular timing and competitive intensity of an entrepreneurial opportunity (Edelman, Manolova, & Brush, 2008; Honig, 2004; Neck et al., 2014). At most colleges and universities, classes focus on the creation of a business plan, where students are challenged to defend the objective characteristics of an entrepreneurial opportunity and how organizing resources can yield known outcomes and known returns (Katz, 2003). The logic for success is driven by the expected return on investment (ROI), which is based on predictions about market penetration, revenues, costs, and expected returns on invested capital (Honig, 2004; Van Osnabrugge & Robinson, 2000). In this model, an entrepreneurial team and venture stakeholders are assembled based on the perceived demands of the particular entrepreneurial opportunity. Participants and stakeholders are expected to implement pre-determined business models that focus on value creation and value capture by targeting specific customer segments (Honig, 2004). While those joining a growing venture may experiment with the venture's value creation activities, there is the presumption that entrepreneurial action will be guided by outlines and contingencies put down in the business plan. The overall process is ends driven.

The creative approach that underpins Babson's ET&A philosophy is based on quite different assumptions (Sarasvathy, 2001). Table 2 shows the core assumptions of the creative approach. The creative approach is means driven and highly interactive (Neck & Greene, 2011; Read, Song, & Smit, 2009; Sarasvathy, 2001). One important difference from the predictive approach is that there is an assumption that outcomes are often intrinsically unknowable, which leads to a different set of behaviors (Sarasvathy, 2001).

Table 2: Entrepreneurial Thought & Action® — Creative Logic.

Creative Approach	Assumptions	Citations
Self-understanding	Skills and capabilities of individuals; opportunities can be made or created	Fiet & Patel (2006) and Alvarez & Barney (2007)
Observation and reflection	Means driven	Neck & Greene (2011) and Read et al. (2009)
Bring along stakeholders	Interactive and social process	Sarasvathy (2001), Jack & Anderson (2002), and Kloosterman (2010)
Act and experiment	Creative and iterative	Neck et al. (2014), Sarasvathy (2001), and Dew et al. (2009)
Build on results	Unknown outcomes	Mintzberg (1978) and Read et al. (2009)
Affordable loss	Maximize options in the present	Sarasvathy (2001)

Instead of identifying opportunities, actions are rooted in the self-understanding of the entrepreneur, and the opportunity is created within a community of self-selected stakeholders (Fiet & Patel, 2006; Jack & Anderson, 2002; Kloosterman, 2010). Different from trying to achieve a predictable and known outcome, the aims of creative logic are to act and experiment with existing or available means (Chandler et al., 2011; Dew, Read, Sarasvathy, & Wiltbank, 2009; Sarasvathy, 2001). In the creative approach, actions, experimentation to clarify opportunities, and the identification of new stakeholders are each embedded within social structures (Granovetter, 1985; Neck et al., 2014). For this reason, entrepreneurs can create their environments through action. New stakeholders, who are often self-selected, alter and reshape perceptions of the environment, which leads to new possibilities about what is desirable, feasible, and viable for the venture. Willingness to join a new venture rests on social interactions and stakeholders help to shape aims and outcomes (Noyes & Brush, 2012).

In contrast to a predictive approach, the creative approach is rooted in an investment logic that considers what losses are affordable (i.e., affordable loss) for a particular set of entrepreneurial actions valued by the stakeholders (Chandler et al., 2011; Sarasvathy, 2001). Considering what one is willing to lose in association with particular actions and proceeding incrementally with this notion are quite different than attempting to specify known returns and known outcomes as is the goal of predictive logic (Chandler et al., 2011; Dew et al., 2009; Sarasvathy, 2001).

During their time on campus, students' interactions with faculty, staff, and other students influence their learning and identity transformation (Abes, Jones, & McEwen, 2007; Baxter Magolda, 2009; Newman, 2013). Newman (2013) finds that a student's identity is socially constructed, and reconstructed, not necessarily in a linear way. Because identity is socially constructed, the campus environment is a major influencer in a student's entrepreneurial identity development. A student's "meaning making capacity" (Abes et al., 2007, p. 6) is the ability to increasingly define his/her own knowledge, self, and social relations rather than having external influencers define these. This is something that students develop over time as they journey to "self-authorship" (Baxter Magolda, 2008, p. 269; Newman, 2013). This process involves reflection (gaining an understanding of who they are), interpersonal engagement (who they know), and development of intrapersonal skills (what they know) (Newman, 2013). The ET&A philosophy which underpins Babson's entrepreneurship classes is in fact a means of "becoming entrepreneurial" through a series of interactions with others and with the environment (Sarasvathy, 2001, 2008). Because entrepreneurial learning and identity development is embedded in specific activities and cultures, the classroom is one important community within which a student's entrepreneurial identity is constructed and shaped (Kempster, 2006; Newman, 2013).

The next section provides two illustrations of how student identities are transformed thorough two unique classes, *Women's Entrepreneurship and Leadership* (an MBA Elective) and *Living the Social Entrepreneurship Experience* (an undergraduate class, required for the Entrepreneurship Concentration). These two classes serve as examples of how ET&A concepts are applied to help students construct their entrepreneurial identities. As shown in Table 3, the dimensions of context, who I am (self-concept), what I know (human capital), who I know (social capital), and entrepreneurial action are the core elements of both classes.

CASE #1 – WOMEN'S ENTREPRENEURSHIP AND LEADERSHIP

The *Women's Entrepreneurship and Leadership* course is about contemporary women's roles in creating and leading organizations. The

Table 3: A Means to Construct Entrepreneurial Identities in Two Course Examples.

	Living the Social Entrepreneurship Experience – Undergraduate	Women's Entrepreneurship and Leadership – MBA Elective
Context	Social Entrepreneurship Typology; Challenges and Opportunities of Social Entrepreneurship by Type – guest speakers, cases, articles, videos, discussion; Stakeholder exercise; Performance Measurement exercise	Labor Economics, Women in the Workforce, Regulatory and Socio-Demographic History of Women-exercises videos, discussion
Who I am – Self-Concept	Self-assessment exercise, regular written and oral reflections on project experiences	Reflection on values, beliefs, and goals
What I know – Human Capital	Self-assessment exercise, discussions	Self-assessment exercise, past jobs, accomplishments, and capabilities
Who I know – Social Capital	Field interviews with customers, stakeholders, and organizations related to project or new venture	Applied networking exercises interview with successful woman entrepreneur
Entrepreneurial Action	Plan and execute a project for an established social venture or take meaningful action on student's existing or new social venture, for example, market tests, forming partnerships, raising capital	Action plan with vision, and implementable steps

course examines the issues, challenges, and opportunities women face in leading or creating companies, explores organizational policies that facilitate women's advancement and participation in companies, and helps students develop strategies for effectively managing their leadership or entrepreneurial career. Multiple perspectives are considered, including macro environmental, organizational policies, and individual roles and leadership. There are three major learning objectives:

- To develop an awareness of the history and perspectives on women in the workforce, in leadership and in entrepreneurship.
- To experience the issues, challenges and opportunities in women's leadership and entrepreneurship.
- To assess and develop personal skills for effective leadership and to plan a career strategy.

The course begins with the history and background of women in the workforce and the trends and progress of women in management, leadership, and entrepreneurship. This is followed by an exploration of the influence of political-economic, socio-cultural, regulatory, and demographic forces as they influenced occupational opportunities and women's role in work. The next part of the course covers women's experiences in leadership, entrepreneurial, and managerial roles. A focus on the effects of organizational policies on women and discussions of topics such as the glass ceiling, career planning, leadership styles, and management challenges are included. The final part of the course is designed to have students apply an entrepreneurial approach, using ET&A, to their career and personal strategies for action. Experiential team exercises on mentoring, networking, managing family and work, negotiation, communication, and vision provide background for creation of a personal action plan. Table 3 shows how the elements of the three theories, self-concept, social identity, and role identity, are applied through the assignments and activities in this women's entrepreneurship course.

This course has been taught for 15 years at two different schools. The effect of the course on women students is dramatic for three main reasons. First, they enter a course that has "women" in the title. This self-selection into a "women's" entrepreneurship and leadership course is central to the students self-identifying as "women" entrepreneurs and leaders, which reinforces their collective social and role identity (Ashforth, 2000). During the sessions, the students consider how their work/career/entrepreneurial experiences are similar and/or different from the traditional (male) stereotype of entrepreneurship (Hogg et al., 1995). Class discussions include debates about what it means to be stereotyped in one way (e.g., women leaders are emotional) and how to manage or over-come stereotypical perceptions that could be negative or conflicting with other perceptions of how an entrepreneur or leader might behave. Another essential assignment is to systematically evaluate their previous jobs and consider the accomplishments and skills gained from these. The result is identification of competencies and capabilities that define their personal role and human capital, and further develop their self-understanding.

Second, students in the class reflect on and consider their self-concept (who I am) or global identity in terms of what is important to them as entrepreneurs (Markus & Nurius, 1986). One of the assignments is a personal time-line that includes two photos, one from when they were 18 and one from today. This allows students to reflect on the changes and beliefs from then and now. Similar to research noted earlier in this chapter, Babson's women entrepreneurial students frequently have a complex of motivations and goals for their business, rather than just financial concerns. They often plan to start businesses or initiatives that create social value rather than just economic value. As a result, discussions in class, guest speakers, and reading materials help students to believe in their values and trust their personal judgment, even if these are conflicting with traditional entrepreneurial profiles.

Third, students are encouraged to develop their networks strategically (who I know). They work on reaching out to successful women entrepreneurs, doing a network analysis to determine gaps, and developing their personal pitch. This is an essential part of developing their role identity as entrepreneurs or entrepreneurial leaders (Stryker, 1987). Exercises around strategically developing and maintaining their networks and how to develop trust in these relationships and using their social capital to reach out to mentors for advice reinforces this aspect of the class.

After the seven weeks of the class, the personal action plan is the culmination of the learning of the course. This assignment requires that students create a vision of where they want to be and to create an action plan for how to get there. An essential component is to identify what matters to them (who they are and their values), what their capabilities are (what they know), and their plan for business and professional support (who they know). These three elements comprise not only their transformation in collective identity (Ashforth, 2000) but are also accomplished through the use of ET&A techniques (Sarasvathy, 2001). One key outcome is the confidence that students have in pursuing their own chosen pathway as women entrepreneurs or entrepreneurial leaders. Their reflections at the end of the semester state that they learned things about themselves that they did not know, and felt more confident in acting on their personal values and career options. Students commenting on their experience in the classroom note the following:

> "I loved that all the assignments were designed to help us search out something about ourselves."

> "This class was informative, inspiring and helpful both personally and professionally. I have more confidence in approaching my work now."

CASE #2 – LIVING THE SOCIAL ENTREPRENEURIAL EXPERIENCE

The class, *Living the Social Entrepreneurial Experience,* has four primary objectives for students:

- To put Entrepreneurial Thought & Action® into practice by developing and taking key action steps to advance students' own social ventures or projects for existing social enterprises.
- To develop an understanding of social issues and ways in which social ventures of all kinds address these problems: for profit, nonprofit, and multiple types of hybrids, including the opportunities and challenges inherent in each form.
- To understand the ways in which for-profit corporations are undertaking more impactful social programs, such as shared value, conscious capitalism, and partnerships with social ventures, for profit and nonprofit.
- To help students more deeply understand and in many cases change their own values, personal motivations, capacities, and abilities for using ET&A and business to address social problems in a business context, much as they would in a standard for-profit company.

Key elements of the process involve secondary research and significant field work to advance student projects or ventures. Field work involves: (1) interviews with potential customers, industry experts, stakeholders, beneficiaries, and analogous/complementary ventures to understand needs and target segments; (2) market testing of value propositions and products/services (including minimum viable products); and (3) engagement of potential investors/donors. Table 3 outlines the core aspects of the three theories, Self-Concept, Social Identity and Role Identity, and describes how aspects of these theories are applied through ET&A for this social entrepreneurship course.

Course readings, guests, videos, cases, exercises, and discussions provide supplemental background and enrich understanding of context for action. Core to the class experience is the question, how do you build and lead a venture or initiative that benefits society and/or the environment? The course begins with an exercise for students to assess their own values with regard to the role of business in generating social and economic value. This is followed by additional classes that provide an overview of social entrepreneurship history, especially the rapidly changing landscape of the past 15 years and theories and approaches for entrepreneurs and established corporations to address social problems. In parallel during the first three weeks, students identify the project or business that they will work on during the 13-week semester and create a preliminary business model and action plan for researching and executing their project or advancing their venture.

The final project for the course involves taking action on a final project for a new or existing social venture by actually carrying out market tests, forming partnerships, or taking other actions. For example, students will study stakeholder management and devise and act on plans to enlist the help and support of stakeholders that are important to their ventures or project. Other topics include customer identification and value propositions, product/service creation, corporate forms, operations, marketing, performance measurement, financing, and alliances.

Throughout the course, students write about/present/share reflections, execute new action plans based on secondary and primary learning, and revise their business models and functional strategies on an ongoing basis. They receive formal feedback from peers and the instructor inside and outside of class, as well as advisers and partners they develop during the course of the semester. The final deliverable consists of two parts: (1) a write-up and presentation on the business model for their venture/project, including major changes and pivots from the initial model and next steps and (2) a deep reflection on what they have learned about their values related to creating social value through business or personal activities, surprises about social entrepreneurship and their own ability to be an actor in the social entrepreneurship space, and ways in which they can add social/environmental mission in their entrepreneurial/corporate careers.

This course has been taught for four years at Babson College. The tangible outcomes range in scope and impact, including:

- Students develop a more effective interviewing, collaboration, testing, and shaping skills.
- Students gain a keener ability to reflect on the results of actions.
- Students develop greater confidence in their own abilities to take actions that have positive, concrete impact.
- Students are inspired with new interest in incorporating social value activities in their personal lives and/or careers and to

develop greater understanding of the idea that solving social problems helps businesses succeed at a higher level.
- Students learn to make tangible contribution to the success of an existing social venture, or to make significant progress on students' existing social ventures or to develop, commit to start, or actually start a new venture.

Living the Social Entrepreneurial Experience has provided many students with an expanded view of how businesses solving social and environmental problems can benefit not only the target beneficiaries or customers but also the health and success of the organization itself, regardless of corporate form. Additionally, students come to appreciate that ET&A works as effectively in social ventures and projects as it does in businesses with primarily economic goals. Perhaps the most important benefit is a student's new self-confidence in being able to create economic and social value via their own agency. Students comment on their insights:

"This class got me so passionate about the social side of things and it is making me love what I am doing more and more!"

"There are many different ways to help and make an impact to society that I haven't imagined before."

Conclusion

This chapter explored the identity transformation of students who do not fit the traditional entrepreneurial profile. Drawing from Social Identity Theory, Identity Theory, and Self-Concept Theory, we developed a framework that reflected how students develop their entrepreneurial identity using an Entrepreneurial Thought & Action® (ET&A) approach. Because a good number of college and university students do not fit the profile of the traditional entrepreneur, we show how two unique courses, one in social entrepreneurship and one in women's entrepreneurship, can lead to identity transformation and greater confidence in pursuit of alternative entrepreneurial pathways for our students. In both classes, the starting point is "self in context" — achieved by framing the historical and socio-economic environment for entrepreneurship. Because the ET&A approach is and interactive and social process, by grounding entrepreneurial activities in context, students can do a better job of assessing their possibilities and opportunities for entrepreneurship (Sarasvathy, 2001).

Figure 1 shows how the three major identity theories are applied using ET&A in identity construction. The figure reflects the theories and how they are applied in practice: "who I am," "what do I know," and "who do I know." Notably, this shows that these identity elements are interactive with each other. Because the two electives are specialized (women and social) rather than general, students can develop a sense of confidence and inspiration for motives or goals that might be social or environmental rather than just economic.

Both courses start with the personal self-assessment, "who am I" (self-concept), which is revisited with reflections and exercises throughout both classes. The two courses also include systematic assessment of capabilities and skills to help students evaluate "what do I know" (role identity) and how these can be applied in an entrepreneurial endeavor. One key technique for doing this is guest speakers who provide role models for the students who help make it seem "possible" to be a social entrepreneur or woman entrepreneur. Finally, the courses also include networking exercises to help students think about their affiliations and who they know, to further help them develop their sense of social identity ("who do I know").

Importantly, the activities of the classes across the elements of ET&A are interactive across the three types of identities. On the one hand, the collective identity might be connected and aligned. For instance, self-concept and personal values (e.g., for education of low income women) may be reinforced with a social identity (e.g., affiliation with a foundation supporting education for low income women) and further supported by role identity (e.g., a manager in the organization). On the other hand, it is important for students to explore possible conflicts or gaps; for instance, if their self-concept

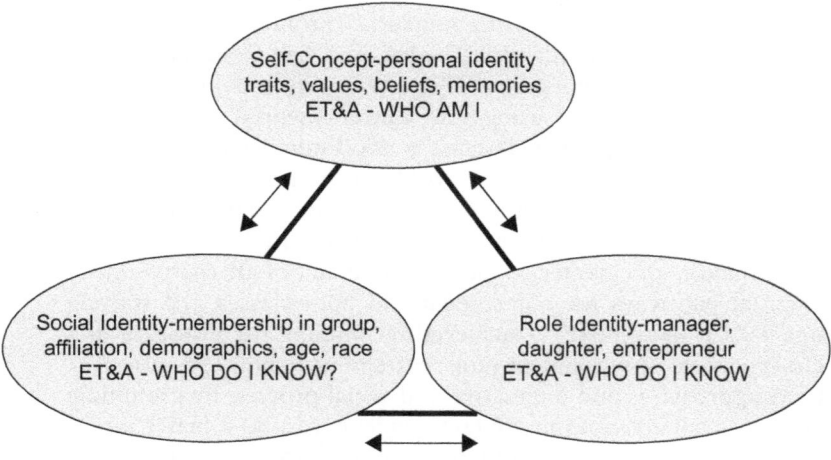

Figure 1:   ET&A Applied to Entrepreneurial Identity Construction.

of being environmentally "green" does not align with the type of company or organization where they presently work.

Finally, the framework applying ET&A concepts for identity transformation has applications across other types of classes. For example, students who wish to start a venture in a family business might also need to consider how their identity transformation might be navigated within a family context where family values, existing business activities, and other factors would influence their journey. Overall, the application of ET&A concepts to identity transformation and construction helps students not only to better understand their collective identity but also develop confidence in their ability to act.

References

Abes, E. S., Jones, S. R., & McEwen, M. K. (2007). Reconceptualizing the model of multiple dimensions of identity: The role of meaning-making capacity in the construction of multiple identities. *Journal of College Student Development, 48*(1), 1−22.

Ahl, H. (2006). Why research on women entrepreneurs needs new directions. *Entrepreneurship Theory and Practice, 30*, 595−621.

Aldrich, H. E., Reese, P. R., & Dubini, P. (1989). Women on the verge of a breakthrough? Networking among entrepreneurs in the United States and Italy. *Entrepreneurship and Regional Development, 1*, 339−356.

Allen, I. E., Elam, A., Langowitz, N., & Dean, M. (2008). 2007 Report on women and entrepreneurship. *Global entrepreneurship monitor.*

Alvarez, S., & Barney, J. (2007). Discovery and creation: Alternative theories of entrepreneurship. *Strategic Entrepreneurship Journal, 1*, 11−26.

Arenius, P., & Minniti, M. (2005). Perceptual variables and nascent entrepreneurship. *Small Business Economics, 24*, 233−247.

Ashforth, B. E. (2000). All in a day's work: Boundaries and micro role transitions. *Academy of Management Review, 25*, 472.

Baxter Magolda, M. (2008). Three elements of self-authorship. *Journal of College Student Development, 49*(4), 269−284.

Baxter Magolda, M. (2009). The activity of meaning making: A holistic perspective on college development. *Journal of College Student Development, 50*(6), 621−639.

Bird, B., & Brush, C. (2002). A gendered perspective on organizational creation. *Entrepreneurship Theory and Practice, 26*, 41−65.

Bruderl, J., & Preisendorfer, P. (1998). Network support and success of newly founded businesses. *Small Business Economics, 10*(3), 213−225.

Carter, N., & Allen, K. (1997). Size determinants of women-owned businesses: Choice or barriers to resources? *Entrepreneurship & Regional Development, 9*(3), 211−220.

Chandler, D., DeTienne, D., McKelvie, A., & Mumford, T. (2011). Causation and effectuation process: A validation study. Journal of Business Venturing., 26(3), 375−390.

Davidsson, P., Delmar, F., & Gartner, W. (2003). Arriving at the high growth firm. *Journal of Business Venturing, 18*(2), 189−216.

Dees, J. G., & Anderson, B. B. (2003). Sector-bending: Blurring the lines between non-profit and for-profit. *Society, 40*(4), 16−27.

Dew, N., Read, S., Sarasvathy, S. D., & Wiltbank, R. (2009). Effectual versus predictive logics in entrepreneurial decision-making: Differences between experts and novices. *Journal of Business Venturing, 24*(4), 287−309.

Edelman, L., Manolova, T., & Brush, C. (2008). Entrepreneurship education: Correspondence between practices of nascent entrepreneurs and textbook prescriptions for success. *Academy of Management Learning and Education, 7*(1), 56−70.

Erez, M., & Earley, C. P. (1993). *Culture, self-identity, and work.* New York, NY: Oxford University Press.

Fairlie, R. W., & Robb, A. M. (2009). Gender differences in business performance: Evidence from the characteristics of business owners survey. *Small Business Economics, 33,* 375−395.

Fiet, J., & Patel, P. C. (2006). Entrepreneurial discovery as constrained systematic search. *Small Business Economics, 30,* 215−229.

Fischer, E., & Reuber, R. (2007). The good, the bad and the unfamiliar: The challenges of reputation formation facing new firms. *Entrepreneurship Theory and Practice, 31*(1), 53−75.

Gannon, A. (2011). *On becoming and entrepreneur: Exploring how African American business owners construct their identities.* Doctoral Dissertation, Boston University Graduate School of Management, Boston, MA.

Granovetter, M. (1985). Economic action and social structure: The problem of embeddedness. *American Journal of Sociology, 91*(3), 481−510.

Gupta, V. K., Goktan, A. B., & Gunay, G. (2014). Gender differences in evaluation of new business opportunity: A stereotype threat perspective. *Journal of Business Venturing, 29*(2), 273−288.

Harding, R. (2006). *Social entrepreneurship monitor, United Kingdom.* London: Foundation for Entrepreneurial Management, London Business School. Retrieved from http://www.london.edu/assets/documents/facultyandresearch/GEM_UK_2006_Social_Entrepreneurship_Monitor.pdf. Accessed on October 15, 2010.

Haugh, H. (2005). A research agenda for social entrepreneurship. *Social Enterprise Journal, 1*(1), 1−13.

Haugh, H. (2006). Social enterprise: Beyond economic outcomes and individual returns. In J. Mair, J. Robinson, & K. Hockerts (Eds.). *Social entrepreneurship* (pp. 180−206). New York, NY: Palgrave MacMillan.

Hechavarria, D. M., Ingram, A., Justo, R., & Terjesen, S. (2012). Are women more likely to pursue social and environmental entrepreneurship? In K. D. Hughes & J. E. Jennings (Eds.), *Global women's entrepreneurship research: Diverse settings, questions and approaches* (pp. 135−151). Cheltenham: Edward Elgar.

Hogg, M. A., Terry, D. J., & White, K. M. (1995). A tale of two theories: A critical comparison of identity theory with social identity theory. *Social Psychology Quarterly, 58*(4), 255−269.

Honig, B. (2004). Entrepreneurship education: Toward a model of contingency- based planning. *Academy of Management Learning and Education, 3*(3), 258−273.

Jack, S., & Anderson, A. R. (2002). The effects of embeddedness on the entrepreneurial process. *Journal of Business Venturing, 17*(5), 467−487.

Jennings, J., & Brush, C. G. (2013). Research on women entrepreneurs: Challenges to (and from) the broader entrepreneurship literature. *Academy of Management Annals, 7*(1), 663−671.

Katz, J. (2003). The chronology and intellectual trajectory of American entrepreneurship Education 1876–1999. Journal of Business Venturing., *18*(2), 283–300.

Keeling, R. P. (2004). *Learning reconsidered: A campus wide focus on student experience*. Washington, DC: National Association of Student Personnel Administrators and American College Personnel Association.

Kelley, D., Brush, C., Greene, P., & Litovsky, Y. (2012). *Global Entrepreneurship Monitor (GEM) women's report*. Wellesley, MA: Babson College.

Kempster, S. (2006). Leadership learning through lived experience: A process of apprenticeship? *Journal of Management & Organization, 12*(1), 4–22.

Kirzner, I. (1973). *Competition and entrepreneurship*. Chicago, IL: The University of Chicago Press.

Kloosterman, R. C. (2010). Matching opportunities with resources: A Framework for analyzing (migrant) entrepreneurship from a mixed embeddedness perspective. *Entrepreneurship and Regional Development, 22*(1), 25–45.

Mair, J., & Marti, I. (2006). Social entrepreneurship research: A source of explanation, prediction, and delight. *Journal of World Business, 41*(1), 36–44.

Mair, J., & Noboa, E. (2006). Social entrepreneurship: How intentions to create a social venture are formed. In J. Mair, J. Robinson, & K. Hockerts (Eds.), 2006. *Social Entrepreneurship* (pp. 121–136). New York, NY: Palgrave MacMillan.

Manolova, T., Brush, C., Edelman, L., & Shaver, K. (2012). One size does not fit all: Entrepreneurial expectancies and growth intentions of US women and men nascent entrepreneurs. *Entrepreneurship and Regional Development, 24*(1–2), 7–27.

Markus, H., & Nurius, P. (1986). Possible selves. *American Psychologist, 41*(9), 954–969.

Meyskens, M. (2010). *How do partnerships lead to a competitive advantage? Applying the resource based view to nascent social ventures*. Doctoral dissertation, Florida International University.

Meyskens, M., Brush, C., & Allen, E. (2011). Human capital and hybrid ventures. In T. Lumpkin & J. Katz (Eds.), *Social and sustainable entrepreneurship: Advances in firm emergence and growth* (Vol. 13, pp. 51–72). Advances in Entrepreneurship, Firm Emergence and Growth. Bingley, UK: Emerald Group Publishing Limited.

Mintzberg, H. (1978). Patterns of strategy formation. *Management Science, 24*(9), 934–948.

Neck, H., Brush, C., & Allen, E. (2009). The landscape of social entrepreneurship. *Business Horizons, 52*(1), 13–19.

Neck, H., & Greene, P. G. (2011). Entrepreneurship education: Known worlds and new frontiers. *Journal of Small Business Management, 49*(1), 55–70.

Neck, H., Greene, P. G., & Brush, C. G. (2014). *Teaching entrepreneurship: A practice based approach*. Northampton, MA: Edward Elgar Publishing.

Newman, E. L. (2013). *A theory on becoming entrepreneurial: A student's developmental journal to a creation-driven mindset*. Doctoral dissertation, University of Pennsylvania- School of Education, Philadelphia, PA.

Noyes, E., & Brush, C. (2012). Teaching entrepreneurial action: Application of creative logic. In A. C. Corbett & J. A. Katz (Eds.), *Entrepreneurial action* (Vol. 14, pp. 253–280). Advances in Entrepreneurship, Firm Emergence and Growth. Bingley, UK: Emerald Group Publishing Limited.

Orser, B., & Elliott, C. (2015). *Feminine capital: Unlocking the power of women entrepreneurs*. Stanford, CA: Stanford University Press.

Read, S., Song, M., & Smit, W. (2009). A Meta-analytic review of effectuation and venture performance. *Journal of Business Venturing*, 7(5), 405–417.

Robinson, J. (2006). Navigating social and institutional barriers to markets: How social entrepreneurs identify and evaluate opportunities. In J. Mair, J. Robinson, & K. Hockerts (Eds.), 2006. *Social entrepreneurship* (pp. 95–120). New York, NY: Palgrave MacMillan.

Sarasvathy, S. (2001). Causation and effectuation: Toward a theoretical shift from economic inevitability to entrepreneurial contingency. *Academy of Management Review*, 26(2), 243–263.

Sarasvathy, S. (2008). *Effectuation: Elements of entrepreneurial expertise.* Northampton, MA: Edward Elgar Publishing, Inc.

Schlesinger, L., Kiefer, C., & Brown, P. (2012). *Just start: Take action, embrace uncertainty, create the future.* Cambridge, MA: Harvard Business Review Press.

Schumpeter, J. (1935). *The theory of economic development.* New York, NY: Oxford University Press.

Seelos, C., Ganly, K., & Mair, J. (2006). Social entrepreneurs directly contribute to global development goals. In J. Mair, J. Robinson, & K. Hockerts (Eds.). *Social entrepreneurship* (pp. 235–275). New York, NY: Palgrave MacMillan.

Shane, S., & Venkataraman, S. (2000). The promise of entrepreneurship as a field of research. Academy of Management Review, 25(1), 217–236.

Stryker, S. (1987). Identity theory: Developments and extensions. In K. Yardley & T. Honess (Eds.), *Self and identity.* New York, NY: Wiley.

Tajfel, H. (Ed.). (1982). *Social identity and intergroup relations.* Cambridge: Cambridge University Press.

Van Osnabrugge, M., & Robinson, R. J. (2000). *Angel investing.* San Francisco, CA: Jossey-Bass.

Xavier, S. R., Kelley, D., Kew, J., Herrington, M., & Vorderwülbecke, A. (2012). Global entrepreneurship monitor: 2012 Global report. Global Entrepreneurship Research Association. Retrieved from www.gemconsortium.org

19 I Am Not a Statistic (Even if Everyone Else Is): A Cross-disciplinary Activity

Nathaniel Karst and Rosa Slegers

Introduction

Many people, including our students, make poor decisions when taking into account quantitative information that is shaped by randomness (Kahneman & Tversky, 1974, 1984, and references therein). In a perfectly quantitative world, a student wrestling with a quantitative problem would avail herself of all available statistical tools. As we all know from personal experience, this is rarely the case. Nisbett, Krantz, Jepson, and Kunda (1983, p. 339) quantify the use of statistical heuristics, which they describe as "judgmental tools that are rough intuitive equivalents of statistical principles," in everyday life. It has been well documented that these heuristics can fail, often quite spectacularly, for any number of reasons (Kahneman & Tversky, 1974). Nisbett et al. (1983) go on to show that statistical training both increases the likelihood that a person will approach real world problems statistically as well as improve the quality of the resulting predictions.

In light of these insights, it seems that one goal of any quantitative education should be to alert students to the inherent biases, blind spots, and foibles in their own quantitative decision-making. We argue that this is especially important in an era when decisions can travel far and fast through a globally connected economy. Often the challenge is not convincing students that these ideas are important (Griffith, Adams, Gu, Hart, & Nichols-Whitead, 2012), but rather that these statistics apply to them.

Zieffler et al. (2008) provide an excellent and detailed review connecting research on the psychology of decision-making to the teaching of college level statistics. In their recommendations for instructors, the authors focus primarily on various forms of assessment to identify areas of misunderstanding that can then be targeted by the instructor for further explanation. This is certainly one important tool in improving overall educational outcomes in a statistics course. In our work here, we pursue a parallel and complementary track of scholarship that encourages students to critically consider and better understand weak areas in their own decision-making processes.

It has been well documented that showing specific examples rather than generalities is a more effective method for communicating the results of data analysis (Borgida & Nisbett, 1977; Nisbett & Borgida, 1975). Moreover, people in general are particularly bad at internalizing statistics if these statistics challenge a view of the self (Borgida & Nisbett, 1977; Kahneman & Tversky, 1973; Nisbett & Borgida, 1975). To combat both of these pedagogical obstacles, we aim to give students specific examples in which *they themselves* make poor decisions based on quantitative information. We first administer a survey to students based on well-known cognitive fallacies featured in Kahneman's *Thinking, Fast and Slow* (2011). The aggregate results of this survey are discussed in class. This approach:

1. Engages students through applicable examples of the ways quantitative reasoning can fail in general;
2. Exposes students to specific instances of inconsistencies in their own decision-making processes;
3. Encourages students internalize concepts through the use concrete rather than abstract examples.

Our approach can also be framed in terms of the traditional investigation of how people make decisions, especially when confronted with randomness and quantitative information. Bell, Raiffa, and Tversky (1988) proposed breaking the study of decision-making into three components:

1. Descriptive: "How do real people think and behave? How do they perceive uncertainties, accumulate evidence, learn and update perceptions?" (p. 16)
2. Normative: "... if the decision maker believes so and so, he should do such and such" (p. 16)
3. Prescriptive: "How can real people — as opposed to imaginary, idealized, super-rational people without psyches — make better choices in a way that does not do violence to their deep cognitive concerns?" (p. 9)

The authors summarize their work in the following way: "We will consider how people do make decisions, how 'rational' people should make decisions, and how we might help less rational people, who nevertheless aspire to rationality, to do better" (p. 9). The inclusion of the prescriptive approach is significant to our work here, because it is fundamentally a question of teaching and learning.

Methodology

Survey questions were adapted from examples given in Kahneman's *Thinking, Fast and Slow* (2011). The survey was administered before the start of the Fall 2014 semester to a group of 49 students pursuing a M.S. in Management in a nine-month program at Babson College. Of the 49 students in the section in which this exercise ran, 18 were women. Fifteen nationalities and over 20 distinct undergraduate majors were represented in the roster.

We adapted some questions featured by Kahneman in order to better fit our international audience. For instance, Q3–Q4 ask students to either first state their total amount of debt and then rate their happiness or to complete the same questions in reverse order. This parallels a study by Strack, Martin, and Schwarz (1988) who asked a group of relatively culturally homogeneous German students to either first rate their happiness and then estimate the number of dates they had been on in the last month or complete the same questions in the opposite order. The study found that in the former case, the number of dates a student had been on and her overall happiness were not correlated; the student had managed to assess her overall happiness, dating included, in forming her estimate. In the latter case, the number of dates a student had been on was tightly correlated with overall happiness, indicating that students may have been substituting an easy question, "How many dates have you been on?" with a difficult one, "How happy are you these days?" Global social norms concerning dating differ widely, and so we have opted for the more universal concept of debt. Even here, our replacement is a rather crude one; students from different cultures could have varying opinions on what an acceptable level of debt is. Still, it seems a step forward.

To protect privacy and encourage forthright responses, instructors could see if a particular student had responded to the survey but could not access any particular student's survey. Of the $N = 49$ students in the course, $n = 41$ completed the survey, with $n_A = 22$ taking survey version A (Appendix A) and $n_B = 19$ taking survey version B (Appendix B). Questions were chosen to encompass a broad range of effects in quantitative decision-making, including:

1. Anchoring (Q1, Q6−Q7)
2. Priming (Q3−Q4)
3. Availability (Q8)
4. Positive versus negative phrasing (Q2)
5. Conjunction (Q5, Q9)
6. Statistics versus sense of self (Q10)

These topics naturally motivated several others whose effects we discussed in class but did not measure, including phrasing questions in terms of frequency or count, the illusions of causality, prospect theory, and the utility of algorithms in place of experts.

The themes under consideration in this lesson do not fall neatly into any one discipline's purview. Elements of philosophy, statistics, and cognitive psychology all play an important role. To help students make connections among these complementary modes of thought, the session was co-taught by philosophy and mathematics faculty. The format was initially conceived as a sequential discussion of the survey results and the associated cognitive fallacies. In practice, the conversation flowed quite freely between students and both instructors.

Results

Virtually none of the resulting differences between the two surveys were statistically significant. This is entirely unsurprising in light of the small sample sizes and the high levels of cultural heterogeneity. That being said, a discussion of the normative responses to the survey questions and a comparison of these rational answers to those observed in the classroom are illustrative of the overall purpose of the project.

Questions 1 and 2 present identical collections of information in different formats; in both questions, Version A frames the information in a more positive light, while Version B frames the same information in a more negative light. In the absence of cognitive biases, we would expect the difference between the average student responses to be zero. Given the p-value of 0.48 as seen in the first row of Table 1, we have insufficient evidence to dissuade us of this belief.

The order of the questions "Roughly how much debt (in US dollars) do you currently have?" and "On a scale of 1 to 10, 1 indicating very unhappy and 10 indicating very happy, how happy are you these days?" is reversed between the two versions. To the perfectly rational student, such a change in order would not matter; average student happiness over a very large sample of perfectly rational

Table 1:   Average Survey Results for Both Versions A and B.

Question	Version A Average	Version B Average	p-value (H_0: $\mu_D = 0$)
1.	4.73	5.18	0.48
2.	6.68	5.94	0.43
3.	$49,205	$13,256	0.30
4.	7.73	7.00	0.18
5.	14,883	6,005	0.19
6.			
7.	84.8	67.9	0.00
8.	8.50	8.82	0.34
9.		95% C.I.: (0.224, 0.552)	
10.		95% C.I.: (0.588, 0.882)	

(Question numbering is with respect to Version A).

students would be the same in both versions. This is not what is commonly observed in the laboratory. Question 3 is intended to induce a priming effect in Version B of the survey; students who think about their level of debt before trying to decide how happy they have been recently naturally over represent the role their level of debt plays in their happiness. This is exactly what we observe in rows 2 and 3 of Table 1: respondents to Version B reported to be less happy than their Version A counterparts. Interestingly, the primed Version B respondents also had lower levels of debt!

Question 5 in Version B, "How much would you pay for a life insurance policy that pays $100,000 in case of death in a catastrophic terror attack?," is intended to invoke images of imminent danger and so influence respondents to pay more for the same insurance offered in Version A: "How much would you pay for a life insurance policy that pays $100,000 in case of death for any reason?" We did not observe the expected behavior and, instead, observed more rational choices as seen in Table 1. A closer inspection of the data calls this into doubt, however, as one respondent to Version A offered to pay $100,000 for $100,000 in coverage — omitting even this single outlier drives the two version averages closer together.

The age of Gandhi at his death, as referenced in Question 6, was shockingly old in Version A (age 114) and shockingly young in Version B (age 35). These outlandish figures are meant to "anchor" student responses to Question 7 which is the same in both versions: "What is your best guess as to Gandhi's age at the time of his death?" Typically, respondents deviate only relatively small amounts from the figure they received in the previous question. This is one of the few questions in which we saw a very strong signal amongst the noise, as students overwhelmingly stayed close to the anchor they received, with Version A respondents reporting an average guess of 84.8 and Version B respondents reporting an average guess of only 67.9.

In Version A, Question 8 asks students to place their impression of Babson College on a numerical scale. Respondents to Version B did the same, but first they were asked to list 20 things they liked about the college. In a typical laboratory experiment, this sort of list-making results in a "depletion" of positivity about the subject; respondents conclude at the end of the list that there is nothing left to like about the entity in question and, therefore, place their impression on the less favorable end of the scale. We observe no such distinction between respondents to the different versions. This may be attributable to several design flaws, including student desire to seem positive about the institution (even under the guarantee of anonymity) and overall earnestness in the first few weeks on campus.

Question 9 presents a classic cognitive error plaguing statistics, that of the conjunction fallacy. After being presented with a series details that portray Linda as a free-thinking liberal, respondents are asked whether it is more likely that "Linda is an insurance salesperson" or that "Linda is an insurance salesperson and is active in the feminist movement." The second option certainly fits better with the narrative presented in the prompt. A moment's thought, however, can convince us that every person satisfying the second description necessarily satisfies the first, and so the first simply cannot be the less likely alternative. We observed a strong signal here. Only roughly 40% of students responded correctly, with a 95% confidence interval of (0.224, 0.552).

We round out the survey with a question that is both light-hearted and fundamental to the discussion of our results, "Are you better than average as a driver?" Assuming that the skill of drivers is approximately symmetrically distributed about the mean, only 50% of rational students would respond in the affirmative. In our sample, nearly 75% of students responded that they were better than average drivers, with a 95% confidence interval of (0.588, 0.882). On some level, we all know that only 50% of people can be better than average, but somehow, we feel that this statistic just does not apply to us.

Discussion

In this section, we draw from Bergson, James, Hulme, and Marcel to explain why students may be reluctant or unable to apply abstract statistical results to their own lives, that is, why it is so important to confront students with concrete examples of how they themselves make poor decisions rather than presenting generalized abstractions.

I AM NOT A STATISTIC (EVEN IF EVERYONE ELSE IS)

"To continue thinking unchallenged," James observes, "is ninety-nine times out of a hundred, our practical substitute for knowing in the completed sense" (James, 1996, p. 206). Our everyday epistemic life is largely geared toward sustaining the sentiment of rationality and the habits that support the feeling of cognitive ease. This is the way we get things done in efficient and time-saving ways – the utility of this attitude cannot be denied. This utilitarian mindset corresponds to the adoption of skills through training – a useful and necessary approach to qualify for and hold down a job and generally cope in a society where certain behaviors and skills are expected. This attitude does not, however, encourage critical thinking of the kind that prefers diversity and distinction to simplification. The utilitarian attitude severely limits our perception because it prevents us from seeing things in their individuality.

Much case-based teaching encourages the simplifying tendency to present reality as a coherent, rational whole. Many business case studies promote the idea that we operate in a world where the necessary and sufficient information to make good decisions is readily available and where the role of randomness and luck can, for the most part, be ignored. It instills the mindset described by Kahneman as "what you see is all there is" (WYSIATI) – the idea that the information available to us is the only relevant information and that any other considerations outside of the set of facts at our disposal is either irrelevant or redundant (Kahneman, 2011). When employed in this narrow way, case-based teaching can instill in students the illusion that once they have a job "in the real world," their decisions and actions will be similarly based in "objective" truth and rational consideration.

Hulme (1924, p. 146, 160, 167) explains in "Bergson's Theory of Art" that because our lives are centered on action, we prefer thinking in terms of concepts to paying attention to detail and uniqueness. We look for common denominators and as a result, "we only see stock types. We tend to see not *the* table but only *a* table" (*ibid.*, p. 159). We rely on patterns and order: "Our normal faculty of knowing is then essentially a power of extracting what stability and regularity there is in the flow of reality" (Bergson, 1946, p. 50). Concepts, patterns, and practical categories make us feel in control of our lives and give us that sense of ease that James calls the sentiment of rationality. As a result, we tend to use the word "true" to indicate what has proven useful: "ideas … become true just in so far as they help us to get into satisfactory relation with other parts of our experience ... working securely, simplifying, saving labor" (James, 1978, p. 34). This phenomenon is parallel to our students substituting the question "how much debt do I have?" for "how happy am I these days?" When faced with complexity, whether it concerns a question or the richness of lived experience, we instinctively look for shortcuts. Parts of experience for which we have no use are disregarded as irrelevant or even untrue so that the labor saving work of our utilitarian intellect can proceed unimpeded (*ibid.*, p. 118).

Deep down, however, we know that "no abstract concept can be a valid substitute for a concrete reality except with reference to a particular interest in the conceiver" (*ibid.*, p. 70). Drop the particular interest and the abstract concept becomes useless or perhaps even offensive. We have all had this experience applying for jobs. Our application relies on abstract concepts that, seen from one perspective, describe us as degrees obtained, years of experience, hard working, great leadership potential, etc. But we know that this list of concepts does not capture who we are, and this knowledge is experienced most keenly when we are rejected. We feel that the abstract version of ourselves does not do justice to the unique individual we in fact are. Yet, the application process as such is set up to reduce us to abstractions, choosing simplification over individuality and diversity. When our students fail to apply statistical tools to their own experience and somehow hold themselves exempt (as in Lake Woebegone, they all consider themselves above average), they refuse to see themselves as a statistic. To reduce oneself to just one case among many feels wrong because the richness of our experience rebels against categorization and conceptualization.

Conclusions and Directions for Future Work

We have argued that if business education is to produce epistemically responsible agents, then the courses and cases offered as part of the business curriculum need to strike a balance between problem and mystery, abstraction and concreteness, analysis and intuition, simplification and diversity, conceptualization and uniqueness, etc. At the moment, business education is still dominated by a utilitarian mindset aimed at preserving the sentiment of rationality.

Lovett (2001) performed a study in which students were either given feedback immediately after attempting a problem or only at the end of the problem set. Students who were given immediate feedback improved more than their peers, in this case on choosing appropriate graphical depictions for data. This effect may extend into "softer" statistical skills, as well. One could imagine administering similar or identical survey questions to students in class and discussing the result immediately. While some issues concerning the need to hide each survey version from half of the participants would need to be solved, the benefit to student learning may more than make up for the added complexity of implementation.

References

Bell, D., Raiffa, H., & Tversky, A. (1988). *Decision making: Descriptive, normative, and prescriptive interactions.* New York, NY: Cambridge University Press.

Bergson, H. (1946). The creative mind *(M. Andison, Trans.).* New York, NY: The Philosophical Library.

Borgida, E., & Nisbett, R. (1977). The differential impact of abstract vs. concrete information on decisions. *Journal of Applied Social Psychology, 7,* 258–271.

Greco, J. (2011). Virtue epistemology. In E. Zalta (Ed.), *Stanford encyclopedia of philosophy.* Stanford, CA: The Metaphysics Research Lab, Center for the Study of Language and Information, Stanford University. Retrieved from http://plato.stanford.edu/entries/epistemology-virtue/

Griffith, J., Adams, L., Gu, L., Hart, C., & Nichols-Whitead, P. (2012). Students' attitudes towards statistics across the disciplines: A mixed-methods approach. *Statistics Education Research Journal, 11,* 45–56.

Hulme, T. E. (1924). *Speculations.* New York, NY: Harcourt, Brace & Company, Inc.

James, W. (1978). *Pragmatism and the meaning of truth.* Cambridge, MA: Harvard University Press.

James, W. (1996). *Essays in radical empiricism.* Lincoln, NE: University of Nebraska Press.

Kahneman, D. (2011). *Thinking, fast and slow.* New York, NY: Farrar, Straus and Giroux.

Kahneman, D., & Tversky, A. (1973). On the psychology of prediction. *Psychological Review, 80,* 237–251.

Kahneman, D., & Tversky, A. (1974). Judgment under uncertainty: Heuristics and biases. *Science, 185,* 1124–1131.

Kahneman, D., & Tversky, A. (1984). Choices, values, and frames. *American Psychologist, 34,* 341–350.

Lovett, M. (2001). A collaborative convergence on studying reasoning processes: A case study in statistics. In S. Carver & D. Klahr (Eds.), *Cognition and instruction: 25 years of progress.* Mahwah, NJ: Erlbaum.

Nisbett, R., & Borgida, E. (1975). Attribution and the psychology of prediction. *Journal of Personality and Social Psychology, 32,* 932–943.

Nisbett, R., Krantz, D., Jepson, C., & Kunda, Z. (1983). The use of statistical heuristics in everyday inductive reasoning. *Psychological Review, 90,* 339–363.

Strack, F., Martin, L., & Schwarz, N. (1988). Priming and communication: Social determinants of information use in judgments of life satisfaction. *European Journal of Social Psychology, 18,* 429–442.

Zieffler, A., Garfield, J., Alt, S., Dupuis, D., Holleque, K., & Chang, B. (2008). What does research suggest about the teaching and learning of introductory statistics at the college level: A review of the literature. *Journal of Statistics Education, 16.*

Appendix A: Survey Version A

1. All applicants to a job in your firm were asked to supply a recommendation. Each recommender was instructed to supply six adjectives in no particular order that described the applicant. The applicant you are currently reviewing was described in the following way:

   intelligent − industrious − impulsive − critical − stubborn − envious

   On a scale of 1−10, 1 indicating "do not hire" and 10 indicating "hire immediately," how would you rank this applicant?
2. The probability surviving a medical procedure is 90%. On a scale of 1−10, 1 indicating low and 10 indicating high, how serious do you consider this procedure?
3. On a scale of 1−10, 1 indicating very unhappy and 10 indicating very happy, how happy are you these days?
4. Roughly how much debt (in US dollars) do you currently have?
5. How much would you pay for a life insurance policy that pays $100,000 in case of death for any reason?
6. True or false: Gandhi more than 114 years old when he died.
7. What is your best guess as to Gandhi's age at the time of his death?
8. On a scale of 1−10, 1 indicating very low and 10 indicating very high, what is your impression of Babson College?
9. Linda is thirty-one years old, single, outspoken, and very bright. She majored in philosophy. As a student, she was deeply concerned with issues of discrimination and social justice, and also participated in antinuclear demonstrations. Which is more likely?
   - Linda is an insurance salesperson.
   - Linda is an insurance salesperson and is active in the feminist movement.
10. Are you better than average as a driver?

Appendix B: Survey Version B

1. All applicants to a job in your firm were asked to supply a recommendation. Each recommender was instructed to supply six adjectives in no particular order that described the applicant. The applicant you are currently reviewing was described in the following way:

   envious − stubborn − critical − impulsive − industrious − intelligent

On a scale of 1–10, 1 indicating "do not hire" and 10 indicating "hire immediately," how would you rank this applicant?

2. The probability surviving a medical procedure is 10%. On a scale of 1–10, 1 indicating low and 10 indicating high, how serious do you consider this procedure?

3. Roughly how much debt (in US dollars) do you currently have?

4. On a scale of 1–10, 1 indicating very unhappy and 10 indicating very happy, how happy are you these days?

5. How much would you pay for a life insurance policy that pays $100,000 in case of death in a catastrophic terror attack?

6. True or false: Gandhi more than 35 years old when he died.

7. What is your best guess as to Gandhi's age at the time of his death?

8. List 20 things you like about Babson College.

9. On a scale of 1–10, 1 indicating very low and 10 indicating very high, what is your impression of Babson College?

10. Linda is thirty-one years old, single, outspoken, and very bright. She majored in philosophy. As a student, she was deeply concerned with issues of discrimination and social justice, and also participated in antinuclear demonstrations. Which is more likely?

    • Linda is an insurance salesperson.
    • Linda is an insurance salesperson and is active in the feminist movement.

11. Are you better than average as a driver?

20 Experimenting with a Flipped Classroom

Steven Gordon

Introduction

Babson College encourages its students and faculty to innovate. Our faculty members teach the principles of Entrepreneurial Thought and Action[1] (ETA) to our students and incorporate them as best we can into our curriculum and pedagogy. So, when I first learned about the flipped classroom, I studied it, liked what I learned, and decided, in the spirit of ETA, to experiment with it. If the experiment failed, I would abandon the effort, but I was confident that I could learn from the experience and adjust my practices to improve my students' learning. This chapter describes why I flipped my introductory computer programming class, how I did it, what the results were, and what I have learned in the process. It is a case study of a flipped classroom experience and of my attempt to bring ETA entrepreneurial principles to the practice of teaching.

What is a flipped classroom? Strictly speaking, it is a pedagogical approach in which activities that are normally performed in the classroom, such as lecturing, take place outside of class, and activities that are normally performed outside of class, such as homework, are undertaken in the classroom. Most often, instructors flip their classroom by requiring students to watch pre-recorded lectures in advance of class. Then, during class time, students work through assignments under the instructor's guidance and with help from their peers.

---

[1]Entrepreneurial Thought and Action is a trademark of Babson College.

The flipped classroom is not a new concept. Faculty at business and law schools have been using the case study method for more than 100 years (Barton, 2007). Students in case study classes read one or more cases before class, often supplemented with readings on theory related to the cases. In business schools, class time is used to argue about how the theory can best be applied to the advantage of the case protagonists. In law schools, class time is devoted to arguing about how theory has been or should be interpreted in court cases. In its pure form, where lectures are absent and the instructors assume the role of facilitators, the case study method should be viewed as a version of the flipped classroom. Eric Mazur, one of the best known advocates of the flipped classroom, has argued in support of this perspective (Mazur, 2013). Seminars in literature and in other liberal arts disciplines often follow a similar approach, using class time to apply concepts acquired out of class rather than deliver content. The STEM disciplines (science, technology, engineering, and math) have been slower to adopt the flipped classroom model. Instructors in these disciplines usually assume that the concepts students need to understand are too abstract and difficult to be delivered in written form. While students might prepare for class by reading a textbook or lecture notes, instructors in the STEM disciplines traditionally redeliver the content in class, probing students with questions to assess their understanding and adjusting the pace and number of examples until they are confident that the large majority of students has grasped the key concepts.

The simple definition of the flipped classroom presented above is not universally accepted. Some researchers require the out-of-class instruction to be computer-based (see, e.g.,, Bishop & Verleger, 2013). This distinction is motivated by research showing that college students often fail to complete reading assignments (Sappington, Kinsey, & Munsayac, 2002) and that students watching video lectures tend to come to class better prepared than those assigned textbook readings (Brecht & Ogilby, 2008; Evans, 2008; Lepie, 2014), especially if the videos are interactive (Zhang, Zhou, Briggs, & Nunamaker, 2006). This definition also differentiates the flipped classroom, as it is most commonly practiced, from case study and seminar pedagogies.

Even within the more restrictive definition of the flipped classroom, many alternative models exist. When the task of knowledge delivery is removed from the classroom, a great deal of in-class time becomes available for activities that can be devoted to higher levels of learning. How instructors make use of this time is an individual decision. In a traditional class, very few options exist for instructors to make use of students' out of class time, so homework and take-home exams are commonplace. But, when the class is flipped, the in-class time does not need to be used in such a mundane manner. It can be used for any activity that requires students to apply and assimilate the knowledge they have acquired. Examples of these activities include peer-to-peer activities, group activities, student-led problem solving, as well as instructor-aided individual problem solving, which is similar to traditional homework with the difference being instructor availability to help students who would otherwise be stuck.

The Decision to Experiment

The flipped classroom concept first hit my radar in 2010. But, not much had been written about it at that time. A search through Babson's library database returns no results for the term "flipped classroom" in 2010 and only 42 results in 2011. However, by the summer of 2012, I sensed that the idea had gained some traction. A retrospective search of Babson's library database verifies that my instinct was correct, as the search returns 175 references published between January and June of 2012, more than an eightfold increase when annualized compared to the previous year. The proponents of the flipped classroom were enthusiastic in their evaluation of the outcome of their own experiences. So, over the summer of 2012, I decided that it was time for me to learn about the flipped classroom by experimenting with it myself.

My first task was to decide which class to flip. I taught several classes, and each was a good prospect for flipping. I ultimately elected to experiment with an introductory computer programming course called "Problem Solving and Software Design." I had taught the course for five consecutive years with high student satisfaction. Because of my long experience with it and the amount of instructional material I had acquired or developed for it, I thought experimentation carried a relatively low risk. Additionally, I had hoped that flipping the classroom would allow me to move at a more rapid pace. Although my students had been happy with the course, I knew that we had been unable to cover some of the basic concepts that they would need to understand if they were to continue to learn on their own or to supervise programmers in their employ. I had previously tried to move my students faster and push them further, but I invariably found that covering more topics resulted only in more shallow knowledge. They may have learned a few more concepts, but they were less able to apply them. The more I demanded from their term projects, the more help they needed to meet my expectations. Furthermore, I found that as I moved more quickly, I would lose some students so badly that they seemed ready to give up. Learning to program is a progressive task in which students have to deal with increasingly abstract concepts. If concepts covered early in the course are not mastered, it becomes impossible to understand later concepts. From what I had read about the flipped classroom, I thought it would be the answer to my problems. The students would learn the programming language syntax and semantics outside of class and I could use class time to ensure that they could apply what they had learned and move them ahead more rapidly.

Preparing to Launch

Babson provides two technology platforms for asynchronous online instruction – Brainshark and Panopto. Brainshark is a cloud-based service that allows the instructor to record voice-overs to PowerPoint presentations and intersperse them with interactive activities, such as questions or quizzes. The instructor records one slide at a time and can rerecord any slide at any time, even after an entire lesson is posted. The instructor can require students to log in before viewing a lesson. Brainshark then records how much time each student spent on each lesson and how many slides were viewed. It also records students' answers to any quizzes or questions embedded in the lesson.

Panopto is a cloud-based service that provides a richer environment than Brainshark at a cost of treating the entire lesson as a unit. Panopto can record the instructor's delivery through the camera on his/her computer along with what appears on the computer screen. This is an ideal solution for demonstrating the use of software or working through an exercise. However, if the instructor is simply presenting a lecture using PowerPoint, revising material in the midst of the lecture can be extremely difficult.

Because I had already developed in previous years a set of PowerPoint presentations to support my lectures, I decided to use Brainshark as my primary delivery platform. However, I also used Panopto selectively to record short videos that could be embedded as "video slides" in a Brainshark presentation.

I spent much of the summer of 2012 preparing to flip my classroom. In the notes section of each PowerPoint slide, I added the text of what I planned to record. This allowed students to read the text, if they preferred, rather than listening to my voice or to do both simultaneously. It also made it easier to record my presentation flawlessly. In addition, I broke each lecture into smaller parts, aiming for presentations of about 20 minutes covering just a single concept. In many of the presentations, I also added an activity or quiz to make the experience more interactive and to allow me to assess students' difficulty in understanding the concept under delivery.

Running the Class

In the past, I had run the Problem Solving and Software Design class as part lecture, part lab. I spent approximately 30 minutes at the start of each class presenting the lesson's key concepts. I used the next 30 minutes to solve a programming problem together with my students. I occupied the podium, obtaining and filtering students' suggestions about how to implement the computer code. My computer screen was projected for all to see, and the members of the class followed my lead as they attempted to understand and copy the solution to their own laptops. In the final 35 minutes, students attempted to solve a similar problem on their own as my teaching assistant and I worked the room to help those who were having problems.

When I flipped the classroom, I came to each class session knowing how much time students had spent viewing each presentation and knowing how well they had performed the activities and answered the questions. As a result, I had a good sense of which concepts posed problems and which were easily grasped. During the first 15 minutes or so of each session, I took questions and used examples to illustrate concepts that I knew students had found to be most difficult during their preparation. Then, as in previous years, my students and I spent about 30 minutes solving a problem together. During the remaining 50 minutes, students solved one or two problems on their own or with a peer, as my teaching assistant and I circled the room. The major differences between before and after the flip were that I reduced and focused the lecture time and students had more time to work problems on their own, although under supervision.

Reaping the Benefits

Among the most commonly cited benefits of the flipped classroom is an increase in interaction between the instructor and the students (Clark, Norman, & Besterfield-Sacre, 2014; Tucker, 2012). Since my class was capped at 20 students and I had previously run it as a lab in part, I had always felt that the student–instructor interaction in my classroom had been strong. So, I did not expect and did not see a great deal of improvement in this interaction. Nevertheless, some improvement was evident because I was able to devote more time to lab work and could more easily assess and address problems at the individual level. Instructors who have not previously used a lab should find, when dealing with small classes (fewer than 40 students), that they will get to know their students better in a flipped environment than in a traditional one because they can attend to each student individually at least once in every class session.

Another benefit of the lab environment is that as their instructor peers over their shoulders, students can ask questions that they think are dumb without fear of ridicule from their colleagues. For me, these questions were quite revealing, as they often reflected a profound misunderstanding of the concept under study. In other words, they really were dumb questions. But, they allowed me to explain the concept patiently, kindly, confidentially, and with examples, until I could see that the student was really on board. This allowed me to move forward confidently from session to session, as I knew that everyone in the class has mastered what they need to advance to the next lesson. The lab format also allowed me to more easily identify trailing students, who I could direct to places where they could get more help and suggest that they visit me during my office hours.

Another benefit of the flipped classroom is that students can learn at their own pace (Phillips & Trainor, 2014; Starzee, 2012). Some can learn quickly and will breeze through the instructional material. Some will watch for a while, take time to assimilate the material, and then watch some more. Others will watch a video over and over again, as repetition is necessary for their learning. For example, in the fall 2014 semester, one of my students watched parts of the lesson on arrays, one of the most difficult concepts in programming, 18 times, averaging 1.75 times per slide each time she watched the lesson. In contrast, many of my students watched the lesson only once and viewed no slide more than once. In a traditional classroom, the lecture cannot be slowed down or repeated, so many students are left behind while others are frustrated by what they perceive to be a slow pace. Some instructors in traditional classes, particularly at medical schools, are recording their lectures, so that even in a traditional environment, students can accord themselves of the pacing benefits of a flipped classroom.

A flipped classroom is a natural environment for today's students, who have grown up in a digital world (Phillips & Trainor, 2014). My students are used to using the Internet, search engines, and digital media to acquire information and knowledge. I know that many of them are more comfortable watching a video, interrupting it to seek confirmation, related data, or material examples, and returning to it, than they are sitting inertly in a classroom absorbing a barrage of information aurally, or occasionally by video. I learned by accident that some of my students have software that will allow them to listen to the audio of the lectures at double or triple speed. They report to be confident that they can absorb the material at that pace and have assured me that they lower the speed and repeat watching a slide if they feel they've missed something or have trouble understanding what was presented.

Ideally, a flipped classroom helps students with self-assessment (McLaughlin et al., 2014). In a traditional classroom, students often have difficulty determining how well they understand what the instructor has explained. They may believe that they understand things well enough and have no need to ask any questions until they are confronted with homework or an exam that exposes their incorrect assessment. With Brainshark, I was able intersperse tests with the instructional material so students could immediately and accurately gauge their understanding. Brainshark even provides an option I did not use to direct the flow of the instruction depending on how students answer the questions. I assumed that when students were confronted with a lack of understanding, they would rewatch the parts of the lecture they misunderstood and they would turn to the Internet, textbooks, or other students for help. Although instructors in traditional classrooms can also help students self-assess by posing questions for them to answer, remediation is more difficult than in the flipped classroom. One solution is to use clickers to determine what percentage of students need remediation, and if that percentage is large enough, provide additional examples and explanations. However, many students still get left behind, which is not the case when the classroom is flipped.

I had expected that a flipped classroom would improve the pace of instruction. To me, that was the most compelling reason for trying it. The literature is not very explicit on this issue. Many writers have claimed that the flipped classroom makes more efficient use of time (see, e.g., Arnold-Garza, 2014; McDonald & Smith, 2013), but they are vague in describing or documenting how the increased efficiency translates into a deeper exploration of concepts or additional learning objectives. I found that by having instant feedback on student comprehension, I could accelerate when desirable and slow down when necessary. As a result, I could move the class faster without fear of losing any students. In the fall of 2012, I was able to add classes on three programming constructs that I had not had time to teach in prior years.

Anticipating the Drawbacks

One of the most intractable problems of the flipped classroom is students' inability to get their questions answered in a just-in-time fashion. If students have a question while watching a video at home, their only alternative is to turn to the Internet, a textbook, or another student for help. Often these alternatives are insufficient. In a traditional classroom, students can raise their hands and get their questions answered immediately. When students cannot get immediate help, they get frustrated and it affects their ability to understand the material that follows. I attempted to address this problem by holding online office hours by Skype the evening before class between 8:30 and 9:30 pm. I encouraged my students to watch the lecture during that hour so that they could get immediate help for any concepts they could not understand. I'm not certain that this was an effective solution. I received very few questions during my online office hours.

Another vexing problem is what to do when a student arrives in class unprepared. The flipped classroom operates on the assumption that all students have done the out-of-class work before attending class. Since the lecture is not repeated in class, a student attending without doing the required preparation will be unable to extract any value from the in-class activities. As a result, students have a strong incentive to prepare adequately. But, sometimes personal problems, a sudden increase of work in other classes, or other factors beyond their control impede their ability to prepare. I occasionally noticed that a student who rarely had a question suddenly needed a lot of help. I assumed, in these cases, that the student had not prepared in advance. As long as this didn't happen frequently, I tolerated it, making sure that the delinquent student did not rob too much of my attention from other students.

Unfortunately, not every class has well-motivated students, and the likelihood of falling behind may be insufficient to persuade the less motivated students to prepare adequately. I experienced this situation in the fall 2013 semester, when several of my students repeatedly came to class unprepared. There seemed little I could do to convince them that they needed to do a better job of preparation, and there was no explicit penalty for arriving in class unprepared. As a result, several fell badly behind, their grades suffered, and they felt frustrated and somewhat dissatisfied with the class. The next time I taught the course, I incorporated course preparation as 12% of the overall course grade so that students were more motivated to prepare well. As explained in the syllabus, the grade for preparation was determined by the percentage of the online lecture that each student viewed as recorded by Brainshark, the percentage of lecture questions that each student answered (they were not penalized for incorrect answers), and their ability to demonstrate when cold-called in class programs they had been directed to create during the online lecture.

Evaluating and Revising the Experiment

My initial evaluation of the experiment in 2012 was overwhelmingly positive. I was able to cover more material while fewer students fell behind or felt lost. However, the average student grade in the course had not changed significantly. And, from my students' perspective, it seemed that nothing had changed at all. Their ratings of their learning and my teaching were nearly identical to what they had been before the course was flipped. I was puzzled by this at first until I realized that my students had no point of comparison. They had not taken the course before it was flipped and had no idea that they had acquired so much more knowledge and skill in programming.

I was encouraged to continue the experiment when I taught the course again in the fall of 2013. That semester, I tweaked very little, but the course did not go as well. A number of students consistently failed to attend class and many of the students who did attend had not viewed the lectures online. Additionally, some students who were conscientious nevertheless seemed to have trouble mastering the work. Although a large majority of the students did very well, a significant minority did not. The average grade for the class fell, as did the students' evaluation of their learning and my teaching. At this point, I was discouraged and unsure whether my 2012 class was exceptionally strong or my 2013 class was exceptionally weak. If a flipped classroom only works when students are strong, I would have to assess it as a failure. But, I also considered the possibility that I was a novice at using the flipped format and had much to learn. I felt that I should continue to experiment while addressing the causes of the poor 2013 outcome.

In the fall of 2014, I made four rather significant changes that I thought would help ensure a more positive result. First, as explained above, I graded students' preparation and provided a rubric to explain how their preparation would be evaluated. Second, I broke the lectures into smaller pieces that would be easier for students to watch. Practitioners seem to agree that at the collegiate level, online presentations should be no more than 15–20 minutes long. My presentations now averaged 11.12 minutes with a median of 10.12 minutes and a maximum of 23.08 minutes. Third, I added examples to each lecture as well as additional exercises for the students to reinforce what they were learning. Finally, I added three sessions on a second computer language. I hoped that students would have a more positive evaluation of their learning if they could see how easy it would be to apply the concepts they had learned in one language to learning a second language. To make room for these classes, I had to drop coverage of two programming concepts and consolidate two others into one class.

My evaluation of the changes implemented in 2014 is largely positive. The reward system seemed to improve my students' motivation, or perhaps I again had an exceptionally strong class. The average student grade returned to its previous high level and students' evaluations of their learning and my teaching was also high once again. Two students struggled somewhat throughout the semester, but they managed to succeed in the end. I remain unsure of the impact of the decision to add a second language. Student feedback on that decision was mixed and I have regretted the need to delete concept coverage to free up the time for this change.

Student Perceptions of the Flipped Classroom

Until 2014, I had not done any systematic analysis of my students' perception of the flipped classroom. However, to continue learning how the class might be improved and in preparation for writing this chapter, I polled my students to see how I might better be able to handle some of the factors I thought might have impeded their progress.

One of my greatest concerns with the flipped classroom format is my students' inability to ask questions when viewing presentations outside of class. In 2014, I attempt to alleviate this concern by increasing the number examples and the number activities that students could do to confirm their understanding of the concept being presented. I continued the practice of holding office hours by Skype the evening before class. Still, I expected there would be questions and I wondered how important it would be that I couldn't be there to answer them. As shown in Figure 1, the inability to ask questions during the presentation was always or quite often a problem for only 4 of the 18 students responding to the survey.

The techniques that students used to deal with this for problem varied considerably. As shown in Figure 2, half of the students who considered the inability to ask questions to be a problem found that their questions were answered later in the presentation or they were able to search the Internet for an answer. But, the plurality waited until class time to ask. This finding is problematic because, as one student responded, by the time class rolled around, the question was forgotten. As shown in Figure 3, more than one-fifth (22%) of the

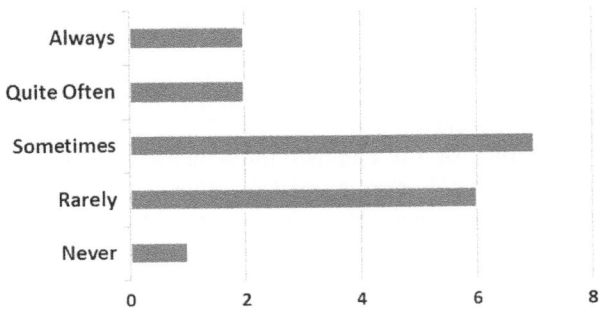

Figure 1: How Often Was the Inability to Ask Questions a Problem for You?

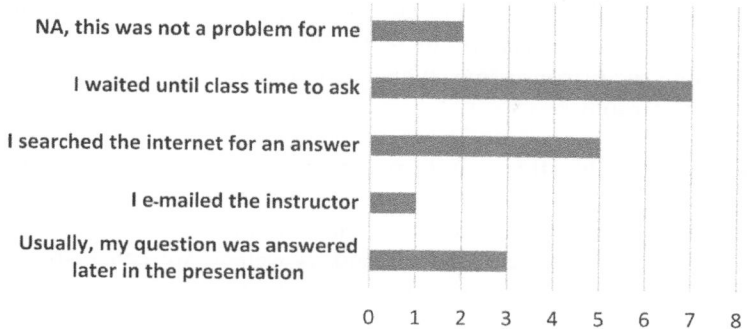

Figure 2: How Did You Resolve the Inability to Ask Questions?

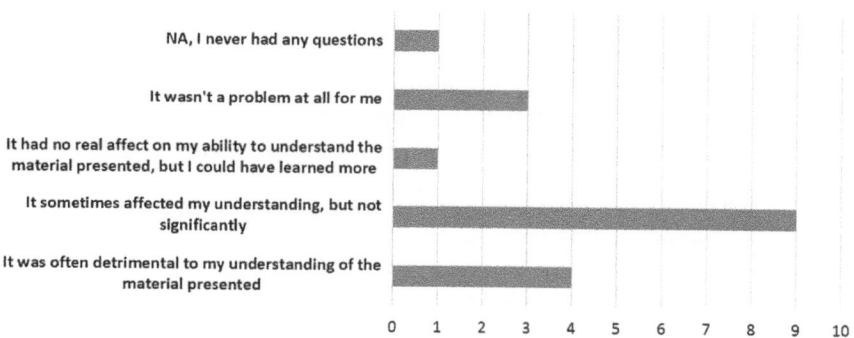

Figure 3: How Did the Delay in Getting Your Question Answered Affect Your Understanding of the Lesson?

respondents said that their inability to ask questions was often detrimental to their understanding and 50% said that it affected their understanding, although not significantly.

Students' perception of the exercises that were embedded into the presentations varied somewhat but not significantly. More than three-quarters of the students responded that they did the exercises most of the time (39%) or always (39%). All but one student felt that the exercises helped with 56% responding that they helped a lot and 39% responding that they helped a little. The one student who felt that they didn't help complained that "it bothered me that I was supposed to do them." Interestingly, despite the fact that the syllabus stated class preparation was a component of the course grade and I made a point of emphasizing it on the first day of class, 39% responded that they were unaware of this until I mentioned it again much later in the term and one student claimed to be unaware of it until filling out the survey.

The overall verdict: Half the class said they would have preferred a traditional classroom to the flipped classroom. Here is a sample of the reasons some students would have preferred the traditional classroom:

- For a class like this ... it is important that they can ask questions when needed. It's hard to ask a question through e-mail, and when I did I found it harder to understand.
- I love having other peers around as well so we can help each other and professor can help all of us if we can't do it together.
- Flipped classroom works if everyone understands the content in the presentations, but has negative effects if even a small majority of the class does not understand the content.
- I feel like I am learning better when a professor teaches, rather than self-teaching, so I don't learn to do something the wrong way. It is learned the right way the first time and engrained correctly.
- I would preferred a traditional classroom to our current format as it allows students to ask questions during the lecture, instead of waiting until the next day (many times forgetting the question).
- The traditional format is also one that we have been used to growing up.

Here is a sample of the reasons some students preferred the flipped classroom:

- The presentations suffice for complete learning.
- I think the flipped classroom is pretty efficient.
- In a collegiate setting, student's core learning should take place independently and be refined in a classroom setting. The flipped classroom was an incentive for more independent learning, since you would not benefit from class time or your advice if you were unprepared.
- It helped in being able to work the code in reality with other students and the professor in class. This type of course would only be effective in a flipped classroom.
- Solving problems in class with the possibility of immediately having questions being answered by the professor is a big plus.

Two factors might have affected my students' lukewarm response to the question about whether they would have preferred a traditional model. First, they had never experienced this class in a traditional model. Second, the survey was structured to get responses that might help me improve the class. In particular, its questions focused on problems, such as not being able to ask questions during the video presentations. As a result, students might very well have been biased to think about the problems of a flipped classroom rather than its benefits.

Concluding Thoughts and Lessons Learned

If you are considering flipping your classroom, be prepared for the amount of work it entails. Even if you've taught the class before, flipping it requires far more work than preparing to teach it the first time in a traditional format. The first time I flipped my class, recording more than 20 class sessions took the better part of an entire summer. When revising the class in subsequent years, you will have much more data on students' responses and reactions than you would have had with a traditional classroom. A considerable amount of time is needed to review this data and respond to it. For my course, it was easy to see where students got bogged down. Typically, it occurred with the more complex concepts. Although I had anticipated this the first time I taught the course, as I reviewed where students spent their time and how they responded to embedded exercises, it was clear that my intuition was insufficient. The data proved that I needed to expand my explanations and create more exercises than I had expected would be necessary.

Many options exist in designing a flipped classroom. How long should the out-of-class videos be? Should the instructor be shown on the video while delivering the content or is it better if the full screen is devoted to the content? How frequently should activities be embedded? How complex should they be? How often should self-assessment exercises be included? Should peer-to-peer instruction be used in the classroom, and if so, in what proportion to instructor-aided activities? There is little data-based research to answer any of these questions, so first-time instructors will need to experiment, as I have. A literature review on best practices for the flipped classroom provides only opinions from those who have used it. Quite naturally, opinions vary depending on the audience. What works for K-12 does not necessarily work in a college environment, and what works in a general college environment will not necessarily work at a medical school or law school. At any level, best practices for a math or physics flipped classroom are probably very different from those for classes in computer science or finance.

In conclusion, designing and implementing a flipped classroom should be seen as an experiment, not just the first time through, but for several times thereafter. Instructors willing to try should be prepared for an occasional failure and for the work necessary to learn from and rectify it. But, the results can be very satisfying for the instructor and beneficial for student learning.

References

Arnold-Garza, S. (2014). The flipped classroom teaching model and its use for information literacy instruction. *Communications in Information Literacy, 8*(1), 7−22.

Barton, B. H. (2007). A tale of two case methods. *Tennessee Law Review, 75*, 233.

Bishop, J. L., & Verleger, M. A. (2013). The flipped classroom: A survey of the research. *American Society for Engineering Education conference & exposition*, Atlanta, June 23−26. Retrieved from http://www.studiesuccesho.nl/wp-content/uploads/2014/04/flipped-classroom-artikel.pdf. Accessed on November 25, 2014.

Brecht, H., & Ogilby, S. (2008). Enabling a comprehensive teaching strategy: Video lectures. *Journal of Information Technology Education: Innovations in Practice, 7*(1), 71−86.

Clark, R. M., Norman, B. A., & Besterfield-Sacre, M. (2014). Preliminary experiences with 'flipping' a facility layout/material handling course. *IIE annual conference proceedings* (pp. 1194−1202).

Evans, C. (2008). The effectiveness of m-learning in the form of podcast revision lectures in higher education. *Computers & Education, 50*(2), 491−498.

Lepie, K. (2014). *Why you should use video in education.* Retrieved from http://www.edudemic.com/use-video-education/. Accessed on November 30.

Mazur, E. (2013). Quoted in "The flipped classroom will redefine the role of educators." Interview dated March 20. Retrieved from http://www.seas.harvard.edu/news/2013/03/flipped-classroom-will-redefine-role-educators. Accessed on November 25, 2014.

McDonald, K., & Smith, C. M. (2013). The flipped classroom for professional development: Part I. Benefits and strategies. *The Journal of Continuing Education in Nursing, 44*(10), 437−438.

McLaughlin, J. E., Roth, M. T., Glatt, D. M., Gharkholonarehe, N., Davidson, C. A., Griffin, L. M., … Mumper, R. J. (2014). The flipped classroom: A course redesign to foster learning and engagement in a health professions school. *Academic Medicine, 89*(2), 236−243.

Phillips, C. R., & Trainor, J. E. (2014). Millennial students and the flipped classroom. *Journal of Business and Educational Leadership, 5*(1), 102−112.

Sappington, J., Kinsey, K., & Munsayac, K. (2002). Two studies of reading compliance among college students. *Teaching of Psychology, 29*(4), 272−274.

Starzee, B. (2012). 'Flipped classroom' model leaps to Long Island. *Long Island Business News.*

Tucker, B. (2012). The flipped classroom. *Education Next, 12*(1), 82−83.

Zhang, D., Zhou, L., Briggs, R. O., & Nunamaker, J. F. (2006). Instructional video in e-learning: Assessing the impact of interactive video on learning effectiveness. *Information & Management, 43*(1), 15−27.

21

Using VoiceThread to Socialize Online Presentations

Salvatore Parise

Introduction

While there has been an increase in social tool use in higher education, the research on its impact, in particular with regards to learning behaviors and outcomes, has been scant. This exploratory research aims to build on this important research stream. This chapter will illustrate the use of VoiceThread, a cloud-based social presentation software, in an undergraduate and graduate business course. VoiceThread takes a Microsoft PowerPoint presentation and allows individual students to add video, voice, or text comments to each slide. While there are other popular tools, such as Brainshark and Panopto, that enable instructors and students to add voice and video to presentations, VoiceThread provides a unique learning environment in that it allows the viewer community to provide rich media comments directly on any slide to engage in an online discussion.

Social media technologies are increasingly being used in higher education courses to enable new ways of delivering education and to improve learning outcomes (Maloney, 2007). A large percentage of today's undergraduate and graduate students have grown up with and are familiar with popular social platforms such as Facebook, Twitter, and YouTube, in addition to mobile apps and cloud-based (i.e., hosted on the Web) software applications. These students are used to working with multimedia, including text, images, audio, and videos. They have a comfort level with complex information spaces and learning through discovery (Seely Brown, 2000). Further, innovative tools serve as motivation for students to engage in the learning experience. For example, new tools such as VoiceThread and SlideShare are changing the way students experience online presentations (Carvin, 2008). Instructors now have to meet the demand from tech-savvy students and create learning designs that align students' technology behaviors with effective learning practices (DeGennaro, 2008).

Social tools and platforms have increased communication and engagement among course participants outside the traditional face-to-face classroom. For example, Facebook can be used as a venue for online class discussion that results in higher levels of student activity that goes beyond the physical and time constraints of the traditional classroom (Kent, 2013). Also, instructors are using video to create multimedia presentations that students view before coming to class. In this way, basic frameworks and lecture material can be delivered through the video presentation medium, while classroom time can be better spent having case discussion. These social platforms also enable sharing of digital materials. Students can use a class-designated Twitter hashtag as a means to post links to Web materials related to class topics. Finally, these social technologies improve social presence and collaborative learning (Orlando & Orlando, 2010). Student identification and awareness can be increased through personal photos and profiles. Ultimately, digital communities allow for online conversations and reflections of course materials, therefore changing the role of the student from a passive learner to an active learner (Hartshorne & Ajjan, 2009).

A big driver for the use of social tools has been a large increase in online courses as well as blended courses (mix of face-to-face and online classes) in higher education during the past decade (Twigg, 2003). Perhaps the most frequently used technology to enable online engagement in a course is the online discussion board. One typical scenario is for the instructor to assign an activity such as a case study assignment and then have students engage in an online discussion centered on case questions using a threaded discussion forum. However, the traditional discussion board is text-based and there are challenges with the effort required by students to develop long text comments, the effectiveness of communicating through text alone, and the student's motivation to use online discussion boards. Social media provides the opportunity to add multimedia components such as voice and video to online discussions, thus improving student motivation, enjoyment, and overall learning.

This chapter focuses on one such social tool, VoiceThread, and its effects on online student discussions. The impacts on the instructor, students, and the learning process and outcomes will also be presented. Interviews were conducted with students from both graduate and undergraduate courses to get their attitudes regarding the tool including: features, ease-of-use, differences with online discussion boards, challenges, and overall effectiveness to the learning process. The instructor perspective, including differences between using the software in the undergraduate and graduate course, will also be discussed. Finally, I also focus on various potential uses of VoiceThread, such as case study discussion, brainstorming sessions, and Q&A activities.

Use of Virtual Media to Support Social Learning

Social technologies support the social constructivism model of learning, where students are active participants in sharing knowledge and content, and therefore learning occurs from student-to-student discussions in addition to instructor-to-class interaction. Rather than knowledge being transmitted by instructors to students in a didactic manner through lecture format, the constructivist view holds that knowledge is constructed by learners through a collaborative process (Jonassen 1994; Vygotsky, 1978). Students develop meaning through interactions with others and by incorporating different perspectives and experiences they arrive at through a shared understanding (Miers, 2004). In particular with more senior and graduate students, learning is situated within a broader community of practice, where individuals develop and share the capacity to create and apply knowledge (Wenger, 1998).

The instructor's role is to facilitate learning and provide feedback, rather than controlling the content and delivery of materials. Because learning is a socially constructed process, students who are active participants as opposed to passive recipients of knowledge will learn more effectively (Flynn, 1992). Learners will generate more diverse ideas, critical thinking, and creative responses in a cooperative environment (Schlechter, 1990).

Social technologies are well suited to supporting the social constructivism model of learning for several reasons. These technologies are often associated with the "democratization of ideas" where participants contribute and share content, ideas, and comments with each other. Another potential benefit from the use of social media technologies in the classroom is that it allows for continuous dialogue among instructor and students outside the traditional face-to-face classroom. This becomes increasingly important as higher management education moves toward both online and blended delivery models. Finally, research has shown that constructs such as fun and enjoyment are important in the learning process (e.g., Bisson & Luckner, 1996). Therefore, it can be argued that video, voice, and other multimedia elements that add to the enjoyment and interest levels of traditional online lectures and discussions delivered via static PowerPoint presentations or text-based discussion boards can increase learning outcomes. As a result, students may be more motivated to use newer technologies in the classroom.

A key tenet of social learning is that higher levels of student interaction lead to increased student satisfaction and learning (Durrington, Berryhill, & Swafford, 2006). Interactions lead to both social benefits (e.g., improving one's presence in the class) and cognitive benefits (e.g., brainstorming different ideas to a problem). There are three types of interactions that are critical for learning: student-to-student, student-to-teacher, and student-to-content (Moore, 1989). Again, social tools can help in all these forms of interaction. For example, an instructor can create a short video explaining a course concept (e.g., key principles of effective digital marketing) and post it to his/her Blackboard discussion board or a more public forum such as YouTube or Facebook. Students are tasked to provide comments, post company campaign examples, and ask questions. In this way, students are interacting as much with their peers and the content itself than with their instructor in a one-way communication.

One distinguishing aspect of social tools and platforms that leads to higher learning is the richness of the experience. In traditional text-based discussion boards, the leanness of asynchronous text communication can result in a sense of loss among learners (Palloff & Pratt, 2007). With richer media including audio and video as part of the discussion, there is increased social presence as students are more aware to whom they are responding. Recent research indicates that adding social presence in discussion through richer media such as audio and video can lead to a more satisfied experience and perceived learning (Caspi & Blau, 2008). In one study, students using an audio discussion board were able to express emotion better and described the experience as more "real," when compared to students using a text-based discussion board (Hew & Cheung, 2012). In another study, students using asynchronous video in their course rated their professor higher than students rating the same professor in the same course delivered in a traditional face-to-face format (Griffiths & Graham, 2009a, 2009b). Finally, students found video feedback more helpful than text feedback (Moore & Filling, 2012).

Based on the existing research, several challenges exist with using social tools in the college classroom. First, the learning curve for both students and the instructor using the technology has to be low. Therefore, ease-of-use for any class activity is a critical design factor. Tech savvy students may be perceived as having an advantage over their classmates if there is a high bar in learning the technology. Second, projects involving social media tend to have less structure than traditional online discussion boards. While the use of video, photos, and audio allows for more creativity, the tradeoff is there is often less structure for students in terms of how to use these newer technologies for class projects.

What is VoiceThread?

VoiceThread (www.voicethread.com) is a cloud-based social presentation tool. VoiceThread takes a common document format, such as a Microsoft Powerpoint presentation or a Microsoft Word document, and converts it into a VoiceThread presentation. This presentation is stored in the cloud and is accessed by individual accounts that students and instructor create for themselves. The key feature of VoiceThread is that it easily allows anyone to add a voice, video, or text comment to any slide. When a comment is created, the user who generated the comment appears as an icon on that particular slide. The icon is typically a picture of the person, but it could be any image that the user uploads. In Figure 1 example, there are a total of 10 comments (appearing on the left and right side of the presentation). A viewer hits the play button and each comment (video,

Figure 1: Features of a VoiceThread Presentation. *Source*: Adapted from https://voicethread.com

voice, or text format) will appear in the order it was submitted to the slide. The viewer can also jump to a particular comment by clicking on that comment icon. The viewer can also move to a particular slide. Finally, anyone making a comment can use the highlighter to point out specific things on the VoiceThread slide.

VoiceThread has been used in many of the top universities in the United States over the past few years (Tu, 2011). Instructors indicate that VoiceThread is intuitive to use and little training is needed. The few studies that have investigated the impact that the tool has had on the classroom have generally found positive results. Pedagogical benefits include: improving social presence, providing a sense of community, and motivation for students, a better understanding of visual concepts, and more meaning to comments as a result of a voice tone (Orlando & Orlando, 2010). In a business policy course, the instructor used the tool as part of an exam review and found initial support that VoiceThread can be used as an effective tool for facilitating learning activities. In another exploratory study, audio and video comments led to higher social presence, and the tool was valued more by graduate students than undergraduate students (Kidd, 2013). Also, undergraduate students seem to prefer text over audio and video comments (Smith, 2012).

INCORPORATING VOICETHREAD INTO THE COURSE DESIGN

For this exploratory study, the instructor used the VoiceThread tool for separate undergraduate and graduate information technology elective courses at a business school starting in the Fall 2012. Both courses were taught in a blended format, with some online weeks complementing face-to-face class sessions. For both courses, VoiceThread was used during an online week, after Blackboard discussion boards were used earlier in the semester for other online weeks. The instructor wanted to experiment with a new, social technology to motivate project discussion among students. This tool was new to all the students, including the instructor. The instructor reviewed the online tutorials on how to use VoiceThread and created a simple set of instructions for students in terms of how to create their account, create a VoiceThread presentation, and comment on other group presentations.

Each student team (five to six students per team) had to create a VoiceThread presentation for a class project. The project involved assessing a specific company's digital property strategy (e.g., website, social media, mobile) and coming up with specific recommendations based on their analysis. Teams were expected to use tools and concepts learned throughout the semester for both the analysis and recommendations aspects of their project. Each team was given one week to develop their VoiceThread presentation. The presentation could not be longer than 30 minutes and 15 slides.

Each student was then tasked to individually comment on two other team presentations assigned to him or her. Links to each team's VoiceThread presentation were posted on the course Blackboard site (and also emailed to the class). Comments could include the following:

- Aspects of the presentation they particularly found interesting (e.g., recommendations).
- Key similarities or differences from their own team presentation.
- Questions that they had for the team.

The instructor encouraged students to use all three comment types: voice, video, and text comments. All students had access to a laptop with a built-in video camera, so it was not difficult to create a video comment. Students were given a few days to comment on other team presentations. They were allowed to comment as many times as they liked and on any of the VoiceThread slides. Students were told to check back on their own presentation periodically to answer any questions that others might have for them. As with other online weeks, all VoiceThread comments were counted as part of the class participation grade for each student.

The instructor's role with this VoiceThread discussion, as it was with the online discussions on Blackboard, was to provide some general comments for each team, ask a few questions, and to spark conversation by raising a point or two where there was not necessarily a clear answer. The instructor did not want to dominate or be the center of the discussion interactions and, as a result, waited a while before providing any comments so as to allow several students to provide their comments first.

Findings

This VoiceThread project was introduced in the Fall 2012 for both the undergraduate and graduate elective course. Subsequently, the same project assignment was used again in the next offering of the same blended graduate elective and in the next four offerings of the same blended undergraduate elective. The number of VoiceThread comments for each class is presented in Table 1. The average class size for the undergraduate course (26) did not change across the five classes. The class size for the Fall 2012 graduate course was 17 and for the other graduate course was 36, resulting in an average of 26.5. So, the average class sizes for the graduate and undergraduate class were essentially the same.

Table 1: Number of Voicethread Comments by Course.

VoiceThread Comment Types					
Class Type	Class Size	Text	Audio	Video	Total
Grad					
Grad1	36	75	150	42	267
Grad2	17	39	80	24	143
Grad average	26.5	57	115	33	205
Undergrad					
UGrad1	26	80	90	30	200
UGrad2	26	85	90	28	203
UGrad3	26	75	95	32	202
UGrad4	26	82	85	25	192
UGrad5	26	78	90	35	203
UGrad average	26	80	90	30	200

Prior to Fall 2012, this same project assignment was used in the same undergraduate and graduate course (roughly the same average class size) but with a different individual student comment activity. Each team was given one week to create a Microsoft PowerPoint presentation. The instructor posted each presentation on Blackboard, and each team had its own text-based discussion board. Individual students were then asked to comment on two different team presentations on the three areas listed earlier (interesting aspects, similarities/differences, questions). The instructor stressed that when posting their comments, students should have a meaningful topic header for their post, so that students can more easily follow the discussion. Table 2 includes a text-based Blackboard discussion as a comparison point for the VoiceThread discussion. To gain insights from students regarding their experiences using the VoiceThread tool, optional interviews were conducted with students for both the Fall 2012 undergraduate and graduate courses. A majority of students in both courses were interviewed.

VOICETHREAD VERSUS BLACKBOARD TEXT DISCUSSION

The total numbers of VoiceThread comments were 64% and 67% higher than the Blackboard text-based comments for the graduate and undergraduate classes respectively (see Table 2). Many of the students pointed out the *"comment-in-context"* aspect of VoiceThread as a major benefit to contributing and learning. According to one student, *"I like that you comment directly to the*

Table 2: Graduate versus Undergraduate Course Comparisons.

Comment Type	Graduate Courses (Avg)		Undergraduate Courses (Avg)		Comparisons
Blackboard total	125		120		Increase in total grad = 64%
VoiceThread total	205		200		Increase in total undergrad = 67%
VoiceThread text	57	28% (of total)	80	40% (of total)	Grad versus undergrad ($P < .001$)
VoiceThread audio	115	56%	90	45%	Grad versus undergrad ($P < .000$)
VoiceThread video	33	16%	30	15%	Grad versus undergrad (no significance)

slide. So, *I'm actually looking at content that I'm referring to as I record my audio comment. This makes things so much easier. With some of my Blackboard discussions, I had to go back, find my presentation hardcopy with my notes, and remember what I read before I could comment. Also, as I'm reading others' comments on Blackboard, many times I have trouble understanding what they are referring to. With VoiceThread, I really like that you can play back all the comments contained in that one slide. It was much easier to follow along and learn from others."* In addition, students enjoyed the highlighting feature in VoiceThread as they made their comments. This was especially useful with slides that had a lot of visuals and chart data, as students could pinpoint what they were referring to in their comments.

Another recurring theme from the interviews was that VoiceThread *increased social presence.* Students pointed out the importance of having icons with their names and pictures as a way to identify themselves. The audio and video capability also created instant recognition of who was contributing to the discussion. As one student pointed out, *"I became much more aware of who was commenting using VoiceThread. To be honest, there are people in class that I'm not quite sure of their names or their background. But, seeing their picture and video as they spoke, I quickly remembered who they were or what they said in class previously. With Blackboard, sometimes I'm not sure who I'm replying to as their text names don't trigger anything with me. With VoiceThread, especially using audio and video, it almost feels like I'm sitting next to the person and therefore I'm much more engaged in terms of what I say and building off of others' comments. I know others will be watching what I post, so I want to say something meaningful."*

Students also indicated a *higher level of emotional connection* with VoiceThread, especially when compared to Blackboard text discussion. With audio and video, students were motivated when hearing others express positive comments about their analysis and recommendations. Several students also pointed out it was easier to express humor and sarcasm with audio/video (e.g., facial expressions or voice connotations) versus text, as others might miss or misinterpret the language or emoticons used in text-based discussions. Some students and the instructor also mentioned it was easier to critique the team's presentations with audio/video versus text. With audio/video, commenters had more time and bandwidth to explain their line of thought and their reasoning behind their critique or line of questioning. As receivers of these critiques, students felt they learned a lot more from the richness of these comments, especially when compared to a sentence or two text comment that they may typically get.

Also, all of the students pointed out that VoiceThread was very intuitive and easy to use. Being a relatively "cutting-edge" virtual presentation tool also *increased motivation*. All of the students had used Blackboard text-based discussion boards previously in this elective or in their previous classes. So, introducing a new way of delivering and commenting on presentations generated excitement and most likely was a factor in the high participation rates. Most students found that creating video and audio comments were interesting, fun, and enjoyable, especially when contrasted with typing long text messages. Many students preferred "watching and listening" to the team presentations and class comments rather than reading lots of sometimes disjointed text comments on discussion boards. Finally, several graduate students had plans to now incorporate VoiceThread into their own workplace since they found the experience so satisfying and useful.

Undergraduate versus Graduate VoiceThread Use

There was very little difference between undergraduate and graduate student VoiceThread use in terms of total number of comments generated. However, there was a significant difference in terms of the types of comments used. According to Table 2, an analysis of variance test indicates that graduate students used audio comments as a percentage of total comments at a higher rate than undergraduate students, while undergraduate students used text comments as a percentage of total comments at a higher rate than graduate students. In particular, graduate students used audio comments at roughly twice the rate than text comments (56% vs. 28%), while the undergraduate students used audio comments at only a slightly higher rate than text comments (45% vs. 40%). Graduate students seemed more comfortable and experienced with using audio. Several mentioned that some form of audio/video conferencing in their current or previous workspace was commonplace.

Graduate students also seemed to be more proficient in organizing their thoughts and posting on more complex topics. VoiceThread gives users the ability to listen to what they just recorded and either delete (and re-record) or post their comment. Many graduate students indicated they posted their comments in a single take and were comfortable if the comments were a little "rough." Undergraduate students, meanwhile, were not as experienced using audio/video conferencing, at least for work/student projects. Several indicated it was more challenging leaving audio comments, as they had to outline what they wanted to say first. Many more undergraduate students reported they posted their final audio comment after deleting several attempts. They also seemed unsure in terms of how "polished" the audio/video comments should be. At the same time, undergraduate students were very familiar with using text comments on their student projects, as well as socially with mobile chats and social media platforms. Some undergraduate students also said it was less work for them leaving text comments. However, they also agreed that audio/video was worth the effort since these comments provided much more richness and thus learning.

Video comments had the lowest percentage of use for both undergraduate and graduate students at roughly 15%. Many said they used video comments as an experiment to try the new technology, and many indicated it was fairly easy to use their laptop's video camera to do the recording. However, some students pointed out it was more work to do video commenting since you had to adjust your sitting position and camera so that your face was being captured. Several students also mentioned they were conscience of their appearance and did not want to use the video comments since they "had just woken up and had not yet showered." Also, for both courses, this assignment occurred toward the end of the semester and everyone in the blended class was at least familiar with everyone else. So, many indicated that a video comment did not provide much value-added when compared to an audio comment that already contained an image of them on their comment icon.

CHALLENGES WITH VOICETHREAD

Since VoiceThread comments were played in the order they were submitted, it was difficult to track the discussion on those slides that had many comments. While students "built" on others' comments, it was sometimes difficult to do this with so many comments since there was no topic header with each comment icon. Also, while users could play any comment by clicking on it, they would not know what the discussion was that led to that comment. Therefore, while VoiceThread provided a forum for more creativity, richness, and visual representation of thoughts and ideas, there was a tradeoff in terms of lack of structure in certain areas to manage the discussion. Another challenge had to do with the international students in the class. Those students who were not as comfortable with English as their learning language seemed to focus on shorter text messages. Finally, some students were unsure of how good the quality of the audio/video comments had to be as well as any length or time restrictions for comments.

Discussion

This exploratory study indicates that the VoiceThread tool has much promise in terms of enabling social learning and improving student engagement for online presentations. However, like with all technology supporting learning outcomes, the instructor needs to carefully think through how and when to most effectively use the tool to support the learning objectives. This tool seems to work well in a blended course format, a mixture of face-to-face and online classes. The project used in the study is ideal for an online week. But, it could also work in a traditional face-to-face course where the instructor wants to add an experiential, hands-on component and break up the monotony of in-class presentations. Also, the results indicate that VoiceThread increases social presence in virtual presentations. In this study, the instructor introduced the project at the end of the course, after everyone had already interacted with their classmates. By introducing the tool earlier in the course, there might be more realized benefits from jumpstarting students' interactions with each other, as well as increasing one's identity and awareness among classmates.

This tool also has the potential to enable social learning by increasing student-to-student, student-to-instructor, and student-to-content interactions. In particular, this study focused on a complex content project that involved analysis (visuals, charts, tables) and recommendations, and VoiceThread seems to have been a good fit for this type of project. The ability to provide and listen to rich comments-in-context on each slide was very conducive to student learning. Students generally felt it was much easier to follow the discussion narrative in this way, versus a complex web of threaded text comments. The instructor needs to think of ways to apply a tool like VoiceThread to other "complex content" projects that benefit from social learning, such as brainstorming activities, case discussions, and Q&A assignments.

The results also indicate that the instructor needs to provide some structure to activities involving new tools such as

VoiceThread. While these tools spur creativity, some students, in particular younger and international students, may need more structure with respect to creating audio and video content. For example, the instructor needs to think through assignment design issues such as: should there be time or length constraints with respect to comments, should students be forced to use certain comment types (e.g., video) or should everything be optional, and how "polished" should the comments be. What is absolutely critical is that the tool be easy to use and intuitive, so the instructor should provide sufficient direction and training in this regard. One limitation of this study is that it involved students in an information technology elective, so there might be a bias toward students who can easily adopt technology. It would be interesting to see this tool be used on a similar project in a nontechnology course.

Future research in the use of rich media in online discussions could look at the impacts that the technology channel has on the content of the message. This exploratory study only looked at the frequency of student postings as a dependent measure. Studies could also measure the impacts that rich media has on the quality or effectiveness of the message, the length or duration of the message, and the types of messages that get generated.

Finally, individual students have learning profiles, personality types, and cultural backgrounds that may or may not be conducive to using social learning platforms. For example, some students may be averse to critiquing other students on more public platforms since it was frowned upon since their early education. Or, some students may be shy and feel awkward in posting short video clips of themselves that the entire class can view. Therefore, an area for future research in this space is to study the relationship between individual learning characteristics and social technologies.

Conclusion

VoiceThread, a cloud-based social presentation tool, was shown to increase student participation in both an undergraduate and graduate business course. The tool increased engagement and motivation, especially when compared to traditional text-based online discussion boards. Also, graduate students were more comfortable contributing audio comments when compared to undergraduate students.

Social media technologies are increasingly being used in higher education courses to improve learning outcomes. In particular, the use of audio and video in online discussions has the potential to increase student engagement and learning. In addition to VoiceThread, popular social presentation software platforms such as Kaltura, Panopto, and Brainshark, utilize rich media features.

Higher education instructors have the opportunity to create innovative learning designs that leverage these social learning tools in various classroom settings.

References

Bisson, C., & Luckner, J. (1996). Fun in learning: The pedagogical role of fun in adventure education. *Journal of Experimental Education, 9*(2), 108−112.

Carvin, A. (2008, April 25). *SlideShare and VoiceThread: Not your father's film strip* [Web log post]. Retrieved from http://www.pbs.org/teachers/learning.now/2008/04/slideshare_and_voicethread_not_1.html. Accessed on December 4, 2014.

Caspi, A., & Blau, I. (2008). Social presence in online discussion groups: Testing three Conceptions and their relations to perceived learning. *Social Psychology of Education, 11*, 323−346. doi:10.1007/s11218-008-9054-2

DeGennaro, D. (2008). Learning designs: An analysis of youth-oriented technology use. *Journal of Research on Technology in Education, 41*(1), 1−20.

Durrington, V. A., Berryhill, A., & Swafford, J. (2006). Strategies for enhancing student interactivity in an online environment. *College Teaching, 45*(1), 190−193.

Flynn, J. L. (1992). Cooperative learning and Gagne's events of instruction: A syncretic view. *Educational Technology, 32*(10), 53−60.

Griffiths, M. E., & Graham, C. R. (2009a). The potential of asynchronous video in online education. *Distance Learning, 6*, 13−23.

Griffiths, M. E., & Graham, C. R. (2009b). Using asynchronous video in online classes: Results from a pilot study. *International Journal of Instructional Technology & Distance Learning, 6*, 65−76. Retrieved from http://itdl.org/Journal/Mar_09/article06.htm. Accessed on December 4, 2014.

Hartshorne, R., & Ajjan, H. (2009). Examining student decisions to adopt Web 2.0 technologies: Theory and empirical tests. *Journal of Computing in Higher Education, 21*(3), 183−198.

Hew, K. F., & Cheung, W. S. (2012). Audio-based versus text-based asynchronous online discussion: Two case studies. *Instructional Science, 41*, 365−380. doi:10.1007/s11251-012-9232-7

Jonassen, D. H. (1994). Thinking technology: Toward a constructivist design model. *Educational Technology, 34*(4), 34−47.

Kent, M. (2013). Changing the conversation: Facebook as a venue for online class discussion in higher education. *MERLOT Journal of Online Learning and Teaching, 9*(4), 546−565.

Kidd, J. (2013). Evaluating VoiceThread for online content delivery and student interaction: Effects on classroom community. In R. McBride & M. Searson (Eds.), *Proceedings of society for information technology & teacher education international conference 2013* (pp. 2158−2162). Chesapeake, VA: AACE.

Maloney, E. J. (2007). What Web 2.0 can teach us about learning. *Chronicle of Higher Education, 53*(18), B26−B27.

Miers, J. (2004). BELTS or braces? *Technology School of the Future.*

Moore, M. G. (1989). Three types of interaction. *The American Journal of Distance Education, 3*(2), 1−6.

Moore, N. S., & Filling, M. L. (2012). iFeedback: Using video technology for improving student writing. *Journal of College Literacy & Learning, 38*, 3–14. Retrieved from http://j-cll.com/files/38_3_MF.pdf. Accessed on December 4, 2014.

Orlando, J., & Orlando, L. (2010). Using VoiceThread to improve educational outcomes. In *Proceedings of the 26th annual conference on distance teaching and learning*. Madison, WI: The Board of Regents of the University of Wisconsin System. Retrieved from http://www.uwex.edu/disted/conference/Resource_library/proceedings/28642_10.pdf. Accessed on December 4, 2014.

Palloff, R. M., & Pratt, K. (2007). *Building online learning communities: Effective strategies for the virtual classroom* (2nd ed.). San Francisco, CA: Jossey-Bass.

Schlechter, T. M. (1990). The relative instructional efficiency of small group computer-based training. *Journal of Educational Computing Research, 6*(3), 329–341.

Seely Brown, J. (2000). *Growing up digital: How the web changes work, education, and the ways people learn*. Retrieved from http://www.johnseelybrown.com/Growing_up_digital.pdf. Accessed on December 4, 2014.

Smith, J. (2012). Facilitating enhanced self, peer and instructor-centered performance assessment with VoiceThread. In P. Resta (Ed.), *Proceedings of society for information technology & teacher education international conference 2012* (pp. 3075–3080). Chesapeake, VA: AACE.

Tu, C. (2011, October 11). *VoiceThread app on iOS* [Web log post]. Retrieved from http://etc647.blogspot.com/2011/10/voicethread-app-on-ios.html. Accessed on December 4, 2014.

Twigg, C. A. (2003). *Improving learning and reducing costs: Lessons learned from round I of the PEW grant program in course redesign*. Troy, NY: Centre for Academic Transformation, Rensselaer Polytechnic Institute.

Vygotsky, L. S. (1978). *Mind in society: The development of higher psychological processes*. Cambridge, MA: Harvard University Press.

Wenger, E. (1998). Communities of practice. Learning as a social system. *Systems Thinker*. Retrieved from http://www.co-i-l.com/coil/knowledge-garden/cop/lss.shtml. Accessed on December 4, 2014.

22

Start Your Class with a "What Do You Know?" Survey

Mahdi Majbouri

Introduction

The first session of each course is known to be one of the most important sessions and sometimes a challenging one. Students try to choose among the many available courses and instructors introduce their courses, wanting to attract the interested students. Most of the time, the instructors do this by going over the syllabus, which turns this important session into a routine and predictable one. Some students have already read the syllabus and some prefer not to attend the first session as they can predict what would be discussed. In many cases, the students cannot clearly tell, after the first session, how the course helps them in their future career or life. So it sometimes remains a puzzle as to how instructors can start their course in an interactive way and engage students in the topic from day one.

This chapter offers an interactive and engaging solution: on the first day of the class, bring a set of well-chosen questions or short cases that refer to concepts that will be covered in the course (I call this a "*What do you know?*" survey). Hand the questions to the students, and give them a few minutes to answer. When they finish, ask the students to bring back this survey on the last class of the semester to measure the improvement in their knowledge and skills. An additional question about learning styles can be added to help the instructor to find out the distribution of learning styles in the class.

This simple but effective technique achieves four goals at the same time: (1) introducing the subject of the course to the students in a very clear way and setting expectations about the course, (2) getting the students invested in class from the first day by offering experiential evidence on the importance of the course in their career or daily life, (3) providing a data point of the knowledge level of students before taking the course; at the end of the semester these data are revisited by students to see how much they learned, and (4) identifying students learning styles on day one; which helps the teacher to tune her teaching style.

Self and social awareness is one of the key elements of *Entrepreneurial Thought and Action*® for *entrepreneurial leaders* (Greenberg, McKone-Sweet, & Wilson, 2011). This *"What do you know?"* survey explicitly addresses this critical element by bringing to light what the student knows about her knowledge, experience, and context. It gives an authentic and insightful understanding of what and who she knows, what her complex context is, and how much she is aware of it. Therefore, from the first day, the course helps the student to evolve into a mindful entrepreneur. The technique that is discussed here can be used to teach *entrepreneurship of all kinds* as it can be applied to almost any course in any discipline. As an *innovation in the Babson classroom*, this is one of the non-traditional experiential techniques that takes part in evolving the entrepreneurial education at Babson.

The rest of this chapter is organized as follows: first, the main steps in designing the survey is introduced followed by a few examples. Then, the additional question to identify learning styles is discussed and the administration of the survey is explained. This chapter ends with a brief conclusion.

The Survey

The *"What do you know?"* survey can be implemented in any type of course but its format depends on the learning objectives of the course. The first step in designing the survey is to choose its format from the following three main types:

- *Case-based*: these surveys are a collection of short cases. Each case is a situation in which a problem or problems exist. The survey briefly explains the situation and asks students to either offer solutions or a rigorous approach to find solutions.
- *Regular questionnaires*: these surveys have a list of questions asking about facts, concepts, and theories, as well as soliciting students' opinions about different issues.
- *Hybrid*: these surveys are a mix of case-based and regular questionnaires.

The appropriate format for the survey depends on the nature of the course and its learning objectives. In order to make the design process simpler and easier, you should categorize the course, based on its learning objectives, into one of the following four broad groups. These groups are based on the Bloom's taxonomy of educational objectives (Bloom, Engelhart, Furst, Hill, & Krathwohl, 1956; Bloom, 1994; Gronlund, 1991; Krathwohl, Bloom, & Masia, 1964) and can be listed as:

- *Knowledge-based*: these courses are conceptual and theory-driven and require students to learn and understand a large body of facts, concepts, and theories. The main learning objectives of these courses are to open new horizons of knowledge to students and make them aware of things that they did not know in advance. Examples include some science and humanities courses. All learning objectives in these courses are knowledge-based and affective.
- *Skills-based*: these are courses that transfer little facts and theories and use previously acquired knowledge to cultivate problem solving skills. Many advanced elective courses in business, law, and medicine are good examples. Almost all learning objectives in these courses are skills-based.
- *Hybrid*: these courses are a mix of knowledge and skills. Introductory, intermediate, and sometimes advanced courses in management, law, accounting, finance, economics, natural and social sciences, as well as humanities fall in this category. These courses have a mix of knowledge-based and skills-based objectives.
- *Affective*: the primary objective of these courses is to change values, beliefs, attitudes, aspirations, or behavior of students. Examples include some elective courses in humanities such as courses related to *social, environmental, and economic responsibility, and sustainability* (SEERS).

In identifying the type of the course, learning objectives would be the best guide. When the learning objectives of the course are to teach skills and expertise in applying knowledge, the course is skills-based or hybrid. Similarly, learning objectives that require students to understand or explain concepts and facts are more likely to be in knowledge-based courses. If the learning objectives are not clear or relevant, the first step for the instructor is to re-write them.[1] Note that there is a spectrum from pure knowledge-based courses to pure

---

[1]See Gronlund (1978) for a guide on how to state objectives.

skills-based courses and many courses are somewhere in the middle, a form of hybrid.

After you find the course category, choosing the format of the survey is simple. If the course is knowledge-based, the regular questionnaire is the best option. If the course is skills-based or hybrid with more than 50% of learning objectives as skills-based objectives, case-based format works best. When less than 50% of learning objectives of a hybrid course is skills-based, a hybrid or regular questionnaire is suitable. For affective courses, a hybrid format is appropriate. You can always revisit the format while designing the questions of the survey. But it would be appropriate to stick to what you have already chosen and try to design the questions accordingly.

The second and probably most important step in designing the survey is to pick the questions or write the short cases. Again, the learning objectives are your guide. Try to create the questions based on them. The questions or cases should be challenging, interesting to students, and have clear answers. The best questions or cases are those that may be asked in a job interview if the interviewer wants to refer to the concepts in the course. Next, I explain these three characteristics briefly and offer a few examples of such questions and case studies:

- *Challenging*: the questions should be puzzling. The students should realize that valuable knowledge and skills could be learned from the course.
- *Relevant and up-to-date*: the questions should easily relate to students personal and/or professional life. The examples should be from the daily activities and challenges the students will face at work or in life. It is disappointing for students to see questions that are irrelevant, because the technologies, discussed in the questions, are obsolete or the problem does not exist anymore. The best source for relevant and up-to-date questions is the popular press or recently published case studies.
- *Having either a clear solution or clear approach toward (potential) solutions*: the questions should have a clear solution or if there are ambiguities involved, the approach toward finding the solution should be clear. Questions that have many solutions depending on people's opinions do not show the benefit of taking the course clearly.

If all of the above are followed, the questions will be interesting enough for the students and accomplish the goal of the exercise well. The best sources for the questions are the stories in the news, recent case studies, the textbook examples, as well as the questions in the assignments, handouts, quizzes, and exams.

In the following sections, I include a few examples.

MANAGERIAL ECONOMICS – FOR BOTH UNDERGRADUATES AND MBAS

This is a course that teaches how to use economic concepts in practice. Here are some of its learning objectives:

- Analyze business news using market equilibrium models
- Understand and use consumer behavior
- Estimate demand and apply elasticities in business decisions
- Understand the cost and cost structure and its applications in business
- Make sound pricing strategies in various markets.

The learning objectives are a mix of knowledge and skills and hence, one would better use a series of short cases in the survey, such as the followings:

1. Recently, publishers had a dispute with Amazon over pricing of e-books. The publishers argue that the price should be higher than what Amazon is currently charging. Amazon disagrees and claims that both publishers and customers lose if the price increases. What information do you need to find out who is right?
2. You have invested $2.5 million to develop a product with interesting features. It is going to be launched in the next quarter if you continue investing in R&D in the next couple of months. The breakeven price is expected to be $500. But, today, you heard that your competitor is going to launch a new product with similar features (and some more) at the price of $300. Considering that you have already invested $2.5 million, should you stop or continue with the project?

DEVELOPMENT ECONOMICS

This course is knowledge-based rather than skills-based and therefore, its survey is a regular questionnaire. At the end of the course, the students are able to:

- Explain the socio-economic characteristics of poor nations and individuals
- Understand the theory of economic growth and its applications
- Describe and criticize the theories of macroeconomic traps of development and the solutions for those traps

- Describe and criticize the theories of microeconomic traps of poverty and the solutions for those traps.

The survey questions are as follows:

1. Why do you think some countries are poor and some are not?
2. What do you think could be done to alleviate the poverty of nations?
3. What are the problems of the poor in the very poor countries?
4. How do you find out whether an initiative to fight poverty is effective?
5. What is microfinance? Do you think microfinance is effective in reducing poverty?

ECONOMETRICS AND BUSINESS ANALYTICS COURSES

These courses have a mix of knowledge and skills-based learning objectives such as the following:

- Understand data, their types, and applications
- Use various techniques and models to explain data. Describe the limitations of these techniques
- Apply various models to infer meaningful patterns from the data
- Use data for forecasting and intelligent decision making.

The recommended survey has the case-based format and may look like the following:

1. Suppose you have data on sale prices of houses in a city as well as the following characteristics of the houses: the lot size, number of bedrooms and bathrooms, number of stories, number of garage places, whether it is located in a preferred neighborhood of the city, whether it has a driveway, a recreational room, central air conditioning, or a full finished basement, whether the house uses gas for heating. A new house in the city becomes available with the following attributes: lot size of 3000 sq. ft., 3 bedrooms and 1.5 bathrooms, 2 stories excluding the basement, one driveway, no recreational room, uses oil for heating, has no central air conditioning, has one garage place, and is not located in a preferred neighborhood. Do you have enough information to say whether the asking price of $635,000 is a bargain for this house?
2. Suppose you have quarterly data on GDP per capita for a country from 1980 to 2014. How do you predict GDP per capita in the first quarter of 2015?

3. Imagine a car. It has features such as horsepower, gas mileage, interior amenities, GPS navigator, wireless capability, color, and many more. How can you find how much each of these features are demanded by customers?

Identifying the Learning Styles

In addition to the survey above, you may want to identify the learning styles of the students with an additional question. Educational theory and research observes four learning styles: assimilating, converging, accommodating, and diverging (Kolb, 1984, 1999). Each of these styles corresponds with one of the statements in the following question and can be identified accordingly. You may add the following question to the survey or hand it to students separately:

With which of the following statements do you identify yourself the most? Note that every one of us is a mix of all the following statements. Try to find one with which you identify yourself *the most*.

- I am very interested in ideas and feel easy with abstract concepts. I can understand a wide range of information and summarize or categorize it into a concise, logical form. I feel comfortable learning theories that have logical soundness rather than practical value.
- Whenever, I learn a new thing, I try to find a practical usage for it. I love solving problems and feel at ease in applying my knowledge and skills when I encounter challenges. I do not relate to theories that do not have practical usage even if they are logically beautiful.
- I love to carry out plans and involve myself in new challenging experiences with teams of people. I believe logic can only take us so far and have a tendency to act on "gut" feeling and emotions rather than relying on logic. In a challenging situation, I would love to hear other people's opinions and feelings rather than making decisions myself.
- I am very interested in hearing various opinions and points of view and can look at a problem myself from different angles. I am imaginative and emotional and have broad cultural interests. I like brainstorming and can participate in it well. I am also very interested in people.

The learning style that is identified with the first statement is called "assimilating." People with this learning style are very good at abstract conceptualization and reflecting on observations. They prefer lectures, exploring analytical models by themselves, and having time to think things through. They perform very well in science and information careers (Kolb, Boyatzis, & Mainemelis, 2001).

The second statement belongs to the "converging" learning style. People who agree with this statement are good with technical tasks and prefer to learn with experiments, simulations, individual games, and practical applications. The third statement applies to "accommodating" learning style. Students with this style prefer to learn by hands-on experience in groups. They enjoy doing group projects and assignments and learn well from others. Group discussions in the class would be a good way for them to learn. The diverging style corresponds to the last statement. People who identify with this statement prefer to work in groups in formal learning environments, listen to people's opinions, and receive personalized feedback on their work (for more information on these learning styles, see Kolb, 1984, 1999).

The instructor needs to know the distribution of students who identify with each learning style in the class in order to adapt its teaching style, exercises, projects, quizzes, and exams accordingly.

Administering the Surveys

You can administer the survey using pen and paper. It would be good to give 2–5 minutes for each case-based question and about 1–2 minutes for a regular question. The students fill out the survey and keep it with themselves until the last day of the class when they bring it back to see how much their answers have changed and how much they learned through the semester. In the last session, you can ask them to even grade their answers. Afterwards, collect the surveys and evaluate them. Alternatively, you can collect the surveys in the first session and return them on the last day.

When the students review their answers, you can hear giggles and laughs, and sometimes sounds of surprise. Some may show others their answers and joke about them. This can be an exciting moment for the instructor as it displays student appreciation of the course and what they learned. You could feel that they realized how much they changed and that a leap of learning has occurred for them. It is an appealing experience for the instructor to feel that the semester long efforts have paid off.

Using this simple technique may also impress students about how much their learning is important to you. They understand that you spend a good deal of time designing a course that taught them valuable skills and/or knowledge which helps them in their professional, intellectual, and personal lives. The rewarding moment for the instructor is when the survey creates a lasting image in the students' minds about the course. A student may later contact you to mention that one of the questions in the survey was so relevant to what she is doing in her job.

The learning style question can be easily administered using modern technologies such as clickers or online survey tools on course management systems such as Blackboard, since the instructor only needs to know the share of the students with each learning style. It can also be done using the traditional pen and paper. But the results should be analyzed before the second session of the class. It would be interesting to students to learn a bit about learning styles in the second session as well. The question can be revisited then. This time each statement would be linked to a learning style so that students potentially learn something new about themselves.

Conclusions

This chapter discussed an intervention on the first day of the class that can be used to introduce the course and its objectives and convey its potential value to the students. The intervention is a "*What do you know?*" survey with questions related to the course objectives that can be asked on a potential job interview. Steps to design a successful survey were discussed and several examples were offered. An additional question is also introduced, to be added to the survey helping the instructor to identify the distribution of learning styles in the class. This intervention helps students to have more realistic expectations about what the course can deliver, understand its value, and use it in their future careers. In addition, it helps instructors to convey the value of the course to students more clearly.

Acknowledgments

The author wishes to thank the Center for Engaged Learning and Teaching (CELT) at Babson College, the editors of the volume, and the anonymous reviewers of this manuscript.

References

Bloom, B. S. (1994). Bloom's taxonomy: A forty-year retrospective. K. J. Rehage, L. W. Anderson, & L. A. Sosniak (Eds.), *Yearbook of the national society for the study of education* (Vol. 93(2)). Chicago, IL: National Society for the Study of Education.

Bloom, B. S., Engelhart, M. D., Furst, E. J., Hill, W. H., & Krathwohl, D. R. (1956). *Taxonomy of educational objectives: The classification of educational goals. Handbook I: Cognitive domain.* New York, NY: David McKay Company.

Greenberg, D., McKone-Sweet, K., & Wilson, H. J. (2011). Entrepreneurial leadership: Shaping social and economic opportunity. In D. Greenberg, K. McKone-Sweet, & H. J. Wilson (Eds.), *The new entrepreneurial leader: Developing leaders who shape social and economic opportunity*. San Francisco, CA: Berrett-Koehler Publishers, Inc.

Gronlund, N. E. (1978). *Stating objectives for classroom instruction*. New York, NY: Macmillan.

Gronlund, N. E. (1991). *How to write and use instructional objectives* (4th ed.). New York, NY: Macmillan Publishing Company.

Kolb, D. A. (1984). *Experiential learning: Experience as the source of learning and development* (Vol. 1). Englewood Cliffs, NJ: Prentice-Hall.

Kolb, D. A. (1999). The Kolb learning style inventory. Version 3: Technical specifications. Boston, MA: Hay Group.

Kolb, D. A., Boyatzis, R. E., & Mainemelis, C. (2001). Experiential learning theory: Previous research and new directions. In R. J. Sternberg & L. Zhang (Eds.), *Perspectives on thinking, learning, and cognitive styles. The educational psychology series* (pp. 227–247). Mahwah, NJ: Lawrence Erlbaum Associates, Inc.

Krathwohl, D. R., Bloom, B. S., & Masia, B. B. (1964). *Taxonomy of educational objectives: The classification of educational goals. Handbook II: The affective domain*. New York, NY: David McKay Company.

23

Quickfire! Increasing Student Engagement Using Competitive Classroom Exercises Under Time Constraints

Jennifer Bailey and Richard C. Hanna

Introduction

Student engagement is a topic which is of critical importance to the college educator, as many theories propose and demonstrate the positive link between engagement and learning outcomes (Carini, Kuh, & Klein, 2006; Prince, 2004). Engagement leads to several positive classroom behaviors. Specifically, Fredricks and McColskey (2012) outline three levels of student engagement: behavioral engagement (level of participation and time on the task), emotional engagement (interest in the task), and cognitive engagement (mental focus on the task). As a result of these behaviors, engagement has carryover benefits in terms of improved learning outcomes and academic performance, as evidenced by higher classroom test grades and standardized exam scores (Carini et al., 2006; Faria, 2001). However, during the delivery of complex course material, instructors are often faced with students who are highly disengaged, often exhibiting feelings and behaviors of boredom, apathy, anxiety and resistance (Fullagar, Knight, & Sovern, 2013; Silver & Perini, 2010; Sashittal, Jassawalla & Markulis 2012). Four factors have been shown to be important for generating student engagement in classroom activities (Parsons & Taylor, 2011; Shernoff & Csikszentmihalyi, 2009; Silver & Perini, 2010; Strong, Silver, & Robinson, 1995). The first factor is the level of challenge of the classroom activity. The second factor is the degree of relevancy of the problem. The third factor is the degree of collaborative learning required for completing the activity. The fourth factor is the level of enjoyment associated with completing the activity. Therefore, as educators, there is an opportunity to improve levels of student engagement by manipulating these drivers. Experiential exercises are perceived by students as being more enjoyable, challenging, relevant, and valuable than other traditional course delivery mechanisms (Karns, 2005), all of which generate higher levels of student engagement (Garrett, 2011). Therefore, we propose an experiential classroom activity which incorporates these four factors which lead to improved student engagement.

Borrowing from the reality show *Top Chef*, we propose an exercise based on the "Quickfire" challenge format, for which the show is popularly known. Similar to the show's format, students participate in a competition in which they are tasked with using a specific concept from class in a real decision setting (i.e., equivalent to using one "ingredient" as the focal point of the decision) and have an imposed time pressure from the shortened time to execute. Having students compete under a time constraint adjusts the level of perceived challenge associated with the task (Roskes, 2015). In addition, the students are challenged with solving a problem which has a direct application to the real world. Therefore, the exercise also adds a level of realism and relevancy with respect to the degree of complexity and ambiguity that students will face outside of the classroom (Erzurumlu & Rollag, 2013). For our proposed activities, students work in a team, which increases learning and engagement by incorporating an element of cooperative learning. Finally, the competitive gaming element of the exercise adds an element of play to the activity, which increases students' enjoyment and, hence, engagement.

Developing students as future entrepreneurial leaders requires building students' capabilities to operate under two complementary types of logic: a prediction logic and a creation logic. Prediction logic is based on an analytical decision-making process, in those contexts in which optimal solutions can be determined under a given set of goals and constraints. On the other hand, creation logic is more appropriate when the future is unknown, and when novel and original ends can be shaped by applying the means at hand (Neck & Greene, 2011). To capture both these contexts, we will present two different applications of the Quickfire exercise, one for an inventory management exercise in operations management (a more quantitative-oriented course, requiring a prediction logic focus) and another for an advertising message strategy exercise in marketing communications (a more qualitative course, requiring a creation logic focus). The format of the Quickfire exercise also underscores the Babson philosophy of teaching Entrepreneurial Thought and Action (ETA), which emphasizes the importance of taking smart action, and making decisions under time pressure, even in the face of limited information and uncertainty (Neck & Greene, 2011), which is a critical skill for entrepreneurs (Pittaway & Cope, 2007). Next, we present the two exercises and the results of the student pre-activity and post-activity attitude surveys as well our own observations of student engagement and progress.

Quickfire Application 1: Operations and Inventory Management

For our first illustration of the Quickfire concept in use, we describe an application to a quantitative topic. The exercise was used to reinforce the economic order quantity (EOQ) concept being taught as an inventory management principle within an undergraduate operations management class. The main premise of the EOQ concept is that managers can use the model to minimize annual inventory costs, by identifying an optimal inventory ordering quantity, when replenishing products from a supplier (or from production). Students are introduced to the inventory sawtooth concept in order to understand the tradeoff between the per-order transaction costs, associated with the placement of each order, versus the holding costs associated with warehousing and storing the inventory once the order has been placed.

As an instructor, this complex topic poses several challenges in terms of keeping students engaged in the subject matter. First, the EOQ concept is heavily quantitative, which increases the level of students' anxiety associated with mathematical problem-solving and numerical manipulation (Desai & Inman, 1994). Second, students typically report that the subject of inventory management is dry and uninteresting. Furthermore, since the inventory management examples are often far removed from the students' experience, it makes it more difficult for them to appreciate the applicability and importance of the subject matter. Finally, more often than not, students simply apply rote memorization and application of the equations, but have difficulty gaining a deeper understanding of the inventory management concepts. As a result, they fail to appreciate the managerial implications of the various cost factors at play and have difficulty applying the concept to more open-ended problems and across varying contexts.

To overcome these issues, we designed an interactive inventory-related Quickfire challenge. Students would assume the role of an entrepreneur who was considering several potential ventures and had to consider the impact of his/her start-up inventory budget as a factor in deciding whether or not to pursue a venture in a particular product category. There were three objectives for conducting this classroom activity related to increasing student engagement: (i) make the topic of inventory management enjoyable and interesting; (ii) increase the degree of realism and relevancy of the exercise; and (iii) move students from rote memorization of the equations to a deeper conceptual understanding of the topic of inventory management.

To engage the students, we intentionally selected high-tech and college-related products to which the students could relate. For purposes of practicality, students are often given oversimplified inventory management examples, which they are able to solve with rote application of the EOQ formula; however, this makes it difficult for them to gain a full appreciation of the power of the EOQ concept. In contrast to this, for the Quickfire exercise, students were given a more realistic scenario with a significant amount of data (six pages). This required them to discern what information and which equations were relevant and necessary, in order to identify the optimal product category. Therefore, the exercise presented students with the challenge of solving a more open-ended and ambiguous problem, and required them to move from rote application to thinking more critically and deeply about the problem and understanding how to apply their previously acquired knowledge (Hmelo-Silver, 2004).

This Quickfire challenge was conducted with a class of 36 students. Prior to the Quickfire class, students had completed two lecture-based sessions on the basics of inventory management and the EOQ concept. For the Quickfire challenge, the professor crafted three alternate potential entrepreneurial ventures from which the students could select: (i) a high-end running jacket, embedded with wearable audio technology; (ii) a high-tech navigation helmet with a GPS system projected on the visor; and (iii) college flip flops (see Appendix A). For each product category, students were given information on the historical demand for this product category for the prior four years, the retail price of the product, the per transaction ordering fee, and the inventory holding cost. For one product category, the running jackets, they were also presented with information on a second ordering option, in which the supplier offered the option for the running jackets to be purchased at a discounted cost, if the jackets were ordered in bulk quantities. However, while the bulk order strategy had a cheaper unit cost, it resulted in a higher per transaction ordering fee. Students were presented with data for all three product category options, in a six-page handout. This exercise is unique from other inventory management exercises (Umble & Umble, 2013), in that instead of making multiple inventory management decisions over time, for a single product, students had to consider the impact of inventory-related costs on profitability, in order to select a final product for investment, from a set of alternative product choices. In this way, the context more realistically reflects how students might apply this knowledge as a future entrepreneurial leader. Students were divided into nine teams of four students each, to compete with each other, and were required to present their final investment decision within a 20-minute time frame. The students were presented with the rules of the game as follows:

> You are considering starting a new company. You have been approached by a venture capitalist (VC) who has offered to provide enough funds to acquire your start-up inventory for the first year. You will have an inventory budget of $25M for the first year of inventory investments. You have to choose which product category you would like to invest in. The VC is waiting for your answer NOW! You have 20 minutes to make your investment choice which must specify the following: (i) the product category you selected to invest in, (ii) how often per year you will order from the supplier, (iii) the quantity per order, and (iv) your annual inventory cost and profit for the first year. The Winning Team must (i) stay within the investor's inventory budget of $25M and (ii) must make the maximum profit relative to the other teams. In the event of a tie for profit, the tie-breaker will be determined by the team who submits their winning decision first.

By putting students in the shoes of an entrepreneur who is comparing three different potential ventures, they can see how inventory management concepts play a broader role in understanding of the profitability of a product. The instructor deliberately selected the product with the lowest retail price (college flip flops), to be the most profitable product, net of inventory costs to reinforce the importance of considering not only a product's revenue potential (retail price) but also the importance of inventory costs. Furthermore, by considering the inventory budget constraint, students had to recognize that, in addition to considering both holding costs and ordering costs (the two factors in the EOQ model), they also had to account for the inventory purchasing costs for acquiring the product from the supplier. In typical classroom and homework problems, the level of annual demand is provided in advance; however, in this Quickfire exercise, detailed historical demand data was given by week for four prior consecutive years. Therefore, students were required to identify the required information by computing trends of year-over-year sales growth, in order to forecast projected future annual demand levels, and to consider the impact of their sales forecast projections on both revenues and optimal EOQ. These calculations had an impact on both their inventory budget, and the profitability of the product.

Results for Application 1

In order to evaluate the impact of the Quickfire exercise on students' engagement levels, we designed a pre-activity and post-activity survey. The actual questions and results of the survey for the Inventory Management Quickfire are shown in Appendix B. Based on the pre-activity survey results, 83% of the students indicated that they felt that they understood the basic principles of inventory management; however, 52% of students thought inventory management was a complex topic. Based on the post-activity results, 80% of the students reported that the exercise was more effective than traditional course delivery mechanisms. Although only three of the nine teams were able to identify the optimal product selection within the time frame given, the exercise allowed students to challenge their existing knowledge and to identify the gaps in their understanding (Hmelo-Silver, 2004). Students' qualitative comments also suggest that the level of realism of the Quick fire inventory management challenge provided them with an opportunity to gain a deeper understanding of the subject matter:

> "The Quickfire inventory management challenge showed me how I would be able to apply these concepts in the real world, which helped them make more sense to me."

> "I did well on the HW so I was surprised that I struggled."

> "Although it was hard because of the time constraint — I think that applying it to a budget made it seem a lot more real because it is not just a number anymore."

> "The most interesting insight was being aware of your constraints e.g. the budget."

The post-activity results also showed that 83% of students indicated that the team structure made the exercise more enjoyable, while 68% reported that the team structure made it easier to ask their teammates questions about difficult concepts. Hmelo-Silver (2004) notes the importance of cooperative learning strategies which facilitate learning as students are required to exchange and defend their ideas. These benefits of using cooperative learning mechanisms as an instrument to engage students is reflected in the following post-activity qualitative comment

> "I loved the team exercise because that's the best way to engage students in a learning fashion."

Surprisingly, in the pre-activity survey, 51% of the students indicated that they enjoyed working with numbers. Consistent with existing research findings, however, 54% of the students indicated that they get anxious when working on quantitative tasks under time constraints (Onwuegbuzie & Seaman, 1995). Nonetheless, the post-activity results confirm that using a time constraint in order to increase challenge component of the exercise was effective in increasing student engagement. In fact, in the post-activity survey, 40% of students agreed that the time pressure made the exercise more enjoyable. Qualitative comments gathered at the end of the exercise provide additional support for the benefits of using a competitive time constraint to increase engagement. Students' comments include the following:

> "I really enjoyed the Quickfire challenge — it was a competitive and fun way to understand the inventory management more thoroughly."

> "The challenge was interesting and engaging. It was enjoyable to work through."

> "Today's class was soo fun!". "Today I was actively engaged in the competition."

However, the results also demonstrate the delicate balance that must be maintained when moving along the continuum between disengagement, engagement, and anxiety (Fullagar et al., 2013). While 40% of students agreed that the time pressure made the exercise more enjoyable, another 40% disagreed. Qualitative comments gathered at the end of the exercise suggest that the same factors, such as a competitive time constraint, that lead to engagement for some students served to reinforce performance anxieties for other students (Fullagar et al., 2013). For example, students' comments included the following:

> "Too Little Time."

> "I'm just a little unsure about inventory management — mainly the Quickfire exercise."

> "I felt stressed because I didn't understand."

Quickfire Application 2: Advertising Message Strategy

For our second illustration, we used the Quickfire concept in a qualitative class for a creative exercise focused on generating a novel outcome. In marketing communications, one of the key topics is determining the message strategy for an advertising campaign.

While this topic explores familiar ideas (e.g., using humor as a strategy), it becomes a complex decision-making exercise because there are 10 major strategies to consider and most have sub-strategies (e.g., persuasive strategies include comparison messages and reasons-to-buy ad messages), each with their own pros and cons and optimal usage opportunities. The strategies, taken from the textbook for the course (O'Guinn et al., 2014) range from simple jingles, the easiest to execute, to transformational experiences, the hardest to execute (see Appendix C, Figure C1).

There are two main issues that we need to overcome when teaching this topic. First, students often overestimate their ability to recall these strategies because of their familiarity with them, having seen many of these strategies executed in commercials they have seen before. Also, because there are many options and several of the strategies either share some components or have been used in combination in commercials seen in real life, students tend to mix them up. Moreover, it is our experience that, regardless of topic, students often assume that reading and memorizing equals a deep understanding of the material, when in fact they only have a cursory understanding. Thus, when subsequently tested to apply this knowledge in a different context than they have read, many students fail the test. Second, and perhaps more importantly, when applying the strategies for a given problem, students tend to pick the most obvious or easiest message strategy to fit the problem without considering more creative options that may be harder to imagine but would be more effective. For example, for consumer products, the easiest strategy to execute and the most obvious choice would be choosing to use a jingle. However, a more difficult strategy to execute, such as trying to leverage social anxiety (see Appendix C, Figure C1), may be more effective and more interesting. This last problem is a real challenge because only a few students will push the boundaries to use the less obvious message strategy. And if they don't experience the creative process themselves, they may not appreciate the benefit of thinking beyond the obvious. Thus, there were two learning objectives for this exercise. First, to improve students' ability to distinguish and recall the different message strategies and require them to apply their knowledge in different contexts. And second, to illustrate that the easiest (and perhaps most obvious) choice in message strategy is not always the most creative.

This Quickfire challenge was conducted with a class of 15 students that had been formed into four agency teams (approximately four students per team) earlier in the semester. Prior to the Quickfire challenge, students had completed two lecture-based sessions covering all of the relevant material on message strategy, including showing multiple examples of the different strategies used in real advertisements. Students were told to review this material before the start of class in preparation for the exercise. Before starting the Quickfire exercise, the professor surveyed the students to gather their opinions and feelings toward the message strategy topic (see Appendix D, Table 1). For the Quickfire challenge, the professor designed the exercise to challenge students to access a large source of qualitative information and quickly decide on the appropriate solution. However, there were some built-in twists that required students to go beyond their comfort zone.

A list of seven consumer products that launched in 2014 was assembled for this exercise. The products were primarily line extensions of existing brands so that students would have some familiarity with the products. However, the extensions were new enough that students would not have seen the actual message strategies used in real executions. At the start of class, the professor informed the students that they would be competing to serve as the new advertising agency for a consumer product goods manufacturer. In order to win the deal, the teams would compete by seeing which student agency could create the most creative message strategy for the recently launched consumer product. They were then provided a list of seven product choices. The students were told each team could choose only one of the seven products for the competition and that once a team selected a product, the other teams could not choose that same product. Teams were advised to take a few minutes to rank order the products so that they would have a backup if their first choice was not available by the time their turn came around. The teams then drew numbers from one through four to determine the order in which they would choose their products. After allowing the teams to deliberate for a few minutes, the professor asked each team in their assigned order to pick a product. Once each team made a choice, they were given a product worksheet for their choice (see Appendix C, Figure C2 for an example) and instructed to develop a message strategy for their chosen product and record their decisions on the worksheet. They were then informed that they had 8 minutes to complete the task and told to begin immediately!

When time was up, the students were handed a "twist." Again, borrowing from the Top Chef concept, the professor introduced a new element to the process that would require the teams to think quickly on their feet and possibly shift into doing things differently. The teams were informed that they should pass their work to the team to their right. After handing out new worksheets, the professor then informed the teams that the client they were competing for was looking for each agency's take on all four of the products used in round 1 and has challenged the new team to come up with a new solution for the product another team had already worked on. The catch, however, was that the new team needed to use a different message strategy than the strategy employed by the prior team. They again had only eight 8 minutes to complete the task. After the next round was over, the teams again exchanged their work with another team and repeated the process. After four rounds, each team had worked on all four of the originally chosen products, but with each round the task became harder as they had fewer message strategy options to choose from, and presumably the easiest strategies were already picked. Once the final round was completed, the teams took turns presenting their strategy for each product while the professor compiled the results on the board. After the presentation of the different strategies, the teams then voted for their favorite strategy for each product. Finally, the students completed a second post-activity survey regarding their experience with the Quickfire and an assessment of how they felt about the material (see Appendix D).

Results for Application 2

The pre-activity survey revealed that more than half of the class had a basic understanding of the message strategy concepts and felt confident regarding how to apply the various strategies. In terms of the actual product choices, the teams chose to generate messaging strategies for four products: Lindt Excellence Dark Assortment, Harmless Harvest 100% Coconut Water, Hershey's S'mores, and Yoplait Greek Yogurt Frozen Bars (the actual message strategies used by the student teams are provided in Appendix E). Throughout the four rounds, the teams used a variety of message strategies for the four products and applied them in different ways. After the teams presented their strategies, the students voted for the one that they thought was the most effective application of the strategy as well as appealing to the most audience. Based on the student vote, the best strategies for Lindt Chocolates and Harmless Harvest Coconut Water were created during the third round, and the best strategy for Yoplait was created on the fourth round. Only Hershey's S'mores had a strategy voted best in the first round. The instructor for the class also evaluated these strategies and, based on both his professional and academic experience in marketing communications, concurred with the student vote. However, the instructor noted to the class that the strategy for Hershey's S'mores created in the third round could be viewed by some as more appealing depending on the target audience.

In examining the post-activity survey results, overwhelmingly, all the students agreed that the exercise strongly reinforced their understanding of the different message strategies and thought the exercise was more helpful than doing a homework problem or case problem in class on the same topic. Students also felt the team structure was helpful in understanding the different strategies. Thus, it would appear the exercise satisfied the first learning objective.

The results of this Quickfire highlight several opportunities and challenges for using time pressure to increase engagement levels on a creative task. In the post-activity survey, 53% of the students indicated the time pressure of the assignment made the exercise more enjoyable. Therefore, the Quickfire exercise was effective in leveraging both the time pressure and the competitive nature of the game to improve engagement. Research suggests that when performing creative tasks, time pressure can serve as a constraint which is associated with a positive challenge and is met with excitement and enthusiasm and results in improved creative performance (Gutnick, Walter, Nijstad, & De Dreu, 2012; Roskes, 2015). In fact, consistent with this finding, two of the teams on the first pass attempted very difficult strategies by trying to tie social meaning to the product with slice of life message strategies in the first round for Harmless Harvest Coconut Water and Hershey S'mores (see Appendixes C and E. Strategy 8, social meaning using a slice of life used by two groups in the first round). On the other hand, others can perceive the time constraint for creative tasks as a negative threat, which induces anxiety and reduces cognitive flexibility (Gutnick et al., 2012; Roskes, 2015). Relatedly, Andrews (1996) suggests that under extreme time pressure, brand managers will often use the easiest and least creative strategies. Consistent with this theory, in the first round, two of the four groups selected relatively easy strategies (see Appendixes C and E. Strategy 2 and Strategy 4 used by two groups in the first round).

Once the simpler strategies were used up, teams needed to think outside of the box and be more creative in order to use one of the strategies that are more difficult to execute. As a result, the third and fourth attempt for a particular product tended to be the most creative. Roskes (2015) suggests that while time pressure could be considered a limiting constraint which initially leads to less creative outcomes, other constraints such as having restrictive goals can counteract this effect, leading to more creative outcomes. During the discussion of the teams' strategies for each product, what students began to realize was how the product concept could be communicated in different ways without any loss of the brand identity. Therefore, as the challenge became more difficult, students rose to the occasion and found ways to use the more difficult strategies and were rewarded by achieving a more creative, and often more effective message for a given product.

Conclusion

We developed an experiential learning exercise which leverages a competitive time constraint to increase the level of challenge and student engagement while presenting a complex topic. The results are discussed for two different contexts: a quantitative course and a qualitative course. The results for both are consistent. Overwhelmingly, students reported that the use of a competitive time constraint made the class exercise more interesting, enjoyable, and engaging. However, for both the qualitative and the quantitative exercise, the time pressure also increased anxiety and decreased engagement for some students. Our findings are consistent with those in the literature, related to the impact of time pressure on both quantitative tasks and creative tasks. Onwuegbuzie and Seaman (1995) find that for high anxiety students, time constraints reduce motivation and impair performance on quantitative tasks. Relatedly, studies also show that while time pressure can increase both intrinsic motivation and performance for creative tasks, those prone to anxiety can perceive the time constraint as a negative threat which decreases both intrinsic motivation and performance on creative tasks (Gutnick et al., 2012; Roskes, 2015).

Educators are required to manage several related issues when teaching complex subjects and designing optimal learning experiences: boredom, engagement, and anxiety (see Figure 1). Boredom and apathy occurs when students are presented with easy, non-challenging activities, and disengage as a result (Sashittal, Jassawalla & Markulis 2012). On the other hand, when students with low skill level are presented with difficult challenges, they may also disengage and

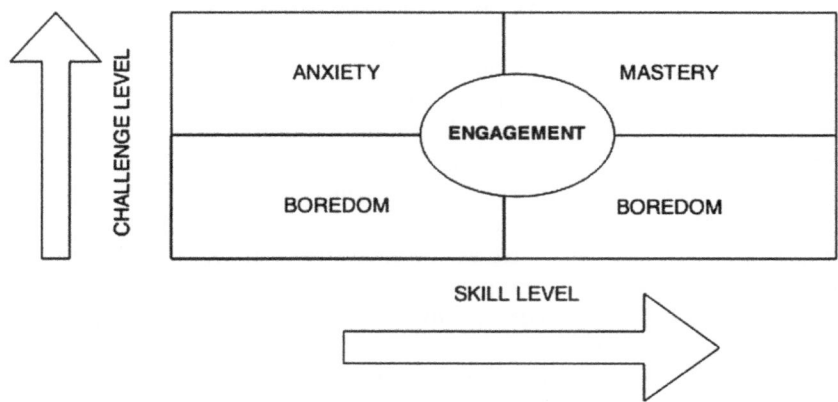

Figure 1: Impacts of Challenge and Skill on Boredom, Engagement, and Anxiety. *Source*: Adapted from Fullagar et al. (2013).

perform poorly because they feel threatened and unprepared to meet the challenge, which increases their levels of anxiety. An optimal level of engagement occurs when students with moderate skill are presented with moderate/difficult tasks which allow them to become engrossed in the task as they strive to attain mastery. This optimal zone of engagement has also been referred to as a flow experience (Fullagar et al., 2013; Shernoff & Csikszentmihalyi, 2009). Therefore, for skilled and capable students, increasing the level of challenge on a task can effectively shift them from boredom to enthusiasm and engagement. However, for poorly skilled students, increasing the level of challenge on a task could result in increased anxiety, resulting in disengagement from the task. The results of our Quickfire challenge therefore suggest that educators must carefully consider both skill levels and potential anxiety levels when designing learning experiences for a diverse student body, and must delicately balance these factors, in order to achieve optimal levels of student engagement.

References

Andrews, J. (1996). Creative ideas take time: Business practices that help product managers cope with time pressure. *Journal of Product & Brand Management, 5*(1), 6–18.

Carini, R. M., Kuh, G. D., & Klein, S. P. (2006). Student engagement and student learning: Testing the linkages. *Research in Higher Education, 47*(1), 1–32.

Desai, K., & Inman, R. A. (1994). Student bias against POM coursework and manufacturing. *International Journal of Operations & Production Management, 14*(8), 70–87.

Erzurumlu, S. S., & Rollag, K. (2013). Increasing student interest and engagement with business cases by turning them into consulting exercises. *Decision Sciences Journal of Innovative Education, 11*(4), 359–381.

Faria, A. J. (2001). The changing nature of business simulation/gaming research: A brief history. *Simulation & Gaming, 32*(1), 97–110.

Fredricks, J. A., & McColskey, W. (2012). The measurement of student engagement: A comparative analysis of various methods and student self-report instruments. In *Handbook of research on student engagement* (pp. 763–782). New York, NY: Springer US.

Fullagar, C. J., Knight, P. A., & Sovern, H. S. (2013). Challenge/skill balance, flow, and performance anxiety. *Applied Psychology, 62*(2), 236–259.

Garrett, C. (2011). Defining, detecting, and promoting student engagement in college learning environments. *Transformative Dialogues: Teaching & Learning Journal, 5*(2), 1–12.

Gutnick, D., Walter, F., Nijstad, B. A., & De Dreu, C. K. (2012). Creative performance under pressure an integrative conceptual framework. *Organizational Psychology Review, 2*(3), 189–207.

Hmelo-Silver, C. E. (2004). Problem-based learning: What and how do students learn? *Educational Psychology Review, 16*(3), 235–266.

Karns, G. L. (2005). An update of marketing student perceptions of learning activities: Structure, preferences, and effectiveness. *Journal of Marketing Education*, *27*(2), 163–171.

Neck, H. M., & Greene, P. G. (2011). Entrepreneurship education: Known worlds and new frontiers. *Journal of Small Business Management*, *49*(1), 55–70.

O'Guinn, T. C., Allen, C. T., Semenik, R. J., & Scheinbaum, A. C. (2014). *Advertising and integrated brand promotion* (7th ed.). Stamford, CT: Cengage Learning.

Onwuegbuzie, A. J., & Seaman, M. A. (1995). The effect of time constraints and statistics test anxiety on test performance in a statistics course. *The Journal of Experimental Education*, *63*(2), 115–124.

Parsons, J., & Taylor, L. (2011). Improving student engagement. *Current Issues in Education*, *14*(1). Retrieved from http://cie.asu.edu/ojs/index.php/cieatasu/issue/view/12

Pittaway, L., & Cope, J. (2007). Simulating entrepreneurial learning integrating experiential and collaborative approaches to learning. *Management Learning*, *38*(2), 211–233.

Prince, M. (2004). Does active learning work? A review of the research. *Journal of Engineering Education*, *93*(3), 223–231.

Roskes, M. (2015). Constraints that help or hinder creative performance: A motivational approach. *Creativity and Innovation Management*, *24*(2), 197–206.

Sashittal, H. C., Jassawalla, A. R., & Markulis, P. (2012). Students' perspective into the apathy and social disconnectedness they feel in undergraduate business classrooms. *Decision Sciences Journal of Innovative Education*, *10*(3), 413–446.

Shernoff, D. J., & Csikszentmihalyi, M. (2009). Cultivating engaged learners and optimal learning environments. In *Handbook of positive psychology in schools* (pp. 131–145). New York, NY: Routledge.

Silver, H. F., & Perini, M. J. (2010). The eight C's of engagement: How learning styles and instructional design increase students' commitment to learning. In *On excellence in teaching* (pp. 319–344). Bloomington, IN: Solution Tree Press.

Strong, R., Silver, H. F., & Robinson, A. (1995). Strengthening student engagement: What do students want. *Educational Leadership*, *53*(1), 8–12.

Umble, E., & Umble, M. (2013). Utilizing a simulation exercise to illustrate critical inventory management concepts. *Decision Sciences Journal of Innovative Education*, *11*(1), 13–21.

Appendix A: Sample Documentation for Inventory Management Quickfire

PRODUCT CHOICE #1

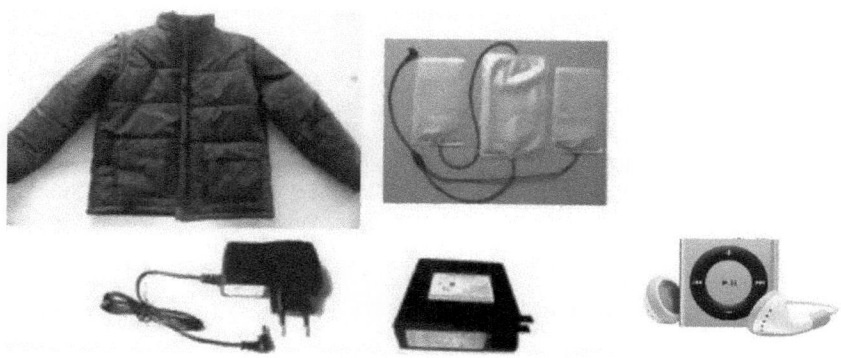

"ELECTRIC BOOGIE WOOGIE"
RUNNING JACKET

The *"Electric Boogie Woogie"* Running Jacket is pre-wired with the latest version of the iPod Shuffle music player to keep you entertained all throughout your run. The Jacket will retail at $250 per unit. You have identified a Supplier in Australia who has offered to produce the jacket and sell it to you at a cost of $190. For each order manufactured and shipped by the supplier, there is a per order cost of $21,000 which will cover all shipping, customs, and transportation costs from Australia to the United States (USA). Once in the USA you estimate that the annual holding cost per unit per year will be approximately $20 per unit held, which will cover all warehousing, insurance, and other inventory carrying costs. The supplier in Australia has also offered you the option to produce and ship a single shipment at the beginning of the year, to cover your demand for the entire year. If you agree to this arrangement, you will be charged a single ordering cost for the year of $2,5000,000. However, to sweeten the deal for this special arrangement, the supplier will also offer you a discount of $40 per unit bought. That is, the supplier will sell the jackets at a cost of $150, if you agree to place a single bulk order. The past estimated demand for the market you will serve is presented here. It is the beginning of 2013, and you will enter the market and place order in anticipation of selling in 2013.

Week	2009	2010	2011	2012
1	1,998	2,198	2,417	2,659
2	1,999	2,199	2,418	2,660
3	2,002	2,202	2,422	2,664
4	1,998	2,198	2,418	2,660
5	1,999	2,199	2,418	2,660
6	1,997	2,197	2,417	2,659
7	1,997	2,197	2,417	2,658
8	1,998	2,198	2,418	2,660
9	1,999	2,199	2,419	2,661
10	1,996	2,196	2,415	2,657
11	2,002	2,202	2,423	2,665
12	2,001	2,201	2,421	2,663
13	1,999	2,199	2,419	2,661
14	2,003	2,203	2,424	2,666
15	2,003	2,204	2,424	2,666
16	1,997	2,197	2,416	2,658
17	2,003	2,204	2,424	2,667
18	2,000	2,200	2,420	2,662
19	1,999	2,199	2,419	2,661
20	2,000	2,200	2,420	2,662
21	2,001	2,201	2,422	2,664
22	2,000	2,201	2,421	2,663
23	2,002	2,203	2,423	2,665
24	2,002	2,202	2,422	2,664
25	1,998	2,197	2,417	2,659
26	2,002	2,202	2,422	2,664
27	2,000	2,200	2,420	2,662
28	1,997	2,197	2,416	2,658
29	2,001	2,202	2,422	2,664
30	2,000	2,200	2,420	2,662
31	2,001	2,202	2,422	2,664
32	1,999	2,199	2,419	2,660
33	1,997	2,197	2,417	2,658
34	1,999	2,199	2,419	2,661
35	2,000	2,200	2,420	2,662
36	1,998	2,198	2,418	2,660
37	2,000	2,200	2,420	2,662
38	2,002	2,202	2,423	2,665
39	1,999	2,199	2,419	2,661
40	2,001	2,201	2,421	2,663
41	2,001	2,201	2,421	2,663
42	2,001	2,201	2,421	2,663
43	2,004	2,205	2,425	2,668
44	2,002	2,202	2,422	2,664

Week	2009	2010	2011	2012
45	1,999	2,199	2,419	2,661
46	2,000	2,200	2,421	2,663
47	2,002	2,202	2,422	2,664
48	1,998	2,198	2,418	2,660
49	1,999	2,199	2,419	2,660
50	2,001	2,201	2,421	2,663
51	1,997	2,196	2,416	2,658
52	2,001	2,201	2,421	2,663
Total	103,997	114,397	125,836	138,420

(Continued)

PRODUCT CHOICE #2

NAVIGATION HELMET

Touchscreen navigators and paper maps aren't that useful to riders while on their motorcycles, so this Navigation Helmet addresses this problem with augmented-reality such as full-color, translucent pictures projected on the visor. It will come fitted with a microphone for voice control, a set of earphones, a light sensor for adjusting image brightness, and batteries along with a G-sensor, gyroscope, and digital compass for head movement tracking. You have identified a possible market where you can retail the helmets at $2,500 per unit. You have identified a Supplier in Russia who has offered to produce the helmets and sell it to you at a cost of $1,900. For each order manufactured and shipped by the supplier, there is a per order cost of $1,000 which will cover all shipping, customs, and transportation costs. The ordering costs are very low because the supplier is eager to get into this new market and is willing to cover most of the shipping and manufacturing setup costs for you. Once in the USA you estimate that the annual holding cost per unit per year will be approximately $19 per unit held, which will cover all warehousing, insurance, and other inventory carrying costs. The past estimated demand for the market you will serve is tabulated here. It is the beginning of 2013, and you will enter the market and place order in anticipation of selling in 2013.

PRODUCT CHOICE #3

COLLEGE FLIP FLOPS

The *College Flip Flop* is a staple for college students. You have identified a possible market where you can retail a pair of flip flops at $2.50 per unit. You have identified a Supplier in Jamaica who has offered to produce the flip flops and sell it to you at a cost of $1.50. For each order manufactured and shipped by the supplier, there is a per order cost of $21,000 which will cover all shipping, customs, and transportation costs. Once in the USA you estimate that the annual holding cost per unit per year will be approximately $0.10 per unit held, which will cover all warehousing, insurance and other inventory carrying costs. The past estimated demand for the market you will serve is tabulated here. It is the beginning of 2013, and you will enter the market and place order in anticipation of selling in 2013.

Appendix B: Inventory Pre- and Post-activity Survey for Inventory Exercise

Table B1:   Inventory Management Quickfire Survey Questions.

ID	Pre-Activity Likert-Scale Questions
Q1	I enjoy working with numbers.
Q2	I find the topic of inventory management to be interesting.
Q3	I get anxious when having to learn quantitative material and math concepts such as inventory management.
Q4	I get anxious when I have to work under time pressure.
Q5	I see the usefulness and importance of learning of inventory management.
Q6	Knowledge of inventory management will be useful for my future job or career.
Q7	I understand the basic principles of inventory management.
Q8	I understand the definition of the various inventory management methods – EOQ, ROP, Safety Stock, Single Period Newsvendor Model, etc.
Q9	Inventory management is a complex topic.

ID	Post-Activity Likert-Scale Questions
Q1	The Quickfire exercise was an interesting, hands-on learning experience.
Q2	I enjoyed working with the numbers in the Quickfire exercise.
Q3	I felt anxious during the Quickfire exercise because I was working with quantitative material and numbers.
Q4	The Quickfire exercise reinforced my understanding of inventory management principles.
Q5	The Quickfire exercise helped me to apply specific inventory management frameworks better than a traditional lecture or doing homework problems.
Q6	The Quickfire exercise helped me to see the usefulness and importance of learning of inventory management.
Q7	The time pressure of the competition made the Quickfire exercise more enjoyable.
Q8	The team structure of the Quickfire exercise made it more enjoyable.
Q9	The team structure of the Quickfire exercise made it easier to ask questions about difficult concepts.

Table B2:   Inventory Management Quickfire Pre-Activity Results.

Rating	Q1	Q2	Q3	Q4	Q5	Q6	Q7	Q8	Q9
Strongly Disagree	3%	0%	9%	9%	0%	0%	0%	0%	0%
Disagree	20%	3%	29%	14%	0%	6%	3%	11%	6%
Neutral	26%	20%	37%	23%	0%	17%	14%	34%	43%
Agree	40%	63%	17%	40%	46%	51%	74%	49%	43%
Strongly Agree	11%	14%	9%	14%	54%	26%	9%	6%	9%

Table B3:   Inventory Management Quickfire Post-Activity Results.

Rating	Q1	Q2	Q3	Q4	Q5	Q6	Q7	Q8	Q9
Strongly Disagree	3%	3%	9%	3%	3%	0%	17%	0%	3%
Disagree	6%	11%	26%	6%	9%	6%	23%	6%	6%
Neutral	11%	29%	20%	23%	9%	6%	20%	11%	23%
Agree	37%	37%	31%	54%	51%	63%	23%	34%	31%
Strongly Agree	43%	20%	14%	14%	29%	26%	17%	49%	37%

Appendix C: Sample Documentation for Marketing Quickfire

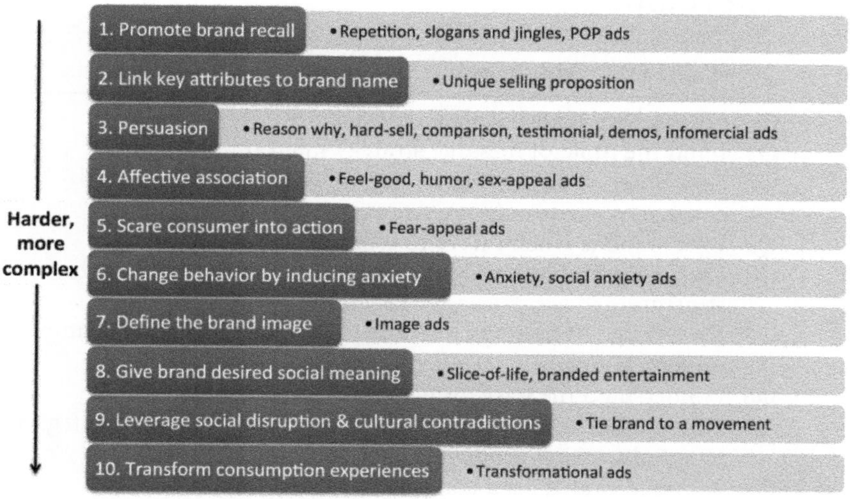

Harder, more complex

1. Promote brand recall • Repetition, slogans and jingles, POP ads

2. Link key attributes to brand name • Unique selling proposition

3. Persuasion • Reason why, hard-sell, comparison, testimonial, demos, infomercial ads

4. Affective association • Feel-good, humor, sex-appeal ads

5. Scare consumer into action • Fear-appeal ads

6. Change behavior by inducing anxiety • Anxiety, social anxiety ads

7. Define the brand image • Image ads

8. Give brand desired social meaning • Slice-of-life, branded entertainment

9. Leverage social disruption & cultural contradictions • Tie brand to a movement

10. Transform consumption experiences • Transformational ads

Figure C1:   Brief Description of Common Message Objectives and Strategies.

Target Market:

Objective:

Message Strategy:

Explanation:

KETCHUP

Figure C2:   Sample Worksheet.

Appendix D: Inventory Pre- and Post-activity Survey for Message Strategy Exercise

Table D1:   Message Strategy Quickfire Survey Questions.

ID   Pre-Activity Likert-Scale Questions

Q1   I find the topic of message strategy interesting.

Q2   I get bored when having to learn qualitative material and concepts such as message strategy.

Q3   I get anxious when I have to work under time pressure.

Q4   I see the usefulness and importance of learning of message strategy.

Q5   Knowledge of messaging strategy will be useful for my future job or career.

Q6   I understand the basic principles of message strategy.

Q7   I am confident that I can properly apply the message strategies in an advertising problem.

Q8   Message strategy is a complex topic.

ID   Post-Activity Likert-Scale Questions

Q1   The Quickfire exercise was an interesting, hands-on learning experience.

Q2   I enjoyed working with different message strategies in the Quickfire exercise.

Q3   I felt anxious during the Quickfire exercise because I was working with so many concepts.

Q4   The Quickfire exercise reinforced my understanding of the different message strategy approaches.

Q5   The Quickfire exercise helped me to apply specific message strategy approaches better than a traditional lecture or doing homework problems.

Q6   The Quickfire exercise helped me to see the usefulness and importance of learning of messaging strategy.

Q7   The time pressure of the competition made the Quickfire exercise more enjoyable.

Q8   The team structure of the Quickfire exercise made it more enjoyable.

Q9   The team structure of the Quickfire exercise made it easier to ask questions about difficult concepts.

Table D2:   Communications Quickfire Pre-Activity Results.

Rating	Q1	Q2	Q3	Q4	Q5	Q6	Q7	Q8
Strongly Disagree	0%	0%	0%	0%	0%	0%	0%	0%
Disagree	0%	47%	7%	0%	0%	0%	7%	7%
Neutral	0%	53%	20%	0%	13%	40%	40%	47%
Agree	20%	0%	53%	67%	67%	47%	40%	40%
Strongly Agree	80%	0%	20%	33%	20%	13%	13%	7%

Table D3:   Communications Quickfire Post-Activity Results.

Rating	Q1	Q2	Q3	Q4	Q5	Q6	Q7	Q8	Q9
Strongly Disagree	0%	0%	0%	0%	0%	0%	0%	0%	0%
Disagree	0%	0%	20%	0%	0%	0%	0%	0%	0%
Neutral	0%	0%	53%	0%	0%	13%	47%	7%	20%
Agree	33%	47%	27%	53%	40%	60%	33%	60%	40%
Strongly Agree	67%	53%	0%	47%	60%	27%	20%	33%	40%

Appendix E: Student Message Strategies

		Strategy		
	First round	Second round	Third round	Fourth round
Product *Lindt Assorted Dark Chocolates*	Link key attributes by using unique selling proposition (USP) of quality (2)	Persuade the customer by comparing to other chocolate brands (3)	Affective Association: Sex appeal-a date with an attractive woman and the product (4)	Promote brand recall with jingle (1)
Harmless Harvest Coconut Water	Social meaning using a slice of life of a workout ending with drinking the product (8)	Persuade the customer with Reasons Why Ads with facts about coconut water (3)	Define Brand Image connecting brand with healthy living (7)	Link brand attributes by using USP of health (2)
Yoplait Greek Yogurt Frozen Bars	Affective Association using sex appeal-attractive woman eating the product (4)	Persuade the customer with comparison ads to regular yogurt brands (3)	Link key attributes by using USP of health (2)	Brand Image-Greek goddess, classy sophistication (7)
Hershey's s'mores	Social meaning Slice of Life Ads-Family cooking together (8)	Promote brand recall with jingle (1)	Affective Association using feel good situation of raising the spirits of a friend (4)	Link key attributes using USP-quality and excellence (2)

Notes: Numbers in parentheses reflect the order of difficulty from Appendix C, Figure C1. Shaded boxes represent the strategies favored by the student vote.

24

A SEERS Approach to Analyzing Impact: Using an Ecology Research Project to Evaluate Product Life Cycle Sustainability

Vikki L. Rodgers

Background

In order to succeed in today's world of rapidly declining natural resources, shifting climate conditions, and deteriorating ecosystem services, students must develop a clear understanding of how their business decisions will impact the environment and future generations. In the past, business students have been disconnected from environmental education (Becker, 1997), until more recently when corporate social responsibility (CSR) policies and sustainability strategies have become widely accepted practices in many major corporations (Hall, Daneke, & Lenox, 2010). In addition, the pursuit of sustainable development is now a primary policy goal of international organizations such as the United Nations, the World Bank, and the World Trade Organization (Elliott, 2012). In fact, sustainability is now considered a primary driver for innovation and business success (Nidumolu, Prahalad, & Rangaswami, 2009).

It is critical for our future business leaders to be aware of the environment and recognize how the choices they make will impact nature and society. As stated originally in the Tbilisi Declaration (1978), the goals of environmental education are to provide knowledge on the functioning of natural environments and skills in recognizing and solving environmental problems. However, environmental education also has a responsibility to raise awareness and create new patterns of behavior to increase concern for the environment and vital economic, social, political, and ecological interdependence (Tbilisi Declaration, 1978). More recently, the United Nations Decade of Education for Sustainable Development (DESD) has stated that its mission "is to integrate the principles, values and practices of sustainable development into all aspects of education and learning …[to] create a more sustainable future in terms of environmental integrity, economic viability and a just society for present and future generations" (UNESCO, 2014). Interestingly, it has been found that simply changing a student's sensitivity to environmental issues can be critical to shaping how individuals consider the environmental implications of their decisions (Cordano, Ellis, & Scherer, 2003).

At Babson, students are challenged to learn and practice Entrepreneurial Thought and Action® (ETA) to create economic and social value. The ETA methodology consists of three components: cognitive ambidexterity; self and contextual awareness, and social, environmental, economic responsibility, and sustainability (SEERS) (Greenberg, McKone-Sweet, & Wilson, 2011). A true SEERS approach investigates both the synergies and the tensions among the social, environmental, and economic perspectives simultaneously (Greenberg et al., 2011), which is often difficult to do in a standard college course. However, our environmental science courses are ideally situated to do just this. Our science courses are designed to emphasize inquiry-based learning and scientific literacy, as the interplay between scientific knowledge and societal concerns (Furtak, Seidel, Iverson, & Briggs, 2012; Hurd, 1958). The project described here has been designed to provide an opportunity for our students to use SEERS to engage in evaluating the impact of economic production.

The Product Impact Project

PROJECT DESCRIPTION AND LOGISTICS

The product impact project simulates the research done in a life cycle assessment (LCA), measuring inputs and outputs of production, use and decomposition of a product (Curran, 1993), and incorporates social impacts and economic considerations. This semester-long project is designed to provide adequate work for groups of 3–5 students within our intermediate level science course, *Case Studies in Ecological Management*. This course is designed as an applied ecology course specifically for business students. It focuses on understanding the ecological principles of natural resource management and the unequal distribution of global supply and demand. There is a strong emphasis on the impact of the human economic production in extracting resources from nature and generating waste and at each step, sustainability-based solutions for product design, supply chain management, and waste generation are discussed.

The goal of this project is for students to examine the overall impact of a simple product they select by researching and estimating impact through the different phases of its life cycle: (1) raw material extraction, (2) manufacturing and packaging, (3) consumer use, and (4) decomposition or end of life. Students are instructed to choose relatively simple products to reduce the number of different raw materials they must research and to allow the time to perform a complete and quantitative analysis. Transportation, distribution, and energy use are intentionally left out of this project to simplify the analyses and because our curriculum has a foundation course, *Sustainable Energy Solutions*, which focuses specifically just on energy issues. Students are made aware that transportation, distribution, and energy use are important parts within a LCA, but that we will not be addressing them.

The project has two deliverables and multiple stages for instructor feedback. It follows closely with course material so students are encouraged to integrate ecological concepts discussed in class into their projects throughout the semester. For the first deliverable, students must perform in-depth research to produce a well-cited, written report, termed a portfolio, detailing the ecological and social impact of their product at each stage (Figure 1). Graphs, figures, flow diagrams, and tables of calculations are embedded within the text. The figures and graphs provide an opportunity for students to practice interpreting graphs and creating graphs from scientific data. In order to encourage focused and quantified research on natural resource implications, ecological impact is broken down into categories of: physical land use, biodiversity and intact ecosystem decline, natural resource consumption, water and air pollution, solid waste generation, and social impacts (human health and labor practices).

For the second deliverable, students propose one change that would best mitigate the negative effects on both the environment and society. This change can be a redesign of the product itself (Figure 1, arrow a), a substitution of raw materials used in production/packaging (Figure 1, arrow b), or utilization of a waste product as raw material or energy (Figure 1, arrow c; i.e., "cradle-to-cradle design;" McDonough & Braungart, 2002). They must justify how the proposed change would specifically decrease each of the negative impacts and perform a cost-benefit analysis to evaluate the economic considerations that would come with such a change. They complete

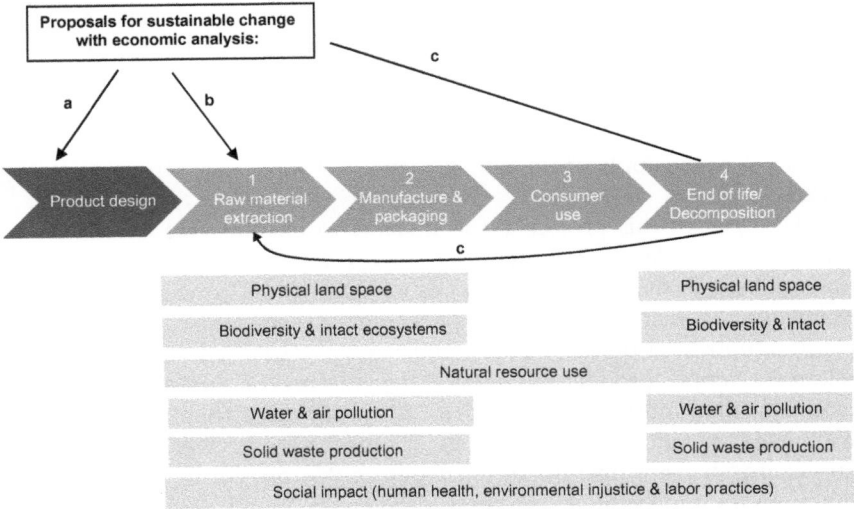

Figure 1: Schematic for How Students Research the Impact of their Everyday Products (Distinct Life Cycle Sections Labeled 1–4) and What Parts of the Environment are Typically Affected by Each of These Stages (Shown in Boxes Below). The Three Possible Areas for Sustainable Change Proposals are Indicated (Shown with Black Arrows and Labeled a–c).

this second part of the project by creating an in-class presentation or video that is designed as a mock-pitch to the company who manufactures the product. Within the presentation or video, students are expected to briefly summarize the ecological and social impacts from their written portfolios in graphical form and then provide in-depth analysis, cited research, and estimated cost-benefit analysis justifying their proposal for change.

At the start of the semester, students sign up for a category of products they are most interested in (e.g., beauty product, food, toy, household item). The group then selects one specific brand of a product within the category and decides what unit they will be investigating. Examples of units are a 5 fl. oz. bottle of Clean and Clear Morning Burst facial scrub, a 2 L bottle of Coca-Cola, a single white 2 × 4 Lego brick, or one Duracell AAA battery.

After this proposal stage, students are given roughly one month to produce individual outlines. The outlines require the students to divide up the group work, demonstrate exactly what material they are covering, and show some initial research with in-text citations and a bibliography. The outlines are grouped together for instructor feedback, but require each student to contribute their own part of the group outline which provides accountability and a chance for the instructor to help manage any problematic group dynamics early in the semester. Although the outlines are not graded, feedback from the instructor is provided to the entire group to signify how the group is progressing as a whole and which sections need to shift direction or include other parts.

GRADING RUBRIC

Roughly one month after the outlines are submitted, the written group portfolio is due. Students are told that the portfolios are graded with 60% for content, broken down into the specific required sections and the remaining 40% of the grade is for research and writing quality (Table 1). One week after the portfolios have been submitted, groups then create a short proposal for one change they would suggest to increase the product's sustainability. They are given feedback from the instructor and approximately three weeks to develop a 10 minute presentation for class. The presentations allow students to share their findings with their peers and to

Table 1:   Grading Rubrics for the Written Portfolio and Oral Presentation Deliverables.

Written Portfolio Grading Rubric		Presentation Grading Rubric	
Content (60%)	Writing quality (40%)	Content (60%)	Presentation (40%)
Raw materials	Writing style	Ecological impact and solution	Overall organization
Manufacturing and packaging	Overall organization and cohesion of document	Social impact	Professionalism and speaker excitement
Consumer use	Use and integration of figures	Economic costs	Quality of visual aids
Decomposition	Research references (number and quality of as well as correctly used internal citations)	Clear and justified recommendation	Timing, pace, and volume
Social impact		Feasibility and creativity of recommendation	
Background (which includes information on the company, product, market share, and target market) and Conclusions (which includes a synthesis of the overall findings)		Adequate research performed	

synthesize the overall environmental and social externalities of their product. They pitch their idea for how to improve sustainability and to detail the economic costs that are associated with this change.

Often students get quite excited, critical, and even defensive of the proposals presented, demonstrating clear engaged and active learning (Auster & Wylie, 2006). The students grade each other's presentations with 50% of their grade from the instructor and the remaining 50% from the average of their peers. The grading rubric for the presentations divides the points into content and presentation ability (Table 1). Finally, students complete the project by filling out a survey that evaluates their own group members for their contributions to the project.

Learning Goals and Outcomes of the Project

A PROJECT-BASED LEARNING STRATEGY

This project allows students to take lessons they learn from class (e.g., habitat degradation, water pollution, or sustainable options for product design) and apply them directly to scenarios of environmental and social externalities in business production. In working together on a project, students are given a certain level of choice and control over their learning and an ability to engage in authentic investigation and problem solving. Previous studies have well-documented the educational benefits of project-based learning strategies, including improvements in critical thinking, self-directed learning, team communication, and retention of knowledge and skills (Dochy, Segers, Van den Bossche, & Gijbels, 2003; Martello, Brabander, & Gambill, 2014). Similar to many project-based learning strategies (Blumenfeld et al., 1991), this project encourages students to gain a deep understanding of the ecological concepts discussed in class by requiring them to acquire, organize, synthesize, and apply knowledge and then create a plan and evaluate solutions. Application of these higher-order thinking skills is essential for students to develop themselves into advanced critical thinkers (Bloom, Engelhart, Furst, Hill, & Krathwohl, 1956; Miri, David, & Uri, 2007).

INCORPORATING SYSTEMS THINKING, CONCEPT MAPS, AND ESTIMATION

Another goal of this project is for students to realize the complex interactions and connections of nature and society. Natural environments are complex systems and therefore identifying ecological impacts through indirect effects and interconnected relationships requires systems-based thinking. This type of thinking guides students through solving difficult problems effectively (Weinberg, 1975) by observing the simultaneously moving parts of a system. Hardin (1985) discusses the importance of "ecolacy" as the ability to take into account the effects of complex interactions of natural systems over time. His idea stresses that due to the interconnectedness of nature and multiple reciprocal cause-effect pathways, changing just one thing in nature is never possible. Therefore, investigating how the environment is impacted by human production challenges students to develop an ecological systems way of thinking and problem solving that is vital for future sustainable development.

Students often get overwhelmed initially when attempting to trace the full impact of a product through the environment and so we spend one class period creating a concept map (Novak, 1990) or flow chart diagraming the effects for their products. Using large tabletop notepads or whiteboards student groups work together to diagram the inputs and outputs of the life cycle of their product with a specific focus on how nature and society is impacted. This visualization often helps to organize and motivate their work.

Another skill that this project builds for students is the ability to address difficult problems, meaning those that are missing some information or do not have one simple solution. Often students cannot find the exact amount of pollution produced by a product or the specific manufacturing process used because their company does not make this information publically available. This is, of course, a part of the project. Because there is often not a simple number to look up or a simple answer to find, students are forced to practice creating well-cited and reasonably justified estimations with whatever information they can obtain. The skill of realistic estimation is one of the most important for developing practical problem solvers and critical thinkers (Sriraman & Knott, 2009). I often find that, initially, students feel uneasy in doing this. But once they realize how to state a reasonable assumption and create calculations, students can be very creative in doing so. A number of groups have utilized our laboratory resources to weigh their products or to run a simple test to add to their calculations. As the future becomes more complex, students will need to feel comfortable making practical assumptions and using cited justification to estimate answers.

OVERALL THEMES IN THE PROJECTS

Student teams have selected a number of everyday products to assess and have developed many creative recommendations for sustainable changes. A sample of different products within different categories is provided in Table 2. This project and the presentations highlight for

Table 2: Sample List of Previous Project Examples, Including their Category, the Product and Brand, the Major Impact Findings by the Students and their Proposed Sustainability Solutions. The Sustainability Solutions Are Indicated as Either a, b, or c as Explained in Figure 1.

Product Category	Product and Brand	Major Impact Findings	Proposed Sustainability Solution
Beauty product	Burt's Bees lip shimmer	Landfill or incineration waste of plastic lipstick tubes	Create cardboard tube for packaging (b)
Beauty product	Clean and Clear Morning Fresh face scrub	Microbeads create nanoplastic waste in oceans when go down drain	Use sand as substitute to plastic microbeads (b)
Food	Chobani Greek yogurt	Large amount of toxic acid whey produced in manufacture process	Use acid whey in agricultural digesters to generate biogas as energy (c)
Toy	Barbie doll	Landfill or incineration waste of doll and petroleum raw material	Switch to corn-based bioplastic for raw material (b)
Household product	Energizer batteries	Release of heavy metals in raw materials extraction and decomposition	Redesign batteries to use less heavy metals (a)
Household product	Bic ballpoint pens	Plastic sleeve is often not recycled, because consumers do not separate from ink part	Design snap apart pen so outside sleeve can be recycled or inside ink refilled (a)
Other	Marlboro cigarette	Pesticides and chemicals sprayed on tobacco crops and also within cigarette	Switch to biocontrol for pests in tobacco production (b)

students some of the main problems with our economic production cycle. Students begin to recognize some similarities among the different projects, which enriches our classroom discussions.

One revealing point often made by students is that even products that are considered to be "environmentally friendly" and "socially responsible" still have substantial negative impacts. One example would be Burt's Bees lipstick. Although the ingredients are 99% natural and responsibly sourced, manufactured at a zero waste plant, and recycled materials are used for packaging (Burt's Bees, 2014), the group that investigated this product performed a detailed analysis of the energy and water used in recycling plastics and the end of life issues of plastic packaging tubes that end up in the garbage. As a solution, this team proposed developing a sturdy cardboard tube to replace the plastic one and eliminating the associated landfill waste.

Reducing or eliminating packaging is another common overall theme for the sustainable change proposals. Students are often quick to realize the excess economic costs associated with overly packaged products. Many groups propose to switch from crude oil derived plastics to bioplastics if these materials are required for the product or the packaging. The environmental benefits that come from changing to corn-based polymers are significant in reducing resource use, decreasing carbon dioxide emissions, and producing zero waste after complete biodegradation at end of life. As we have discussed in class, students must also recognize the social concern of using corn, a potential food product, as a plastic and therefore diverting it from people who use corn for food. Many teams point out that the bioplastic material is typically very expensive and can cause an increase in food prices, so I encourage them to investigate some companies like Stonyfield Farms who have been able to do this successfully and what benefits they have received from doing so.

Lastly, a number of groups get invested in the project when we start discussing ways to redesign products and processes to copy nature, utilizing the principles of biomimicry (Benyus, 2002). Although taking on a full biomimetic design change would be too much within the limited time and scope for this project, we plan to pair this *Case Studies in Ecological Management* course with a *Biomimicry* course and utilize a similar group project across the two courses. In these integrated courses, we will encourage students to redesign their products and reenvision how business can work when ecological systems and societies are used as sources for inspiration, rather than degradation.

Conclusions

At Babson College, science has the unique opportunity to ignore the typical disciplinary boundaries and connect scientific course material to relevant business applications. This allows for the development of projects that can use science to develop critical integrated thinking and problem-solving skills. Projects can also challenge students to consider both their personal and their potential future business role in a larger context by considering large-scale societal and environmental problems. Also projects can be used to interest students by integrating associated business skills, such as LCAs and cradle-to-cradle design. This project promotes problem-solving strategies using scientific inquiry and forces students to unite their perspectives of impact for society, the environment, and economics. It is becoming increasingly imperative for successful business leaders to see themselves and their businesses as connected to the natural world and to understand how healthy ecosystems function in order to be financially sustainable (Willard, 2012).

Acknowledgments

I am grateful to Babson College for actively encouraging innovative teaching and learning strategies. I also thank Jodi Schaefer for her helpful review of a previous version of this manuscript and the students in my courses for their effort and enthusiasm in completing the projects described here.

References

Auster, E. R., & Wylie, K. K. (2006). Creating active learning in the classroom: A systematic approach. *The Journal of Management Education, 30*(2), 333–353.

Becker, T. (1997). The greening of a business school. *Journal of Environmental Education, 28*(3), 5–9.

Benyus, J. M. (2002). *Biomimicry: Innovation inspired by nature.* New York, NY: Harper Perennial.

Bloom, B. S., Engelhart, M. D., Furst, E. J., Hill, W. H., & Krathwohl, D. R. (1956). *Taxonomy of educational objectives book 1: Cognitive domain.* New York, NY: David McKay Company, Inc.

Blumenfeld, P. C., Soloway, E., Marx, R. W., Krajcik, J. S., Guzdial, M., & Palincsar, A. (1991). Motivating project-based learning: Sustaining the doing, supporting the learning. *Educational Psychologist, 26*(3–4), 369–398.

Burt's Bees. (2014). *Sustainability.* Retrieved from http://www.burtsbees.com/Sustainability/sustain-landing,default,pg.html

Cordano, M., Ellis, K. M., & Scherer, R. F. (2003). Natural capitalists: Increasing business students' environmental sensitivity. *Journal of Management Education, 27*(2), 144–157.

Curran, M. A. (1993). Broad-based environmental life cycle assessment. *Environmental Science and Technology, 27*(3), 430–436.

Dochy, F., Segers, M., Van den Bossche, P., & Gijbels, D. (2003). Effects of problem-based learning: A meta-analysis. *Learning and Instruction, 13*, 533–568.

Elliott, J. (2012). *An introduction to sustainable development.* New York, NY: Routledge.

Furtak, E. M., Seidel, T., Iverson, H., & Briggs, D. C. (2012). Experimental and quasi-experimental studies of inquiry-based science teaching: A meta-analysis. *Review of Educational Research, 82*(3), 300–329.

Greenberg, D., McKone-Sweet, K., & Wilson, H. J. (2011). *The new entrepreneurial leader: Developing leaders who shape social and economic opportunity.* San Francisco, CA: Berrett-Koehler Publishers, Inc.

Hall, J. K., Daneke, G. A., & Lenox, M. J. (2010). Sustainable development and entrepreneurship: Past contributions and future direction. *Journal of Business Venturing, 25*(5), 439–448.

Hardin, G. J. (1985). *Filters against folly: How to survive despite economists, ecologists, and the merely eloquent.* New York, NY: Viking.

Hurd, P. D. (1958). Scientific literacy: Its meaning for American schools. *Educational Leadership, 16*, 13–16.

Martello, R., Brabander, D., & Gambill, I. (2014). Paradigms, predictions, and joules: A transdisciplinary, project-based course approach to sustainability. *CUR Quarterly, 35*(1), 20–26.

McDonough, W., & Braungart, M. (2002). *Cradle to cradle: Remaking the way we make things*. New York, NY: North Point Press.

Miri, B., David, B.-C., & Uri, Z. (2007). Purposely teaching for the promotion of higher-order thinking skills: A case of critical thinking. *Research in Science Education, 37*, 353–369.

Nidumolu, R., Prahalad, C. K., & Rangaswami, M. R. (2009). Why sustainability is now the key driver of innovation. *Harvard Business Review, 87*(9), 56–64.

Novak, J. D. (1990). Concept mapping: A useful tool for science education. *Journal of Research in Science Teaching, 10*, 923–949.

Sriraman, B., & Knott, L. (2009). The mathematics of estimation: Possibilities for interdisciplinary pedagogy and social consciousness. *Interchange, 40*(2), 205–223.

Tbilisi Declaration. (1978). *Connect, 3*(1), 1–8.

UNESCO. (2014). *Education for sustainable development*. Retrieved from http://www.unesco.org/new/en/education/themes/leading-the-international-agenda/education-for-sustainable-development/mission/

Weinberg, G. M. (1975). *An introduction to general systems thinking*. New York, NY: Wiley.

Willard, B. (2012). *The new sustainability advantage: Seven business case benefits of a triple bottom line*. British Columbia, Canada: New Society Publishers.

25

Sexism and Gendered Marketing: Exploring Critical Issues in the Marketing Classroom

Victoria L. Crittenden

S exism and gender stereotyping occurs in a wide variety of products and services. One of the most prominent examples to hit the press in the 21st century is that of children's toys, with gender stereotyping expected to have an effect on how a toy is perceived and who is meant to purchase it. The National Association for the Education of Young Children (2014) explored the notion of gender-typed toys, with researchers commenting on what their research found on toys, children, and play. Not surprisingly, one of these researchers concluded that girls' toys associated with physical attractiveness, nurturing, and domestic skills and boys' toys related to violent, aggressive, competitive, exciting, and dangerous. But sexism and gender stereotyping is not limited to the toy aisle. The power of the "gaze" is evidenced throughout marketing approaches to reaching consumers (Streeter, Hintlian, Chipetz, & Callender, 2005). That is, provocative advertising depicts sensuous looking men and women, lounging against beautiful cars, flirting with various scents, or eyeing one another over drinks. Additionally, physical attractiveness ("faux fitness") has resulted in the opening of new markets for long-time products (Spindler, 1996).

Many observations about gender are constructed societally. For example, Lucal (1999, p. 784) notes, "A person uses gender displays to lead others to make attributions about his or her gender." Marketers pick up on this gender attribution and utilize gender displays in the segmentation process to tap into the personal gender demographic of the targeted consumer. This personal gender attribution tends to follow the traditional demographic norm of male and female, the two-sex system in our society (Fausto-Sterling, 2000). Given this two-sex system norm, gender signals sent by marketers are so ubiquitous and routine that they are likely left unheeded unless brought to someone's attention (Lorber, 1994).

Some suggest that sexism and gendering by marketers are driven by consumer capitalism (Bordo, 1999), while others note that the same consumer capitalism has led to a blurring of gender roles since consumers have become more comfortable with gray areas instead of the two-sex stereotype (Sanburn, 2013). Regardless of the intent, marketing is often blamed for the stereotyping of the sexes, particularly since market segmentation is a key component of the marketing concept that is taught very early in the core marketing course. However, some might think that marketers are just really smart and utilize their understanding of human psychology and demographics to sell products.

The intent of this "sexism and gendered marketing" project in the capstone marketing course is not to engage in the debate as to the virtues (or lack thereof) of marketing and its premises. Rather, the project's purpose is to assess marketing's actions in the 21st century as related to its role with regard to gender issues. One of Babson College's core values is that of diversity: *We value our membership in a lifelong community that is broadly diverse. We believe that differences make Babson a richer community and provide the necessary contexts for shared accomplishment. We welcome and value people and their perspectives and respect the interests of all of the members of the community.* In addition to delivering on this core value, the project also enables the exploration of the Global & Multicultural Perspectives and Ethics, Social, Environmental, & Economic Responsibility learning objectives.

The Social Construction of Culture

Before exploring sexism and gendering from a marketing approach, it is important to frame the topic within a broader social context as there are various views on the subject. These views cover a wide range of overlapping explorations. Butler (1988) explores sex and gender from a phenomenology and feminist theoretical perspective. Within this framework, she suggests that "the existence and facticity of the material or natural dimensions of the body are not denied, but reconceived as distinct from the process by which the body comes to bear cultural meaning" (p. 520) and suggests that "the body becomes its gender through a series of acts which are renewed, revised, and consolidated through time" (p. 523). In her work, Davis (2008) explores "intersectionality" within the context of feminist theory and looks at how the concept's vagueness enables researchers to use it in a variety of ways. Regardless of the uncertainty surrounding intersectionality, it provides a context for understanding interactions with regards to gender, race, social practices, institutional arrangements, and cultural ideologies (Davis, 2008). With regards to these interactions, Tyler and Cohen (2008) pursue Butler's (1988) phenomenological understanding culturally using critical insights from Queer theory. Queer theory suggests that gender and sexuality cannot be categorized into two sexes within a single restrictive sexual orientation and takes into account biological, linguistic, and socially given categorizations (Sherry, 2004). With these theoretical/conceptual frameworks as foundations, cultural studies have occurred with regards to the two traditional sexes and the intersections thereof.

With regards to the social context of gender theory (which is where marketers operationalize their actions), Connell (1983) explores the social construction of the body in boys' and men's practices. Later work by Carrigan, Connell, and Lee (1985) further developed and reformulated the notion of hegemonic masculinity in which homosexuality was brought into the discussion of masculinity. Thus, Hearn (2004) emphasizes the need for examination of the gendered processes in marketing, particularly as related to commercial mass media, advertising, and persuasion.

This sexualization of culture, in particular the sexual explicitness of women, has long been a component in the marketer's toolkit in the discourse around consumerism (Evans, Riley, & Shankar, 2010). Historically, women have been the object of "the gaze" rather than the possessor of it (Bordo, 1999). But, shifts in sexual liberalization by the early 21st century enabled women to possess "the gaze" and participate in consumer practices where female sexuality is explicit (Evans et al., 2010). But, even explicit sexuality encounters intersectionality in that age, race, sexual orientation, and appearance interact with different discourses and, as such, intersectionality is exhibited regularly in marketing materials.

According to Bordo (1999), however, marketers also exploit sexual ambiguity. By doing so, marketers can speak to homosexual consumers and straight consumers simultaneously, all while using both male and female bodies as objects of consumption. Thus, the consumer can apply whatever message is fitting for the recipient. This does, however, call into question how marketers utilize the social construction of our culture in practical applications of the profession.

SOCIAL CONSTRUCTION IN MARKETING

> As long as we stick to things and words we can believe that
> we are speaking of what we see, that we see what we are
> speaking of, and that the two are linked.
>
> —Deleuze (2006, p. 55)

Marketers utilize representations where visuals and sounds are tethered to the material world. The representations thus serve to imply meaning to the recipient of the marketer's message about a product or service, and representations are entrenched deeply in our culture (Barad, 2003). Students of marketing are taught that market success is dependent upon the positioning of a product or service so that it can occupy a distinct and valued place in the target customer's mind (Kates, 2002). With this criticality in mind, representations abound in marketing with product positioning taking on nuanced interpretations within contextualized cultural frameworks (Holt, 1997). At the heart of these nuances, however, is consumption which gets at the heart of marketing — that of the target market for products/services.

Consumption — Target Marketing

According to Nava (1991), the consumer culture has had a particular significance for women as it has tended to privilege the "female" consumer over the "masculine" producer. Thus, modern marketing has basically relied on the traditional two-sex gender and has taken for granted that consumers are female (Catterall, Maclaran, & Stevens, 2005). As noted by Sandlin and Maudlin (2012), the feminization of consumption made it possible for women to be targeted as primary consumers, particularly in the domestic sphere. In contrast, Thompson and Holt (2004) found that men's everyday consumption practices were based on the socio-cultural articulation of phallic masculinity. Holt and Thompson (2004) describe consumption and masculinity within three models: the breadwinner model, the rebel model, and the man-of-action hero model. In general, the conclusion is that men and women take different approaches in the buying decision process (Kraft & Weber, 2012).

Bordo (1999, p. 21) says that marketers have long utilized a "middle class, performance-oriented, no-nonsense version of 'masculinity'." But, she also highlights the concept of dual marketing in which marketers creatively appeal to both gay and straight consumers simultaneously. Thus, while a two-sex gendering has occurred in mainstream marketing, the gay and lesbian market has attained recognition as its own market segment (Penaloza, 1996). Branchik (2002) chronicled three phases of gay market segmentation in the United States and suggested that businesses have been marketing to gay consumers, either advertently or inadvertently for over 100 years. These three phases are: the underground phase (pre-1941), the community-building phase (1941–1970), and the mainstream phase (1970–present).

Branding and Advertising

Grier and Brumbaugh (1999) suggest that marketers and potential consumers can construct different meanings based on their own cultural, social, and individual experiences. The two major areas in which the role of gender and sexism are prone to influence consumption via these different meanings are branding and advertising, particularly since interpretations of messages are inferred by a gendered perspective (Brown, Stevens, & Maclaran, 1999). For example, Maynard and Taylor (1999) found that Japanese and American magazines portrayed teenage girls in different ways, with the differences corresponding to the country's central concepts of self and society. Kates (2004) suggests that consumers cocreate brand meanings, and he explores the dynamics of that brand legitimacy within the context of the North American gay community. According to Tuten (2005, p. 442), "the term, gay-friendly, is widely used in discussions of marketing brands to gay and lesbian consumers," and she goes on to suggest that brands utilize "gay vague" (i.e., sexual preference of person in ad is not clear) appeals in advertising so as to simultaneously target the gay/lesbian and heterosexual markets. Borgerson, Isla, Schroeder, and Thorssén (2006) note that it is only in recent years that homosexual consumers have received personal attention from advertisers. Stern (1999) notes that advertising research has begun to adopt pluralistic meanings by integrating race, class, and sexual orientation so as to become more sensitive to a wider meaning of gender.

With this social construction as a background for marketing actions, the sexism and gendered marketing project described here sought to create awareness of issues for which business school students might not otherwise pursue. That is, our marketing courses seek to instill the need for developing marketing content and products that speak specifically to a particular target market. Unfortunately, our marketing courses do not encourage students to pursue alternative interpretations of that same content and product offerings.

Teaching about Sexism and Gendered Marketing

Babson College recognizes the importance of collaborating with and celebrating people across cultures, countries, and capabilities.

According to Bal and Langowitz (2015), Babson College follows a multilayered approach to diversity through programmatic learning goals, curricular, and cocurricular activities, and an increasingly diverse campus community. However, a review of marketing course syllabi at Babson showed that, while diversity is a theme across campus, it was captured largely in our course content as diversity across countries. Interestingly, issues surrounding gender appeared to be left to the Center for Women's Entrepreneurial Leadership (CWEL), with no overlap between CWEL and marketing course content development and delivery. As well, there is a strong Lesbian, Gay, Bisexual, Transgender, Queer/Questioning (LGBTQ) presence on campus; yet, again, no appearance in marketing course content. Seeking to bridge this gap and expand the marketing division's focus on diversity issues, a sexism and gendered marketing project was developed for delivery in the undergraduate capstone marketing course.

SEXISM AND GENDERED MARKETING PROJECT OVERVIEW

This group project, which was 30% of the final course grade, was introduced and described on the course syllabus as shown in Box 1. Each student team was comprised of four to five students. Since group formation is considered an important element of a successful team experience (Crittenden, Crittenden, & Hawes, 1999) and particularly relevant give the nature of this group project, there was no effort to create gender-balance in the teams as that would have corroborated the two-sex conception of gender. Rather, the students self-selected teams (with assistance as needed from the professor). Five teams were comprised only of females and two teams were males-only; the remaining 10 teams were balanced between male and female. Yet, this two-sex conception of gender was not referred to or discussed in class since other gender-related classifications were not readily apparent visually. For example, some members of the class were members of the LGBTQ group on campus, but membership alone does not signal a particular sexual orientation.

The sexism and gendered marketing topic was included on the syllabus and described briefly on the first day of the class. The topic's placement in the course was about mid-point of the semester, and the students were assigned readings by Bordo (1999), Corporate Conspiracies (2013), Sanburn (2013), Spindler (1996), and Trebay (2004). The readings provided the motivation for four class sessions, which began with the definitions of gendered and sexism from www.merriam-webster.com: *Gendered* — reflecting the experience, prejudices, or orientations of one sex more than the other and reflecting or involving gender differences or stereotypical gender roles; *Sexism* — behavior, conditions, or attitudes that foster

Box 1:   Project Description.

Marketing is often blamed for the stereotyping of the sexes. However, some would say that marketers are just really smart and utilize their understanding of human psychology and demographics to sell products. With this project, we will explore how marketers use sexism and gendered marketing in today's marketplace.

1. Each group will identify a product or service ("gendered objects") that at least perceptually stereotypes the sexes.

2. The group will create a visual depiction of the sexism/gendering that occurs with this product or service.

3. The paper to accompany the visual depiction should address the following: (a) the aspects of the product or service that construct sexism or gendering, (b) why we, as marketers, utilize this sexism/gendering, and (c) a discussion as to whether or not marketers are guilty of exacerbating stereotyping of the sexes. Be sure to reference materials from the class (readings, films, etc.) and/or any other outside sources (articles, people, etc.).

The final paper should be around five double-spaced pages, plus the visuals. Be sure to write well and proofread appropriately. Each group will also give a presentation in class. This presentation will be a part of the final project grade. (Individual group evaluation will be completed by all group members to assess the impact each member had on the final project.)

The reading on Blackboard (Gendered Objects) about magazines at Barnes & Noble will give a general idea of what we will be doing in this project. But, keep in mind that this chapter was not written by a marketing or business person, and it was written for a gender studies class. (Since magazines are the object in this chapter, magazines are not a viable subject for this chapter.)

stereotypes of social roles based on sex. The fourth class session was the viewing of a documentary by Liz Canner entitled *Orgasm Inc.* (http://orgasminc.org). Additionally, a paper written by a student at another university for a cultural studies class was posted on Blackboard (with the student's permission). This paper explored magazines as gendered objects and provided the Babson College marketing students with an example of the type of analysis that needed to be done for the class project.

In brief, the "Magazines as Gendered Objects" paper explored the construction of gender as represented by the magazine display at one Barnes & Noble location. This particular student's conclusions were that:

- Mainstream retailers and magazine publishers targeted gender specifically as male or female,
- Magazine retailers and magazine publishers did not adhere to anything other than the two-sex system,
- The magazine covers for men and women portray women in a sexual way but did not portray men sexually in quite the same way,
- Magazine displayed separate women's interest with almost a line of sexual demarcation,
- The traditional roles of male and female were depicted clearly in the display arrangements at Barnes and Noble,
- The traditional role modeling was exemplified in the layout of the displays, and
- The magazine covers themselves were indicative of the issue that gender oppression within society is not an independent concept.

Not only did this sample paper provide an example of the analytic approach that should be pursued in the current marketing project, it also enabled considerable class discussion about viewing magazine displays from the cultural perspective without having the business perspective of why retailers do what they do. Thus, the students were presented with a one-sided, nonmarketing perspective of the issue.

STUDENT PROJECTS

Since the students had read the paper that focused on magazines as gendered objects, magazines were not allowed for the group project. As well, considerable class time had been devoted to the toy product category so that category was banned from further consideration. Aside from those product categories, any product or service was allowed for exploration by the groups.

The breakdown of final product/service categories examined by the students included:

- Food — five groups focused on food items (yogurt, colas, candy, and frozen food) with products such as Powerful Yogurt, Dr. Pepper, Coca-Cola, Yorkie, Hungry Man, and Lean Cuisine.

- Personal Care Products — five groups explored products such as body wash, hygiene items, and razors from Old Spice, Gillette, Dove, and Axe.
- Alcohol — three groups examined the alcohol marketplace, looking at the marketing of wine, beer, and liquor in general as well as including specific brands such as Skinnygirl and Ketel One.
- Children's Movies — one group provided a look at Disney as related to its popular children's movies.
- Halloween Costumes — one group analyzed the Party City, Costume Super Center, and Spirit Halloween websites with regards to the promotion and selling of Halloween costumes.
- Cleaning Products — one group looked at the marketing of Procter and Gamble's Mr. Clean Magic Eraser.
- Fitness Products — one group explored a wide range of protein powders and fitness supplements.

Based on the professor's observations, there might have been an orientation toward a particular product category as related to group composition. Female-only teams explored products such as Dr. Pepper, Coca-Cola, Powerful Yogurt, Skinnygirl, and Halloween costumes. Male-only teams may have been more prone to "masculine" products as these two teams examined Dove's products for men and Old Spice. At the same time, however, mixed teams (as per male-female) also looked at products in the same or similar product categories. Thus, it is impossible to draw any clear conclusions based on team composition with regard to the two-sex system.

A variety of observations were made by the students with regards to their products/services and marketing in general. Excerpts from a sampling of comments from student paper include:

- Marketers play into the two-sex stereotyping, and the taglines and descriptions of products feed into the sexist mantra that all women want to lose weight and all men want to be muscular.
- The company still believes in the stereotype that mothers are the only ones completing the housework.
- Women are expected to be "sexy" or "flirty"; men are expected to be "macho" or "masculine"; society accepts these gender tags.
- The biggest anxiety of almost any man is not being manly enough.
- The company has contributed to the sexist, gendered societal view built upon gender binaries, heterosexuality, and traditional sex roles.
- The company is not shy about its concept of "sex sells" as it has continued to use highly sexualized and gender-biased material in

its advertisements in order to generate an artificial demand for its products and its social media content is no exception.

The overarching goal of the project was to raise awareness of sexism and gendering in marketing efforts, while also understanding why marketers do what we do, and it appears that this was accomplished. Unlike the student paper from the cultural studies course which had taken a one-sided approach and largely condemned business actions, the intent was to combine cultural and business perspectives so as to make marketing leaders of tomorrow more aware of their actions in the pursuit of success. Thus, while enjoyment of the project itself was exhibited by students, the awareness intention was attained as noted by student comments throughout the semester.

FEEDBACK

Professors have a tendency to rely on course evaluations for feedback on student perceptions of the course. Naturally, such feedback was important, with students expressing enjoyment of the sexism and gendered marketing project. However, what might be more important as related to the raising of awareness among students were email comments that came in throughout the semester. These unsolicited comments from students included:

- Following today's class — I thought you might like these videos, in case you haven't already seen them.
- Maybe you've already been familiarized with the article but there was a headline on NYT today on gendering in marketing for girls toys.
- I hope you're having a wonderful break. I was online and found an interesting video about role reversals of gendered marketing and thought it really applied to the class.
- Here is the link to the article I was telling you about in class.
- Went on AdWeek and saw probably the first commercial with a gay couple portrayed and targeted throughout the entire clip. Very wholesome and warm commercial. Thought you'd like it.
- I came across an article that I thought you might like. Enjoy!
- I came across this article and thought you might be interested in it. It's about a company giving a makeover to Barbie to create a doll that has the average measurements of a typical 19 year old. They're also planning on making bendable body parts like the ankles so the doll will be able to move around and "play sports" instead of being ready to put on some high heels. This started a few months ago, so you may have heard about it already, but I thought it was really interesting after learning about sexism and

gendered marketing in class. They're focused on capitalizing on the trend of parents wanting to empower their daughters and spread the message that girls can be athletic and powerful.

- I had to run to the CVS in Wellesley and look what I found!
- I am excited for this course and the topics that are on the syllabus, especially the sexism and gendered marketing project. I became interested in the topic after seeing the film Misrepresentation and am looking forward to exploring it in greater detail. On that note I thought I would share the clip below.

Based on these types of comments, it would seem that awareness about the issue of sexism and gendered marketing was increased via including the topic on the syllabus, the class discussions, and the group projects/presentations. The comments began filtering in even prior to the actual focus on the topic/project.

The group projects were presented in class over two class sessions. With two sections of the course, this resulted in four sets of presentations all of which were attended by various faculty and administrators from across campus. These attendees included an associate dean of the graduate school, the director of CWEL, the director of the Center for Engaged Learning and Teaching (CELT), and faculty members from the History and Society Division and the Marketing Division. Sample feedback from the faculty and administrators included:

- Your class was the best part of my day yesterday! Should have taken a picture so I could tweet it out. The students did a great job. I was very impressed with their work.
- I had the privilege of attending presentations yesterday and the students did an amazing job. The project on sexism and gendered marketing gave students the opportunity to pick any category of product they were interested in and consider the gender issues that might underlie the brand positioning. The students did an amazing job of analysis based on all the appropriate marketing details and clearly presented the issues in the brand campaigns in connection with prevailing stereotypes. The most surprising product category? Frozen food! I think this was an eye opener for many in the room — even something seemingly innocuous as frozen food or shampoo can be highly gendered in its brand positioning. Comments and questions from the students were insightful.
- This was a great Babson learning experience. You are doing the kind of work in the classroom that is so important to developing entrepreneurial leaders and also to education. As a former sociology major (undergrad), it was quite fun to see your students connecting marketing lessons with sociological issues.

Conclusion

As noted by Tanner and Whalen (2013), top teachers search for ways to innovate in their courses. At Babson College, innovation is key to delivering value to our students, and faculty members are constantly seeking innovative projects and processes. The sexism and gendered marketing project described here is an innovative project that attempts to bring together cross-disciplinary issues as related to how we, as marketers, conduct business. Repeated exposure to concepts is expected to be critical to learning retention (Raska, Keller, & Shaw, 2014), and this marketing class project actually re-exposed students to diversity issues for which other parts of campus (e.g., CWEL, LGBTQ, and arts and humanities courses) highlight specifically.

Babson College professors engage in a process of continual innovation, which is not necessarily conducive to capturing longitudinal data on a particular project's repeated use since course content is changing constantly. However, the immediate response to this project was positive from both students and classroom observers. In addition to the direct feedback about the project, professors across campus were also hearing about the project as students shared course content information with other professors. For example, a student in the marketing course was sharing course content with her "gender in history" professor and vice-versa.

From an implementation perspective, the difficult part of the project was identifying appropriate readings for the course. Once these readings were selected, the project was relatively easy to bring to fruition since the students were excited to embark on the cross-disciplinary, yet marketing-centric, project. The value programming and socialization process of our business students are shaped by classroom topics, and this particular project touched upon so many areas for which Babson College students have been acclimatized over the course of their undergraduate education.

References

Bal, A., & Langowitz, N. (2015). A multi-layered approach to diversity in management education. In V. Crittenden, K. Esper, N. Karst, & R. Slegers (Eds.), *Evolving entrepreneurial education: Innovation in the Babson classroom*. Cambridge, MA: Emerald Group Publishing Limited.

Barad, K. (2003). Posthumanist performativity: Toward an understanding of how matter comes to matter. *Signs: Journal of Women in Culture and Society, 28*(3), 801−831.

Bordo, S. (1999). Gay men's revenge. *The Journal of Aesthetics and Art Criticism, 57*(1), 21−25.

Borgerson, J. L., Isla, B., Schroeder, J. E., & Thorssén, E. (2006). Representation of gay families in advertising: Consumer responses to an emergent target group. *European Advances in Consumer Research, 7*, 143–152.

Branchik, B. (2002). Out in the market: A history of the gay market segment in the united states. *Journal of Macromarketing, 22*(1), 86–97.

Brown, S., Stevens, L., & Maclaran, P. (1999). I can't believe it's not Bakhtin!: Literary theory, postmodern advertising, and the gender agenda. *Journal of Advertising, 28*(1), 11–24.

Butler, J. (1988). Performative acts and gender constitution: An essay in phenomenology and feminist theory. *Theatre Journal, 40*(4), 519–531.

Carrigan, T., Connell, R. W., & Lee, J. (1985). Towards a new sociology of masculinity. *Theory and Society, 14*(5), 551–604.

Catterall, M., Maclaran, P., & Stevens, L. (2005). Postmodern paralysis: The critical impasse in feminist perspectives on consumers. *Journal of Marketing Management, 21*(5–6), 489–504.

Connell, R. W. (1983). *Which way is up?* London: Allen & Unwin.

Corporate Conspiracies. (2013). *Gender stereotyping.* Retrieved from http://corpora teconspiracies.wordpress.com/2013/04/19/gender-stereotyping/

Crittenden, V. L., Crittenden, W. F., & Hawes, J. (1999). The facilitation and use of student teams in the case analysis process. *Marketing Education Review, 9*(3), 15–23.

Davis, K. (2008). Intersectionality as buzzword: A sociology of science perspective on what makes a feminist theory successful. *Feminist Theory, 9*(1), 67–85.

Deleuze, G. (2006). *Foucault.* London: Continuum.

Evans, A., Riley, S., & Shankar, A. (2010). Technologies of sexiness: Theorizing women's engagement in the sexualization of culture. *Feminism & Psychology, 20*(1), 114–131.

Fausto-Sterling, A. (2000). The five sexes, revisited. *The Sciences*, (July–August), *40*(4), 18–23.

Grier, S. A., & Brumbaugh, A. M. (1999). Noticing cultural differences: Ad meanings created by target and non-target markets. *Journal of Advertising, 28*(1), 79–93.

Hearn, J. (2004). From hegemonic masculinity to the hegemony of man. *Feminist Theory, 5*(1), 49–72.

Holt, D. B. (1997). Poststructuralist lifestyle analysis: Conceptualizing the social patterning of consumption in postmodernity. *Journal of Consumer Research, 23*(4), 326–350.

Holt, D. B., & Thompson, C. J. (2004). Man-of-Action heroes: The pursuit of heroic masculinity in everyday consumption. *Journal of Consumer Research, 31*(2), 425–440.

Kates, S. M. (2002). Barriers to deep learning in student marketing teams. *Australasian Marketing Journal, 10*(2), 14–25.

Kates, S. M. (2004). The dynamics of brand legitimacy: An interpretive study in the gay men's community. *Journal of Consumer Research, 31*(2), 455–464.

Kraft, H., & Weber, J. M. (2012). A look at gender differences and marketing implications. *International Journal of Business and Social Science, 3*(21), 247–253.

Lorber, J. (1994). "Night to his Day": The social construction of gender. In J. Lorber (Ed.), *Paradoxes of gender.* New Haven, CT: Yale University Press.

Lucal, B. (1999). What it means to be gendered me: Life on the boundaries of a dichotomous gender system. *Gender and Society, 13*(6), 781–797.

Maynard, M. L., & Taylor, C. R. (1999). Girlish images across cultures: Analyzing Japanese versus U.S. seventeen magazine ads. *Journal of Advertising*, *28*(1), 39–48.

National Association for the Education of Young Children. (2014). *What the research says: Gender-typed toys.* Retrieved from http://www.naeyc.org/content/what-research-says-gender-typed-toys

Nava, M. (1991). Consumerism reconsidered: Buying and power. *Cultural Studies*, *5*(2), 157–173.

Penaloza, L. (1996). We're here, we're Queer, and We're going shopping! A critical perspective on the accommodation of gays and lesbians in the U.S. marketplace. *Journal of Homosexuality*, *31*(1–2), 9–41.

Raska, D., Keller, E. W., & Shaw, D. (2014). The curriculum-faculty-reinforcement alignment and its effect on learning retention of core marketing concepts of marketing capstone students. *Marketing Education Review*, *24*(2), 145–158.

Sanburn, J. (2013). *Selling to the other sex.* Retrieved from http://business.time.com/2013/06/19/transgender-marketing-12-campaigns-that-defy-sexual-stereotyping/

Sandlin, J. A., & Maudlin, J. G. (2012). Consuming pedagogies: Controlling images of women as consumers in popular culture. *Journal of Consumer Culture*, *12*(2), 175–194.

Sherry, M. (2004). Overlaps and contradictions between Queer theory and disability studies. *Disability and Society*, *19*(7), 769–783.

Spindler, A. M. (1996). It's a face-lifted, tummy-tucked jungle out there. *The New York Times.* Retrieved from http://www.nytimes.com/1996/06/09/business/it-s-a-face-lifted-tummy-tucked-jungle-out-there.html

Stern, B. B. (1999). Gender and multicultural issues in advertising: Stages on the research highway. *Journal of Advertising*, *28*(1), 1–9.

Streeter, T., Hintlian, N., Chipetz, S., & Callender, S. (2005). *This is not sex: A web essay on the male gaze, fashion advertising, and the pose.* Retrieved from http://www.uvm.edu/~tstreete/powerpose/index.html

Tanner, J., & Whalen, D. J. (2013). Teaching moments: Opening the pipeline to teaching innovations. *Marketing Education Review*, *23*(3), 265–274.

Thompson, C. J., & Holt, D. B. (2004). How do men grab the phallus? Gender tourism in everyday consumption. *Journal of Consumer Culture*, *4*(3), 313–338.

Trebay, G. (2004). Cultural studies: When did skivvies get rated NC-17? *The New York Times.* Retrieved from http://www.nytimes.com/2004/08/01/style/cultural-studies-when-did-skivvies-get-rated-nc-17.html

Tuten, T. L. (2005). The effect of gay-friendly and non-gay-friendly cues on brand attitudes: A comparison of heterosexual and gay/lesbian reactions. *Journal of Marketing Management*, *21*(3), 441–461.

Tyler, M., & Cohen, L. (2008). Management in/as comic relief: Queer theory and gender performativity. The Office. *Gender, Work & Organization*, *15*(2), 113–132.

PART 4
The Role of Centers in Enhancing the Educational Environment

26

The Heart of Entrepreneurship Practice at Babson College: The Arthur M. Blank Center for Entrepreneurship

Candida Brush, Andrew Corbett and
Janet Strimaitis

Introduction

In many ways, this entire volume can be viewed as an inside look at
some of the core parts of the entrepreneurship education ecosystem
of Babson College. So far you have seen chapters that examine the
creative process of educational scholarship, cross-disciplinary teaching and learning, and innovative pedagogical techniques that gird
our foundational paradigm of Entrepreneurial Thought & Action®.
Here, we shift the discussion from a focus on curriculum to practice
by exploring the Arthur M. Blank Center for Entrepreneurship
(AMBCE) and its constituent programs. In doing so, we examine the
two other elemental parts of the entrepreneurial education ecosystem: cocurricular programs and applied research.

Babson College has a history of teaching entrepreneurship
and running programs and cocurricular activities since 1978.
Entrepreneurship is a learning objective for all students, meaning
100% of our students are required to take entrepreneurship

courses.[1,2,3] First-year students take a two semester integrated course Babson's **Foundations of Management and Entrepreneurship (FME)** which is year-long immersion into business, giving students a strong entrepreneurial foundation from the start. Throughout the year, two dedicated faculty members – industry professionals – teach students the ins and outs of entrepreneurship, marketing, accounting, organizational behavior, information systems, and operations, while emphasizing the integrated role these functions have in a business. Classes of up to 40 students form teams of 10 students, and the College loans up to $3000 as start-up money for each business. The ideas for the businesses come from the students, and whether they are selling a tangible product or providing a service, they are encouraged to think about how their business meets a human need. Teams also establish a partnership with a local social services agency, emphasizing the importance of corporate social responsibility. Collectively, each team donates 80 hours of community service, plus all profits from their business, to that organization. Since 1999, these undergraduate FME businesses have donated nearly a half million dollars to local charities. At the graduate level, students in all four MBA programs also take a required entrepreneurship course that covers the basic elements of Entrepreneurial Thought and Action®, and a practice-based approach to entrepreneurial activity. Students in the Master of Science in Management program take a two semester team taught course where students working as part of a team, define, design, and develop a business or initiative that solves a problem.

While entrepreneurship is required of all students, only part of the answer to our uniqueness lies in the required courses and curriculum. At the AMBCE we are also guided by the following important question: *What percentage of a university student's "entrepreneurial education" happens in the classroom?* To our knowledge no one has ever formally studied this question, but preliminary research suggests that the percentage is low (Newman, 2013). The important outcome of asking such a question, however, is that it spurs scholars to think more deeply about how and where our students both learn about entrepreneurship and practice it.

---

[1] Babson's MBA program has been ranked #1 in entrepreneurship by U.S. News and World Report for 21 consecutive years and its undergraduate program has been similarly ranked for the past 18 consecutive times.
[2] In 2014, Babson was recognized for Outstanding Venture Acceleration by the Global Consortium of Entrepreneurship Centers and was rated #1 among all colleges and universities in the U.S. in Money Magazine's first ever college ranking (2014).
[3] http://www.babson.edu/about-babson/at-a-glance/babsons-history/timeline/Pages/default.aspx

Most full time undergraduate students spend about 15−17 hours in the classroom per week and an additional 30 hours studying and doing homework. After subtracting time for sleeping, eating, and recreational activities − students have roughly 50−60 hours of time for cocurricular activities.

Taking all of this into account, the leadership at Babson College has always thought deeply about entrepreneurship focused cocurricular programs and their alignment with the curriculum. Centers and Institutes at Babson College are places where our students both learn about and practice entrepreneurship and the AMBCE is the most recognized of these institutions on campus. We see it as the "heart" of entrepreneurship practice for the campus because it not only delivers such a wide array of activities[4] and events but because it represents a place where students can immerse themselves in entrepreneurial activity and practice entrepreneurship by interacting with other students and alumni entrepreneurs.

We continue this chapter by first briefly describing an entrepreneurship education ecosystem and articulating what is unique about Babson's ecosystem. Using this framework as our guiding principle, we then outline the cocurricular curricular programs of the AMBCE highlighting one (the John E and Alice L. Butler Venture Accelerator) as an example. We then turn our attention to the applied research programs of the center and similarly highlight one of these scholarly endeavors (the Successful Transgenerational Entrepreneurship Practices (STEP) project) before describing the other research programs in the center's portfolio. In both cases we explore how these programs are aligned with the broader institutional objectives of Babson by underscoring their symbiotic relationship with other parts of the ecosystem both on and off campus.

An Entrepreneurship Education Ecosystem View

Developed from physical and environmental science literatures, an ecosystem encompasses all of the physical and biological factors within a defined environment; their relationship to each other, and mutual dependence (Tansley, 1935). Christopherson (1997) defines an ecosystem as "a natural system consisting of all plants, animals, and microorganism (biotic factors) in an area functioning together with all of the non-living physical (abiotic) factors of the

---

[4]The monthly calendar of activities offered through the AMBCE averages about two dozen events.

environment." Ecosystems include living and nonliving organisms; they can be large or small, natural or manmade, or bounded in scope. There are significant interdependencies, and they are always dynamic and changing.

Entrepreneurship ecosystems are defined as areas where a conducive culture, enabling policies and leadership, availability of finance, quality human capital, venture-friendly markets for products, and a range of institutional and infrastructural supports entrepreneurial development (Isenberg, 2010). The World Economic Forum (2013) identifies seven similar components: markets, culture, education and training, regulatory framework and infrastructure, funding and finance, and human capital. In these cases, regional or community efforts are involved to develop a vibrant ecosystem. Generally, the idea of entrepreneurship ecosystems is perceived as a solution to both social and economic problems (Xavier, Kelley, Kew, Herrington, & Vorderwulbecke, 2013). Online conversations and articles in the popular press describe the interactions among universities, the finance community, service providers, faculty, and entrepreneurs that help to support economic development and innovation.[5]

Fetters, Greene, Rice, and Butler (2010) present the concept of university-based entrepreneurship ecosystems (U-BEE's). As Fetters et al. (2010) note, universities are central to economic development around the world, providing infrastructure, resources, and means to develop entrepreneurial communities. They argue that entrepreneurial ecosystems evolve and expand through specialization of knowledge and innovation. Following Aulet (2008), they argue that the relevant aspects of entrepreneurship ecosystems are alignment of institutional objectives, access to the university and other regional resources, coordination of research initiatives, and the participation of the business community and local government. They suggest that the necessary dimensions of an entrepreneurship ecosystem are governance, innovation, infrastructure, and culture. Their book analyzes three universities focused on the new venture creation aspects of an entrepreneurship ecosystem. The case studies include details of internal university activities as well as external interactions within the community and provide recommendations appropriate to policy-makers, administrators, educators, and practitioners interested in creating or expanding a U-BEE. The U-BEE includes multiple levels — the individuals (student, faculty, staff, practitioner, and administration), groups (faculty, students), organizations

---

[5]http://www.technologyreview.com/article/14761/
http://www.xconomy.com/boston/2008/02/25/universities-an-entrepreneurs-ecosystem/

(incubators, centers), events, and community stakeholders (government, policy-makers, industry, funders). Central to the U-BEE are internal entrepreneurship activities, revolving around curricular, cocurricular, and research activities.

BABSON'S ENTREPRENEURSHIP EDUCATION ECOSYSTEM

The entrepreneurship education ecosystem is a central component of the U-BEE, but focused primarily on the entrepreneurship activities across a campus or school and within the departments directly connected to entrepreneurial activity. Internal entrepreneurship activities are nested within the community and school, and comprised a "domain" which includes curriculum, cocurricular activities, and research — as the primary activities universities and colleges engage in with regard to entrepreneurship (Alberti, Sciascia, & Poli, 2004; Brush, 2014; Kuratko, 2005) (see Figure 1). Below we describe the three dimensions of the entrepreneurship education ecosystem, the curriculum, the cocurricular, and the research and consider how these are interrelated at Babson College.

Entrepreneurship Curriculum

A curriculum is organized by discipline, program, or concentration for a degree. It is a set of courses and their content, and the courses are based on a syllabus which specifies learning objectives, topics, and grading criteria. This involves decisions about which materials are used in courses, which cases, choices of exercises, pedagogies, concepts, and delivery mechanisms. The courses are linked to the school's definition of entrepreneurship in a curriculum. The role of

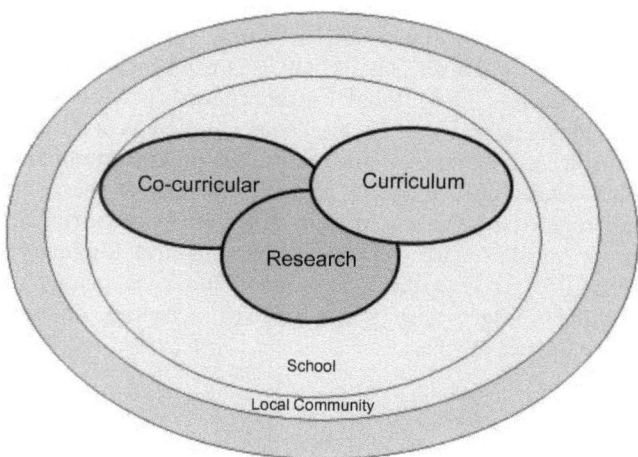

Figure 1:   Internal Entrepreneurship Education Ecosystem.

theory and integration across classes and disciplines are all decision points for entrepreneurship curriculum. At Babson College, all students take entrepreneurship; entrepreneurial thinking is a measurable learning outcome assessed for students in many core classes. The College has a stand-alone Division of Entrepreneurship with more than 50 faculty members all of whom have entrepreneurial experience of some kind.

Entrepreneurship Cocurricular Activities

These activities are all nondegree bearing activities that enrich the student learning experience. These include, but are not limited to programs, clubs, living experiences, workshops, guest speakers, forums, business competitions, networking, and other programs. Decisions about cocurricular activities focus on the choice of leadership (faculty and staff), resources, audience served, faculty incentives, and resource allocation. At Babson College, significant resources (space, funding) are committed to student participation in entrepreneurial activities. Faculty advisors in the venture accelerator are also teaching in the classroom, insuring alignment of concepts and learnings across curricular and cocurricular activities.

Entrepreneurship Research

Research at Babson covers both theoretical and applied issues across a broad domain, but primarily focuses on *"the actors, actions, resources, environmental influences and outcomes associated with the emergence of entrepreneurial opportunities and/or new economic activities in multiple organizational contexts, and (b) the characteristics, actions, and challenges of owner-managers and their businesses."*[6] At Babson College, there is an institutional commitment to applied entrepreneurship research supported in terms of faculty, funding, and staff. The AMBCE is the home to three global research projects — The Global Entrepreneurship Monitor (GEM), the STEP Project, and the Diana Project. GEM is a multicountry study of start-up behaviors and attitudes of entrepreneurs in 70 economies. The STEP program is a consortium of 42 institutions across all regions of the world that study entrepreneurial activities of business families with a focus succession and longevity issues. The Diana Project is a research consortium that brings together hundreds of scholars who study growth activities of businesses owned by women.

---

[6]Academy of Management Entrepreneurship Division Mission Statement; http://division.aomonline.org/ent/index.php?option=com_content&view=article&id=46&Itemid=34

Going forward, we now draw out the relationships of two distinct parts of the AMBCE and show how they enhance the student experience and foster entrepreneurship education at Babson College. We first examine cocurricular programs before we transition to applied research.

Cocurricular Programs at Arthur M. Blank Center for Entrepreneurship (AMBCE)

The AMBCE at Babson College focuses on expanding the practice of Entrepreneurship of All Kinds™ through innovative cocurricular programs and global collaborative research initiatives that inspire and inform Entrepreneurial Thought and Action®. The center provides a base for the cocurricular portion of Babson's entrepreneurial ecosystem and is also the home for the Entrepreneurship Division faculty. Working in close proximity with each other provides substantive opportunities for both formal and informal collaboration among faculty and staff. Each of the programs in the AMBCE is aligned with the broader goals of the curriculum of the Entrepreneurship Division (Department) of the College and of the College itself. The cocurricular programs provide students an outlet to put into practice their nascent venture ideas in a nurturing supportive environment. The hands-on experiential environment provides them with tangible learning experiences not generally found in the classroom. They gain self-awareness and have the opportunity not only to develop their venture ideas but to develop themselves as entrepreneurial actors. The effectiveness of cocurricular programming at AMBCE is perhaps best seen through two events: the Rocket Pitch and the B.E.T.A Challenge.

The Rocket Pitch is an annual event that happens late fall where student entrepreneurs from Babson College (and our affiliated, local partner schools – the Franklin W. Olin College of Engineering, and Wellesley College) pitch their business ideas to their fellow students, faculty, and to entrepreneurs, investors, and other stakeholders from the Boston entrepreneurship ecosystem. The Rocket Pitch is Babson's take on how to efficiently present one's venture concept: three slides in three minutes with a call for action. Pitches happen in rapid succession in multiple rooms on campus with no questions from the audience. An open networking reception follows the event and allows for audience members to connect directly with entrepreneurs.

The AMBCE's B.E.T.A. Challenge (Babson Entrepreneurial Thought and Action® Challenge) is the modern version of traditional business plan competitions. Recognizing that a formal business plan is not the most appropriate vehicle for student and early-stage entrepreneurs to use to communicate and connect to stakeholders, the Blank Center created the B.E.T.A. Challenge format in 2012. Applications and presentations do not focus on what the entrepreneur plans to do, but rather on the actions and concrete milestones achieved to date and their plans for future action based upon these achievements. Winners in the undergraduate, graduate, and alumni tracks each receive a $20,000 cash prize plus additional "in kind services" from corporate sponsors.

While the annual Rocket Pitch and B.E.T.A. Challenge events are substantive examples of cocurricular programming at AMBCE, the John E. and Alice L. Butler Venture Accelerator illustrates what happens to animate our students and their entrepreneurial ventures every day. Thus, the accelerator is a demonstrable exemplar of the on-going, daily relationship between the curriculum and cocurricular activities.

JOHN E. AND ALICE L. BUTLER VENTURE ACCELERATOR

The Butler Venture Accelerator, through its staff of directors, advisors, faculty, and associated partners (lawyers, accountants, and other local service providers), helps undergraduates, graduate students, and alumni move their ideas forward from initial concepts to flourishing businesses. Each year the accelerator is the home to nearly 400 participants and over 300 nascent business concepts. Through its programming and events the accelerator aligns its content to support and integrate with the formal in class curriculum. It is also a conduit to allow students to more easily reach out into the other parts of the Babson entrepreneurship ecosystem and to the Boston-area entrepreneurship ecosystem. Students are able to put into practice what they learn in the classroom and test it in the real world. All the while. they receive guidance from faculty advisors, experienced entrepreneurs, and other business partners.

The Butler Venture Accelerator is an important part of the ecosystem as it provides a safe, nurturing support system that allows students to take action and move their ideas forward with minimal costs (financial, reputational, and other) and maximum learning. The product and service ideas, concepts, new business models, and nascent ventures that most of the students bring to the accelerator on day one do not endure, but instead are reimagined over time. Through their own actions and experience we are teaching students a method for entrepreneurship (Entrepreneurial Thought & Action®) while they explore and develop their ideas. While the accelerator does generate a number of new start-up companies each year, our primary goal is to develop individuals who think and act

Figure 2: Framework of the John E. and Alice L. Butler Venture Accelerator at Babson College.

entrepreneurially. Through the practical application of exploring and pursuing their venture ideas, students grow as entrepreneurs regardless of whether their current idea is ready to take off, or whether they need to begin exploring a new concept. Given this, the accelerator is structured in three distinct phases: explore, pursue, and launch and grow (see Figure 2).

Explore

The explore phase is where the majority of accelerator participants begin their experience within the program. This initial phase is for students who have a concept that they are just beginning to consider. Some students come to the accelerator just with the thought and desire to be an entrepreneur; but they have no idea for venture. These students begin here as well. Given this, all participants are required to do some self-assessment of their capabilities. We also reacquaint them with the foundation of Entrepreneurial Thought & Action® that they have experienced in their classwork and elsewhere on campus. The initial activities in the explore phase direct students to gain a better understanding of "who they are," "what they know," and "whom they know" in order to build a foundation for developing and screening their initial ideas.

The explore stage helps students explore both themselves and their fledgling ideas. The goal of this stage is to discover whether the student's concept is a true opportunity – whether it is feasible. Participants have peer-to-peer mentoring sessions guided by an accelerator mentor or advisor. They have access to free coworking space, informal gatherings, and workshops. Once a student demonstrates that their concept is viable and feasible for them, they move on to the pursue stage.

Pursue

Participants in the pursue stage have access to the same resources as those in the explore phase and more. The accelerator parses its resources via a staged model so that as the students move their concepts forward they are provided access to more specific and focused resources. In the explore stage, many of the mentoring sessions are group sessions; in the pursue stage mentoring is provided in smaller groups and often in one-on-one session. In pursue the goal is for students to establish the real business case through building a business model and developing a team. Students focus on things such as prototype development, in-depth customer interviews, and creating plans for implementation. They may also apply for seed funding and hatchery office space.

Launch and Grow

The launch and grow phase is the most advanced level of the accelerator program, but it is just the beginning for Babson entrepreneurs. Here, participants focus on creating their recurring revenue stream and developing their venture as a self-sustaining business. Individuals refine their team, lock in suppliers and customers, and perhaps secure investors. There is also a focus on pitching, business planning, and bootstrapping. Participants receive one-on-one advising and may also apply for hatchery workspace and seed funding. They are also expected to give back by mentoring those in the earlier stages.

Summer Venture Program

The accelerator program runs throughout the academic year (September–April) and also provides an on-ramp to a full immersion initiative during the summer. The Summer Venture Program (SVP) supports some of the most promising students from Babson as well as from Olin College of Engineering, and Wellesley College. Each year up to 15 student teams participate in this 10-week intensive experience designed to fast-track the development of their entrepreneurial ventures. Teams receive housing, workspace, advising, and other resources to help their businesses develop throughout the 10 weeks.

Although SVP participants forgo internship and job opportunities by choosing to work on their businesses full time from mid-May through July, this commitment pays off by speeding up their time to market or by helping them decide that the venture as currently defined needs to be modified or abandoned. The program concludes with the Summer Venture Showcase, a culmination of the students' hard work where they present their accomplishments and learnings to professional investors and the local community.

There are two very important features of the Butler Venture Accelerator not normally found in most university and college cocurricular support for entrepreneurship, accelerators, incubators, or student activities. First, all the advisors to the accelerator are also faculty members that teach in the classroom and have real world entrepreneurial experience. This means the knowledge transfer for curricular to cocurricular practice is very tightly aligned. Second, the Venture Accelerator is completely aligned with the curriculum. Both the undergraduate and graduate curriculum are organized in the same fashion as the accelerator – explore, pursue, and launch and grow. Courses are taught that help students explore ideas through design thinking, ideation, and all aspects of exploring opportunities. These are followed by courses that teach feasibility analysis, proto-typing, and building a team. And finally, courses that have students practice taking entrepreneurial action – launching and growing, complete the series. In other words, the concepts, handouts, and materials taught in the curriculum are completely aligned with the cocurricular support. Importantly, there is no single form or path-way that is emphasized – students can approach their venture initia-tive in any context (family, corporate, small, new, large, social venture) and through any means of entry (bootstrapping, buying the business, transferring technology, franchising, licensing, etc.). In other words, the curricular and cocurricular are tightly aligned to reinforce students practicing entrepreneurship both in and outside of the classroom with a focus on taking action, learning from the results, and building the concept/venture from these tests. We call this methodology "Act – Learn – Build."

Applied Research at AMBCE

Research plays an important role integrating curricular and cocurri-cular activities at Babson College. As the founder of the premier research conference for entrepreneurship in the world in 1981, the Babson College Entrepreneurship Research Conference (BCERC), the College has provided a forum linking researchers around the world through spirited dialogue and presentations. Each year the conference attracts more than 350 scholars who come to hear pre-sentations of more than 200 papers. In addition, for the past 15 years, Babson has led the three globally collaborative (multiyear, multicountry, multi-university) research projects dedicated to differ-ent aspects of entrepreneurship noted above: the Diana Project, the GEM Project, and the STEP Project.

The *DIANA Project* was launched in 1998 to investigate factors leading to growth for women entrepreneurs and their businesses worldwide, and in particular factors that enable or constrain women entrepreneurs to contribute fully to economies around the world.[7] The Diana International Forum held every other year, attracts more than 100 top researchers from around the world to share research findings and methodologies. Most importantly, The Diana Project communicates this work to a variety of research, educational, and policy audiences.

The GEM was initiated in 1999 as a joint venture of Babson College and the London Business School. Starting with 10 participating countries, the project, now in its 15th year of operations, has expanded to include 70 economies.[8] GEM is the largest and most developed research program on entrepreneurship in the world. GEM is unique because, unlike most entrepreneurship data sets that measure newer and smaller firms, *GEM studies the behavior of individuals with respect to starting and managing a business.* GEM teams are members of an exclusive research project which provides access to the collective knowledge of some of the world's most renowned researchers and institutions involved in entrepreneurship research. Over the years GEM data has influenced numerous national economic policies around the world.

Unique to Babson's entrepreneurship education ecosystem, is the STEP research project. Just as the accelerator exemplifies the curricular/cocurricular nexus, this project highlights the commitment and alignment of research activities with the curriculum and cocurricular programs in the Babson Entrepreneurship Ecosystem. Here we explore STEP in depth.

SUCCESSFUL TRANSGENERATIONAL ENTREPRENEURSHIP PRACTICES (STEP)

Families are the dominant form of business organization worldwide — they play a leading role in the social and economic wealth creation of communities and countries. Founded in 2005 by Babson College in collaboration with six academic affiliates in Europe, the STEP Project is a global applied research initiative that explores the entrepreneurial process within business families and generates solutions that have immediate application for family leaders.[9] To achieve continued growth and continuity, they must pass on the entrepreneurial mindsets and capabilities that enable them to create

---

[7]http://www.babson.edu/Academics/centers/blank-center/global-research/diana/Pages/home.aspx

[8]http://www.babson.edu/Academics/centers/blank-center/global-research/gem/Pages/home.aspx

[9]http://www.babson.edu/Academics/centers/blank-center/global-research/step/Pages/home.aspx

new streams of wealth across many generations. The STEP Project for family enterprising conducts leading edge research, generates applied entrepreneurship practices, and provides a shared learning environment. The project also examines how families generate new economic activity through venturing, renewal, and generation. Academics participating in the STEP Project have a strong interest in creating a practical nexus between entrepreneurship theory and family-influenced wealth creation, and their institutions have committed to exploring research and practice solutions for how families build their entrepreneurial legacies through growth.

The STEP Project is designed to:

- Conduct leading edge research on the entrepreneurial capabilities and contribution of business families worldwide
- Generate an applied stream of entrepreneurship powerful practices that lead to family business continuity and growth
- Provide a shared learning environment where researchers and professors interact with family business leaders to generate solutions that have immediate impact.

The STEP Project operates in four regions of the world — Europe, Latin America, Asia, and North America. Each region utilizes the same model, but organizes its research collection and dissemination as independent groups. Forty-two institutions currently participate. Each affiliate must complete three research case studies in order to be a member in good standing. The project recently launched a multicountry, multi-respondent survey to examine entrepreneurial activities in family businesses.

The STEP research model (see Figure 3), developed from the qualitative research cases, includes internal and external factors influencing the entrepreneurial behavior of the family business, as well as the role of the family members in leading and governing the business. Because this is an applied research project, regional summits are held each year that include family businesses and academics. Workshops are held to present key findings of research to families.

On the Babson Campus, over 40% of undergraduate students identify themselves as part of a family business.[10] The graduate school admissions office estimates that the number graduate students is approximately the same. As such, the STEP research is integral to curricular, cocurricular, and executive education activities. The Blank Center's Institute for Family Entrepreneurship (IFE) supports

---

[10]According to a Babson College survey of all Freshmen FME students over two year period, 2013, 2014.

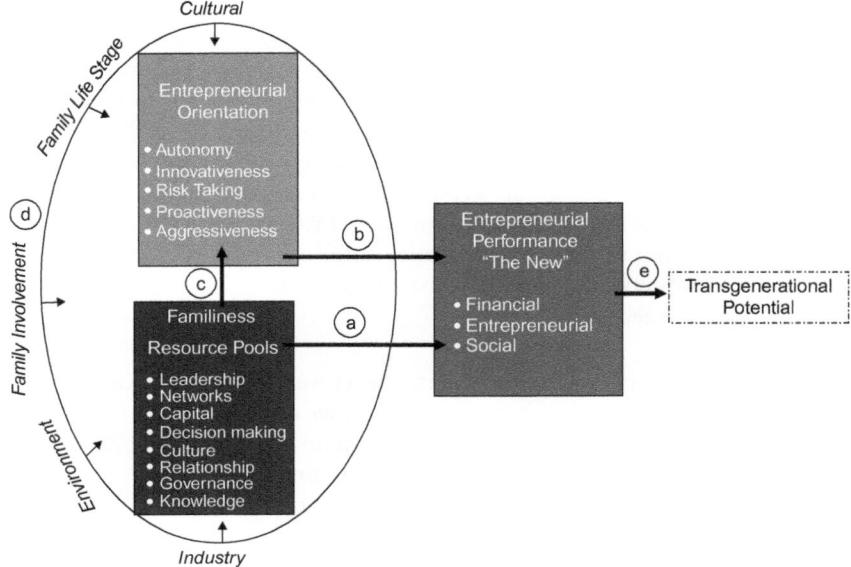

Figure 3: The STEP Research Model.

a family entrepreneurship club for both graduate and undergraduate students and brings programming to students through cocurricular activities. Executive education events include students, parents, and alumni, with the goal of helping families to understand how entrepreneurship works in the family business context and how to grow their businesses through entrepreneurial leadership.[11]

In addition to the IFE and family business clubs, courses are offered in both the graduate and undergraduate curriculum, focusing on entrepreneurship in families. The faculty members teaching these courses have direct involvement in the STEP research project and are able to bring the lessons, findings, and best practices directly into the classroom.

Conclusion

This chapter provides a brief overview of many of the programs and activities of AMBCE. However, the critical message for readers is

---

[11]http://www.babson.edu/executive-education/non-public/Pages/family-entre preneurship.aspx

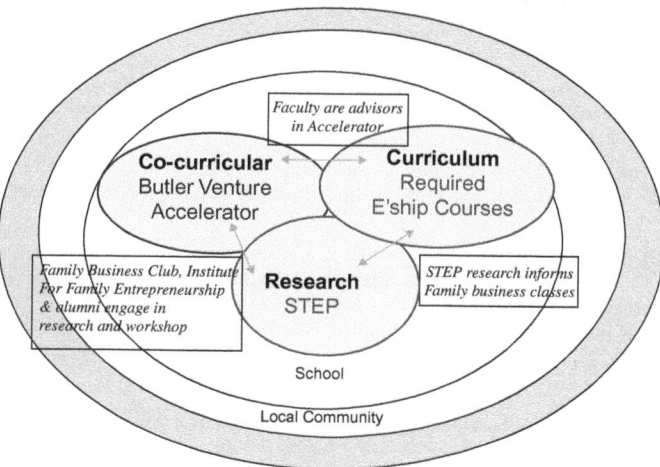

Figure 4: Integration and Alignment in the Babson College Entrepreneurship Education Ecosystem.

not just an interesting list of activities for student entrepreneurs to take part in, but rather how these efforts are integrated. As we show, by taking an ecosystems perspective, developing a center or institute for entrepreneurship requires alignment and coordination with other parts of the campus ecosystem and in the larger environment. The importance is not only what programs are offered for students but how they are connected to all of the other parts of the ecosystem in order to strengthen them all. We showcased the Butler Venture Accelerator and the STEP Project to demonstrate the contributions that the Blank Center makes with respect to creating new knowledge and learning for all stakeholders within our ecosystem (see Figure 4).

For those in the process of developing their entrepreneurship curriculum for the first time or reevaluating their current offering, we cannot stress enough the importance of first examining your entire ecosystem. It is also important for others to recognize that it would be a fool's errand to try to replicate Babson's ecosystem or that of any other college or university (Corbett, 2011). Benchmarking others is an important first step, but each school must use its own "discretion while being cognizant of their own unique resources and mission" (Corbett, 2011, pp. 29–30) in order to develop appropriate curricular and cocurricular programs. Only by clearly aligning with your institution's mission and goals can you construct the center that is "right" for your ecosystem and begin building the true heart for entrepreneurship for your campus.

References

Alberti, F., Sciascia, S., & Poli, A. (2004). Entrepreneurship education: Notes on an ongoing debate. *Proceedings of the 14th annual international entrepreneurship conference*, Naples, Italy.

Aulet, B. (2008). *How to build a successful innovation ecosystem: Education, network and celebrate*. Retrieved from http://www.Xconomy.com. Accessed on October 14, 2008.

Brush, C. G. (2014). Exploring the concept of an entrepreneurship education ecosystem. In D. Kuratko (Ed.), *Innovative pathways for university entrepreneurship in the 21st century* (Vol. 24, pp. 25–39). Advances in the Study of Entrepreneurship, Innovation and Economic Growth. Bingley, UK: Emerald Group Publishing Limited.

Christopherson, R. W. (1997). *Geosystems: An introduction to physical geography*. Upper Saddle River, NJ: Prentice Hall.

Corbett, A. C. (2011). Finding your own way: Entrepreneurship course development, strategic fit, and the problems of benchmarking. *International Journal of Entrepreneurship and Small Business, 13*(1), 18–31.

Fetters, M., Greene, P., Rice, M., & Butler, J. (2010). *The development of university-based entrepreneurship ecosystems: Global practices*. Northampton, MA: Edward Elgar Publishing.

Isenberg, D. J. (2010). How to start an entrepreneurial revolution. *Harvard Business Review*, June, *88*(6). Reprint R100A.

Kuratko, D. F. (2005). The emergence of entrepreneurship education: Development, trends and challenges. *Entrepreneurship Theory and Practice, 229*(5), 577–598.

Newman, E. L. (2013). *A theory on becoming entrepreneurial: A student's developmental journal to a creation-driven mindset*. Doctoral Dissertation, University of Pennsylvania – School of Education, Philadelphia, PA.

Tansley, A. G. (1935). The use and abuse of vegetational concepts and terms. *Ecology, 16*(3), 284–307.

Xavier, S. R., Kelley, D., Kew, J., Herrington, M., & Vorderwulbecke, A. (2013). *Global entrepreneurship monitor: 2012 global report*. Wellesley, MA: Babson College.

27 Arts and the Entrepreneur: The Sorenson Center for the Arts

Beth Wynstra

Arts and Business on the College Campus: An Historic Glance

The relationship between business and the arts on American college campuses is one that has interested faculty, staff, and students for over a century. In the early 20th century, when American universities first began establishing performing arts departments and centers, faculty teaching dramatic literature, visual arts, acting, and playwriting were asked to consider how their respective fields connected to and supported a new and emerging goal set for colleges and universities: to prepare American students for the workforce, particularly in managerial roles. As Shannon Jackson argues,

> the late 19th to early 20th century was a period of debate, change, retrenchment, and more debate as U.S. colleges and universities grappled with their relationship to a changing American society ... as numerous historians of higher education have demonstrated, this period would also usher in the era of "professionalism," an economic and discursive formation that differently but pervasively inflected both professors' sense of their students' educational goals and their own sense of their positions as "career academics."
>
> —Jackson (2001)

Indeed, at the very time that Babson College was founded (1919), colleges and universities across the country were focused on how to best prepare students for the professional careers that awaited them after graduation. As colleges began to open their doors to women, immigrants, African Americans and to "the children of both the industrial bourgeoisie and the working classes," (Jackson, 2001) institutions of higher learning were no longer just the domain of the privileged white male who had the time and resources for a university setting. Rather colleges and universities were becoming places, for a wider swatch of the population, of not only serious learning but also of serious preparation. Faculty from all disciplines, arts included, began to think critically about the specific links between classroom content and real-world application. Jackson goes on to argue that

> as the role of the U.S. university was increasingly positioned as preparation for entrance into the managerial classes, academics worked to maintain a separate social position outside the so-called professions while simultaneously legitimating themselves curricularly and institutionally within professionalizing terms.
>
> —Jackson (2001)

Those in arts-related fields had to legitimatize themselves in this sphere of professional training being supported by colleges and universities. Those at the helm of arts education in top colleges and universities did not shy away from this professional-training challenge presented to them however. An important figure in American theater history who was keenly interested in the links between classroom content and the professional realm was George Pierce Baker. Baker, who in 1924 founded the Yale School of Drama, began his career at Harvard University as Professor of Rhetoric in the English Department and later created the famed English 47 Workshop, a playwriting program where such artists as Eugene O'Neill, Thomas Wolfe, John Mason Brown, John Reed, and Hallie Flanagan (director of the Federal Theatre Project) first honed their crafts. Baker was a revolutionary theater professor in the way that his pedagogy emphasized both humanistic and economic concerns. Baker's students in English 47, or Baker's dozen as they came to be known, left his playwriting class with effective ways to create commercially and critically successful works. In other words, his students learned how to craft works that would be appealing to a given audience at a given time. Mark Hodin argues that

> in English 47, he [Baker] assured his students that addressing conventional audience desires and expectations was

not inconsistent with their ambition to be literary artists. Quite the contrary, as in successful public address, mastery of rhetorical situation enabled the expression of "the individual mind upon the material"....

—Hodin (2005)

Baker's classroom lessons weaved economic concerns with artistic ones. He asked his students to be entrepreneurs, to create original artistic productions that would fulfill and exceed audience desires. He had an eye on the professional future of his students while he taught the mechanics of playwriting. Baker's pedagogical tactics have a rich legacy of success; his roster of prominent students certainly were able to straddle artistic and commercial success, and institutions like the Yale School of Drama are still graduating students who have a rich history of navigating commercial and artistic realms.

Arts and Business on the College Campus: The 20th and 21st Century

In 1991, the *Harvard Educational Review* published a volume dedicated to Arts as Education. In an introductory essay of the volume the editors argued:

The arts can be, for both students and teachers, forms of expression, communication, creativity, imagination, observation, perception, and thought. They are integral to the development of cognitive skills such as listening, thinking, problem-solving, matching form to function, and decision-making. They inspire discipline and dedication.

—Bucheli, Goldberg, and Phillips (1991)

Such sentiments put late 20th century and early 21st century arts faculty in a different position than their early 20th century predecessors. Buoyed by extensive research about the vast benefits of arts education in notable academic publications, like the *Harvard Educational Review*, as well as in more popular magazines and periodicals, arts faculty and leadership find that they no longer just tasked with connecting classroom content with the professional realm (see Clapp & Edwards, 2013; Merrion, 2009). Rather their role has become more nuanced and complex. Although some arts faculty still may feel that they have to justify their existence on a college campus and fight against the harmful arts-are-frivolous reputation, for the most part, arts on top college campuses enjoy a prominent and significant place. In November 2014, *New York Times* article Russell reported,

> Elite campuses across the country have emerged from the recession riding a multibillion-dollar wave of architecturally ambitious arts facilities, even as community arts programs struggle against public indifference. The current tide of building developed over years, as universities reassert the essential value of the arts to a well-rounded education ....
>
> —Russell (2014)

But with these financial resources and state-of-the art facilities come important responsibilities. A "well-rounded education" today, for instance, must take into account the tremendous leaps made in technology and media over the last 25 years. Thus the arts, too, must keep up with these advances in the work that is showcased at a college, the way the arts are taught, as well as how art is produced. What role do the arts play in a changing educational landscape and ever developing curriculums? How can theater, dance, and drawing help to prepare students for the increasing professional fields where arts and industry collide? What unique lessons do the arts provide in developing young entrepreneurs? It is these questions that the leadership team at the Richard W. Sorenson Center for the Arts asks on a daily basis.

Housed at Babson College, a college without a formal theater or visual arts department yet with a strong, interdisciplinary liberal arts program, the Sorenson Center serves the needs of students, faculty, staff, and greater community members. Our methods for creating compelling, educational, and entertaining productions and events are guided by Babson's mission as well as a firm belief in the vast benefits of synergizing arts and business. Through the work of the Sorenson Center as well as several faculty and staff across campus, Babson College is demonstrating how creative thinking and thoughtful performance are key to entrepreneurship and how business strategies are fundamental to successful arts initiatives. Our arts programming at Babson reflects this fascinating reciprocal relationship.

THE RICHARD W. SORENSON CENTER: A LABORATORY FOR ENTREPRENEURIAL THOUGHT AND ACTION

Constructed in 1997, the Richard W. Sorenson Center was designed to expand and enhance the presence of the arts and culture on Babson's campus while serving as a paradigm of creative thinking and entrepreneurial practice for academic programs across the business and liberal arts spectrum. The Center features a state-of-the-art

441 seat proscenium theater, a dance/rehearsal studio, and band and music practice rooms. The Sorenson Family Visual Arts Center features a ceramics/sculpture studio, a black and white photo lab, a drawing/painting studio, artist-in-residence studio, and student gallery.

From 1997 until 2013, the Sorenson Center was overseen by one director who produced an array of programming by visiting performing and visual artists as well as supported faculty initiatives and student performance groups. In the Fall of 2013, the Sorenson Center underwent a momentous change. As Babson welcomed the Commonwealth Shakespeare Company (CSC) as the college's new theater-in-residence, the Sorenson Center welcomed a new leadership structure and team. Steven Maler, Artistic Director of CSC, assumed the role of Director of the Sorenson Center. Beth Wynstra, Assistant Professor of English, became the Center's first Faculty Director. Adam Sanders, the Associate Artistic Director of Commonwealth Shakespeare, took on the role of the Center's first Associate Director.

This new leadership structure is designed to ensure that all stakeholders and audiences of the Sorenson are served. Maler is responsible for ensuring that the Sorenson programming is aligning with the goals of the college and the vision of Babson's president; Wynstra ensures that the productions, exhibits, and performances produced by the Sorenson support Babson's academic curriculum and speak to the research and pedagogical interests of faculty; Sanders works with Babson's student groups to bring rigor and professionalism to the works these groups produce. Danielle Krcmar, Babson's Artist-in-Residence, continues her work in creating greater visibility for the visual arts programs and exhibits on campus.

One of the first projects the new leadership team initiated in the Fall of 2013 was a series of interviews with key stakeholders across campus. These interviews were conducted by consultant Janet Bailey. Interviewees included faculty members from both business and liberal arts disciplines, staff members from disparate departments such as financial aid, student activities, and health and wellness, as well as individuals in prominent administrative positions such as the Dean of the Undergraduate School and the Dean of Faculty. The feedback the leadership team received from these interviews was that there was great interest in arts programming at Babson, but that the work was under-marketed, under-supported, and not well integrated into the curriculum. There was a strong interest in more professional activity on campus and a desire to see the student activities held to a more rigorous standard.

Using the feedback from the interviews as well as the parameters established by Babson's signature teaching approach, Entrepreneurial Thought and Action® (ETA), the Babson leadership team began formulating a new mission statement for the arts at Babson. ETA® is a methodology that teaches undergraduates, graduates, and executives to balance action, experimentation, and creativity with a deep understanding of business fundamentals and rigorous analysis as the ideal approach to creating economic and social value (see Greenberg, McKone-Sweet, Wilson, n.d.). The Sorenson leadership team recognized (and continues to recognize) the unique educational experience that Babson offers, and thus our vision and goals reflect the institution's distinctive approach to teaching entrepreneurship.

In the Spring of 2014, the Sorenson leadership team launched a season of events under the umbrella name of BabsonArts. BabsonARTS presents performances, exhibitions, films, and conversations designed to entertain, extend and supplement the classroom experience, and shine a spotlight on global issues, social and environmental concerns, the creative process, and the arts as a business. Our mission is both to serve the educational needs of students and enhance Babson's reputation as an institution that values innovation and creativity.

BABSONARTS: THE FIRST TWO SEASONS

The first season of BabsonArts (2014) was an exciting one, with an array of diverse offerings in theater, visual arts, dance, film, and music. Babson's theater-in-residence, CSC, provided several new and special events and productions for the Babson community. CSC is dedicated to bringing vital and contemporary productions of Shakespeare's works to the people of Greater Boston and is best known for their annual free productions on Boston Common that play to thousands of people each summer. At Babson, CSC artists provided a number of workshops for students, staff and faculty in voice, movement, and improvisation. Anthony Rapp, a notable CSC alumnus and actor who originated the role of Mark in the Broadway smash hit *Rent*, came to campus for screening a film version of *Rent*. The screening was part of the existing Sterns Family Film Series on campus, but Rapp's presence allowed for a master class with students as well as a performance of Rapp singing "Seasons of Love," the signature song from *Rent*, with Babson's student a cappella group, the Rocket Pitches. The master class allowed 10 students to work on a song or monologue of their choosing while receiving feedback from Rapp. While master classes at other institutions allow for an interaction with a notable actor or artist, the master classes we offer at Babson are intimate experiences for our participants which allow for discussion and critique.

BabsonArts supported existing faculty initiatives in new and innovative ways. Our interviews in 2013 revealed that faculty-driven programs in the performing and visual arts were not well publicized.

By providing a more systematic marketing approach, the Sorenson leadership team was able to generate substantial on and off-campus visibility. These marketing efforts paid off both in higher audience numbers and in a significantly increased profile in the media. The Sorenson team also worked with the Alumni office to create engagement opportunities for area alumni. Faulty initiatives such as The Empty Space Theater (TEST), a theater company directed by faculty with the goal of producing produce socially relevant plays and musicals that speak to and extend the classroom curriculum, the Thompson Visiting Poet Series, a program that brings internationally poets to campus to read their work and engage with students, and The Global Film Series, a program that screens four films a year with talkbacks and activities led filmmakers and scholars, all benefitted in new ways from the increased exposure and support by BabsonArts.

The Sorenson team developed a new program designed to reflect the interest Babson students have in careers in which business and the arts collide: Arts and Business Conversations. These conversations bring prominent arts leaders to campus to discuss the challenges of leading nonprofit organizations. Conversations are held over lunch and are intimate enough to allow for students and Babson community members to engage with the arts leaders. The Sorenson team works to ensure that we are bringing representatives from all arts disciplines and that the conversations include extensive descriptions of how business acumen and entrepreneurship are crucial ingredients in successful artistic initiatives. Professors across campus are beginning to require these conversations as part of their courses as students have the opportunity to better understand how the lessons they are learning in Babson classrooms are not only applicable but necessary in the professional realm. In Spring, 2014 BabsonArts featured conversations with Jill Medvedow, Director of the Institute for Contemporary Art; Michael Maso, Managing Director of the Huntington Theater; and Pedro Alonzo, Independent Curator. These talks were moderated by Sorenson staff or by faculty members.

BabsonArts produced two visual arts exhibits, Kiyomiziu and SURGE, and offered several master classes in drawing and sculpture. The Sorenson team, in particular Wynstra and Sanders, worked deliberately to integrate programming into the student experience. Sanders worked closely with Professors Betsy Newman and Kathleen Kelly to bring Shakespeare to life in their classrooms. Sanders visited Newman and Kelly's courses several times during the Spring 2014 semester and led students in workshops focusing on language, movement, and vocal capabilities. Although the work Sanders did with students was focused on Shakespeare, the lessons students gained in bodily and vocal awareness and critical reading are some that will help them in any field or profession. Many other initiatives and programs of the Sorenson Center were incorporated into the student experience through partnerships with faculty, Arts and History Foundation (AHS) courses, student clubs, and the Babson LGBTQ Action Group.

Finally, BabsonArts produced performances by visiting artists, including Babson alumnus Jamie Kent and classical guitarist Colin Thurmond playing Latin music at Glavin Chapel, a presentation by Israeli Stage of Savyon Leibrecht's *Dear Sigmund and Carl*, which was a featured event for the AHS foundation courses, and a cabaret-style performance by Charles Busch.

During both the Spring 2014 and Fall 2015, the Sorenson team realized that a faulty infrastructure was not allowing us to promote and market the events we were producing in an effective way. The Sorenson team engaged a Marketing Coordinator to be the point person for all promotion and advertising of BabsonARTS in general and each specific event and to be sure all our materials are professional and consistent with Babson branding. We hired an Audience Services Manager to handle the box office and front-of-house at every performance; this position is critical to ensure safety and security in the theater, to see that audience members are treated with courtesy and professionalism, and to curb inappropriate behavior in the theater. The Sorenson team acquired directional signage so that off-campus visitors can actually find the theater and are working on more prominent signage on the building itself. We worked with staff from Information Technology and Marketing to create a better looking and more functional website, and a more attractive brochure. We acquired a professional box office and customer relationship management system, which allows us to fulfill ticket requests and track useful information about audiences and marketing initiatives.

At the conclusion of the Spring semester 2014 we conducted an all-campus survey to gauge reactions to what we had done and to generate ideas for the future. The survey received over 500 responses, suggesting that there is tremendous interest and support for the arts across the campus. Some quotations from the survey include:

> "The arts events at the Sorenson invigorated the cultural life on campus, helped to integrate students, faculty and staff, and enriched the life of the campus. They made me think, and they made me happy to be at Babson."

> "I love the arts and business talks. As a grad student aspiring to arts leadership, these were valuable, relevant, and inspiring. I also think that this is an important topic.

Babson is known for creativity and entrepreneurship, which ties SO closely to the arts, but the arts are not very present at Babson."

"I enjoyed everything about Anthony Rapp's visit and screening of the movie. The most special part of the evening was when the Babson Choir Group sang with Anthony. The event was a great night of all things wonderful about Babson. It was a classy, informative, intimate and enjoyable event."

This survey as well as several informal conversations and meetings helped to guide our programming for the Fall of 2014.

Some highlights of the Fall 2014 season included a production of Samuel Beckett's *Happy Days* with Brooke Adams and Tony Shalhoub, presented on the campus by CSC, which drew well over 1000 audience members onto the Babson campus and generated a huge amount of press coverage. Master classes taught by CSC artists continued in the Fall but under a new title: "The Public Speaker's Toolbox." This series of classes offered guidance in voice and speech, physicality, and presentation skills for students across campus. BabsonArts continued its Arts and Business conversations featuring Bill Taylor of American Ballet Theatre; Spring Sirkin, Broadway producer; and Susan Rodgerson of Artists for Humanity. The latter was accompanied by exhibition of Artist for Humanity works around campus. Last, BabsonArts continued to make faculty initiatives a priority supporting the existing and new works faculty produce at the Sorenson Center.

The off-campus work of CSC has become increasingly important for expanding the visibility of Babson College. During CSC's annual summer production on Boston Common, large groups of Babson faculty and staff as well as alumni were in the audience and Babson signage was very prominent. In the Fall, CSC celebrated its 20th year with a "Shakespeare at Fenway Park" event, which garnered publicity both locally and nationally. At this event, Babson President Kerry Healey spoke and Babson was recognized as CSC's institutional home.

LOOKING AHEAD: ARTS AS PART OF THE ENTREPRENEURIAL EXPERIENCE

The Sorenson team is both enthusiastic for the performances and productions coming to campus as well as reflective about the successes and areas of improvement for arts programming at a unique place like Babson. At this juncture, there are several principles informing our programming decisions:

- Our events should have multiple components that reach across several disciplines and categories.
- We intend that each event will include a talkback, a Q&A, an artist talk, or some other mechanism that gives the Babson community an opportunity to interact with the artists who are coming to campus.
- We are working closely with at least one, and in many cases more than one, faculty member on most of the programming, as a way to build visibility across the campus and ensure that our offerings are relevant to the academic side of the institution.
- We have established a Faculty/Staff Advisory Committee, whose purpose will be to guide us toward our goal of providing quality arts programming that speaks to and extends the classroom experience, supplements faculty and staff's research and pedagogical interests, and provides Babson community members with experiential opportunities in all arts disciplines.

The Spring 2015 season continues to be crafted by energy surrounding the intertwining of the arts and Babson College's mission. There is the production of *Basetrack Live*, a theatrical collaboration between award-winning theatre company En Garde Arts and corpsman and families of the 1st Battalion/8th Marines. This multifaceted production includes multimedia, a live orchestra, and theatrical performances all focusing on war. BabsonArts will also be screening *Underwater Dreams*, a film by Babson's filmmaker-in-residence, Mary Mazzio. This film documents a robotics team from Arizona, comprised mainly of children of undocumented immigrants, who built an underwater robot that won a major competition at the University of California, Santa Barbara. The screening will also include a panel discussion with Mazzio, a Babson professor who specializes in design, and the Babson Vice Provost for International and Multicultural education, who will discuss the immigration issues in the film. The Spring season will end with a special cabaret performance by major Broadway, television, and film star Jeremy Jordan.

We are confident that we have established a set of programming principles that will guide us as we make selections in the future and that we have a professional staff and systems in place to support that programming. We intend to continue to work with faculty and student groups to ensure that we are addressing their needs for events that are both enjoyable and enriching, that enhance the curriculum, and that bring visibility to the College. We are also working with the Alumni and Development offices to establish a non-fiduciary Advisory Board whose members will offer resources, connections, and expertize to help us have greater sustainable impact on the College.

As we look to the future for BabsonArts, the entire Sorenson team is committed to finding more ways to highlight the intersection of arts and innovation and entrepreneurialism as well as explore the vast benefits of such intersections. Business leaders today need to be able to communicate well, have a good sense for design, and consider multiple ways to complete projects and initiatives. The arts train and prepare students for these important tasks, and Babson seems to be the only college in the country where the synergies between arts and business not only are celebrated but also shape the season of arts programming for the greater campus community.

References

Bucheli, R., Goldberg, M. R., & Phillips, A. (1991). Symposium: Arts as education. *Harvard Educational Review*, 61(1), 25.

Clapp, E., & Edwards, L. (2013). Expanding our vision for the arts in education. *Harvard Educational Review*, 83(1), 5–14.

D. Greenberg, K. McKone-Sweet, & H. J. Wilson, Entrepreneurial thought and action: A methodology for developing entrepreneurial leaders. Retrieved from http://www.babson.edu/executive-education/education-educators/babson-insight/articles/pages/entrepreneurial-thought-action-methodology-developing-entrepreneurial-leaders.aspx.

Hodin, M. (2005). 'It did not sound like professor's speech': George Pierce Baker and the market for academic rhetoric. *Theatre Survey*, 46(2), 232.

Jackson, S. (2001). Professing performance: Disciplinary genealogies. *TDR*, 45(1), 86.

Merrion, M. (2009). A prophecy for the arts in education. *Change*, 41(5), 16.

Russell, J. (2014). On Elite campuses, an arts race. *New York Times*.

28 ETA-ing from the Center: The Story of the Design of a Course, the Creation of a Book, and an Ongoing Adventure at The Lewis Institute at Babson College

Cheryl Kiser and J. Janelle (Jan) Shubert

This is a story. A story about how as educators, as practitioners and as students, we used Entrepreneurial Thought and Action® as the compass for acting our way into real innovation around intellectual concepts, around the processes of teaching and learning, and around the role of centers in colleges and universities. Like all good stories, it has a colorful cast of characters, scenes of (cerebral) jousting, and (spoiler alert!) a happy ending. With the exception of "Time" and "Enthusiastic but Unintentional Ignorance," there are no real villains, although there are lots of heroines and heroes.

In the best tradition of storytelling, it is an adventure, a quest, a journey, an exploration, and a treasure hunt that all began in 2011 and is still in progress. To make it easy to follow, we have mapped the narrative using key elements of Babson's Entrepreneurial Thought and Action® to tell the story of our actions in the first year, our experimentation and revisions for the second year, and our learning and planning for the future.

Before you begin, we want to offer a very transparent disclaimer: The reality of our journey was *never* this tidy! We began with one map that got us lost and more than a little confused. We wandered around and found new paths. We sought out guides and encountered fellow travelers who pointed new ways forward; some even joined us to form an expeditionary force – a tribe. We created, and abandoned, routes and navigational charts. Eventually, we caught sight of a place on the horizon that we could never have imagined when we began. It was only when we looked back that we could fully appreciate how much our journey and adventure had been hardwired to Entrepreneurial Thought and Action® – the cornerstone of how Babson approaches leadership education.

In the "chapters" that follow, we invite you to not just read and enjoy what we hope is a good story, but join us and enlist for the next phase of this journey. Explorers of all kinds are welcome!

Chapter 1: A Desire Sufficient to Get Us Started (2011)

Well, it wasn't "A dark and stormy night"! In fact, it was in the eagerly awaited mild days of the spring of 2011 that an opportunity appeared. The then-dean of the Babson MBA program approached Cheryl Kiser, Executive Director of The Lewis Institute, about working with him to create an experimental elective focused on Strategic Leadership for MBA students. The conversation no sooner began than the dean accepted a position at another institution and suggested that Jan Shubert (who at that point was the Executive Director for The Center for Women's Entrepreneurial Leadership and Faculty Co-Chair for the MBA core course, Babson Consulting Alliance Program) should join Cheryl in creating this experimental elective. We immediately and enthusiastically agreed.

In our very first conversation, we quickly realized that while both of us had a strong desire to work together again (we had collaborated on other projects and programs) and to create an experimental elective focused on leadership, our *real* shared passion was fueled by what at the time we saw as a fairly narrow question: "What kind of leadership does the world need to foster social value creation?" It wasn't that we didn't see this kind of leadership as "strategic" – we did. But even in this early batting-ideas-around phase, we found that we kept coming back to an approach to leadership that *we* cared deeply about and that we felt was tightly aligned with the mission, values, and resources of both Babson College and The Lewis Institute in new and exciting ways.

Our next discovery (the journey had begun!) was that both of us were drawn to, and felt strongly about, the pedagogical power of what we'll call here "Action Learning" and "Living Cases." (Babson College, overall, and the college's graduate programs support a wide, rich array of courses and programs that operate under the oversight of the Office of Experiential Learning.) We wanted the students to do more than read about or "discuss" leadership in class. We wanted them to see and hear and *really* interact in a substantive way with real leaders, from real companies about real, meaty, messy issues. Equally, we wanted the people who represented those companies, although already acknowledged leaders in social value creation, to join the class in the spirit of co-created learning, to be willing to share not just *what* they and the organization had done (and were still doing) but also the complex issues surrounding the *how*. What were the leadership opportunities and challenges they had faced/were facing/were anticipating? What did a day in their "leadership lives" look and feel like? And, most importantly, what did they want or need to hear and learn *from the students*?

To be perfectly honest, at that point our "intriguing idea" looked pretty much like a mash-up of "Inside the Actors Studio," a hands-on learning laboratory, a graduate symposium, and a set of lively face-to-face conversations, complete with interruptions and talk-overs and challenges and (yes) laughter. Now all we had to do was to shape this into something that carried academic credit and counted toward completion of a Babson MBA. So we scribbled "Leading for Social Value: Inside the C-Suite" across the top of a page — and took off running.

Chapter 2: Start with the Means at Hand or What and Who We Knew and Our "Affordable Loss" (2011)

By the summer of 2011, we had the first cameo appearance of one of the pseudo-villains — Time. We would be launching this half-term, experimental elective for MBA students (seven weeks, a three-hour session each week) in late October. With a very short planning runway, we didn't have the luxury of a leisurely, "scholarly" approach to course design. The Graduate Program Office was breathing down our necks (in the nicest possible way) for a course description, and we knew that invitations needed to go out quickly (yesterday?) to the extremely busy executives we planned to feature. So, like all good ET&A'ers, we just took a deep breath and went with the means at hand. What did we know? Who did we know? How could we enroll others in this journey? What was our "afford-able loss" — what was the risk in undertaking this adventure?

Cheryl brought invaluable resources, including a massive rolo-dex and deep relationships with companies that were already on the path to creating social value in ways that went beyond corporate social responsibility (or, as she preferred to call it "corporate social relevance"). As the previous Managing Director of the Center for Corporate Citizenship at Boston College, she had also been at the forefront of actually creating the foundational knowledge about this domain; she not only "saw" but had actively shaped the intellectual roadmap we wanted to follow. Although Jan had a more modest rolodex and set of relationships in this particular domain, she too had decades of experience building relationships with executives in the corporate world and brought 30 plus years of academic and pro-fessional experience designing and teaching in action learning envir-onments and creating "living cases."

In some circumstances, it can feel like the "What you know" and "Who you know" are interrelated but still very independent ele-ments in the ET&A® process. For us, these were immediately highly *interdependent* and ultimately became critical, necessary multipliers. What we knew connected us to who we knew, who in turn knew things we didn't know and to people we didn't know. The "what" and "who" quickly morphed into a "virtuous circle of knowing" that was both exciting and extremely productive and (again speak-ing candidly) sometimes overwhelmingly complicated.

But above and beyond these not insignificant "means at hand," the thing that created the strongest foundation for our ET&A'ing was the environment — being imbedded at Babson and having the Lewis Institute (as a college "Center") as our supporting platform. The Lewis Institute was barely two years old when we set off on this journey. But it already had an impressive track record of inno-vation inside Babson and was launching a robust, aspirational, and inspirational roster of outwardly facing initiatives. On the college side, Babson had a decades-old tradition of both formal and infor-mal process in place for "trying things out" in the classroom (the experimental elective being just one), which in turn permitted small-scale "beta testing" (a half-term elective), which in turn could then be developed in a wide variety of ways into "regular" curriculum.

As you discovered in other sections of this book, the college also has a long tradition of encouraging and supporting very permeable disciplinary and cross-campus collaborations. This made it not just "permitted" but actually very easy for the Lewis Institute (which is a nonacademic center) to take the lead in proposing a course that could be offered under the academic umbrella of the Graduate

Management Division. Of course, it certainly didn't hurt that Babson, overall, is absolutely crawling with folks who, because they too are ET&A'ing all over the place in their research, teaching and practice, could (and did) offer advice, support, inspiration, and collegial engagement at multiple levels and at critical junctures.

This environment also helped us understand our "affordable loss" — what we could risk. First and foremost, we had the convening power of both The Lewis Institute and the college that we could draw on and leverage as resources. We had a student body that was already imbued with the fundamentals of Entrepreneurial Thought and Action®. We had a college-wide mission of educating "… entrepreneurial leaders who create great economic and social value — everywhere."

Even in the earliest stages of our enthusiastic optimism, although we understood that "failure" at some level was probably inevitable, we also knew that unless it involved legal or ethical violations, "failure" in the design or delivery of the course would be tolerated as "experimentation" and as "learning" and that we would be encouraged — even expected — to learn from what we did and try again. It was Babson.

Chapter 3: Acting — Launching the 2011 Course

If you had been enrolled as one of the 22 students in the first iteration of the course or had been a guest from the C-Suite of one of the six organizations we spotlighted in the fall of 2011, you would have been following a Syllabus that is presented in an abbreviated form in Appendix A. In Appendix B, you will see the roster of C-Suite organizations we included in the 2011 iteration of the course.

Unless you, too, are designing a course focused explicitly on social value creation, the details of this overview are we hope interesting and informative but not essential. Rather, it is the "big picture" gestalt of the design *process* that had (and continues to have) critical implications for our — and we hope your — on-going exploration of entrepreneurial education.

For us, this has meant the continuous design and re-design of the pedagogy (how we will teach, who are the "students" and how they learn), the broadening and deepening of both the scope of the content (the rapidly evolving definition of social value creation and of "leadership" within that arena), and the landscape for the dissemination of knowledge (the equally rapidly growing thirst for information from an ever-expanding range of stakeholders). But perhaps most critical to our journey has been the discovery of a more nuanced understanding of how to align with and leverage the power of an operating environment — in our case The Lewis Institute and Babson College.

Chapter 4: Act, Learn, Repeat, Building on What (and Who) We Knew — The 2012 Re-Design

The 2011 experimental elective was gratifyingly successful. It got very strong, positive evaluations and feedback from the students, enthusiastic endorsements from the executives who participated, questions and engagement from other interested parties (internally and externally), and led to a publishing contract to turn what we had originally envisioned as a Babson-produced handbook for students into a book that would have broad distribution and application.

There was also unplanned-for (albeit perfectly understandable in the Babson environment) value-add for the students, the faculty, and the College. The organizational executives featured in the course were energized and excited about what they saw as opportunities to engage with Babson. They quickly began seeking out ways to be partners and collaborators in a much broader array of activities including supporting programs and projects through the auspices of The Lewis Institute, developing cases for broad use across the curriculum (and beyond Babson), and signing on to become organizational partners for an MBA core course (The Babson Consulting Alliance Program). All of this and more created pathways for student internships and even employment.

In 2012, the second offering of the experimental elective enrolled 25 students. Flush with our 2011 success, we changed the name of the course to "*Social Value Creation Matters*" and featured a slightly revised partner organization roster (see Appendix B). Pedagogically, we ultimately changed little else except to say that the "deliverables" (assignments) produced by the students (individually and in teams) would be incorporated into "a book" that was under contract.

However, for 2012, we made multiple additions and modifications to *what* we were teaching, including a much heavier focus on leadership characteristics and on the power of communication (and even more particularly, "narratives") to build stakeholder buy-in. With the wisdom of hindsight, we can see that although we were still constrained by seven three-hour sessions and still required essentially the same student deliverables, we over-enthusiastically built in an ever-expanding list of "themes" that kept cropping up both inside the classroom and in our interactions with academic and corporate colleagues and prospective collaborators. To say that each three-hour session was "action-packed" would be an understatement!

Chapter 5: Act, Learn, Re-Learn, Repeat — A Way Forward

So, then what happened? The good news was that, despite a frenetic pace and sometimes on-the-fly adjustments, the 2012 iteration was also very "successful" in terms of strong, positive student evaluations and corporate engagement and enthusiasm. In the year following the end of the course, the book was completed and launched (*Creating Social Value: A Guide for Leaders and Change. Makers*, Greenleaf Publishing, 2014). It has sold out once, been adopted by organizations such as Ashoka and Net Impact, and nominated for awards.

We also gained the approval of the college and the graduate school to offer *Social Value Creation* as a regular intensive elective beginning in the fall semester of 2015. (See Appendix C for an overview of the proposed intensive elective.) We believe that this fresh venue for delivery will better align with our aspirations for increasing thought leadership in this domain, more fully integrate our partner organizations with Babson students and Babson colleagues, and be a much stronger platform for very powerful hands-on experiential learning.

With over 40 "alumni" of the course, more than 10 corporate partners, a vibrant cadre of "collaborators," and an expanding readership, we also now have a much larger "tribe" as well as a larger, more varied platform for our ideas. In many respects, we succeeded beyond our wildest expectations. Yet, in other respects, it could be said that we also "failed." Fortunately, here at Babson, that "failure" translates into: we acted, we experimented, and we learned. It also means that we can (and will) continue to learn and act, with support and encouragement.

Chapter 6: Starting All Over Again with a Strong Desire and the Means at Hand

In 2011, we began with a shared passion and with what we knew and who we knew. That's exactly where we are now in our thinking and planning for the 2015 launch of an intensive elective. What we now know (the big "ah-ha's" from our journey) definitely have multiple implications for academic thought leadership and for pedagogy. But perhaps the most important — and somewhat embarrassingly belated — realization has been that both the thought leadership and the pedagogy can, and should, be dramatically enhanced by a much more intentional, thoughtful recognition of, and alignment with, our operating environment. We were, and are, thinking, designing, teaching, and learning in one of the most flexible, fertile educational laboratories imaginable. As we re-set our compass for the next phase of this journey, we are concentrating on the five broad and challenging "Take-Aways-for-Moving-Forward." Each of these five represents recognition of how we have begun organizing our thinking about the exciting thought-leadership opportunities for social value creation. Each of the five also serves as an ET&A® compass for guiding not just *what* we are teaching but also as a reminder to be more intentional about knitting together the inextricable, intertwined variables of teaching *what, to whom, how and in what context.*

> Take-Away-for-Moving Forward #1: *Social value creation is a newly-emerging, growing, but also already robust field of intellectual inquiry.*

Our original starting point was a shared passion/interest, which became a course, which morphed into a book. But as we re-start the journey from a very different entry point, we know that this time it is not just about a course or about a book. The conceptual, thought-leadership implications and opportunities are heady! We accept that we really are hip-deep in discovering and creating new paths of knowledge. We also fully accept that this new starting point carries the imperative of a much more thoughtful and intentional leveraging of the convening power of The Lewis Institute and Babson College, overall, to encourage and support the cross-disciplinary, academic research of our colleagues and cross-industry sharing of "best practice."

Moving forward, we aspire to expand and enhance proactive collaborations with our colleagues in Babson's other centers (e.g., The Blank Center for Entrepreneurship, The Cutler Center for Investment and Finance, The Babson Center for Executive Education, and The Center for Women's Entrepreneurial Leadership). We aspire to create more mutually aligned and mutually beneficial venues (e.g., conferences, symposia, workshops, and case writing) to showcase social value creation of all kinds.

Take-Away-for-Moving Forward #2: *Social value creation is about co-creation.*

This follows hand-in-hand from the previous Take-Away, but it bears emphasizing and expanding. Our journey is a case in point of where the "what" we are teaching and writing about can also be, and perhaps even arguably should be, the "*How* we educate about the *what*." In creating the course and the book we learned (*really learned*) first-hand that companies we were showcasing and studying had *not* created social value in a vacuum. In every instance, unlocking social value was a process of *co-creation* between company leadership, stakeholders, and the complex forces of a broader societal landscape. We learned that companies — for-profit and not-for-profit, large and small — created sustainable social value by fully considering the economic, environmental, and social aspects of the impact of their initiatives. We also learned that a course, a book, a workshop, and a conversation on this topic should also, as much as possible, mirror the same kind of co-creation and integration.

In addition to the aspirations in the section above, we also aspire to make this mirroring a reality in our 2015 elective by (a) doing more up-front design co-creation with Babson colleagues across disciplines around their research interests, (b) structuring the course so that our guests/partner organizations have the opportunity to spend substantive, meaningful time co-creating/really working together with our students to find solutions to tough problems, and (c) use this same structure to create more opportunity for our guests/partner organizations to work together and with others here at Babson to share "best practice," learn from one another, and co-create "learning communities."

Take-Away-Move-Forward #3: *Social value creation success depends on accessibility and a well-designed infrastructure.*

Over the two years of designing and teaching the course and gathering and shaping the information for the book we were shown countless examples of ideas that organizations had for creating social value that were ultimately abandoned. Often these abandoned pilots or projects were the result of the organization not finding, using, or creating the organizational infrastructure to support them; that is, the leadership, the broad-base of talent, the financial resources, or the processes for embedding and spreading the idea were missing. Sometimes the failure was the result of the idea not having a clear, unambiguous link to the mission of the company, its overall business strategy, or its values. Sometimes ideas faltered or faded for lack of "ownership" by the very people it sought to engage.

Moving forward, we aspire to strengthen *our own* infrastructure and create more robust accessibility to, and ownership of, ideas, best practice, on-going experimentation, and learning. The more-than-a-little-embarrassing truth is that in the two successful offerings of the course, while *we* were having one heck of great time *in the classroom*, too few of our colleagues on campus or collaborators off campus had any clue this was happening!

In the previous section, we sketched out some of our moving-forward plans in terms of strengthening internal collaborations and revising how the course itself will be structured, but we aspire to enhancing our own infrastructure and increasing accessibility by communicating much more proactively and doing a better job of sharing the course, its content, and its access to world-class leaders with our internal Babson colleagues and collaborators and with those beyond the borders of Babson. We also aspire to containing "scope creep" which can, as we learned from several of our organizational partners, irreparably erode infrastructure and muddle understanding and, thus, accessibility. The delineations between the big picture intellectual landscape of social value creation and the by-necessity-time-bound themes for the course often got hopelessly blurred and tangled in our first two offerings of the course. Our experience taught us that, as a subject for intellectual inquiry and research and for real-time learning and innovation in partnership with organizations, Social Value Creation has almost no boundaries and limitless potential. The infrastructure at Babson and within The Lewis Institute is suited perfectly to enhancing this scope and potential. On the other hand, that same experience taught us that infrastructure matters and that the themes and issues covered in a course will always be constrained by the number of weeks the course meets and the number of hours for each session in that course. Put baldly: The infrastructure of the intensive, experiential learning course we are now designing cannot − and should not − support the limitless potential of the broader intellectual subject. We are aspiring to making wise choices.

> Take-Away-Move Forward #4: *Social value creation requires new definitions of "leadership," as well as new models of leadership education and development.*

Time after time, over the two iterations of the course, we and the students listened spell-bound as the leaders of social value creation described their roles and their responsibilities. To be sure, there were elements of their leadership that bore the theoretical markings of "authentic leadership," "transformational leadership," "innovation," and "change management." There were also the themes of "deep functional expertise" and "a track record of success" in almost all of the stories.

But, ultimately, what emerged loudly and clearly and resonated for the students and for the leaders themselves was how the "leadership" of social value creation was, at its core, fundamentally about being an entrepreneur inside – about using ET&A®. So, moving forward, we aspire to create learning that helps students and leaders discover how to act their way into a new way of thinking, rather than thinking their way into a new way of acting. We aspire to designing not just a course centered on social value creation, but a course that is also a living laboratory for being an entrepreneur inside an organization. We aspire to creating not just a time-bounded course, but rather a vibrant community of stakeholders and problem-solvers. Finally, moving forward, we aspire to creating a learning environment where students have more opportunities, more incentives, and more rewards for moving entrepreneurial thinking all the way through to leading entrepreneurial action.

> **Take-Away-for-Moving-Forward #5:** *Social value creation requires a powerful narrative – and even a new language.*

In the two years of listening to our organizational partners describe how they grappled with finding ways to tell their story of social value creation and in the countless hours we spent "transcribing and translating" those stories into the book, we discovered two key things. First, we discovered the enormous power of a compelling narrative that engages others in an endeavor. Leader after leader shared the mind-bending challenges of creating messages that resonated inside the organization and aligned with the core business, while at the same time creating messages that had relevance and resonance for multiple, complex, and often impossibly incongruent stakeholders inside the organization and with customers, vendors, communities, and even competitors – and sometimes doing this globally. Our second key learning was discovering the critical importance of creating our own narratives about the intellectual domain we were exploring, the pedagogy we were using to foster learning in this domain, and the ongoing narrative of an expanding infrastructure – the "tribe" of partners, colleagues, learners, collaborators who are sharing the journey.

The story we are telling on these pages is a beginning for creating that narrative. Our aspirations for keeping the narrative dynamic and vital include: (a) staying open and curious about the rapidly changing language being used in this domain and the "plots" (intellectual paths) being developed, (b) nurturing our relationships with the existing cast of characters (our academic and organizational partners) while also continuing to "audition" a widening cast of characters and providing a venue for their emerging narratives, (c) expanding the "narrative template" to include more in-depth collaboration with colleagues around cross-disciplinary research, and (d) enliven and enrich the narrative by creating more venues for student voices.

Chapter 7: Just Do It

In both of the experimental offerings of the social value creation elective, students either breezed in the door of the first session naively optimistic about "doing good" and triumphing over capitalistic greed or, conversely, sidled into the room cynical and skeptical about efforts they saw as little more than "greenwashing" or just smoke and mirrors. Over the space of seven weeks, their knowledge expanded and their perspectives fluctuated widely — and sometimes wildly — sometimes even within a single three-hour session! Based on their written assignments, their course feedback, on the blogs many of them have subsequently created for The Lewis Institute, and our ongoing conversations with them, we know that the majority of them walked out the door on the last evening sobered by the complexity of what they had learned from leaders of the partner organizations, yet buoyed by possibilities for organizations, for communities, and for themselves as future leaders.

Having Babson MBA students grapple with the big, unimaginably complex and tangled issues surrounding social value creation, right alongside of some of the world's key players in this domain, gave both the students and the leaders the opportunity to reflect on and test their own knowledge and beliefs about social value creation, their own capacity for curiosity and exploration, and their own leadership strengths and aspirations in this realm. In our own ongoing journey as academics and practitioners, we began with the knowledge that social value creation was beyond philanthropy and the belief that, at its robust best, it is beyond the triple bottom line. Along the way, we learned in profound and compelling ways that creating social value is a *business essential*, driving innovation both inside and outside the organization. When successful, it aligns societal dilemmas with business models and creates new market opportunities. It acts as a furnace for forging a new brand of leadership.

As noted earlier, the "business" of Babson is educating "… entrepreneurial leaders who create great economic and social value – everywhere." When it is successful, it, too, is about "alignment"; aligning societal dilemmas with organizational capacity to drive innovation, both inside the college and in the world. It creates new "intellectual market opportunities" and real professional opportunities. It is a powerful furnace for forging strong, future leaders.

Our story of using Entrepreneurial Thought and Action® to create a course and then a book, of experimentation and learning and re-designing and re-inventing, is also the story of the "business" essentials of alignment and leverage. It is the story of mirroring – aligning with – the fundamentals of the same social value creation issues we were exploring. It is the story of mirroring the realities of the organizational leadership issues we hoped to better understand. It is the story of mirroring (albeit sometimes not as successfully as we had hoped) the same ET&A® "paths" we teach our students and prepare them to use in the world beyond Babson College.

But, in the end, our story is the story of a very unique operating environment – The Lewis Institute and Babson College. It is what grants permission, offers encouragement, minimizes barriers, and provides resources to "Just Do It." And so we did. And will again.

Reference

Kiser, C., Leipziger, D., & Shubert, J. J. (2014). *Creating social value: A guide for leaders and change makers.* Sheffield: Greenleaf Publishing Limited.

Websites for More Information:

Babson College. Retrieved from http://www.babson.edu/about-babson/at-a-glance/Pages/mission

The Lewis Institute, Babson College. Retrieved from http://www.babson.edu/Academics/centers/the-lewis-institute

The Office of Graduate Experiential Learning, Babson College. Retrieved from http://www.babson.edu/Academics/graduate/mba/experiential

APPENDIX A

ABBREVIATED SYLLABUS FOR 2011 "LEADING FOR SOCIAL VALUE: INSIDE THE C-SUITE"

The Learning Objectives:

- Gain a broad and deep understanding of the multiple ways in which modern organizations create both social and economic value
- Demonstrate the ability to identify and assess (qualitatively and quantitatively) an organizations efforts at "doing well" and "doing good"
- Assess the skills and competencies needed to build the leadership capacity to drive and influence social value creation
- Create a portfolio of resources that can guide your journey around social value creation within an organization, including how to align, integrate, measure, and communicate social value creation

Overview of Process and Outcomes:

Each week the course will host a guest from the C-Suite of an organization, drawn primarily from private sector, but many will also have had experience in not-for-profits or entrepreneurial start-ups and most have had extensive track records working in the world of polity/inter-governmental agencies and building cross-sector alliances.

Each C-Suite guest will (a) Submit two or three leadership challenges/opportunities they would like to have an in-depth learning conversation with the class about, and (b) Share their company's best practice approaches and their ideas for strong leadership development.

Each week the class will:

- Be guided by an assigned "Lead Team" that will present a high-level briefing analysis on the industry and the company, introduce the C-Suite guests and their background/experience, and take responsibility for moderating the session
- Use a combination of team and individual preparation and contributions to create a lively, robust session and learning conversation
- Make individual contributions to the session through well-researched, thought-provoking questions for the C-Suite guests
- Individually and in teams, create the Final Project Report

The Evaluation Requirements

- Lead Teams have the responsibility for introducing the C-Suite guests, moderating the discussion and creating a 2–3 page high-level industry and organization analysis, which should be posted to the course Blackboard site no later 48 hours prior to class so the entire class can come prepared for discussion. The Lead Team will be asked to review these, post session, revise if appropriate and incorporate this analysis into the Final Project Report.
- Individuals will submit 3–5 questions each week that they want to engage the C-Suite Guests in discussing. These questions should focus on the opportunities for leadership. These must be submitted 24 hours in advance of each session and will be posted to the course Blackboard site. The Lead Team will have the discretion to select questions to pose. (10%)
- Individuals will each week prepare a written memo (maximum one page) addressed to C-Suite guests with observations and recommendations that grew out of the discussion. These will be reviewed by the instructors, revised if needed by the student, and forwarded electronically to the guests. These memos are due, in class the week following the session where the guests were present. (15%)
- Individual Participation includes being present and proactively engaged, participating fully in each session, conversation, exploration and debate. Individuals are expected to facilitate the engagement and learning of their classmates and guest, use professional standards for discussion and disagreement and professional standards for notifying the instructors and their classmates when they will not be present or not able to meet a deadline. (25%)
- The Final Project requires students to work within their team and as individuals to create the first issue of what is being planned as an ongoing publication "Babson Students Explore the Role of Business Leadership in Today's World. This will be a written report that brings together the issues from each session, the responses from the C-Suite guests, a focused analysis of business possibilities and a set of recommendations for business, for students and for educators. (30%)

APPENDIX B

ROSTER OF PARTNER ORGANIZATIONS AND BUSINESS LEADERS
(ARRANGED ALPHABETICALLY BY NAME OF ORGANIZATION)

2011 Course and Book
Jon Carson, CEO, **BiddingForGood**

2011, 2012 Course and Book
Dave Stangis, Vice President — Public Affairs & Corporate Responsibility at Campbell Soup Company; President, Campbell Soup Foundation, **Campbell Soup Company**

2011 Course
Deborah Holmes, Americas Director, Corporate Responsibility, **Ernst & Young**

2011, 2012 Course and Book
John Viera, Global Director of Sustainability, **Ford Motor Company**
David Berdish, Executive-in-Residence at Virginia Commonwealth University, formerly Social Responsibility, **Ford Motor Company**

Book
Mike Brady, CEO, **Greyston Bakery**
Ariel Hauptman, Director of Business Development & Benefit Corp Chair, **Greyston Bakery**

2012 Course and Book
Kevin Thompson, Director of Marketing — IBM Commerce, Mobile and Social for North America, **IBM**

Book
Eric Hudson, Founder & CEO, **Preserve**

2011, 2012 Course and Book
Shainoor Khoja, Managing Director at Better Business Enterprise Ltd as well as Managing Director, Roshan Community, **Roshan**

2012 Course and Book
Rachel Weeks, Founder and CEO, **School House**

2011 Course
Holly Fowler, Senior Director, Sustainability & CSR, **Sodexo**

2012 Course and Book
Shawn Grensch, Co-Founder and CEO at iAMroyalist Inc., formerly, SVP Marketing, **Target**
Nate Garvis, Founder of Naked Civics, formerly of **Target**

2012 Course and Book
Lynnette McIntire, Director, sustainability, **UPS**

2011, 2012 Course and Book
Rose Stuckey Kirk, President, Verizon foundation, **Verizon**
Kathy Brown, President and CEO, The Internet Society. Formerly, Senior Executive **Verizon**
Chris Lloyd, Executive Director — Public Policy and Corporate Responsibility, **Verizon**

APPENDIX C

OUTLINE OF 2015 INTENSIVE ELECTIVE "LEADING SOCIAL VALUE CREATION"

Fall Semester 2015

Two 2.5 day sessions (Friday evening through Sunday evening)
Breakfast, lunch, and dinner sessions will be designed to include Babson colleagues and collaborators whose research and program initiatives are aligned with the partner's industry and challenges.

Friday Evening 1:

- Overview/introduction to the course, the domain of social value creation, the pedagogical framework for exploration and to one another as a community of learners and ET&A™ doers.

Saturday 1:

- Interactions with executives/leaders from three partner organizations. Partners will share their narratives with the students, engage in directed dialog about the leadership challenges they have faced and present a real-time "case" for the students to help them work on.

Sunday 1:

- Student teams (with faculty facilitation) will engage with the partner organization guests in a "design thinking studio" format that produces real, viable options and opportunities for the partner organization to meet a social value creation challenge.

Friday Evening 2:

- Review and Reflections from Week One and Personal Aspirations for Leadership Growth.

Saturday 2:

- Interactions with executives/leaders from three partner organizations. Repeat format from Week 1.

Sunday 2:

- Student teams, partner organizations and faculty facilitators, per format from Week 1.

29 The Center for Women's Entrepreneurial Leadership: Creating Gender Enlightenment on and Beyond a Business School Campus

Susan Duffy, Marjorie Feld and Nan Langowitz

Imagining and Creating a Possibility

My ideas are of the blossoming kind ...

−Female applicant in letter to Babson (1999)

In the fall of 1999, a taskforce gathered with a simple question as its charge: What could Babson be doing for women? This charge came from the President and arose from the realization that while Babson had been accepting women for more than 30 years, and while it had become accustomed to seeing women across the campus among students, faculty, and staff, we had in fact lost ground in terms of student population as compared with competitor schools at both the undergraduate and graduate levels. A quick decision was made to create a scholarship that targeted women leaders and created a women's leadership program for its recipients, but the longer range solution was not evident and what came to be known as the Women's Leadership Steering Committee taskforce was formed. That group of some 40 individuals fanned out to tackle some of the possibilities: what *could* Babson be doing for women? When the various sub-committees reunited to share findings, the idea for a Center crystallized. Then, as now, we knew we were on a journey of continuing innovation and evolution. The report from the Women's Leadership Steering Committee (WLSC) said the following:

> And, while many questions remain unanswered, we know that the essence of what draws students lies in the educational environment. The proposed center would establish Babson as a leader in creating an educational environment that intentionally prepares women for success in the business world ..... We firmly believe that by creating an intentional program for women at Babson, we will draw more women here and increase the likelihood of their success. We also believe that such a program will enrich the educational environment for all, both men and women, in the same way that a new lens creates new potential for knowledge and understanding. And, by intentionally focusing on advancing women in their business, entrepreneurial, and related life pursuits, Babson can take the lead on a question critical to management education and practice — how to more fully leverage the talents of women.

The steering committee was mindful of the recently published book *Taking Women Seriously* (Tidball, Tidball, Smith, & Wolf-Wendel, 1998) which identified elements contributing to the success of women's colleges that might be transferred to the co-educational environment. Among these were the notion of having a place where women's voices could be heard and treated with respect; having a place where women's issues could be at the center rather than at the margin; having positive peer groups and support for development; having women role models among faculty and staff; and holding high expectations for what students could dream and achieve. These became the areas of impact that the taskforce envisioned for a Center and for the creation of a gender-enlightened campus community. While feminist scholars have more recently argued that researchers of gender differences need "to consider how organizations as socio-cultural contexts shape these differences" (Ely & Padavic, 2007), Babson has been working on reshaping the context of the campus environment through the creation of the Center for nearly 15 years.

This chapter highlights the key points in the development of what came to be called The Center for Women's Entrepreneurial Leadership at Babson College. There have been twists and turns in the journey, with lessons learned along the way. It is our hope that both the story of the journey and the sharing of the lessons may be instructive to others seeking to transform the educational context of their institutions.

Start with the Means at Hand: Act, Learn, Build

Every entrepreneurial endeavor begins with an aspiration and needs to build from a series of actions based on the resources at hand. The WLSC report laid out a clear aspiration and a series of potential activities that would allow us to create a robust Center. Our early focus was to change the gender mix on campus. We wanted to enhance the representation of women among the student population, among the speakers available to students through campus activities, and among the faculty who might become their role models. The Center's early activities focused on admissions, events, and research that would highlight the success and advancement of women in business and entrepreneurship. The Women's Leadership Program was created for a cadre of select undergraduate and graduate women at the point of admission each year. The program included financial support through a scholarship as well as co-curricular leadership development activities. A mentor program – in which each woman student was matched with a successful woman mentor, typically an alumna or friend of the College – quickly became the centerpiece of the Women's Leadership Program. This program has evolved over time but remains an important offering to women students, now across the campus community. In addition, a series of events was planned: some leveraging existing programs such as the "Women Building Business" panel session that had annually been held by the Babson Entrepreneurship Club or the Graduate Women in Business annual "Women in Business" conference; others newly developed to expand the range of programming that would elevate the visibility of women leaders in the business arena. This robust mix of programming continues to shape the campus environment today though the strategy for how programming is enacted and co-sponsored has evolved. Adding to the mix of events was a growing body of research highlighting the roles and impact of women in business and entrepreneurship. This work was conducted by Babson faculty, sometimes in collaboration with outside organizations, and served as a means of bringing visibility to the opportunities and challenges for women seeking professional advancement.

These early actions provided a strong platform from which to build and deepen the Center's work. The focus on changing the gender mix on campus yielded important outcomes. The undergraduate female population grew from comprising just 34% of the student body in 1999 to achieving near parity in 2014. Similarly, the graduate MBA population shifted from 24% female to 34% female overall in the same timeframe. In Babson classrooms, students experienced an increasing mix of female faculty as their role models. In 2014, 36% of full-time faculty were women compared with approximately 25% in 2000. The composition of women faculty has also changed. While in 2000, the predominance of female Babson faculty was among the liberal arts division, women now account for 32% of the business discipline faculty; this compares quite favorably with the 21.4% level of women in top MBA business school faculties as reported by *Bloomberg BusinessWeek* (Choi, 2014). (The average percentage of women on the full-time faculty at AACSB accredited schools has been rising in the last decade, from 20.8% in 2002 to 25.3% in 2009. See Barber & Palmer, 2009.)

The campus climate has also shifted, with events and activities featuring women leaders and role models happening on a weekly basis as compared with the few "Women in X" events held annually at the time of the Center's founding. While attention is still required to ensure a mix of women speakers as classroom visitors, on event panels and as speakers for student-run conferences, it's fair to say that it's no longer the uphill battle to broach the conversation that it once was. Research activity focused on women and gender issues has also blossomed. The Center benefited from the outset by the presence of at least a dozen researchers on campus with a focus and keen interest in women in business and gender issues in society and organizations. Over the Center's first decade, this faculty group grew to 21 scholars whose work was funded internally by 19 summer stipends, six course releases, two major research awards, and two external grants. As a result of this, the Center published 13 research reports and held eight research-based symposia; in addition, individual faculty members published numerous articles, chapters, and books.

The development of a distinct web presence to showcase the Center and its related events and research helped make this scholarly work visible to the outside world as well as to the campus community. In addition, the Center engaged in significant outreach to collaborate with external organizations as well as to welcome participation in activities. These collaborations extended Babson's reach and presence as a source of research and expertise with respect to women in business and entrepreneurship. Through the Center's initiative, Babson become a founding Forte Foundation school, a supporter of Springboard Enterprises (hosting some of their workshops and venture capital forum), partnered with the Federal Reserve Bank of Boston to disseminate and discuss GEM Women (Global Entrepreneurship Monitor) data, partnered with The Commonwealth

Institute to study and disseminate findings on women CEOs, collaborated with the Center for Women's Business Research on symposia for women entrepreneurs of color, and worked with EY on their Entrepreneurial Winning Women program. By the end of its first decade, the Center had partnered with more than 31 organizations, enriching its connection to like-minded institutions and enhancing its ability to influence the macro-environment into which its students would graduate.

A study published in the *Journal of Business Ethics* (Ibeh, Carter, Poff, & Hamill, 2008) suggested that graduate business schools could be evaluated with respect to the education of women by looking at dimensions such as the percent of women students, whether the institution had a center, the types of educational offerings, availability of fellowships or scholarships, external partnerships, and events and activities. In its first decade, the Center had achieved high marks on these dimensions.

Lessons in Institutional Support

As has been seen with scholarship on women's corporate networks (see Donnellon & Langowitz, 2009) a key factor enabling the empowerment of women in organizational contexts is the consistent investment of resources and sponsorship of activity by senior leadership. Toward the end of the Center's first decade, resource constraints and questions of strategic fit within the institution were the main challenges. Programs that had once been leading edge were in need of refreshment and re-imagination. Budget and staffing had been reduced with concomitant challenges for enacting the Center's mission. Following the 2008–2009 recession, a change of institutional leadership brought with it an updated strategic vision for the College. The Center came under scrutiny and the Provost requested a review of progress, positioning and potential. A new taskforce was created, working for six months to assess the Center and make recommendations. This "2020 taskforce" concluded that the Center needed "re-focus and re-investment. It has been under-resourced and under-leveraged. There is a perception that women's leadership and engagement issues are solved at Babson, but this perception does not match reality. There has been some progress, but there is much work to be done, presenting great opportunity." Recommendations called for enhanced staffing, clarification of the strategic focus of the Center in alignment with the College strategy, and re-dedication to the Center's mission to develop and advance women as entrepreneurial leaders at Babson and beyond. Babson gained momentum with its own refreshed institutional mission to "educate leaders who create great economic and social value — everywhere;" in line with this vision, support for a reinvigorated Center was plentiful. The College President, Provost, and Dean of Faculty embraced the taskforce findings and committed the resources to produce the Center's Second Act.

A Center for all

In 2011, a reimagined Center was launched with the hiring of a new Executive Director and the appointment of a Faculty Director who received two course releases in exchange for her service. Together the two leaders brought a portfolio of expertise that spanned business and the liberal arts, pedagogy and program development, research, and operations. The collaboration worked seamlessly largely because both were deeply committed to the potentially transformative power of the Center: they often spoke about how their work for a more equal distribution of power and resources for women at a business college would translate into greater equality in the larger business world and beyond. The live question, then, was how to begin this new chapter in the life of the Center. The duo decided to lead the Center like a growing early stage venture in the Babson tradition of "entrepreneurial thought and action" (ETA): learn as much as they could about the current state, and then begin a series of small, smart experiments to move the Center forward.

The taskforce report served as the road map, and top priorities included developing a fully institutionally-aligned strategic plan, building a management team to guide the Center's progress, and executing a revitalized portfolio of programs that would deliver value to Babson and beyond. As a signal of the transformation afoot, the Center was renamed the Center for Women's *Entrepreneurial* Leadership (CWEL) to align closely with the larger mission and reputation of the College. With a new name and a mandate for change, the new leadership team set out to learn first-hand from the campus community regarding their ideas for the opportunities ahead.

Given the high profile of the Center's new chapter, the team was much in demand from all corners of campus. In the fall of 2011, with a strong ally in the president, and an eye toward identifying additional allies and advocates, they embarked on a "listening tour" with stakeholders from across the College. They also met with faculty and student leaders in order to gather information on expectations and needs on campus. In gathering this data on their listening tour of campus, they became increasingly aware of the role of intersectionalities on campus, as they found that their work against sexism and male-dominated hierarchies necessarily led them to new priorities and programming around other -isms and overlapping hierarchies. The team became members of the Diversity and Inclusion Council and the Lesbian, Gay, Bisexual, Transgender, and Queer/Questioning (LGBTQ) Action Group. To assure that ongoing dialogue between the Center and all key stakeholders continued, an internal advisory board was created. This group of administrators, faculty, staff, students, and alumnae agreed to serve as ambassadors of the Center, to convene once a semester to receive detailed updates of Center activities, and to offer input as requested on key challenges facing the Center.

CWEL Act Two: ETA in Action

The second priority of the new team was to synthesize the data generated on the listening tour into a cohesive strategy that aligned with Babson's mission and commitment to entrepreneurial thought and action of all kinds. This required that the Center address two inextricably linked sets of activities: *preparing women to lead the world* through women-centered educational programs, events and research; and, *preparing the world for women leaders* through initiatives for women and men that cultivate a "gender-enlightened" campus and broader business context within which all could thrive. After multiple iterations, the CWEL adopted three guiding and aspirational strategic goals:

- To become the U.S. academic leader for women's entrepreneurial leadership training, education and research;
- To be THE thought and action authority for gender-enlightened and inclusive business schools; and
- To achieve positive directional progress toward a sustainable revenue model.

The Center's mission was also updated to reflect renewed priorities:

> Babson's Center for Women's Entrepreneurial Leadership (CWEL) educates, inspires and empowers women entrepreneurial leaders to reach their full potential to create economic and social value for themselves, their organizations, and society. The center does this through innovative education programs and events, and by supporting and widely disseminating research about the unique skills and experiences of women entrepreneurial leaders. Additionally, CWEL supports and advances gender equality as a growth

strategy for individuals and for organizations of all sizes, everywhere in the world.

The aspirations set forth in both the strategy and mission required the evaluation of all programs and activities and tough decision making with regard to the Center's portfolio of offerings. This job was made more complex by the range of opinions across campus regarding the perceived value proposition of the CWEL. The team also went to work to develop new offerings that more closely aligned with Babson's "learning laboratory" approach of thinking, acting, and experimenting in any setting. They also made a firm commitment to actively contribute to the College's mission to lead the world as entrepreneurship educators. This meant accepting the challenge of external brand building through widespread thought leadership and developing programs with future potential for replication and scale.

Given the scope of the new vision for the Center, the team decided to focus first on rebuilding the Center's internal value proposition for students, faculty and staff, and then reemerge as a thought leader and educator in the broader business ecosystem. In order to execute against this strategy, the CWEL formally requested and was granted the resources to hire two additional team members. Both positions were approved on a temporary two-year contract basis with explicit requirement of proving success before making the positions permanent. An Associate Director of Programs was hired to reimagine the program portfolio, and an Associate Director of Outreach and Communication was charged with rebranding and reintroducing the Center to first the internal, and then the external community. The College had invested in institution building to build value and reputation, to be sure, and many stakeholders also were deeply invested in the idea that the Center could be a catalyst for broad cultural change on campus and beyond. The stage was set for action.

As a learning laboratory in an institution committed to ETA, the Center was poised to enter its second decade with an act, learn, build approach. The team piloted new programs on a small scale using the resources of the existing budget. Innovations were tried with mixed success, but all led to useful learning about how the Center could best move forward to serve students, faculty, and staff. The newly expanded CWEL team decided on a set of common elements for all activities. These included underpinning all programs with pedagogy so that formal learning objectives complemented skill-building outcomes, such as making network connections. In addition, all student-centered programs incorporated near peer role models and CWEL engaged in partnering with other campus or external groups to maximize resources, reach, and impact. With these parameters, the Center's Act Two saw an explosion of programming and initiatives as highlighted in the paragraphs below. This work related both to transforming women's entrepreneurial potential into entrepreneurial impact of all kinds and to creating gender-enlightened leaders for today and tomorrow.

CWEL's Program Portfolio

Program changes began with a full redesign of the original undergraduate Women's Leadership Program. Using a competency-based approach, the renamed CWEL Scholars Program offered a cumulative learning and development experience across all four undergraduate years, set new requirements for scholar accountability, and engaged the scholar members in co-creating many of the learning experiences. The Center and Admissions teams successfully committed themselves to diversifying the applicant pool for the program — the new class of scholars looked more like the world, with wider representation of historically underrepresented groups and of international students — with results that met with praise throughout the College.

An important part of the Center's work was geared toward providing spaces to have provocative and important conversations, real time learning laboratories for the CWEL team and others. Toward those ends, a feminist film series was started where the topics ranged from gender and American politics to the explosion of yoga as art, practice and business, to the so-called college "hookup culture." The Center began an undergraduate group self-named the "Gender Justice League" which met once a month in the evenings with two faculty members to talk about developments on campus. And twice each semester, they convened a Faculty Gender Research Luncheon, where one or two faculty members spoke about their gender-inflected research. Importantly, the team extended invitations to faculty and staff to be audience members at these gatherings, intentionally modeling the inclusive and non-hierarchical approach to which the Center was committed. This gathering built community around commitments to gendered topics and encouraged collaborations. It also rebuilt a solid group of CWEL allies from across campus. Some of the projects presented were the product of the Center's faculty research funds, distributed internally through the Babson Faculty Research Fund.

Many faculty colleagues expressed their desire to see gender integrated more broadly into the curriculum. With that in mind the Center leaders created a module on gender for the First Year Seminar, or FYS, a one-credit course required of all new undergraduate students. Titled "Gender Works," the module included an experiential exercise and a set of basic gender lessons about what attributes are rewarded and punished in women and men, especially in a business context. Many staff members reported positively about the impact of those lessons on later conversations about college culture in FYS. The CWEL team saw this as a successful way to reach a large cohort of students – along with the many faculty and staff members who are integral to FYS – and alert them to the Center as an educational resource for all. In that same spirit, the Center sponsored several programs that drew the spotlight on the role of men in gender enlightenment. Renowned feminist Jackson Katz brought his bystander pedagogy to campus in speaking about the role of men in undoing violence toward women. His program was required of all campus athletes. The Center also facilitated a meeting of male allies of the Center and brainstormed ways to reach male students on campus with messages and resources. In addition, a campus-wide gender assessment provided baseline data on the number of men and women in a wide range of roles on campus from presidents of first-year Foundations of Management and Entrepreneurship (FME) businesses, to student government leaders, to participants in Babson's celebrated rocket pitch, venture accelerator, and summer venture entrepreneurship programs. These data, which showed significant leadership differentials between male and female students, reinforced the CWEL mission to address both women's development and gender dynamics more broadly, and led to even more innovation in CWEL offerings. By year two of the Center's Second Act, disrupting the status quo became the new mantra. Babson had a unique opportunity to move beyond focusing on entrepreneurial process and work toward changing the face of entrepreneurial leadership. The CWEL would lead the way.

Rewriting the Script

Reinforced by Alfred Bandura's concept of self-efficacy (1994), the Center began to challenge the traditional narrative and optic of entrepreneurial success. If the world were to benefit from the entrepreneurial leadership of all of its citizens, a move from the unchallenged norm of the white, male, entrepreneurial hero, to a more representative, gender-balanced model of success was necessary. Entrepreneurial leadership requires acting into the unknown and Bandura found that one's confidence in his or her ability to be successful, regardless of competence, was a significant driver of forward motion toward any objective. An important way to build that confidence was by watching others in action: all students deserved confidence-building "vicarious learning" opportunities through access to role models who looked and sounded like them. The role model challenge in schools of business is not minor given the industry's masculine heritage. In fact, one of the earliest pieces of CWEL-related research examined the coverage, or lack thereof, of women entrepreneurs in business media (Langowitz & Morgan, 2003). Fortunately at Babson, the CWEL was fully supported by faculty and administration in initiating efforts to address the prevalence of male versus female guest lecturers in classrooms, the predominance of male case protagonists in required course readings, and the common male majority of expert speakers at campus-wide events. Students soon joined the effort by gender-balancing the high profile MBA-run "forum" conferences. The College's widely acclaimed Entrepreneurship Forum was likely the first large entrepreneurship conference in the country not specifically targeted for women which had an equal number of men and women speakers.

Perhaps the most significant gender-balancing disruption came in the form of a new accelerator program for high potential women entrepreneur students. The Women Innovating Now (WIN) Lab is a nine-month residential program for women entrepreneurs that accelerates the entrepreneurial path, from ideation to launch of big, bold businesses. Underpinned by earlier CWEL research on effective entrepreneurship education approaches for women (see Langowitz, Sharpe, & Godwyn, 2006), the WIN Lab challenges the traditional venture accelerator model — considered by many to privilege a masculine norm — by providing a sector agnostic alternative that considers and develops the unique skills and experiences of diverse women entrepreneurial leaders. The Lab is differentiated from traditional programs in terms of people: role models, experts, and coaches; process: collaborative learning and community-centered pedagogy; and place: a safe zone for discovery, reflection, and change. The WIN experience also explicitly addresses gendered elements of the entrepreneurial process at the individual level (i.e., capabilities perception, failure calculus, and growth ambitions); and the institutional level (i.e., access to capital, sector norms, and homophily hazards). This unique model of venture acceleration is creating a new pipeline of entrepreneurs positioned to generate crucial economic growth in their communities, their countries, and the world.

From the outset, the WIN Lab aligned with the Center's broader strategic goals to both build reputation and create programs for replication. In the second year of the program, the Lab was named one of Boston's 2014 "50 on Fire" in education, a recognition of innovation and game-changing impact in the region; it was also a finalist in the 2015 United States Association for Small Business and Entrepreneurship pedagogy awards in the "Outstanding Specialty Entrepreneurship Program" category. After securing its position in

Boston in 2015—2016, the WIN Lab will execute a five-year, five-city, national growth plan as it simultaneously considers opportunities that complement Babson's international impact strategy.

Other Center programs such as the annual Women's History month celebration also afforded opportunities to assess the gendered environment, evaluate the means at hand, and act forward. In March 2013, as the issue of body image continued to emerge for women students, the Center held a fashion show unlike any one might have seen before: the designers were entirely female entrepreneurs, and the models — of diverse bodies, backgrounds, abilities, sexualities, and ages — all offered brief testimonies about their lives and their beauty while on the runway. That same year, a panel on Working Parenthood presented research and life experiences about the delicate task of life balancing to a packed room of faculty, staff, students, and alumni. A natural outgrowth of this panel was a collaboration with Human Resources for working parents: an Employee Resource Group called Parent Connections, where Babson employees who are also parents serve as resources to each other.

Select calendar offerings built on the Center's history, such as the annual women's faculty gathering and the Nan Langowitz Women Who Make a Difference Awards, which honor women students, faculty, and staff whose work has had a significant, positive impact on the Babson community in the last year. Others charted new territory, such as the matching of faculty advisors to the Babson Association of Women MBAs. This program supported these graduate students to design and fund a robust calendar of programs that engaged senior women leaders, offered opportunities to develop new skills (e.g., negotiation, strategic networking, and raising capital), and develop resource networks. The Center also re-engagedwith the external community to host and co-sponsor educational events for women leaders and entrepreneurs.

Research, Thought Leadership, and Brand Building

From its inception, research has always been a part of the CWEL mission, and its research work has ranged from funding scholarly contributions for academic publication to producing third party sponsored applied reports useful for practitioners and policy makers. It is important to note that the Center has never had dedicated researchers on its team. Instead, it provides research support and convenes conversations among campus scholars, on occasion working to translate faculty scholarship into accessible, high quality reports. In addition to research stipends, the CWEL team identifies funding partners, serves the function of project manager, designs and manages production of research reports, and amplifies research findings through sophisticated media strategies. This model maximizes outcomes by increasing outlets for faculty research, contributing to institutional brand building, generating revenue, and deepening relationships with sponsoring partners. Like other elements of the Center's work, finding the right fit for the applied research agenda took a series of experiments. The most recent success story is the publication of the highly anticipated DIANA Project Report: *Women Entrepreneurs 2014: Bridging the Gender Gap in Venture Capital* (Brush, Greene, Balachandra, & Davis, 2014). This study launched a movement among investors to rethink gender and capital, resulted in a billion media impressions for Babson, and will be the foundation of at least two scholarly articles. More work is in the pipeline.

CWEL: On and Beyond

At the writing of this chapter Babson is approaching CWEL's fifteenth anniversary. Looking back to the time of the Women's Leadership Steering Committee, the establishment of the Center has certainly made a difference on the campus. The refocusing and reinvestment that emerged out of the 2020 Taskforce has contributed to broader transformations in the community. Over nearly a decade and a half, the Center has diversified and deepened student programming, convened campus-wide conversations, developed and funded scholarly research, developed new educational components, supported and enriched entrepreneurial leadership development, and changed the tenor of discourse and focus in the academic community and the broader entrepreneurial ecosystem. The continuous theme has been to create a gender-enlightened campus community that alters the perspectives of students, faculty, and staff. Indeed, the Center's work offers lessons on what organizations can do to shape behavior and understanding, and its work reshaping the context of the business campus environment sets an important model for addressing the role of gender in education and indeed in the wider world.

References

Bandura, A. (1994). Self efficacy. In V. S. Ramachaudran (Ed.), *Encyclopedia of human behavior* (Vol. 4, pp. 71–81). New York, NY: Academic Press.

Barber, B. M., & Palmer, D. (2009). *Women faculty in US business schools* [Electronic copy]. Retrieved from http://ssrn.com/abstract=1490084. Accessed on October 2009.

Brush, C., Greene, P., Balachandra, L., & Davis, A. (2014). *DIANA report: Women entrepreneurs 2014: Bridging the gender gap in venture capital.* Babson College. Retrieved from http://www.babson.edu/Academics/centers/blank-center/global-research/diana/Documents/diana-project-executive-summary-2014.pdf

Choi, A. S. (2014). Faculties at Elite business schools still skew heavily male. *BloombergBusinessweek.* Retrieved from http://www.businessweek.com/articles/2014-02-20/faculties-at-elite-business-schools-still-skew-heavily-male. Accessed on February 20, 2014.

Donnellon, A., & Langowitz, N. (2009). Leveraging women's networks for strategic value. *Strategy and Leadership*, 37(3), 29–36.

Ely, R., & Padavic, I. (2007). A feminist analysis of organizational research on sex differences. *Academy of Management Review*, 32(4), 1121–1143.

Ibeh, K., Carter, S., Poff, D., & Hamill, J. (2008). How focused are the world's top rated business schools on educating women for global management? *Journal of Business Ethics*, 83, 65–83.

Langowitz, N., & Morgan, C. (2003). Women entrepreneurs: breaking through the glass barrier. In *New perspectives on women entrepreneurs* (Vol. 3). Research in Entrepreneurship and Management. Greenwich, CT: Information Age Publications.

Langowitz, N., Sharpe, N., & Godwyn, M. (2006). Women's business centers in the United States: Effective entrepreneurship training and policy implementation. *Journal of Small Business and Entrepreneurship*, 19(2), 167–182.

Tidball, M. E., Tidball, C. S., Smith, D. G., & Wolf-Wendel, L. E. (1998). *Taking women seriously: Lessons and legacies for educating the majority.* American Council on Education/Oryx Press Series on Higher Education. New York, NY: Praeger.

Websites for More Information

CWEL activities. www.babson.edu/cwel

List of business schools with opportunities for women. Retrieved from http://www.princetonreview.com/schoollist.aspx?id=711#/

The Global Entrepreneurship Monitor project includes a special topic report on women entrepreneurs. www.gemconsortium.org/reports

Index